From Barbie

to
Mortal Kombat

The MIT Press—Cambridge, Massachusetts—London, England

From Barbie to Mortal Kombat

Gender and Computer Games

edited by

Justine Cassell and Henry Jenkins

This book was set in Caecilia by Graphic Composition, Inc.

Printed and bound in the United States of America.

Library of Congress Cataloging-in-Publication Data

From Barbie to Mortal Kombat : gender and computer games / edited by Justine Cassell and Henry Jenkins.
    p. cm.
    Includes bibliographical references and index.
    ISBN 0-262-03258-9 (hc : alk. paper)
    1. Computer games—Social aspects—Congresses. 2. Games for girls—Congresses.
I. Cassell, Justine, 1960– . II. Jenkins, Henry, 1958– .
GV1469.17.S63F76 1998
306.4′87′0285—DC21   98-23562
                                                    CIP

Contents

Part Three: Rethinking the Girls' Games Movement

Acknowledgments

This book arose out of a one-day symposium on gender and computer games, sponsored by Women's Studies at MIT. Our original intention was to gather industry representatives and academics in one place to discuss the topic of computer games for girls. The symposium was lively, noisy, and highly interactive, with a range of points of view expressed that fell not at all neatly on any spectrum we could have imagined. Thanks to the participants of the symposium, both in front of the podium and in the audience, for their interest in the topic and for their willingness to bring all of themselves (as parents, academics, technologists, feminists, and entrepreneurs) to the table. Thanks to Michele Oshima for her help in organizing the conference and to her team of student staff, including Eliza Dubroff, Jennifer Noonan, Lorraine Cable, Amy Ashbacher, Christa Ansbergs, Amanda Johnsen, Radika Bhaskar, Emily Cooper, and Milos Komarcevic. Funds for this conference came from the MIT Program in Women's Studies, the Program in Film and Media Studies, the Media Lab, the Program in Science, Technology and Society, Dean Robert Brown, School of Engineering, and Dean Philip Khoury, School of Humanities and Social Science.

Justine Cassell

Since coming to MIT, I have been blessed and cursed with students who talk back. Thanks to all my students, but in particular Tess Algoso, Jennifer Glos, Nick Montfort, Manny Perez, and Marina Umaschi for their research efforts on Rosebud, Renga, and SAGE, and for giving me lip. They challenged my point of view on this work at every stage, leading me to a better understanding of the issues, and of what I believed. Jennifer Glos, along with Shari Goldin, also conducted the interviews of industry people. Their hard work on the questions and their probing interviewing technique resulted in the fascinating material presented here.

Thanks to Lynn Liben for first introducing me to research on the development of gender stereotypes, to Fred Martin for finding the *Saturday Night Live* segment that sets the stage for the introductory chapter, to Seymour Papert for so insightfully questioning my notion of "first-person-ness", and to Nancie S. Martin for first discussions on computer games for girls (over good food and drink, in various cities). I come to issues of narrative and gender from a linguistics perspective. I am lucky that others have tread this path before me, and set up such instructive signposts along the way. Thanks to those scholars, Penny Eckert, Kira Hall, Sally McConnell-Ginet, Bonnie McIlhenny, and Sara Trechter for updating my understanding of the societal and linguistic construction of gender, through their writing, teaching, and many fascinating discussions. I am grateful to Cathy O'Connor for extraordinarily perceptive readings of these chapters and other writing, as well as for general good advice, to the other three members of the Four Seasons for making MIT a hospitable place, and to Mitchel Resnick for sharing his knowledge and his good sense with me about—but not limited to—the topic of technology for children. I am grateful to participants in the symposia and conferences where I have presented this work, and especially to Anita Borg, who came up with a one-line response to a tough question and has since shared many more lines of wisdom. Finally, personal thanks to Mireille and Marin, the Mas de Trifontaine, and Suzan for shelter of all sorts.

Much of my work is funded by industry sponsors. I thank the sponsors of the MIT Media Lab for their generosity, among them the representatives of Lego, Mattel, Nike, Pixar, Purple Moon, Swatch, and other companies who have shared their points of view on designing with girls in mind and have been so open to mine.

Very warm thanks to Glen Sherman for keeping track of everything (in this book and in the rest of my professional life), for tirelessly formatting, reformatting, and getting documents from everybody to everybody else, all with an unflappable good humor.

Most of all, thanks to Henry Jenkins, for first inviting me to help in the planning of the Gender and Games symposium, and then for being a wonderful coeditor, in the best feminist tradition of collaboration, respect for the point of view of the other, and mutual instruction.

Henry Jenkins

My thinking about gender and games has been strongly shaped by a series of engaging encounters organized by Sega of America and hosted by Lee McEnany. Sega brought together researchers from across many different fields to reflect on the impact of video games on American life. I am especially grateful to the cultural studies contingent at these events, Marsha Kinder and Ellen Seiter, who are role models on how one can work with industry and still be a politically committed scholar. I am also thankful for the insight and inspiration of Brenda Laurel, who confronts the same issues from the opposite side of the industry/academic divide.

Thanks are also due to the students in two MIT courses, Understanding Children's Fictions and Media, Culture, and Society, who helped me work through many of the topics discussed here and who were characteristically blunt about the strengths and limitations of the girls' game approach. I also am thankful to the editors of *Next Generation* magazine who pushed me to think more fully about the implications of this research for current debates about video game violence.

I remain grateful to the members of the Women's Studies Steering Committee at MIT, who have accepted me as their "token male" member, especially Ruth Perry, Isabelle de Courtivron, Elizabeth Wood, Margery Resnick, Jean Jackson, Evelyn Hammonds, Evelyn Fox Keller, Brenda Cotto-Escalera, and Lela Kinney. You made me feel welcome within your community and have supported my work on gender and sexuality even when it took me places most of you were unlikely to go yourselves.

I have also learned a tremendous amount about new media and their potential from Janet Murray, Peter Donaldson, Bill Mitchell, Edward Barrett, Gilberte Furstenberg, Shigeru Miyagawa, Kurt Fendt, Doug Morgenstern, Greg Smith, Tara McPherson, Virginia Nightingale, Marc Davis, Warren Sacks, Amy Bruckman, Alan Wexelblatt, Lenny Foner, and Angela Ndalianis, among many others.

During the time this book was being prepared, my research was generously supported by MIT's Class of 1942 fund and by the John and Mary R. Markle Foundation. I also benefited from the patronage of Robert Metcalfe, who overcame his distrust of "deconstructivist litcrit types" to support this particular media scholar.

Many, many thanks are owed to Shari Goldin, who has worked well beyond the call of duty in making sure this project came together, who assembled information that was foundational for the MIT conference, who developed questions, conducted interviews, and wrote the introductions for the interview sections, who read and commented on multiple drafts of the text, who was instrumental in locating the game grrlz sites and showing us their importance for our overall project, and who got excited enough about the project to play games—not only on "company time" but on her own time. I also owe thanks to Chris Pomiecko and his student staffers, who knew how to come to my rescue whenever I confronted technical problems and who did the technical support for the conference; Janice Ellertsen and Janet Sahlstrom, who knew how to translate my oddball expenses (Purple Moon? Barbie?) into something the accounting office understood, and Briony Keith, who makes the MIT Literature Section a more humane place to work.

My son, Henry Jenkins IV, is really the one to blame for my involvement in this project, since he was the one who years ago begged and pleaded until we bought our first game system, who has been showing me level after level since he was five (and still at 16, is willing to take time out from life to walk me through "Nights into Dreams" at a moment's notice), who asks the questions about my work and about the media that get my creative wheels spinning, and who may someday surpass me as a writer. Henry, you are a source of tremendous pride.

Cynthia Jenkins, my partner in life, also remains my intellectual partner, someone who can challenge my thinking and incite my curiosity, even when I am so tired I can hardly keep my eyes open (which is how she sees me too much of the time!). I will almost certainly run out of new ways to thank you long before you run out of new ways to help me.

Collaborating with Justine Cassell surely counts as one of the intellectual highpoints of my life. She has been generous with her time, her budget, her staff, and her ideas, has shared the burden of pulling together this book in record time, and owes the lion's share of the credit for assembling such a diverse and interesting set of contributors. If I can write in this book with some optimism about finding a digital playspace where boys and girls might play, learn, and grow together, it is because of my friendship and collaboration with Justine, who has the tools, the commitment, and the vision to make such a dream become a reality.

Finally, I want to thank the kingdoms of Jungleloca and Freedonia, whereever they may be.

About the Authors

Vangie "Aurora" Beal

When twenty-two-year-old Vangie Beal isn't busy writing articles and reviews for GameGirlz.com (http://www.gamegirlz.com), she can usually be found hanging out with friends, playing "Quake," "NetStorm," or "Dark Reign." Aurora organizes and runs a group of twenty-six female "Quake" players (Clan PMS) and is an affiliate for one of the top games news sites, Planet Quake. By trade she is a digital imaging technician, but she enjoys working as a freelance writer, covering computer games. Along with running GameGirlz.com, Vangie also contributes to several computer games websites and helps run several other women and games resources.

Dorothy T. Bennett

Dorothy T. Bennett is a senior project director and senior research associate at Education Development Corporation Center for Children and Technology. She has twelve years' experience researching and developing educational media, curricula, and teacher-enhancement programs in science, mathematics, and technology. Bennett has conducted several studies investigating the role of gender in science and technology and the social dimensions of networking technologies, most recently as an investigator on the widely recognized, NSF-funded *Telementoring Project*, an Internet-based mentoring program for high school girls in project-based science and engineering programs. Through several research and development projects, she has explored how design can serve as a powerful pathway into science for children, most notably on the NSF-funded *Imagine Project*, an innovative computer software package that aims to increase middle school girls' interest in engineering. As part of a national research project on alternative assessment, Bennett also has worked collaboratively for six years with teachers and students at numerous New York City high schools to investigate ways in which technology can be used to conduct authentic assessments of students' design-based work in science and mathematics. Prior to joining the Center, she did four years of formative research testing the comprehension and appeal of video segments for the Children's Television Workshop's award-winning mathematics series, *Square One TV*. She has a master's of science in education from Bank Street College of Education, with a focus on adolescent development.

Stephanie Bergman

Stephanie Bergman (aka, Bobbi, PMS-Bobbi) works fulltime in the legal department of a New York publishing company. In her free time, she is a staff writer for GameGirlz (http://www.gamegirlz.com), maintains a few personal webpages, is an avid "Quake" player, and an all-around internet junkie who misses her MUD.

Cornelia Brunner

Cornelia Brunner has been involved in the research, production, and teaching of educational technology in a variety of subject areas for thirty years. In addition to conducting research projects about the relationship between learning, teaching, and technology, she has designed educational materials incorporating technologies to support inquiry-based learning and teaching in science, social studies, media literacy, and the arts. She has worked extensively with staff and students in a variety of school environments on curriculum-development projects, teacher support and training, and informal education. She has taught experimental courses at Bank Street College and the Media Workshop in New York, in which teachers are introduced to new technologies, and learn to integrate these technologies into their curriculum and use multimedia authoring tools to design their own educational programs. For the past thirty years, Brunner has also been an industry consultant for the design of educational and entertainment products for children of all ages.

Mary Bryson

Mary Bryson teaches in the faculty of education at the University of British Columbia. Her research looks at gender issues and uses of new information technologies. Mary wishes she were a Lesbian Avenger, but can only claim to be absolutely fascinated with "Riven," Japanese Koi, and Great Danes. She is also intrigued with queer theory as it pertains to understanding marginal identities and with the implications of radical constructivism for understanding and implementing "inclusion" in schools.

Justine Cassell

Justine Cassell is a faculty member at MIT's Media Laboratory, where she heads the Gesture and Narrative Language Research Group. She holds a license in Literature from the Université de Besançon, an M.Phil. in linguistics from the University of Edinburgh, and two doctorates from the University of Chicago, one in linguistics and one in psychology. On the basis of this interdisciplinary training, Cassell studies how artifacts—such as computer interface agents and technological toys—can be designed with psychosocial competence, based on a deep understanding of human linguistic, cognitive, and social abilities. Her current projects include integrating gesture, speech, and facial expression in autonomous animated conversing agents; generating interactive storytelling agents; and designing technological toys that take advantage of gender differences in play styles to encourage children to try new kinds of toys and new kinds of technologies. She has published extensively in journals as diverse as *Poetics Today* and *Computer Graphics*.

Suzanne de Castell

Suzanne de Castell is a professor of curriculum and instruction in the faculty of education at Simon Fraser University. She holds a doctorate from the University of London, and has published widely on educational history, philosophy and theory, literacy studies, and technology/gender studies. Co-edited books include *Literacy, Society and Schooling* (with Alan Luke and Kieran Egan; Cambridge University Press, 1980), *Language, Authority and Criticism* (with Alan and Carmen Luke; Falmer Press, 1986), and *Radical Inventions* (with Mary Bryson; State University of New York, 1997). Video work includes "Deviance and Design" and "Just the Way You Are" (in progress). Studying the epistemological implications of technologies of representation is her long-standing interest. She has recently completed the second year of a three-year federally funded research project, "Learning to Make a Difference" (with Bryson, University of British Columbia). The research explores gender, equity, and new information technologies in education.

Nikki Douglas

Nikki Douglas is the creator of two successful webzines: RiotGrrl (http://www.riotgrrl.com), for Gen-X women, and GrrlGamer (http://www.grrlgamer.com), the first site dedicated to the female gaming experience. She is an author and freelance writer living in Key West, Florida.

Jennifer Glos

Jennifer Glos earned her BS in Psychology and her MS in Media Arts and Sciences, both from MIT. In between these two degrees, she worked as program manager at Microsoft in the Consumer Division, overseeing research on social user interfaces. Glos designed the Rosebud system reported on this volume (Cassell), and also carried out the interviews of industry representatives, in conjunction with Shari Goldin.

Shari Goldin

Shari Goldin has a background in anthropology and is completing her PhD in communication arts through the University of Wisconsin-Madison. Her dissertation is a social history of childhood and radio from the 1920s through the 1940s. Her research interests include historical studies of childhood, children's use of new media technologies, broadcast history, and the history of children's play. She has taught at both Emerson College and MIT. Currently she is assisting Henry Jenkins at MIT in the development of a graduate program in comparative media studies.

Michelle "Kittress" Goulet

Michelle "Kittress" Goulet lives in a small town in Northern British Columbia. After graduating from high school, she obtained an Early Childhood Education certificate and plans to continue her education in this field . . . and many others. Her ultimate career goals include computers, so she finds herself writing articles and editorials for various websites including The 64 Source, where she holds the title of "Female Perspective Editor." Goulet is very much involved with the gaming community and hopes to make it more open and "girl friendly."

Patricia M. Greenfield

Patricia Greenfield is Professor of Psychology at UCLA. Her central theoretical and research interest is in the relationship between culture and human development; she considers electronic media as a key component of modern culture with a profound role in socialization and development. She is a past recipient of the American Association for the Advancement of Science Award for Behavioral Science Research and the author of *Mind and Media: The Effects of Television, Video Games, and Computers*, which has been translated into nine languages. In 1996, Ablex published *Interacting with Video*, which she coedited with Rodney Cocking of the National Academy of Sciences.

Margaret Honey

Margaret Honey is associate director of the Center for Children and Technology (CCT) and served as associate director for the national OERI-funded Center for Technology in Education connected with CCT. She has fifteen years experience in researching and developing educational media for children, including computer software, television programs, and print materials. She directed the first national survey study to look at K-12 educators' use of telecommunications. She continues to direct a number of projects that are examining the role telecommunications technology can play in students' learning and teachers' professional development. These projects include an Annenberg/CPB Math and Science Project that uses a combination of telecommunications and video-based technologies to deliver in-service seminars to teachers in mathematics, an NSF/NIE initiative that is developing a comprehensive model for district-wide networking infrastructures, and Bell Atlantic's *Project Explore*, which is using a combination of ISDN and ASDL technologies to deliver networked multi-media materials to students and teachers at school and at home. Honey has also worked in the area of gender equity and technology, serving as the principal investigator on two NSF-funded initiatives: *Telementoring Young Women in Mathematics and Science* and *Designing for Equity*. She has a doctorate in developmental psychology from Columbia University.

Henry Jenkins

Henry Jenkins is the director of the Media Studies Program at MIT where he is spearheading efforts to create a master's program in comparative media studies. He is the author or editor of eight books, including *Hop on Pop: The Politics and Pleasures of Popular Culture, The Children's Culture Reader,* and *Textual Poachers: Television Fans and Participatory Culture.* He is currently developing *The Virtual Screening Room,* an interactive-media project designed to teach students how to critically analyze aspects of film style. He is also the codirector of the Media in Transition Project, which is sponsoring a yearlong series of events juxtaposing the so-called "digital revolution" with research on earlier periods when media underwent profound transformations, such as the advent of the printing press and the rise of modern mass media.

Cal Jones

Cal Jones has been writing game reviews for more than six years and works as Reviews Editor for *PC Gaming World,* the U.K.-based sister magazine of *Computer Gaming World.* In addition, she writes a weekly column for ZDNet and has also written for the *Observer, PC Review,* and *Computer and Video Games,* among others. She is a keen "Quake" player and, under her nickname, Damballah, was voted Quake's sexiest female player on Siren's Pic Page, a well-known "Quake" website. Cal Jones was born in 1967.

Yasmin Kafai

Yasmin Kafai is an assistant professor at the UCLA Graduate School of Education and Information, where she also heads KIDS (Kids Interactive Design Studios), a research group dedicated to exploring interactive multimedia design environments for young children. Her current research focuses on young children as designers of artificial worlds and builders of digital archives for science learning, both projects funded by the National Science Foundation. Further projects include the study of video games as learning environments in children's homes and schools via the WWW. She recently published and edited two books, *Minds in Play: Computer Game Design as a Context for Learning* and *Constructionism in Practice: Designing, Thinking and Learning in a Digital World* (with Mitchel Resnick), and various articles in the fields of education, developmental psychology, and computer and information science. Before coming to UCLA, she was at the MIT Media Laboratory for five years and worked at various other advanced technology laboratories in the United States. She holds a doctoral degree from Harvard University.

Aliza Sherman

Aliza Sherman is president of Cybergrrl, Inc., a media and entertainment company at the forefront of creating online programming, products, services, and virtual communities for women. She is the first spokesperson for women in new media, and her cartoon creation Cybergrrl^{SM} is the Internet's first cyber-celebrity. Ms. Sherman is the founder of Webgrrls^{SM}, a networking group for women interested in the Internet that currently has more than 100 chapters worldwide. She is also a freelance writer whose work has appeared in national publications such as *USA Today, Ms., The Net,* and *Exective Female,* and on the Clinique and Lifetime TV websites. She has been profiled in publications including the *Wall Street Journal, US News and World Report, Time Digital,* and *Elle* magazine, and on CNN, CNN-FN, MSNBC, Bloomberg TV, C/NET, and CNBC. She was named one of The Most Powerful People in their 20's by *Swing* magazine in 1997 and was called one of the Top 50 People Who Matter Most on the Internet by *Newsweek.* She is also the author of *Cybergrrl: A Woman's Guide to the World Wide Web* (Ballantine, 1998).

Kaveri Subrahmanyam

Kaveri Subrahmanyam who received her Ph.D. in developmental psychology from UCLA in 1993, is an assistant professor of child development at California State University, Los Angeles. Her interest in computer games goes back to the late '80s, when she and Patricia Greenfield conducted a controlled study investigating effects of video-game practice on spatial skills. Currently she is exploring questions of gender differences in the use of computers and the Internet. Her other research interests include children's reasoning and communication about the physical world. In her spare time, she likes to try out new software (marketed for girls) with her daughter, age eight.

Part One: The Girls' Games Movement

Chapter 1

Chess For Girls?
Feminism and Computer Games
Justine Cassell and Henry Jenkins

Chess for Girls: A Parable for Our Times

A recent *Saturday Night Live* show (Dec. 6, 1997) featured a pseudocommercial for "Chess for Girls." The skit opens with a brother and sister playing chess; the boy soon moves to checkmate his sibling. The girl replies, "Chess is no fun!" and sweeps the pieces off the board in disgust. An announcer comes on and says, "Don't worry, now there's Chess for Girls!", and the commercial launches into a montage of images: a chessboard filled with doll-like pieces, girls brushing the hair of the queen, girls prancing around with the knights, which are beautiful ponies, the brother exclaiming, "Hey, you can't move like that!", and the pieces driving around in a convertible and relaxing in their beach house.

The issues raised by this parody parallel, and serve to introduce, the issues discussed in this book. It is true that more boys play chess than girls. It is also true that chess teaches skills that are important for other arenas of life—skills such as logical thinking, strategic planning, and memory. It might therefore be argued that girls, because they are not enjoying chess, are also not enjoying the cognitive effects of chess. Should this worry parents and teachers? Should this push educators to "open up chess to girls?" If so, what would this opening up look like? Would we encourage girls to take pleasure in the (often minimally social, and not-always-cool) activity of chess by pointing out the benefits to be gained by chess playing? Or would we start companies designed to bring chess closer to pursuits that are more associated with girls—perhaps, as this parody did, by constructing chess pieces that resemble dolls? Or, finally, would we look into the contexts in which girls might appropriate chess, leaving the rules the same but setting up clubs that had the purpose of beating boys at their own game? Might chess-set companies realize that only 50 percent of the youth population was spending its dollars on chess sets, chess books, and electronic chess teachers and implement advertising campaigns aimed at cultivating girl players? Which of the above three strategies would educators and parents choose, and which strategy would the game industry choose? As cultural theorists, psychologists, and theorists of education, which strateg(ies) would we stand behind, and which strategies would we criticize?

Why does a "Chess for Girls" movement seem absurd, while a movement to bring computer games to girls has evoked such strong allegiances? The difference may stem from the fact that while chess has been around long enough for most parents to be comfortable with it, the computer has not. The personal computer, and digital media in general, have come into our lives very recently. Consequently, our children are more likely than us to see the computer as an essential part of their lives, and we are less likely than our children to be entirely comfortable with the technology. This situation leads naturally to parental discomfort: what is this technology, and what is it doing to/for my children? How do I get my children comfortable with this technology (when I am not) so that they can reap the benefits that I see touted everywhere? In addition, whereas it would be difficult to argue that chess—as it is played today—reproduces and reflects inherently sexist images of women (except through exclusion), there are abundant reasons to judge the video games of today as reaffirming sexist ideologies and circulating misogynistic images. For this reason too, parents may worry about the ubiquity of such technology, knowing that the game console may represent the technological equivalent of a "headstart" program, preparing children for participation in the digital realm, and yet at the same time potentially socializing boys into misogyny and excluding girls from all but the most objectified of positions.

In this volume we have united essays representing diverse points of view on each of the questions posed above: chapters by cultural theorists (Jenkins; Kinder), educational theorists (de Castell and Bryson), developmental psychologists (Subrahmanyam and Greenfield; Kafai), academic technologists (Brunner, Bennett, and Honey; Cassell), computer game industry representatives (Duncan and Gesue; Kelley; Laurel; Martin; McEnany), and female game players (the Game Grrlz). We hope this anthology will encourage all of us to examine our core assumptions about gender and games, and propose different tactical approaches for bridging the digital gender gap. This introduction outlines some of the basic factors motivating a critical analysis of existent video games, and the desire to design new ones, and explores some of the political contradictions that surround the initiative to create girls' games.

The "girls' games" movement has emerged from an unusual and highly unstable alliance between feminist activists (who want to change the "gendering" of digital technology) and industry leaders (who want to create a girls' market for their games). Some question whether it is possible to fully reconcile the political goal with the economic one. Some argue that the core assumptions of the girls game movement involve a "commodification of gender" that will necessarily work against any attempts to transform or rethink gender assumptions within American culture. However, these issues represent less a divide between academic and entrepreneurial feminism than mixed feelings and competing impulses that everyone involved with this movement must confront. In many ways, these debates within feminism mark feminism's successes in reshaping public opinion and gaining a foothold in the competitive marketplace (as well as setbacks and areas of concern that feminists hope to address by redesigning technologies and by reconstructing the culture of childhood). This introduction will map the range of different feminist responses to the girls' game question, offering a picture of competing and fluid ideological visions that suggests the inadequacies of media stereotypes of American feminists as doctrinaire and "politically correct." As women gain control over the means of cultural and technological production, they are having to struggle with how to translate their ideals into material practices. This book documents one moment in that process of translating feminist theory into practice.

What Do We Mean by Gender?

In this chapter we introduce the concepts that will arise again and again in the essays that follow. Our approach in this introductory essay is openly feminist in two senses. First, we concentrate on the representation of women in computer games—both their cultural representation (how they are portrayed as characters and the options women are offered as players) and the proportional representation of women in computer game companies (as entrepreneurs or programmers, producers or CEOs). In this context we examine the new wave of women-owned computer game companies as examples of "entrepreneurial feminism." The second sense in which we are feminist researchers comes from our belief that equity between boys and girls, men and women, is a laudable goal. "Equity" here refers to equity of access to education and employment, equity of access to the tools necessary for education and employment, and equity in opportunity to be successful in the path that one has chosen, whatever that path might be. In this context we examine the different ways in which we might strive for equity: equity through separate but equal computer games, equity through equal access to the same computer games, equity through games that encourage new visions of equity itself.

We are conscious that the word "gender" is often used in feminist research where the word "woman" or "girl" might have substituted. And, in line with this observation, all but one of the essays in this volume (Jenkins) primarily address the experience of girls. We defend our choice of title in two ways: in terms of a rejection of biological determinism, and in terms of an acceptance of the the study of women and girls as fundamental to the study of culture. The use of the word "gender" among feminists in the 1970s was meant to underline the fundamentally social or cultural quality of distinctions based on sex. The word denoted a rejection of the biological determinism underlying the earlier term "sexual difference." In this book we are fundamentally concerned with one relationship between sex and culture—between girls and the form of popular culture known as computer games. Too often, the study of computer games has meant the study of *boys* playing computer games. In fact, too often the very design of computer games for children has meant designing computer games for boys (Huff and Cooper 1987, described further below). Here, on the contrary, the study of computer games entails the study of girls. This study will lead us further in the understanding of what computer games can be, and what girls are (and are not). It also leads us to examine the hidden gendered assumptions that have existed in the design of computer games, which in turn leads us to understand better what boys are and are not.

One of the primary issues dealt with by the chapters in this volume, then, is the difference between boys and girls, who they are and what they want in their computer games. What leads us to ask this question in the first place? Would it occur to us to question the difference between light-haired and dark-haired children, who they are, and what *they* want in their computer games? Or, as one (male) computer game company executive told HerInteractive's Sheri Granier, "I have more left handed players than I have female players and I don't make games for left-handed people. Why should I make games for you?" (Weil 1997). In fact, gender as an analytic category has only emerged in the late twentieth century (and even more recently for some industry executives). Though earlier theories may have depended on what they described as a primary opposition between men and women, or may have treated the "woman question," they did not employ gender as a way of talking about systems of sexual or social relations (Scott 1986). Today, however, the binary opposition between the sexes carries much weight, and leads us to speculate about "masculine" and "feminine" qualities, likes and dislikes, and activities. We are used to seeing "masculine" and "feminine" as natural dichotomies—a classification system that mirrors the natural world. This classification is so omnipresent, and so binary, that people have no problem characterizing pairs of inanimate objects with genders (e.g., given the pair "knife/fork," subjects characterized "knife" as masculine and "fork" as feminine). This so-called metaphorical gender is highly relational, however. When people were asked to characterize the pair "fork/spoon," then "fork" became masculine (Rosenthal, cited in Cameron 1992).

And, indeed, much empirical research—as well as market research—finds that boys and girls like different things, act in different ways, have differential success at various tasks. However, we need to be careful that the lens not obscure the view. Hurtig and Pichevin (1985) showed that when asked to categorize the people in a photograph of "successful executives," viewers named the photo as being of "men and women." When different viewers were asked to categorize the people in the same photograph, this time called a photograph of "a group of friends," the categories of male and female did not come into play. Hurtig and Pichevin conclude that sex is only a variable when gender is at issue—that is, only when socially constructed categories are evoked having to do with what we expect of men and women. The binary opposition between masculine and feminine is a purely cultural construct—and a construct that is conceived of differently in different cultures, historical periods, and contexts. Thus, in some cultures fishing is women's work, and in others it is exclusively the province of men. In medieval times, women were considered to be sexually insatiable; the Victorians considered them naturally frigid (Scott 1986). The Malagasy of Madagascar attribute indirect, ornate, and respectful speech that avoids confrontation to men; women are held to be overly direct and incapable of repressing their excitability and anger (Keenan 1974, cited in Gal 1991). In the United States, however, men's speech is described as "aggressive," "forceful," "blunt," and "authoritarian," while women's speech is characterized as "gentle," "trivial," "correct," and "polite" (Kramarae 1980, cited in Gal 1991). In fact, recently it has been shown that even the terms "man" and "woman" do not describe as clear-cut a dichotomy between biological sexes as was once thought (Fausto-Sterling 1993 and Kessler 1994 on biological sex as an infinitely divisible continuum).

What Do We Mean by Computer Games?

What exactly do we mean by computer game, and what were computer games like before the girls' game movement?[1] In this section, we examine the nature of the portrayal of women in traditional computer games, and the nature of the action or plot in these games. We take as examples some of the top-selling console (or video games) and computer games from the late 1980s until today. First, however, a question of terminology. There are two kinds of home electronic games: console and PC. Console games are played on a television set with a converter box: Nintendo NSES is a console system, as is the Sega Saturn and the Sony Playstation. PC games, on the other hand, are loaded into personal computers and started up much like any other software. Both genres arose from electronic arcade games, but they became top-selling household products in the late 1980s. Despite the advent of the home PC, console systems remain big sellers, as does software for these systems. Currently, around 35 million homes in the United States own one of the console systems—that means that 30 percent to 40 percent of American homes own a video game play console (and another 10 percent to 20 percent rent these consoles, or share with neighbors). And the total amount spent on console and PC games in 1997 was $5.8 billion— so it's big business.

Let's turn now to look at what computer games have been like—until now. Video games provide a prime example of the social construction of gender. Women rarely appear in them, except as damsels requiring rescue, or rewards for successful completion of the mission. Most feminist analysis of gender and video games to date has been concerned with the proliferation of violent, aggressive, gory, and often overtly misogynistic images within the video game marketplace. The game "Nighttrap" (with its slasher-movie premise, featuring the bloody murder of scantily clad young coeds), for example, became the focus of a nationwide protest by feminist activists.

In a study of one hundred arcade games (cited in Provenzo 1991), 92 percent contained no female roles whatsoever. Of the remaining 8 percent, the majority (6 percent) had females playing the "damsel in distress," and 2 percent had females playing active roles. However, of these active roles, most were not human (such as "Ms. Pacman" and "Mama Kangeroo"). A study of the cover art of video games turned up similar findings: in looking at forty-seven video games currently on the market, Provenzo (1991) discovered that representations of men outnumbered representations of women by a ratio of thirteen to one (115 male, 9 female) and that twenty men were depicted in "dominant poses," while no women adopted similar postures. There are some inherent problems in Provenzo's methodology, starting with the fact that video game ads and covers are more likely to exaggerate the gender address of the product in order to reach their dominant market. There is some evidence that video game companies are making progress toward including more powerful and competent women in their action games. However, a more recent study by Christine Ward Gailey found that characters continued to be constructed according to a fairly traditional set of gender stereotypes, including the portrayal of good but passive princesses as objects which motivate the action, and bad, eroticized women as competitors who must be beaten back by the protagonist: "The urban violence games imply that women in the streets are dangerous, lower-class and, like the males in the games, sexually mature. . . . The implied message is that, if women are going to be in public (in the streets), they have to be like tough men and expect the hard knocks (literally) that men deliver" (Gailey 1993). In 1998, *Next Generation* magazine concluded that, despite dramatic increases in the number of female game characters, "they all seem to be constructed around very simple aesthetic stereotypes. In the East, it's all giggling schoolgirls and sailor uniforms, but in the West the recipe appears to be bee-sting lips, a micro-thin waist, and voluminous, pneumatic breasts." The article cited a number of female game-company executives, on and off the record, as protesting the continuation of "degrading and offensive images of female characters [that] are still being promoted in games."

The plots of most computer games have depended on violent action or the exploration of space (see Jenkins, this volume). The top-selling video and computer games—until very recently—have all fit into the following categories: action, adventure, driving or flying, fighting, airborne combat, sports, role playing, simulation. And within each category it is often the more violent of the games that has sold the most copies. When one of us (Cassell) advertised for an undergraduate research position on the topic of gender and computer games in 1995, one young man replied:

> It sounds really fascinating, as I am an avid video game player, having both a Super Nintendo and a Sega. What caught my eye about your ad is that it isn't quite right. Take my girlfriend and I for instance: I buy mostly combat/fighting games, which she doesn't really care for. But, I have a game called "Donkey Kong Country" that she just loves to play. So most of the time we sit there like "I want to play Mortal Kombat" and she answers "How about Donkey Kong?" I think that it's not

so much video games that girls/women don't want to play, it's the kinds of games they want to play that make the difference.

The "Mortal Kombat" that this young man refers to is a classic example of a top-selling game in the fighting category—perhaps *the* example of what computer games have been. In "Mortal Kombat," the player uses his warrior skills and powers to kill each of eleven opponents, so as to remain the last warrior alive. The player can choose which warrior he wants to be, and each warrior has a distinct appearance and unique fighting style. None of the warriors is female. As the player kills off his opponents, he is rewarded with more fighting powers. In some cases the warrior rescues helpless damsels, but no women play active roles. The pace is rapid, and the game is accompanied by graphic images of spurting blood and exploding bodies, as well as vivid sound effects of blows. Top-selling games of a similar style are the "Virtua Fighter" series from Sega (recently updated with a female street fighter; see McEnany, this volume) and the "Street Fighter" series from Nintendo, the action games "Quake," "Doom," "Duke Nuke'm," and "Maximum Carnage," and the role-playing games such as "Ogre Battle" and "Lunar the Silver Star."

Of course, some games have always been attractive to girls as well as boys, although they were not explicitly targeted for the girls' market. The most successful examples of androgynous games have been abstract-pattern games such as "Tetris" and "Baku Baku," puzzle-based games such as "Myst," and exploration games such as "Donkey Kong Country," "Sonic the Hedgehog," "Ecco the Dolphin," and "Nights into Dreams." The premise of "Donkey Kong Country" is that somebody has taken the ape's stash of bananas, and he is looking for them with the help of his friend Diddy, a smaller ape. The duo advance through every habitat imaginable, from jungles to abandoned mines to underwater landscapes, in search of the bananas. As the characters make their way through each obstacle course, they win extra lives and extra powers. The draw of "Donkey Kong Country" is beautiful 3D graphics and lush sound effects linked to everyday objects in the environment. In most of these cases, girls were an incidental part of the intended market—a lucky byproduct rather than a consciously pursued demographic.

The arrival of games from the small company Sierra On-Line changed things somewhat. The cofounder of Sierra On-Line was Roberta Williams, one of the first women in the computer games field. By 1989, with her fourth title in the "King's Quest" series, she started incorporating female protagonists into her games—although she admits that she was worried that she would lose her male audience in doing so (LaPlante 1994). Following her lead (and after it became apparent, through the stunning sales of "King's Quest IV," that men were not turned off by such a game), other companies began providing one female character for the user to choose. This character was not always a draw for girls, but it was a nod in the direction of the female audience. As one twelve-year-old girl said after switching from the single female character in the game "Odyssey" to one of the male characters, "I don't like the way she dies. The male characters scream when they're slaughtered. The female character whimpers."

Then, in 1994, a new company called Sanctuary Woods released the first game targeted specifically to girls, "Hawaii High: The Mystery of the Tiki." Its designer was Trina Roberts, a writer for Barbie Comics and designer of Wonder Woman. The game was not successful, probably due to the low budget accorded such a ground-breaking project. It was followed, however, by four or five other games targeted towards girls, and it did introduce some of the features that would dominate the girls' games movement discussed in this volume: more character-centered plots, issues of friendship and social relationships, and bright colorful graphics. Until "Barbie Fashion Designer," none of the games targeted toward girls sold significant numbers of copies. In fact, until very recently, for both console and PC games, girls made up no more than 25 percent of the market.

Violent games without positive representations of women, on the other hand, continued to dominate the field. Parents and critics began to suggest that if video games are a primary means of socialization for young boys in our culture, then feminist mothers and fathers needed to be concerned about their content. Some argued that games reaffirmed or reinscribed dominant and patriarchal conceptions of gender roles through their frequent dependence upon rescue-plot structures with male heroes and female victims, or more frighteningly, that they foster a culture which sees violence, especially violence directed against women, as acceptable. And given the link between early use of technology and later facility with technology, parents and educators also needed to be concerned about the lack of computer games appealing to girls.

The Facts (and Ramifications) of Girls' Differential Use of Computer Games
Parents might argue (and many do) that there is nothing wrong with girls' not being attracted to computer games. Perhaps, they simply don't like computer games. Maybe this will mean that they'll spend more time with other children, or playing outdoors. Isn't this a good thing? There is also a substantial differ-

ence in numbers of men and women who use power mowers, but no "girl power mower" movement has arisen. The problem in the differential attraction to computer games stems from the fact that here, as is often the case, the cultural constructions of gender are not separate from those of power. It is not just that girls seem to like today's computer games less than boys do, but that these differential preferences are associated with differential access to technological fields as the children grow older, and this differential access threatens to worsen as technological literacy increasingly becomes a general precondition for employment. Thus, approximately 75 percent to 85 percent of the sales and revenues generated by the $10 billion game industry are derived from male consumers. And men hold the more powerful jobs in technology-related fields, both in companies that design computer games and in all other digital technologies. This pattern exists even though a woman, Ada Lovelace, invented the notion of a binary computing system, and women, including Grace Hopper, initially programmed ENIAC, the very first full-scale computer. In fact, strikingly small numbers of women hold high positions in the computer industry or in academic computer science. Meanwhile, President Clinton has pledged to connect every school in the United States to the Internet by the turn of the century, ensuring at the very least that more computers will be around for some children to experiment with.

The relationship between boys' comparatively higher interest in computer games and their comparatively larger representation in high-power computer jobs is not accidental. Computer and video games provide an easy lead-in to computer literacy (Loftus and Loftus 1983; Greenfield 1984; Greenfield and Cocking 1996; Kiesler et al. 1985), and so those children who aren't playing them at young ages may end up disadvantaged in later years. In addition, girls report stress when working with educational software that has violent themes (while in the same study, boys report stress when working with software that requires verbal agility and cooperation, and does not contain agressive content) (Cooper, Hall, and Huff 1990). Girls may not simply avoid computers but actually experience stress when using them, even in educational situations. It has been shown, for example, that the violent nature of many video games specifically alienates girls (Malone 1981; Greenfield 1996), reducing the number of female game players (although see Gailey 1993; Sherman 1997). Finally, psychologists have discovered that children learn important cognitive skills by playing video games, such as the ability to maintain attention and to orient things in space, and these skills differ between boys and girls, apparently because of their differential exposure to this medium (Subrahmanyam and Greenfield 1994).

We might argue that video games are not attractive to girls, but that they can catch up by using computers in school. This is not the case, because computers in general are used more by boys than by girls, and perceived to belong more to boys than to girls. Even kindergarten children assign a gender to video games, viewing them as more appropriate toys for boys (Wilder, Mackie, and Cooper 1985). This perception can become a self-fulfilling prophecy: among fourth- through sixth-grade students, "heavy users" of computers are over-whelmingly boys—the ratio of boys to girls is four to one (Sakamoto 1994). Among secondary-school aged children (eleven to eighteen years), boys are at least three times more likely to use a computer at home, participate in computer-related clubs or activities at school, or attend a computer camp. In 1982, only 5 percent of high school girls, as opposed to 60 percent of boys, enrolled in computer classes or used the computer outside of class time (Lockheed 1982). And despite the increasing prevalence of computers in schools and homes, these figures have not changed significantly. (Goldstein 1994). While the majority of studies have examined the state of affairs in North America, the same situation is found internationally (Reinen and Plomp 1993; Makrakis 1993). Thus, in school as well as at home and in after-school programs, boys use computers much much more than girls do.

Things don't look much different when we ask adults how they feel about computers. Men are more interested in computers than women are (Giaquinta, Bauer, and Levin 1993; Morlock et al. 1985), and men are more likely to work in computer-related fields. In 1990, approximately 70 percent of all employed computer specialists were men, a figure which had not changed throughout the 1980s, despite the fact that the computer fields were growing rapidly. In addition, the 30 percent of women in these fields appear to be concentrated in lower-paid, less prestigious jobs (Kramer and Lehman 1990). Although the computer industry continues to grow and to diversify, the statistics are still dismally weighted towards men. According to the most recent (1996) CRA Taulbee Survey, only 16 percent of the bachelor's degrees in computer science were awarded to women. Women received 20 percent of the master's degrees, 12 percent of the Ph.D.s, and were 16 percent of enrolled Ph.D. students. In addition, in the universities surveyed only 19 percent of assistant professors, 10 percent of associate professors, and 6 percent of full computer science professors were female.

Is the disparity one of inherent ability, of interest, or something else? Are girls biologically less able to use digital technology, or is our culture steering them away from it? There is evidence that at the earliest ages, the problem is not one of inherent interest or ability but of access. Kiesler et al. (1985) report:

Even in preschool, males dominate the school computers. In one pre-school, the boys literally took over the computer, creating a computer club and refusing to let the girls either join the computer club or have access to the computer. As a result, the girls spent very little time on the computer. When the teachers intervened and set up a time schedule for sharing computer access, the girls spent as much time on the computer as the boys.... Apparently, girls can enjoy the computer and do like to use it, but not if they have to fight with boys in order to get a turn. (p. 254)

This anecdote reflects the conclusions of a growing number of studies that in the school context, girls are not getting to try out computers, and boys are appropriating the computer as their own. Remember, however, that both boys and girls participate in naming the computer a boys' toy. For whatever reason, by third grade differential access to computers has resulted in different attitudes toward the technology. Giacquintta, Bauer, and Levin (1993) found that boys conceptualize computers differently than girls. Boys are more likely to play games, to program, and to see the computer as a playful recreational toy. Girls tend to view the computer as a tool, a means to accomplish a task, such as word processing or other clerical duties (Ogletree and Williams 1990; Culley 1993). In fact, when a group of educators with software design experience was asked to design software specifically for boys or for girls, they tended to design learning tools for the girls and games for the boys. When they were asked to design software for generic "students," they again designed games—the type of software that they had designed for boys. That is, "[male and female designers] may have been simply using 'male' as the default value of 'student'" (Huff and Cooper 1987). Kiesler et al. (1985) describe this phenomenon as creating an alien culture for girls, a culture that makes them less likely to get involved in the new technology. An informal study of children in an inner-city computer afterschool program (Cassell) showed that the few girls who attended did so because they thought that learning about computers would help them "get ahead in the world," while boys attended because they enjoyed playing with the computers. Adult women are also more likely than men to report that they see the computer as a tool rather than as an interesting artifact in its own right (see Bennett et al. this volume).

But none of this research shows that girls are inherently less skilled at computer tasks than boys. In fact, continued exposure to computer games decreased preexisting gender differences (Greenfield 1996), and when educators really make an effort to ensure that girls have equal time to spend on the computer, girls show equal ability in programming (Linn 1985). Woodrow (1994) found that boys' greater experience and more positive attitude towards computers did not result in higher performance in computer courses. And Kafai (this volume) shows that gender differences in computer game preferences may be context dependent: in a study of children's computer-game design preferences, girls and boys designed very different educational software for teaching math but very similar educational software for teaching science.

In sum, although boys and girls can be equally skilled at using computers and computer games, boys are more likely than girls to choose to play with them, and children of both sexes consider both computers and computer games to be boys' toys. The fact that more boys play computer games means that more games are targeted toward boys. As a spokesperson for Nintendo said, "Boys are the market. Nintendo has always taken their core consumers very seriously. As girls get into that core group, we will look for ways to meet their needs" (Carroll 1994). And the fact that more boys play computer games leads to more men in computer-related fields, fields that are growing in scope and importance every day. The problem becomes compounded as more and more fields (commerce, science, journalism, law, etc.) are becoming heavily dependent upon computers.

Why Are Things Changing Now? A New Market, A New Entrepreneurial Feminism

So parents and educators have reason to wish to change the nature of the technological playing field through the design of new kinds of computer games. The game industry has its own reasons for exploring this issue. The widespread success of video games with young boys has resulted in almost total market penetration. As described above, 80 percent of American boys play video games on a regular basis. And between 30 percent and 50 percent of families in America own or rent game systems and buy or rent games. This saturation has occurred at the same time that Sony Playstation, Sega, and Nintendo have entered a phase of heightened competition. A context like this requires some means of expanding the market, of reaching new consumer groups, particularly if all three "major players" hope to enjoy continued economic growth rather than stagnation, and this problem has turned their attention back towards the long dismissed "girl market" as a potential outlet for new products. Game industry representatives claim that one of the biggest obstacles in creating a girls' market has to do with the gatekeeping functions played by chain toystores, such as Toys 'R' Us and Kaybee. Most of the chain stores demand almost immediate success or the game is taken off the shelf. The window of opportunity can be as narrow as a few weeks, a period hardly long enough to introduce a game and create a new market aimed at girls. Many industry leaders suggest that parents are eager to find games and software that will interest girls in taking their fair share of time on the family computer, even if they are reluctant to invest in the stand-alone platforms for their daughters. Thus it is possible that the increase in PC-based games provides a golden opportunity to open the girls' market. The challenge remains, then, to convince chain toystores and computer stores to stock and showcase the new girls' titles, and then to draw these girls and their parents to the computer stores and game counters, which remain largely male ghettos. HerInteractive's Sheri Granier Ray (Weil 1997) argues that girls are no more comfortable in computer stores than they would be in "a men's underwear department." Purple Moon has sought tie-in arrangements with girls' fashion companies, such as Jonathan Martin, as a way of breaking their "Rockett's World" and "Secret Paths" products into more female-friendly sections of the stores.

As long as the boys' market was sufficient to fuel the growth of the game industry, corporate executives felt little motivation to market to girls. And early games, such as "Hawaii High," did nothing to change their minds. The extraordinary success of Mattel's Barbie Interactive line, however, called attention to the potential market that could be reached by spanning the gender gap. "Barbie Fashion Designer" sold more than 500,000 copies its first two months, outstripping such industry megaliths as "Doom" and "Quake," and demonstrating that interactive media aimed specifically at girls might have strong market appeal. Part of Mattel's success had to do with the figure of Barbie itself. Barbie enjoys a 99 percent market share of American girls between three and ten. On average, the typical American girl owns nine Barbies (Weil 1997). However, there have been many previous and largely unsuccessful attempts to exploit the Barbie trademark via video games. Many argue that the product's success has more to do with the kinds of activities it facilitates than the Barbie name per se. As Subrahmanyam and Greenfield (this volume) discuss, "Barbie Fashion Designer," unlike earlier digital representations of Barbie, is less a computer game than an accessory for play with physical Barbies. As such, "Barbie Fashion Designer" is less subject to the attitudes of girls—and their parents—concerning the appropriateness of playing with the computer. On the contrary, as Nancie Martin, executive producer of the BFD, suggests, (this volume) both parents can feel good about purchasing the program for their daughter—mothers may make the association with the Barbie of their youth, while fathers may feel good about giving their daughters a leg-up into the technological domain.

The new focus on creating the "girls' market" also reflects another significant and broader trend in the American economy, the emergence of what has been called "entrepreneurial feminism." Between 1975 and 1990, women started businesses at more than twice the rate of men. Women now own more than 7.7 million firms, and it has been estimated that by the year 2000 nearly half of all American businesses will be owned by women (Moore and Buttner 1997). Advocates of entrepreneurial feminism (Barrentine 1993) point to the private sector as offering a new site for the empowerment of women, one where economic successes may compensate for political setbacks in the struggle for equal participation and equal compensation. According to Goffee and Scase (1985), "Setting up a small business . . . can represent an explicit rejection of the exploitative nature of the capitalist work process and labor market. In this sense, then, business proprietorship may be seen as a radical—albeit short-term and individualistic—response to subordination . . . . Thus, women who both own and manage business enterprises—especially those in male-dominated sectors—serve to undermine conventional and stereotypical notions about 'woman's place'" (p. 37). Some female entrepreneurs have entered into traditional feminine spheres of activity (such as beauty products, catering and food services, or child care); others have embraced economic enterprises that further the political and social goals of the feminist community (ranging from women's health clinics to feminist presses and bookstores and female-oriented pornography and sex toy shops); still others have sought to open a female market for goods and services traditionally associated with men (including cars, investments, computers, and sports) (Edwards and Stocker 1995). Economists argue that female entrepreneurship has often been most strongly felt in the expanding information and service sector, which has been open to new management techniques (based more on collaboration than on competition, more on networking than on hierarchy) and new forms of customer relations (based on stronger "community ties" to potential consumer groups and a greater dependence upon humanistic modes of audience research).

Many of the companies which have been central to the girls' game movement, such as HerInteractive, Girl Games, Girltech, and Purple Moon, closely parallel these trends—smaller start-up companies that are female-owned and largely female-staffed, and that are motivated both by a desire to transform gender relations within American culture and to create a new and potentially profitable market. Their founders fit the profile of female entrepreneurs in other industries—women who had struggled to get their ideas accepted within the male-dominated fields, which they found largely closed to female-oriented products. Their focus on the girl market reflects an economic reality (the need to open new consumer demographics in order to gain a competitive foothold in a largely closed market) as well as a political commitment to female empowerment, one consistent with their own nontraditional career choices. One sign of a management strategy oriented toward collaboration is the collaboration between the companies themselves. In the fall of 1997, eleven game and software publishers, including not only girl-specific companies such as HerInteractive, Purple Moon, and Girl Games, but also major industry players such as Broderbund and IBM, joined forces to create GIRL, the Girl Interactive Library, working in cooperation to increase visibility for their efforts to broaden the female game market (Just4girls 1997). Their website, Just4girls, became a central source of information about girl-oriented software, a carefully crafted collaboration that allowed all of them to promote their products. The site was designed so that its opening screen would prominently display a different product every thirty seconds, while age-specific categories helped parents to locate appropriate software for their daughters.

In this context, we can't maintain any simple division or split between the feminist academic and the media-industry insider. An increasing number of game designers and producers are women, many work for female-run enterprises, and many make their choices based as much on their political commitments as on their economic goals. Even the lines between academic and market research are blurring. Most of these smaller companies have grounded their design and development of girls' games upon extensive sociological, psychological, and cognitive research into girls' cultural interests and their relationships with digital technologies. Many of the key players in the girls' game movement have written dissertations or books exploring their ideas about gender and game design. The existence of such articulate and thoughtful feminist industry leaders enables the kind of dialogue that is represented by this book.

It is too easy for academic feminists to stand on the outside of this complex process doing ideological critiques rather than struggle with the pragmatic challenges of putting their politics into practice in the marketplace. Some academic feminists, including Marsha Kinder, Justine Cassell, Ellen Seiter, and Henry Jenkins, have consulted with the game companies as they have sought to rethink what a feminine (and feminist) approach to digital media might look like. While some other academics are critical of these activities as reflecting the "corporate takeover" of higher education, these feminists defend their interventions and collaborations with industry by analogy to the role that political activists and academics play in shaping government policies affecting media and culture in Canada, Australia, and the United Kingdom. Such collaborations are necessarily "risky," since they are compromised from the start and are sure to produce "ideologically impure" results. However, just as cultural scholars elsewhere have been willing to work hand-in-hand with government officials, who often come from profoundly different political backgrounds, to shape cultural policy, media academics need to join forces with industry insiders in the American context, where cultural policies are shaped less by government intervention and more through private enterprise. Scholars need to be asking the same practical questions that the industry people are asking, if we hope to set a realistic agenda for social and political change.

Computer Games to Change Gender Relations, or to Satisfy the Girl's Market?
For many industry people, the goal of creating a girls' market involves identifying the existing predilections of girls, often through extensive focus-group research, and then catering to their tastes and needs. Purple Moon's Brenda Laurel told *Wired* (Beato 1997), "I agreed that whatever solution the research suggested, I'd go along with. Even if it meant shipping products in pink boxes." A press release for Purple Moon (1997) describes its products as "guided by the complete and unique understanding of girls and girls' play motivations" that emerged from "thousands of hours" of research. Feminism, on the other hand, has been historically committed to transforming rather than simply responding to existing gender roles. As MIT's Sherry Turkle explained during a *Nightline* (1997) discussion of the girls' games movement, "If you market to girls and boys according to just the old stereotypes and don't try to create a computer culture that's really more inclusive for everyone, you're going to just reinforce the old stereotypes. . . . We have an opportunity here to use this technology, which is so powerful, to make of ourselves something different and better."

As Susan Willis (1991) notes, feminists in the 1960s saw children's toys, books, and media as playing a major role in socializing children to accept gender-specific and highly restrictive social roles. Therefore, hoping to create a "nonsexist" environment in which their children could grow and learn, as Willis writes, "Dress codes were condemned, coed sports flourished, fairy tales were rewritten, and toys were liberated." *Ms.* magazine instituted a special column aimed at feminist mothers which provided gender-neutral or pro-female fairy tales, often drawing on earlier folk traditions or reworking traditional stories to create more empowered images of girls. (For a review of this process, see Zipes 1989.) Marlo Thomas's *Free to Be ...You and Me* (1974) as a book, record, and television special, encouraged boys to explore their feelings and to play with dolls, and sought to encourage more competitive attitudes in girls. *Free to Be* broke down the fixed ascription of gender roles, promoting a unisex ideal where everyone was free to choose identities and activities they found most comfortable. Despite this rhetoric of individual choice, the focus was clearly on transforming the play environment to foster a transformation of traditional stereotypes and to encourage a fusion of masculine and feminine identities. Echoes of this politics of transformative play can be seen in the recent efforts of the Barbie Liberation Organization (Spigel 1994) to switch the voice boxes on talking G. I. Joe and Barbie dolls so that consumers would be more aware of the ways they encouraged stereotypical gender traits, such as a distaste for math and a pleasure in shopping (Barbie), or competitiveness, aggression, and militarism (G.I. Joe). Despite this push toward a unisex vision of play, Willis (1991) finds "a much greater division of toys defined by very particular gender traits [in the contemporary toy market place] than has ever existed before." The feminist goal of encouraging boys to play with dolls so they will become more nurturing caregivers was coopted by toy companies which marketed "action figures" for boys that reflected traditional masculine public-sphere identities, such as professional wrestlers or crime fighters.

Willis (1991) concludes that "It matters little that many nursery schools now mix the dolls and trucks on their play-area shelves if everyone—children in particular—perceives toys as originating in a boy-versus-girl context." The color-coding of products, the narrow casting of children's programs, and the targeting of advertisements for specific genders results in a culture which gives children very clear signals about gender-appropriate fantasies and desires (Fleming 1996). Not surprisingly, the market research which supports the growth of the girls' game movement has located fairly stereotypical conceptions of feminine taste. It is no accident, for example, that girls *do* want their products shipped in pink or purple boxes rather than in royal blue (associated with boys) or black (favored by academic feminists); such desires are manufactured by the toy industry itself long before the researchers get a chance to talk with the girls and find out "what girls really want from technology" (Groppe, cited in Weil 1997). It's difficult to carry out empirical research that doesn't result in children giving as answers what they think they're supposed to say (see de Castell and Bryson, this volume). Appeals to such empirical research as a justification for design and development decisions run the risk of reinforcing (and naturalizing) this gender-polarized play culture rather than offering girls an escape from its limitations on their choices.

Girl game companies defend their choices by arguing that one must get a foot in the door first, starting with existing consumer tastes and trying to broaden them rather than shooting toward an ideal that might meet resistance in the marketplace. Girl Games' Heather Kelly argues that the risks surrounding the production and development of girls software at this point are too high to base decisions on anything other than market research. Rather than shape change, industry insiders hope to respond to girls' shifting tastes as they have greater exposure to digital technologies: "If new representations of gender, including new software designs, emerge, we're going to be responding. . . . We'll always be listening to them and, as they change, because they're more techno-literate, we will change along with them. . . . In some ways, we are pushing the cultural envelope for these girls but in other ways, we're responding to where our culture is right now. We're not trying to change the world from a small company of seven women." (Kelley, this volume) Throughout the interviews in this book, game developers cite instances where their own political commitments—such as the desire to provide more frank information about birth control or queer sexuality—ran up against imperatives of the marketplace or the threat of boycotts by schools and parent groups. These developers argue for some pragmatic compromises in order to foster girls' interests and access to the technology. As many of these entrepreneurs argue, it's exactly the girls who are attracted to pink and lavender, hairspray and nail polish, who need to be turned on to technology. Of course, there are exceptions, girls who are already playing the games made and marketed to boys (i.e., the women who constitute 14 percent to 25 percent of the existing market). The challenge is to reach girls who would previously have displayed little or no interest in technology. Girls' game developers hope to reach a female consumer that Purple Moon (1997) describes as "a contradiction in terms: adventurous, smart, competitive and shy, self-conscious and unsure . . . a mystery to most adults." These particular consumers, according to game designer Heidi Dangelmaier, are searching for "experiences where they can make emotional and social discoveries they can apply to their own lives," and often respond to male-centered games as a "waste of time" (Weil 1997; Dangelmaier). Building on these properties, Purple Moon markets its products not as games but as "friendship adventures for girls." Such designers and developers hope to accent features of digital technology that have been ignored in the push for the male market and to develop software that reflects a fundamentally different conception of what a computer can do. However, the impulse to specifically attract the girl consumers results in everything from the creation of pink and lavender control pads to the development of prettier graphics and lusher soundtracks that reflect a perceived feminine aesthetic sensibility. *Salon* magazine documented a story conference for Her-Interactive's "Nancy Drew" game that started with ideas that radically broke with traditional girls' culture themes and motifs (Nancy Drew as a hacker, Nancy using plastique) before settling back on the discovery of a purse (complete with lipstick and compact) as a major plot device. One of the designers protested, "We're going to get hit with, it's so stereotypical. It's such a girl game. But what are you going to do, you know? Girls like lipstick" (Weil 1997).

Moreover, we need to be careful about dismissing traditional girls' interests too easily. Much feminist scholarship in recent years has centered around reclaiming and revaluing women's traditional cultural interests and competencies, recognizing, for example, the political power of gossip or the community-building functions of quilting. As Ellen Seiter (1993) has suggested, broad-based attacks on sweet and frilly girls shows, such as *My Little Pony* and *Strawberry Shortcake,* as "insipid" often resemble earlier dismissals of adult women's genres such as melodrama, romance, or soap opera. These criticisms are grounded in a distaste for women's aesthetic preferences toward character relations and emotional issues, and they are rooted in the assumption that nonprofessional women (whether they are the housewives who read Harlequin romances or their daughters who buy Care Bears) are mindless and uncritical consumers of patriarchal culture. But, as Radway (1984) shows, if one examines not just the content but also the social event of reading, one finds that for many romance readers reading itself is a combative act, carried out during stolen moments of privacy, and contesting the usual self-abnegation of their lives. Seiter (1993) calls on us to value girls' cultural tastes and interest, even as we push toward more empowering fantasies, since there are so many other forces in society that belittle and demean girls. As Seiter notes:

> Something was gained and lost when marketers and video producers began exploiting little girls as a separate market. Little girls found themselves in a ghettoized culture that no self-respecting boy would take an interest in, but for once, girls were not required to cross over, to take on an ambiguous identification with a group of male

characters. . . . The choice is not made out of identification with an insipid and powerless femininity but out of identification with the limited sources of power and fantasy that are available in the commercial culture of femininity.

Game producers defend their efforts on precisely these grounds, insisting that they want to respect and value aspects of traditional femininity even as they seek to open up new spaces for girls. Girl Games' Laura Groppe argues, "I want girls to know that it's OK to be a girl!" (Russo 1997). Often, they cite books like *Reviving Ophelia: Saving the Selves of Adolescent Girls* (Pipher 1994) or *Schoolgirls: Young Women, Self Esteem, and the Confidence Gap* (Orenstein 1995) that point toward a devastating loss of self-confidence experienced by preteen girls as they enter into a culture that consistently devalues their interests, skills, and abilities. Games and software which reaffirm girl tastes are offered as an attempt to counteract such pressures, to help girls recognize that they are not alone and that the things they like are not stupid. Many of the commercial products, such as Girl Games' "Lets Talk About Me!", struggle to reconcile an expanded sphere of activity for girls with their traditional interests in fashion, personal appearance, and dating, by offering information about women in sports or about the professional lives of successful women, and by developing role models like Tech Girl, who combines pink lips and cheeks with a "can-do" attitude towards technology.

One implication of Seiter's analysis of *My Little Pony* in this context is to guard against knee-jerk feminist horror over Barbie and to reflect on what kinds of pleasures and interactions young girls' interests in Barbie enables. Erica Rand's remarkable *Barbie's Queer Accessories* (1995) and Lynn Spigel's Paper Tiger video, *Twist Barbie* (1994), both point the way towards queer and feminist reappraisals of Barbie that complicate any easy account of her place in young girls' lives. After an extensive investigation of Barbie Culture, Rand concludes: "one thing I learned from talking to people about Barbie is that we need to be very humble about our own ability to inscribe meaning in objects, to discern the meanings that others attribute to them, or to transfer conclusions about resistance, subversion, and hegemony from person to person, object to object, context to context" (p. 195). Mattel's Nancie Martin (this volume) adopts a similar argument in defending Barbie as opening up a broad range of fantasies for young girls, including both traditionally feminine careers (such as cheerleader and fashion model) and more unconventional ones (such as astronaut or corporate executive): "We girls can do anything! Barbie started out with a career. She began as a teenage fashion model. So there's a long history of saying, 'Your job is not to get married. Your job is not just to be pretty. You can have a job. You can do stuff in the world. And if you want to wear a hat and high heels while you're doing it, you can do that, too.'" However, much of Rand's defense has focused on the prospect of appropriative play in the hope that girls can use Barbie to enact a broader range of fantasies (including "dyke coming out" stories) than Mattel can commercially market. Increasingly, guidebooks for progressive parents, such as Dr. Montana Katz's *The Gender Bias Prevention Book* (Ivinski 1997), encourage teaching children to "play games with Barbie in which she engages in assertive, self-determined behavior and words. . . . Just because Barbie has been manufactured and marketed to fit and encourage a certain mindset doesn't mean we need to keep her stuck there for good." Some of the girl-oriented websites promote an active questioning of the media's constructions of femininity. For example, a Tech Girl website (Ivinski 1997) encourages readers to "send Disney an e-mail and ask it to make more animated movies featuring girls who have more to think about than finding someone to fall in love with." However, as Pamela A. Ivinski (1997) notes, the structured interactivity of "Barbie Fashion Designer" restricts the potential for appropriative and resistant play, facilitating the creation of "miniskirts and wedding dresses" but not of the work clothes needed to create "Barbie Auto Mechanic or Barbie Police Officer."

Working outside the commercial context, USC's Marsha Kinder (this volume) has been able to prototype a game, "Runaways," that radically questions cultural assumptions about sex, gender, and sexuality. Although Kinder hopes to turn her prototype into a commercial product, she recognizes that her academic-based production context frees her to experiment with digital media in a way that would be difficult for those working in more commercial settings: "This is an experimental project. And if you're already thinking about how it's going to be censored from the time that you're beginning to design it, you're not going to be able to really do anything different. You've got to be willing to take some risks." Kinder hopes that her game will be able to take more risks because it will build on the proven track record of Barbie Interactive and the other girl games, yet she concedes that many aspects of the game's design will prove controversial with parents.

Some game-industry insiders have criticized the over-reliance on market research from another angle. Theresa Duncan, one of the creators of "Chop Suey," has been one of the sharpest critics of the new "girl games," commenting, "I feel like they take their inspiration from MacDonalds and I take mine from

Maurice Sendak" (Weil 1997). Duncan stresses the need for less market research-driven development and more creativity in inventing the game genres to satisfy alternative tastes and sensitivities. In a *Feed* forum on the state of video games (Feed 1997), she attacked the "earnest blandness" of the girls' games, which she said reminded her of "the filmstrips we had to watch in junior high health class." Market research, Duncan argues, "ensures the maximum return on investment, but it also seems to ensure the minimum amount of personality and warmth," resulting in a "perfunctory" feminism she finds even more meaningless than "slapping the pink bow on 'Pacman.'" Game designer Heidi Dangelmaier agrees: "What all these new girl products should have done was open up different ways the interactive medium can integrate into our free time and our social time, and instead what's being produced is really cheesy and petty. What needs to happen is for girls' games to get out of the realm of gender and into the realm of design" (Weil 1997). These critics argue that the call for girls' games should be an invitation to explore new formats, to develop alternative models of software rather than simply to conform to assumptions about gender that are created and reinforced by existing market pressures. They fear that the market research-driven development will result in too narrow a conception of what girls' games might be, leading to stale and formulaic products and an over-harvesting of the potential girls' market. Market research of this sort may also perpetuate an essentialist position on the difference between what boys and girls want from digital media, which is but one short slippery step away from the biological determinist position that argues that boys and girls want different things because of the fact that they are boys and girls.

Computer Games for Girls (Whatever Girls Are)

For the most part, the girls' game movement has operated under the assumption that girls and boys want something fundamentally different from digital media, that it is possible to find out what they want from market research, and that the best way of responding to this situation is to create girls-only or girl-directed media that stand alongside more boy-centered media. One girls' game designer has suggested she wanted to give her product "Cooties" so that boys would stay away, and girls would see it as their own space and feel comfortable playing there without boy interference. *Time* referred to the movement as an attempt to create "a rom of their own" (Krantz 1997). On the other hand, as we have seen, feminists often have harshly criticized the widening separation of the pink and blue sections of the toy store, pushing for a more unisex approach to children's toys and play. Jan Russo (1997), a mother writing for *Superkids Educational Software Review,* expressed concern that the labeling of girls' games might encourage girls to shut themselves off from the broader range of products on the market: "Why create gender-specific software? Doesn't its generation imply that the myriad of excellent educational programs already in existence is not for girls—the underlying message being that girls can't truly enjoy the currently popular math, science, reading, and problem-solving titles? Or more pointedly, that those titles will prove to be too difficult for girls, that we need to paint computer software pink to make it girl-friendly?" Cascade Pass's series of software aimed at preparing girls for entry into professions, such as "You Can Be a Women Engineer" or "You Can Be a Woman Architect," suggests the tightrope to be walked: on the one hand, potential for marginalization and ghettoization; on the other hand, a "leg up" into traditionally male fields. Women's professional organizations have long fought against such gender-specific designations, hoping for women to gain recognition as "architects," not as "women architects." Such products may unintentionally reinforce the perception that technical, scientific, and professional fields are predominantly male turf, even as they try to provide girls with earlier access to the skill sets and knowledge bases necessary to compete in such vocations.

Underlying the position that there are fundamental differences between what boys and girls want from computer games is a discourse that posits essential differences in girls' and boys' cultural tastes, interests, and competencies, entering into what *Wired* jokingly called "the land of sweeping generalizations" (Beato 1997). Throughout most of the essays and interviews in this book, you will encounter phrases such as "girls like. . .," "girls prefer. . .," or "girls want. . . ." Despite the clear dangers of such "sweeping generalizations," the ability to determine what girls want may seem necessary at a time when we are trying to open up a space for girls to participate within this medium at all. Historically, gender was an unexploited category in video game design, with male designers developing games based on their own tastes and cultural assumptions without considering how these approaches might be anything other than gender-neutral. *Nightline* (1997) quoted Id's Todd Hollenshead, "What we try to do is make games that we think are fun and they're not targeted to any specific gender." Yet, as feminist critics note, as long as masculinity remains the invisible norm, the default set within a patriarchal culture, unselfconscious efforts are likely to simply perpetuate male dominance. And, this does seem to have been the case with video game design—remember Huff and Cooper's finding that when game designers designed for "children," they designed products identical to those they designed for boys (and different than those they designed for girls). As game designer John Romero ("Revolution" 1997) explained, "Men design games for themselves because they understand what they know is fun. They don't understand what women find fun." Female game designers consistently complain that their ideas were rejected because they did not conform to their company's often implicit assumptions about what made for a "good game" or a "fun" product.

The development of market research that examines girls' actual tastes and preferences may help to challenge the stereotypes and assumptions that shaped previous attempts to market games for girls. Those initial attempts amounted to putting boys' game iconography and structure in drag (an approach parodied by a series of "Byte Me" (Stamatiadis and Passfield 1997) cartoons that depict game designers introducing "Barbie Quake" or painting the tanks in their combat games pink) or simplifying the game for girls, an approach that Brenda Laurel (this volume) argues took the game industry in exactly the wrong direction. Laurel protests that girls seek different kinds of complexity than boys, complexity in terms of the character relations, not in terms of the action elements. The recognition of gender differences in tastes and preferences may be the first step in broadening who has access to the technology and expanding the range of functions that digital media play in our lives.

However, we run the risk of flattening the diversity of girls' cultural interests. British sociologist Angela McRobbie (1991) notes that from an early age, male-centered magazines start to differentiate boys according to hobbies, sports, professional ambitions, and so on, while girl-centered publications have tended to be organized purely around age levels, assuming that all girls are interested in romance, make-up, physical fitness, cooking, and fashion. McRobbie traced women's magazines across a life cycle that starts with teen romance, acknowledges the budding of late-adolescent sexuality, and then settles into "marriage, childbirth, home-making, child-care, and Woman's Own." Girl Games' "Lets Talk About Me," with its sections devoted to "my body," "my scene," "my life," or "my personality," comes eerily close to the British teen girls' magazines (such as *Jackie*) that McRobbie critiqued almost two decades ago. As McRobbie notes, these female-targeted publications establish "the personal" as "the sphere of primary importance to the teenage girl," treating it as an "all embracing totality" that precludes other forms of social and political intervention and that acknowledges only a narrow range of acceptable lifestyle choices.

"Let's Talk About Me"'s morphing, multicultural logos reflect a conscious attempt to expand the range of female identities, yet it has done little to broaden the range of topics deemed central to girls' lives, except to add "my computer" to the mix.

Feminism has struggled to break down univocal conceptions of gender and open a space for many ways of being masculine and feminine. The development of girls' games needs to be careful to reflect the diversity of women's lives and to foster acceptance of a range of different feminine styles and identities. Industry insiders, however, note that to do so would necessitate fragmenting an already small, marginalized, and developing market, insisting that such specialization of interests will be possible only when the girls' game industry is more firmly established. For the moment, they claim that they are forced to market to a "normative" or "average" conception of femininity, while inserting alternative interests around the margins. Purple Moon's "Rockett's World" series reflects this impulse, casting the red-haired, thin, middle class, and white Rockett as the American everygirl around whom is arrayed a broader range of gender, racial, and cultural types.

In addition, we might wish to question the very essentialist binary opposition between boys and girls. That is, we might ask in what contexts girls play with computers differently than boys do, and in what contexts their play styles are similar? How do race and class intersect with gender in explaining differences in play styles? Laurel (this volume) describes focus-group research that entailed bringing a girl in with her best friend "in order to keep her honest." What if the presence of two girls, instead, perpetuated a girl's need to act in the manner that she thought was consistent with her evolving sense of gender roles?

Recent feminist inquiry suggests that the behavior of men and women is often explained in terms of gender differences, regardless of its content, and despite the fact that the same behavior might be explained in terms of any one of a number of other analytic constructs. Books such as *Men Are from Mars, Women Are from Venus,* and Deborah Tannen's best-selling book on men and women's language differences, *You Just Don't Understand,* testify to the special interest that gender-based explanations hold for Americans in the 1990s. In this sense, the theory of gender differences constructs gender practices. That is, when one looks for differences between the sexes, and does not take into account other crosscutting variables, one is likely to find those differences. An alternative position might posit that we "do" gender, and that we do it differently in different contexts. This performative view of gender (in the sense that we perform particular gender roles, as described by Butler, 1990) is discussed further in deCastell and Bryson, and Cassell (both in this volume). In terms of the issues discussed here, we might analyze computer games in terms of their reproduction of static forms of gender identities, noting that certain computer games allow girls to feel comfortable in their girlhood. Those games fit comfortably into what a girl believes (consciously or unconsciously) is expected of her in order to merit the label "girl." For example, Martin's analysis of how girls play with Barbie (this volume), suggests remarkable similarities in the way that all girls play with Barbie, and remarkable constancy between how different generations of girls have played with Barbie, as well as remarkable loyalty to ensuring that if one has a Barbie doll, one's daughter should have one too. Such a description leads us to the conclusion that Barbie play is a central part of the construction of girlhood. These meanings do not so much arise from the Barbie doll itself as from social norms about the appropriate way to play with Barbie. Martin's analysis of "universal" Barbie play contrasts with Rand's account (1995), which sees the Barbie doll as an object that lends itself particularly well to appropriation, and to a variety of self-identifications and types of gendered behaviors. Such an analysis does not deny that there may be empirically observable associations between certain kinds of behaviors and children of a particular gender. We simply question the "single-genderedness" of these associations by asking what other variables are present (race, class, sexual orientation). The computer game "Runaways" (Kinder, this volume) challenges the notion of gender by splintering it, demonstrating that biological sex and gender are not the same, and that neither is the same as self-perceived gender identity or sexual orientation. SAGE and Rosebud (Cassell, this volume) take an alternative approach to challenging the notion of binary, ontological gender by creating access to computer games for children who engage in a variety of gendered activities. In fact, these games rely on the computer, which so readily reflects us to ourselves (Turkle 1984), as a site for the very construction of gender and other aspects of the child's social reality.

Thus, we might understand the kinds of activities that have been described as "what girls really do" not as neutral or isolated acts but instead as involving the person becoming and acting in the world as part of the construction of a complex identity. In this case, designing "games for girls" misses the point. We should, rather, expand the range of activities we can perform on a computer so as to encourage identity formation as a part of the game. Otherwise, we are teaching girls to act like girls are supposed to act.

New Computer Games for Girls, or a New Look at the Old Games

In much of what's been said above, it's been assumed that the existent selection of game genres are fundamentally wrong for building female access to the technology. We are told that girls simply don't like to play fighting games or that they don't respond well to sport and violence. However, a closer look at trends in popular culture suggests that every one of these generalizations is subject to challenge. The success with women of self-defense classes and of female-centered action films, such as *Thelma and Louise* or *Aliens*, shows that violent imagery is compatible with not only feminine taste but feminist politics. Female action protagonists, such as television's Xena (Sheff 1997) and the comic-book heroine, Tank Girl (Whelehan and Sonnet 1997), have attracted strong female followings, including many lesbians, who celebrate their refusal to conform to traditional gender roles and their ability to hold their own against male opponents. Much of what gets read as female empowerment within popular culture represents feminist appropriation of violent images for their own ends. The popularity of women's sports, the emergence of "soccer girls" and "soccer moms" as increasingly central categories of social analysis (Gailey 1997), suggests a potential girls' market does exist for sports-centered games. If we consider the dominant genres of video and computer games, such as horror and the supernatural, science fiction, sword and sorcery, and mystery, each of them has historically had tremendous participation by women as writers and attracted strong interests by women as consumers (Penley, Lyon, Spigel, and Bergstrom 1991; Jenkins 1992; Bacon-Smith 1992; LeFanu 1989; Donawerth 1997; Wolstenholme 1993; Pinedo 1997). Many of the female-authored works in these genres offer untapped sources for stories, characters, plots, and iconography that might be exploited by the game industry in its search for games that display a strong crossover potential.

Some industry insiders, such as Sega's Lee McEnany (this volume), argue that what is needed to breach the gender gap are not new game genres designed specifically for girls but the successful development of traditional boys' games with stronger female characters. Sega's approach has been to introduce female protagonists into many of its fighting games, giving them strengths and capabilities that are attractive to both male and female players. McEnany, who is herself an enthusiastic fan of traditional video games, believes that better marketing of existing game genres to female consumers may help to close the gap between male and female players. Fantasy role-playing games have proven especially successful in attracting female gamers to games designed and developed primarily for male consumers.

Core Design's "Tomb Raider" (Whitta 1997) hit the shelves around the same time as "Barbie Fashion Designer" and with sales stretching well past 2.5 million has done its own part to shake up industry assumptions about gender. "Tomb Raider"'s protagonist, Lara Crofts, a female archeologist modeled loosely after Indiana Jones, has become one of the most familiar icons in the contemporary game industry, spurning not only game sequels but discussions of other spin-off products, including feature films and television series. Core Design sought to center its action-adventure game around a strong female protagonist, one who is muscular and acrobatic and capable of holding her own in all kinds of dangerous situations. "Tomb Raider" creator Toby Gard told *The Face* (as quoted in Whitta 1997): "Lara was designed to be a tough, self-reliant, intelligent woman. She confounds all the sexist cliches apart from the fact that she's got an unbelievable figure. Strong, independent women are the perfect fantasy girls—the untouchable is always the most desirable." Gard sought to balance traits that would make Crofts an attractive role model for game-playing girls and a sexually attractive figure for their core male market, a balance not that radically different from the formula that made *Xena* such a cult success on television. Female gamers have objected, however, to many of the company's efforts to promote the game to male players, including the hiring of a scantily clad female model to impersonate Crofts at computer trade shows, or the development of an ad campaign based on the theme "Where the Boys Are" and showing lusty boys abandoning strip clubs in search of Lara (Brown 1997a; Jones 1997; Game Girlz 1997). An underground industry in home-developed nude shots of Lara Crofts, including a Nude Raider (1997) website, and rumors that someone has developed a hack which allows one to play the game with a totally naked protagonist suggest the dangers in linking female empowerment to images couched in terms of traditional sex appeal (Whitta 1997). And game magazine coverage of Lara Crofts and the attempts of other game companies to imitate "Tomb Raider"'s success explain the phenomenon almost entirely in terms of her erotic appeal to young male players. Corrosive Software's Kate Roberts asks, "Would Tomb Raider have sold as many copies if Lara had been wearing a nice warm sweater and sweatpants?" (Next Generation 1998). Crofts' popularity may represent the success of a female protagonist (albeit one conceived in terms of male visual pleasure), but she would seem to have done little to alter the relations between girl gamers and the game industry.

Arguments explaining male gamers' close trans-gender identification with Lara Crofts closely parallel Carol Clover's discussions of the "final girl" convention in 1980s slasher films (1992). In both cases, male identification with a female figure allowed a heightened sense of vulnerability or risk that did not endanger conventional conceptions of masculine potency and courage. The result was, in films like *Halloween, Friday the 13th* and *Scream,* and in video games like "Tomb Raider," a more thrilling experience for male players. In other words, Clover's analysis might suggest that Lara Crofts (the digital equivalent of the "final girl") exists not to empower women but to allow men to experiment with the experience of disempowerment. Interestingly, Clover argued that the androgynous personae of the 1980s slasher heroines (including tomboy traits and gender neutral names in many cases) were a key factor in enabling male fans to overcome their resistance to transgender identification, while the success of "Tomb Raiders" has been linked to the exaggeration of Lara Crofts' feminine characteristics. Clover's attempts to explain the appeal of such figures for male horror-film fans, however, may foreclose too quickly the possibility that women may also find such figures sources of identification (however compromised by male interests and fantasies) within scenarios of empowerment. Increasingly, research into the horror audience suggests strong female participation, and the recent success of the *Scream* films has been ascribed in part to their popularity with teenage girls. When Jenkins teaches a class in "Horror and the Supernatural" at MIT, female students consistently outnumber men.

In general, though, male- and female-centered examples of these genres reflect different interests and reward different kinds of competencies. If we compare Anne Rice's vampire novels with splatterpunk horror, for example, we see a difference between traditionally female interests in character relations and emotional issues and traditionally male interests in action and gore. Studies of female fan fiction based on male-centered action-adventure series find that the women often use the existing genre elements as a backdrop for elaborating on themes of romance, friendship, partnership, and community (Jenkins 1992; Bacon-Smith 1992; Penley 1997; Clerc 1996). Henry Jenkins (Tulloch and Jenkins 1995) asked male and female fans of *Star Trek* to say what came to mind when the names of series characters were mentioned: in most cases, male fans identified the characters' capacities as "autonomous problem-solvers," while women consistently fit the characters into a web of complex relationships (romances, friendships, mentorships, partnerships). Those commercial products that have built strong fan followings—*Star Trek* is a classic example—consciously build in both action and character elements and thus reward multiple reading competencies. On the other hand, digital manifestations of *Star Trek* systematically strip away the elements most attractive to female fans, while preserving those having high appeal to male consumers (Jenkins and Murray forthcoming). "Star Trek" games have been innovative in their use of Quick-Time VR, for example, to reproduce the ship as part of an interactive technical manual, but they show a relentless focus on issues of hardware, and depend—like most other video games—on situations of conflict rather than negotiation and exploration. In most cases, the technical choices made by the game designers strip character differentiation to its bare minimum and focus on iconographic rather than cultural differences between the series' alien races. As in the example of Barbie, the digital manifestations of *Star Trek* allow a far narrower range of interactions and appropriations than its previous manifestations.

A core question we need to ask is whether opening the girls' market involves changing the generic base of the game industry (focusing more on romantic, melodramatic, and fairy tale genre traditions, moving from a male sphere of public action toward a female sphere of domestic relations) or shifting the kinds of cultural competencies recognized within the existing generic repertoire (creating horror games that are more like the novels of Anne Rice, imagining games that facilitate play on multiple levels, or developing strong female protagonists, like Lara Crofts, without the overt pandering to adolescent male interests in "tits and ass"). Both scenarios require more responsiveness to female consumers than has historically been visible from the major games companies. The first approach, however, presumes the need for a girls-only game market (the approach taken by Girl Games and Purple Moon), while the second presupposes the possibility of expanding or broadening the existing game market to include both male and female consumer interests (the approach taken by Sega).

The most powerful challenge to the separatist logic behind the girls' game movement has come from an unlikely corner—organizations of female gamers who have embraced traditional fighting games, especially "Quake," as a space where they can confront men on their own terrain and literally beat them at their own game (Abroms 1997; Brown 1997b; Sherman 1997; Brown 1997c; Cavanaugh 1997). Embracing an ethos of empowerment through head-on competition, celebrating their pleasure in "fragging" men, these women have formed all-female clans, such as Die Valkarie, Clan PMS (Psycho-Men-Slayers), and Crack Whores, to do battle in on-line "Quake" tournaments.

In some cases, these groups see themselves as loosely linked to the Riot Grrls, a post-feminist, post-punk movement that has stressed female empowerment through participation in traditional male spheres ranging from motorcycle racing to punk rock and computer games (For further information on Riot Grrls, see Duncombe 1997; Riot Grrls 1997). Like the Riot Grrls, the Game Grrls seek to escape all fixed identities, whether they are the exploitative images of scantily clad women fostered by the traditional game industry ("Babette, the curvaceous redhead with giant overflowing cantaloupe boobs who had to be melted and poured into a glistening black latex bodysuit and has all the muscles of a limp noodle" (Gilbert 1998) or the "stereotypical 50s 'nice girl'" images promoted by the girls' game industry (Douglas 1997). The Riot Grrls have overtly criticized the "victimization" approach taken by many "second wave" feminists, an approach they see as destroying female confidence and fostering the ghettoization of women. Responding to a comment made by Sherry Turkle on *Nightline* bemoaning young males' interest in militaristic games, Game Grrl Nikki Douglas (this volume) protested, "Maybe it's a problem that little girls don't like to play games that slaughter entire planets. Maybe it's why we are still underpaid, still struggling, still fighting for our rights. Maybe if we had the mettle to take on an entire planet, we could fight some of the smaller battles we face everyday."

Often, Game Grrls play with juxtapositions of traditional feminine iconography and aggressive fighting-game images, as can be suggested by such persona names as Fear-No-Man, Goddess, Hellkitten, Icequeen, Killer Bitch, or Lethal Lady. As one of the Crack Whores told *Wired,* "Under every floral print dress lies a lady wearing black garters, carrying a big fucking gun!" (Brown 1997c). The Crack Whores (1997) construct on-line personas based on the cliches of pornography, stressing their measurements and their pleasure in "fucking" and "fragging." Responding to a woman who wrote to say she was uncomfortable with the overtly sexual tone of their website, a Crack Whores (1997) spokesperson explained, "Part of the online multi-player gaming experience is the use of wild and extreme personas. Who would you rather deathmatch against, sweet Barbie from Clan Doll or Street Fightin' Mona from the CrackWhores. The name IS intended to shock and stimulate. My suggestion? Don't bother explaining it to your friends. :)" Such play with overtly sexualized identities reflects the Riot Grrls' political stance as pro-sex feminists who urge women to claim control over their bodies and who sharply criticize what they see as the repressive morality of anti-porn activists. Other groups embrace amazonian imagery, drawing on a whole tradition of images of women warriors and mythological goddesses. The Crack Whores' website plays with this tradition, running a contest for the best digital transformation of "Quake"'s beefy protagonist into a warrior princess.

Although their all-female membership might suggest some forms of separatism, these Game Grrls proudly report on their victories over male clans as well as acknowledge their partnerships with male gamers. Q. Girlz (1997) features a special "whipping boys" section, where they acknowledge what they have learned from the men in their lives and jokingly suggest the following "whipping boy" requirements: "1. Do what we say; 2. Don't think; 3. Pick up after us; 4. Bring us gifts; 5. Kiss our ASSes." Their websites provide a location for discussions of male and female interests in digital media, including such regular features as "he sez, she sez" game reviews, as well as occasional discussions about how female players may deal with online harassment. The Game Grrls refuse to give into ridicule or harassment from male players, many of whom are reluctant to believe they "really are" female "Quake" players. As Mona of Crack Whores explained to *Wired*, "Since you're a girl, the guys expect you to really play poorly. So we take pride in ripping them to sorry little shreds" (Brown 1997c).

The "Quake Grrls" movement gives these women, who range in age from their mid-teens to their late thirties, a chance to "play with power," to compete aggressively with men and to refuse to accept traditional limitations on female accomplishments. Their unconventional rhetoric playfully flaunts their militarism, yet their ties to traditional feminism remain firm. Q. Girlz' website (1997), for example, quotes Sylvia Plath ("out of ash I rise/with read hair and/eat men like air") and includes links to both Riot Grrl and traditional feminist sites. The "Quake Grrls" represent a radically different conception of the girls' market than proffered by girls' game industry insiders, refusing a separatist culture based on feminine interests and fantasies, insisting that women can hold their own in the realm of traditional fighting games and that they may take pleasure precisely in doing things that are not prescribed for women in our culture. The "Quake Grrls" are, on the whole, older than the girls being targeted by the girls' games movement, more self-confident, more comfortable with technology, and more mature in their tastes and interests. These Quake Grrls are lobbying the game industry to generate games that more directly reflect their desires, treating female characters neither as victims nor as sex objects but as "a vicious, bloodthirsty, take-no-prisoners kind of grrl" ready to fight for her place in the world.

Conclusion

In this chapter we've presented arguments from all sides of the console on how to construct a space for girls' play with computer games. The comments of the Game Grrls allow us to boil the issues down to their essentials: do we encourage girls to beat boys at their own game, or do we construct a girls-only space? The problem is that both sides, ultimately, start from the assumption that computer games are boys' own games, and thus both scenarios can result in the disparaging of girls' interests. Girls have always enjoyed greater freedom than boys to engage in transgender play. Tomboys carry far less stigma in our culture than sissies do. This ability to cross gender boundaries may be related to the fact that girls have had fewer choices: there are more games and activities that feature boys or cater to their play styles (Vaughter et al. 1992). In more general terms, boys' tastes constitute the unmarked option in the world. Markedness is a concept taken from linguistics to express the nature of relationships between members of a binary opposition where one member is more regular or simple than the other, more frequently found, more neutral in meaning, and more generic. For example, in grammar the singular number of the English noun is unmarked with respect to the plural—the singular is simpler in that it doesn't have the suffix (for example, the s in *pots*), it is more often found than the plural, and it does not have the added meaning that the plural does. When this concept is applied to gender, it is clear that the way in which boys dress is seen by American society as the unmarked option. That is, girls can dress as boys do, but the opposite is not true (girls can wear jeans, but boys don't wear dresses). Thus, boys' dress is found more frequently, is more generic (found on boys and girls), and more neutral in meaning (it means nothing for a girl to wear jeans, but there is always some kind of meaning attached to finding a boy wearing a dress). In the case of computer games, the unmarked association between children and computers is that boys play with computers and girls don't. Note that girls can play boy games ("Quake," "Tomb Raider"), but it is highly marked behavior for boys to play with girl games (imagine giving your son "Barbie Fashion Designer").

Thus, in playing with computers games that are not explicitly targeted for girls, are girls simply showing their increased flexibility—their ability to engage in both girls' and boys' play—or are they making of computer games a real girls' space? The danger is that when girls take over games that have been traditionally male, the norm is not questioned. Game Grrls can always be read as a harmless aberration. Boys' games remain the norm, and they remain games for boys. Independent of the personal benefits that playing "Quake" might bring them (experimenting with power and autonomy), the presence of girl gamers might do nothing to lessen the identification of "Quake" with boys. Still then, "men and women are not simply considered different from one another, as we speak of people differing in eye color, movie tastes, or preferences for ice cream. In every domain of life, men are considered the normal human being, and women are 'ab-normal,' deficient because they are different from men" (Tavris 1992). On the other hand, if we target games toward girls, we may find ourselves falling into the trap of targeting only the most stereotypical aspects of current girlhood. In doing so, we are ensuring that boys will not play with girl-targeted games, once again ghettoizing girls' interests as the marked option. Judging from this summation, it looks like we are caught in an impasse: play will always be gendered, and female play will always constitute the marked option. How to avoid the impasse? Our answer has to do with the highly unstable situation that we examine in this volume. The girls' games movement is brand new, as is the presence of Game Grrls. With time we expect that, by pushing at both ends of the spectrum of what games for girls look like, a gender neutral space may open up in the middle, a space that allows multiple definitions of both girlhood and boyhood, and multiple types of interaction with computer games of all sorts. We haven't found *the* answer yet. There is almost certainly not a single answer to the challenges surrounding gender and games, but as we broaden the range of available options, we also open up new space for a broader range of experiences and identities for both girls and boys.

Notes

1. *In this essay we will use the terms "computer game" and "video game" more or less interchangeably. In truth, "computer game" refers to games that are played on a home computer, while "video game" refers to games that are played in arcades or on game systems such as Sega or Nintendo.*

References

Abroms, J. 1997, Girl Gamers, http://www.cs.duke.edu/nia/

Bacon-Smith, C. 1992. *Enterprising Women: Television Fandom and the Creation of Popular Myth*. Philadelphia: University of Pennsylvania Press.

Barrentine, P. 1993. *When the Canary Stops Singing: Women's Perspectives on Transforming Business*. San Francisco: Berrett-Koehler.

Beato, G. 1997. "Girl Games: Computer Games for Girls Is No Longer an Oxymoron." *Wired*, April.

Becker, H. J. and Sterling, C. W. 1987. Equity in School Computer Use: National Data and Neglected Considerations. *Journal of Educational Computing Research* 3: 289–312.

Brown, J. 1997a. "Game Girl." *Maximag*. http://www.maximag.com/imitate/laurelwis/lara. html.

Brown, J. 1997b. "GameGirls Turn on to Female Gamers." *Wired*, 11 November. http://www. wired.com/news/culture/story/8434.html.

Brown, J. 1997c. "All-Girl Quake Clans Shake Up Boys' World." *Wired*, 11 November. http:// www.wired.com/news/news/culture/story/1885.html.

Butler, J. 1990. *Gender Trouble*. New York: Routledge.

Cameron, D. 1992. *Feminism and Linguistic Theory*. 2d edition. New York: St. Martin's Press.

Carroll, N. 1994. "Designing Electronic Games to Win Over Girls." *USA Today*, 10 November, p. 4D.

Cavanaugh, K. 1997. "Girls Just Want to Have Fun." *The Web Magazine*, October.

Clan Crackwhore. 1997. Clan Crackwhore website. http://www.crackwhore.com

Clan Quake Girlz. 1997. Qgirlz homepage. http://qgirlz.hec.ohio-state.edu/qgirlz/

Clerc, S. 1996. Estrogen Brigades and "Big Tits" Threads: Media Fandom Online and Off. In L. Cherny and E. R. Weise, eds., *Wired Women: Gender and New Realities of Cyberspace*. Seattle: Seal.

Clover, C. 1992. *Men, Women and Chain Saws: Gender in the Modern Horror Film*. Trenton: Princeton University Press.

Cooper, J., Hall, J., and Huff, C. 1990. "Situational Stress as a Consequence of Sex-Stereotyped Software." *Personality and Social Psychology Bulletin* 16: 419–429.

Cottrell, J. "I'm a Stranger Here Myself: A Consideration of Women in Computing." *Communications of the ACM* 33(11): 47–57.

CRA Taulbee Survey Results, 1996. http://www.cra.org/Statistics/survery/96.pdf, 1997.

Dangelmaier, H. (date not available) "Gender and the Art of Designing Interactive Media." http://www2.sva.edu/readings/HEIDI/Heidi1.html.

Donawreth, J. 1997. *Frankenstein's Daughters: Women Writing Science Fiction*. Syracuse: Syracuse University Press.

Douglas, N. 1997. "Grrls and Gaming on ABCNews." *Grrl Gamer*. December. http://www.grrlgamer.com/news.htm.

Duncombe, S. 1997. *Notes from Underground: Zines and the Politics of Alternative Culture*. London: Verso.

Edwards, L. and Stocker, M. 1995. *The Woman-Centered Economy : Ideals, Reality and the Space in Between*. New York: Third Side Press.

Fausto-Sterling, A. 1993. "The Five Sexes: Why Male and Female Are Not Enough." *The Sciences*, March/April, 20–24.

Feed (1997). "Game Theory: The Feed Dialog on Videogame Culture." http://www.feedmag.com/html/dialog/97.07dialog/97.07dialog3.html.

Fleming, D. 1996. *Powerplay: Toys as Popular Culture*. Manchester: Manchester University Press.

Frenkel, K. A. 1990. Women and Computing. *Communications of the ACM* 33(11), p. 34.

Gailey, C. 1997. Remarks, "From Barbie to Mortal Kombat," Gender & Games Conference, Massachusetts Institute of Technology, Cambridge, MA.

Gailey, C. 1993. "Mediated Messages: Gender, Class, and Cosmos in Home Video Games." *Journal of Popular Culture* 27(1): 81–97.

Gal, S. 1991. "Between Speech and Silence." In M. di Leonardo, ed., *Gender at the Crossroads of Knowledge: Feminist Anthropology in the Postmodern Era*. Berkeley: University of California Press, 175–203.

Game Girlz. 1997. Game Girlz Forum: "Lara Crofts: One of the Game Girlz?" 27 December. http://www.gamegirlz.com/index2.html.

Giacquinta, J. B., Bauer, J. A., and Levin, J. E. 1993. *Beyond Technology's Promise*. Cambridge, England: Cambridge University Press.

Gilbert, A. 1998. "Quake-A-Licious." Grrl Gamer Website. http://www.grrlgamer.com.

Goffee, R. and Scase, R. 1985. *Women in Charge: The Experience of Female Entrepreneurs*. London: Allen and Unwin.

Goldstein, J. H. 1994. "Sex Differences in Toy Play Use and Use of Video Games." In J. H. Goldstein (ed.), *Toys, Play, and Child Development*. New York: Cambridge University Press, 110–129.

Gray, J. 1992. *Men are from Mars, Women are from Venus: A Practical Guide for Improving Communication and Getting What You Want in Your Relationships*. New York: HarperCollins.

Greenfield, P. M. 1996 "Video Games as Cultural Artifacts." In P. M. Greenfield and R. R. Cocking eds., *Interacting with Video*. Norwood, N.J.: Ablex Publishing.

Greenfield, P. M. 1984. *Mind and Media: The Effects of Television, Video Games, and Computers*. Cambridge, MA: Harvard University Press.

Hart, S. 1996. "Gender and Racial Inequality in Video Games." http://www.physics.arizona.edu/~hart/vgh/genracinequal.html.

Huff, C. and Cooper, J. 1987. "Sex Bias in Educational Software: The Effect of Designers' Stereotypes on the Software They Design." *Journal of Applied Social Psychology* 17(6): 519–532.

Huff, Charles W., Fleming, John H., and Cooper, J. 1992. "Gender Differences in Human-Computer Interaction." In C. D. Martin and E. Murchie-Beyma, eds., *In Search of Gender Free Paradigms for Computer Science Education*. Eugene Ore.: International Society for Technology in Education.

Ivinski, Pamela A. 1997. "Design New Media," *Print,* May/June.

Jenkins, H. 1992. *Textual Poachers: Television Fans and Participatory Culture.* New York: Routledge, Chapman and Hall.

Jenkins, H. and Murray, J. "Before the Holodeck: Digital Manifestations of Star Trek." Forthcoming in G. Smith, ed., *CD-ROM 101: Critical Approaches to Digital Media.* New York: New York University Press.

Jones, C. 1997. "Lara Croft, Female Enemy Number One?" *The Mining Company Guide,* 30 December. http://quake.miningco.com/blara.htm.

Jones, D. 1980. "Gossip: Notes on Women's Oral Culture." *Women's Studies International Quarterly* 3.

Jupiter Communications. 1997. "Myths About Girl Users Dispelled." 18 August. http://www.geekgirl.com.au/geekgirl/011crime/myths.html

Just4Girls. 1997. "Eleven Girls' Software Publishers Join Forces to Promote Product Sales, Girls' Software Category Growth." Press Release, 27 October. http://just4girls.com/press.html

Kessler S. J. 1994. "The Medical Construction of Gender: Case Management of Intersexed Infants." In A. Herrmann and A. Stewart, eds., *Theorizing Feminism: Parallel Trends in the Humanities and Social Sciences.* Boulder: Westview Press, 218–37.

Kiesler, S., Sproull, L. and Eccles, J. 1985. "Poolhalls, Chips and War Games: Women in the Culture of Computing." *Psychology of Women Quarterly* (4): 451–62.

Klein, S. S., ed., 1985. *Handbook for Achieving Sex Equity Through Education.* Baltimore: Johns Hopkins University Press.

Krantz, M. 1997. "A Rom of Their Own." *Time.* 9 June.

Kubey, R., and Larson, R. 1990. "The Use and Experience of the New Video Media among Children and Young Adolescents." *Communication Research* 17: 107–130.

LaPlante, A. 1994. "The Other Half." *PC Week* 11(11): 1–4.

Lefanu, S. 1989. *Feminism and Science Fiction.* Indianapolis: Indiana University Press.

Linn, M. C. 1985. "Fostering Equitable Consequences from Computer Learning Environments." *Sex Roles* 13(3/4): 229–240.

Lockheed, M. (1982). *Evaluation of Computer Literacy at the High School Level.* Princeton: Evaluation of Computer Services.

Loftus, G.R., and Loftus, E.F. 1983. *Mind at Play.* New York: Basic Books.

Makrakis, V. 1993. "Gender and Computers in Schools in Japan: The 'We Can, I Can't' Paradox." *Computers and Education* 20(4): 191–198.

Malone, T.W. 1981. Toward a Theory of Intrinsically Motivating Instruction. *Cognitive Science* 5: 333–370.

McRobbie, A. 1991. *Feminism and Youth Culture: From Jackie to Just Seventeen.* London: MacMillan.

Moore, D. P. and Buttner, E. H. 1997. *Women Entrepreneurs: Moving Beyond The Glass Ceiling.* London: Sage.

Morlock, H., Yando, T., and Nigolean, K. 1985. "Motivation of Video Game Players." *Psychological Reports,* 57: 247–250.

Next Generation. 1998. Girl Trouble. January, 98–102.

Nude Raider 1997. The Nude Raider Page. http://ourworld.compuserve.com/homepages/cgration./raider.htm

Ogozalek, V. Z. 1989. A Comparison of Male and Female Computer Science Students' Attitudes Toward Computers. *SIGCSE Bulletin* 21(2): 8–14.

Orenstein, P. 1995. *Schoolgirls: Young Women, Self-Esteem, and the Confidence Gap.* New York: Anchor.

Pearl, A., Pollack, M., Riskin, E., Thomas, B., Wolf, E., and Wu, A. 1990. Becoming a Computer Scientist. *Communications of the ACM* 33(11): 47–57.

Penley, C., Lyon, E., Spigel, L. and Bergstrom, J. 1991. *Close Encounters: Film, Feminism, and Science Fiction.* Mineapolis: University of Minnesota Press.

Penley, C. 1997, *NASA/Trek: Popular Science and Sex in America.* New York: Verso.

Perry, R. and Greber, L. 1990. "Women and Computers: an Introduction." *Signs* 16(1): 74–102.

Pinedo, I. C. 1997. *Recreational Terror: Women and the Pleasures of Horror Film Viewing.* New York: State University of New York Press.

Pipher, M. 1994. *Reviving Ophelia: Saving the Selves of Adolescent Girls.* New York: Putnam.

Provenzo, E. 1991 *Video Kids: Making Sense of Nintendo.* Cambridge: Harvard University Press.

Purple Moon. 1997. "Purple Moon Ships Highly Anticipated CD-ROM Friendship Adventures for Girls." *Purple Moon Press Kit,* September 15.

Q. Girlz. 1997. http://www.neurogamer.com/qgirlz/">QGIRLZ New Home</a.

Radner, H. 1995. *Shopping Around: Feminine Culture and the Pursuit of Pleasure.* New York: Routledge.

Rand, E. 1995. *Barbie's Queer Accessories.* Durham: Duke University Press.

Reinen, I. J., and Plomp, T. 1993. "Some Gender Issues in Educational Comparative Study." *Computers and Education* 20(4): 353–365.

"Revolution in a Box, Part 12." ABC Nightline. Dec. 15 1997. Transcript available at http://www.abcnews.com/onair/nightline/html_files/transcripts/ntl1215.html.

Riot Grrl. 1997. Riot Grrl website. http://www.riotgrrl.com

Rotundo, E. A. 1994. *American Manhood: Transformations in Masculinity from the Revolution to the Modern Era.* New York: Basic.

Russo, M. 1997. "Software for Girls: A Mother's Perspective." *Superkids Educational Software Review.* http://www.superkids.com/aweb/pages/features/girls/jrc1.shtml.

Sakamoto, A. (1994). Video Game Use and the Development of Socio-Cognitive Abilities in Children: Three Surveys of Elementary School Students. *Journal of Applied Social Psychology,* 24: 21–24.

Scott, J. 1986. "Gender: A Useful Category of Historical Analysis." *American Historical Review,* 91(5): 1053–75.

Seiter, E. 1993. *Sold Separately: Children and Parents in Consumer Culture.* New York: Rutgers.

Sheff, D. 1997. "Xena: Web Princess." *Yahoo! Internet Life.* May. http://www.zdnet.com/yil/content/mag/9705/xenainterview.html.

Sherman, A. 1997 "This Girl Wants Games." *Cybergrrl Sez.* 5 November. http://www.cybergrrl.com/planets/sez/index23.html

Spigel, L. 1994. *Twist Barbie.* New York: Paper Tiger Television.

Stamatiadis, S. and Passfield, J. 1997. Byte-Me. http://www.geewhiz.com.au/byte/welcome.html.

Subrahmanyam, K., and Greenfield, P. M. 1994. "Effects of Video Game Practice on Spatial Skills in Girls and Boys." *Journal of Applied Developmental Psychology* 15(1): 13—32.

Task Force on Women, Minorities, and the Handicapped in Science and Technology. 1988. *Changing America: The New Face of Science and Engineering (Interim Report).* Washington: The Task Force.

Tannen, D. 1990. *You Just Don't Understand: Women and Men in Conversation.* New York: Morrow.

Tavris, C. 1992. *The Mismeasure of Women.* New York: Simon & Schuster.

Thomas, M. 1974. *Free to Be . . .You and Me.* New York: McGraw-Hill

Tulloch, J. and Jenkins, H. 1995. *Science Fiction Audiences: Watching Doctor Who and Star Trek.* London: Routledge.

Vaughter, R., Sadh, D. and Vozzola, E. 1992. Sex Similarities and Differences in Types of Play in Games and Sports. *Psychology of Women Quarterly* 18: 85–104.

Walcott, I. 1996. Edequity mailing list. October, 1996.

Weil, E. 1997. "The Girl-Game Jinx." *Salon*, 21 (December). http://www.salonmagazine.com/21st/feature/1997/12/cov-10feature.html.

Whelehan, I. and Sonnet, E. 1997. "Regendered Reading: Tank Girl and Postmodern Intertextuality." In D. Cartmell, I. Q. Hunter, H. Kaye and I. Whelehan, eds., *Trash Aesthetics: Popular Culture and Its Audience.* London:Pluto.

Whitta, G. 1997. "If Looks Could Kill. . ." *PC Gamer.* August.

Woodrow, J. 1994. "The Development of Computer-Related Attitudes of Secondary Students." *Journal of Educational Computing Research* 11(4): 307-338.

Wilder, G., Mackie, D., and Cooper, J. 1985. "Gender and Computers: Two Surveys of Computer-Related Attitudes." *Sex Roles,* 13: 215–228.

Willis, S. 1991. *A Primer for Daily Life.* London: Routledge, Chapman and Hall.

Wolstenholme, S. 1992. *Gothic Revisions: Writing Women As Readers.* New York: State University of New York Press.

Young, R. 1997. "Females and Computer Games." *Quandary* 10. http://www.iinet.net.au/~quandary/issue10/femgame.html

Zipes, J. 1989. *Don't Bet on the Prince: Contemporary Feminist Fairy Tales in North America and England.* London: Routledge, Kegan and Paul.

Chapter 2

Computer Games for Girls: What Makes Them Play?
Kaveri Subrahmanyam and Patricia M. Greenfield

In this chapter, we address the problem of girl appeal in game software.[1] Into a market that had long been dominated by male consumers sprung "Barbie Fashion Designer" in November 1996. Produced and developed by Mattel Media for girls six and older, it sold more than 500,000 copies in its first two months of sales. We are not sure if it should be classified as a game (and this point will be discussed later), but the significance of "Barbie Fashion Designer" is that it is the first piece of entertainment software to garner a mass market with girls.

We analyze why and how the "Barbie Fashion Designer" CD-ROM succeeded with young girls, where so many others failed before it. To develop an account of game features that girls find appealing, we draw from recent research on computer and video games, research on children's play and television preferences, and research by software developers. Our hope is that this analysis will illuminate for parents, educators, researchers, and software developers general principles for girl appeal in computer software.

Background

Ten years ago when we embarked on our research on the effects of video games on cognitive processes, we were struck by the fact that video games were a largely male pastime. Not only did young boys play video games more often than girls both at home and in arcades (Dominick 1984; Lin and Lepper 1987; Rushbrook 1986), but this difference persisted into the college years (Morlock et al. 1985). Moreover, one of the most comprehensive survey studies of the 1980s found that even kindergartners of both genders viewed video games as more appropriate to boys (Wilder, Mackie, and Cooper 1985). At the same time, games were generally the first and most frequent childhood computer experience. Therefore we, like others, were concerned that females might be at a disadvantage where computer usage was concerned because of the speculation that computer and video games provide an easy lead-in to computer literacy (Loftus and Loftus 1983; Greenfield 1984; Greenfield and Cocking 1996; Kiesler et al. 1985).

Our interest in the question of gender specificity in video games was heightened by our own observations during a training study with a nonviolent game, "Marble Madness," conducted in the late 1980s (Subrahmanyam and Greenfield 1994, 1996). Our goal in that study was to assess the effects of video game training on spatial skills. Even before we had started testing, we were struck by how difficult it was to recruit girls—in a coeducational sports camp, not one girl signed up to participate in our study. This was so despite our consent letter clearly stating that participants would have to play either "Marble Madness," an action-maze game, or "Conjecture," a word game. We had deliberately selected a nonaggressive game, "Marble Madness," to ensure that the game would be equally appealing to both genders (Malone 1981). Yet we found that the boys in our study were much more enthusiastic about the training sessions in which they played the video game.

We also found that very soon into the training session, the boys figured out the intricacies of the game, such as the different levels and the strategies appropriate to each; they were also seen comparing notes about the levels they had reached and the scores they had obtained. This whole-hearted absorption in the game was missing among the girls, who were not overtly enthusiastic about playing and seemed almost relieved when they finished their training session. Interestingly, many of the boys in the control group who had to play the word game, "Conjecture," during the training, begged for and were given an opportunity to play "Marble Madness" at the conclusion of the experiment; none of the girls in the control group either asked for or played "Marble Madness" when given an opportunity to do so at the conclusion of the experiment. Although anecdotal, our observations were in line with other findings that females are not as interested in video games as males are.

In the years since, despite efforts by software developers to attract girls to video games, they have remained largely a male province. Most commercially available video games still do not reflect the interests and tastes of half of the potential game-playing population, namely girls (Kafai 1996). In one survey, Kubey and Larson (1990) found that 80 percent of game playing among nine- to fifteen-year-olds was done by boys. With the recent advancement of multimedia interactive computer systems, and the powerful animation and sound effects available in CD-ROMs, the arcade environment has invaded our homes, causing more concern among educators, parents, and industry watchers that girls are not big consumers of computer games. There has been some industry response to these concerns, and games targeted exclusively for girls have come out on the market. The early attempts to make video games appealing to girls largely consisted of having female protagonists and making the content nonviolent. The gendering of games was furthered by the advertising, promotion, and packaging of the games in the ubiquitous pink and purple boxes (Kinder 1996). Despite these efforts, software designed for girls has not caught the fancy of girls, and the crowds in the video game aisles of toy stores and in arcades are mostly boys (Goldstein 1994). It is also relevant that the readership of magazines addressed to video game players is at least 90 percent male (Kinder 1996).

Why Did "Barbie Fashion Designer" Succeed?: Features That Attract Girls

Undoubtedly "Barbie Fashion Designer" benefited from the Barbie franchise and the retailing clout of Mattel's $1.7 billion industry behind it; yet the fact that other Barbie-based games such as "Barbie Story Maker," "Barbie Print and Play," and "Barbie as Rapunzel," all released simultaneously, were not such runaway successes suggests that there might be more to its success than the presence of Barbie and the hot pink packaging.

Our analysis of the success of "Barbie Fashion Designer" is strongly influenced by the seminal work of Yasmin Kafai (1996), who explored what nine- to ten-year-old children wanted in video games by studying what they produced when given the skills and opportunities to create their own games. Her work revealed consistent gender differences in the kinds of games boys and girls create—not only do girls prefer less violence, but they also prefer different kinds of games, game characters, and game worlds.

Kafai (1996) concluded that whereas boys designed games resembling commercially available games such as Nintendo, girls did not; furthermore, at the time of the study, the girls stated that "they had no particular interest in pursuing video game-playing because they did not like the games, their content, and their violent aspects"(p. 62). Thus, existing games generally reflected boys' but not girls' tastes. Because this led to less video game experience for girls, we believe that the girls' designs in the study were less influenced by available video game models than boys' games were.

Most importantly, we assume that game designs reflect game preferences, even if these preferences have been accommodated by the market; action video games accommodate the tastes of boys, who therefore have more environmental experience with computer games than girls. However, prior experience is a two-way street. Children, like adults, are active selectors of their environments; they are not simply passive recipients of environmental influences (Scarr and McCartney 1983). At the same time, their selections are influenced by what environmental opportunities are available. It follows that children's active preferences would be operating as they designed games, just as these same preferences would operate as they selected games to play.

Given this line of reasoning, analysis of the game themes, settings, animations, and interactions developed by the children in Kafai's study (1996) can provide us with clues about the game features that are likely to appeal to the different genders. Our analysis is organized into subsections, each of which examines game features identified by Kafai and others: type of action, game genres and themes, game worlds, game characters, and modes of interaction. We will show that every one of the features that distinguish girls' game preferences from boys' are also found in "Barbie Fashion Designer."

At an even more basic level, we show that basic child-development research on boys' and girls' play and television preferences could have predicted the gender appeal of different kinds of computer software. Our thesis is that it is the concatenation of features identified in research studies on gender and play of various kinds that defines the success of "Barbie Fashion Designer." In other words, the research on the television shows that girls watch, the play activities that they engage in, and the computer games that they design have turned out to have both predictive and practical value in solving the longstanding problem of mass-market "girl appeal" in entertainment software. We believe that our analysis can be of general use in developing better software for girls.

"Barbie Fashion Designer" and Other Barbie Software Titles

Before presenting our account of play and gender, we first describe "Barbie Fashion Designer," as well as some of the other Barbie software titles as a comparison. This comparison is important because the other Barbie titles, released simultaneously with "Barbie Fashion Designer," were not as successful as "Barbie Fashion Designer." It may be that the overwhelming popularity of Barbie dolls with young girls was a necessary element in the success of "Barbie

Fashion Designer"; however, the lack of comparable success of the other Barbie software titles shows that the Barbie doll theme is not sufficient to explain the mass-market appeal of "Barbie Fashion Designer."

Using "Barbie Fashion Designer," girls design clothes for their dolls by choosing from a menu of themes such as vacation outfit or party outfit, styles such as jacket or pants, patterns, and colors; then they print the outfit on special paper-backed fabric that can be run through an inkjet or laser printer. At that point, the players use color markers, fabric paint, and other materials that come with the package to further enhance their designs. Finally, they assemble the parts of the outfit following the instructions provided by the software.

Other products using the Barbie franchise include "Barbie Story Maker," in which players create animated stories starring Barbie and all her friends, "Barbie Print 'n' Play," in which players create personalized print projects featuring Barbie, and "Barbie as Rapunzel," a computer adventure in which players help Barbie rescue the prince.

Violent Action: A Barrier for Girls

Violent Action in Computer Games

It is widely believed that the violent content of much video game activity is a major factor in turning girls off video games (Malone 1981; Greenfield 1996). While there is considerable awareness that aggressive themes are not appealing to girls, we revisit the issue of aggressive content as a starting point of our analysis.

Although violence remains a prominent aspect of most commercially available video games (Provenzo 1991), this was not always the case. The first game, "Pong," was nonaggressive. Aggression started in the second generation with "Breakout," which involved destruction but no human aggression. "Pacman" started animate, but nonhuman aggression. The next generation of games, such as "The Empire Strikes Back," involved human aggression, which took on a more fantastic form with "Super Mario Brothers." It became more personal, with hand-to-hand combat, in games such as "Mortal Kombat." Violence continues to reign in the current generation of action games, which includes titles such as "Doom," "Duke Nuke'em," "Mace," "Hexen II," and "Mortal Kombat 2." These games often have the goal of blasting an enemy to smithereens; generally, mouse clicks fire off laser weapons, and the player has to zoom through tunnels or mazes to escape getting destroyed. The central theme in most games involves someone getting killed, finding out why someone was killed, or taking over the world (Beato 1997; De Witt 1997).

Research suggests that girls do not find this violence appealing. For instance, Malone (1981) found that girls did not like a video game when an aggressive fantasy theme was added to it compared to the same game without the aggression. Others (Kafai 1996; Nancy Deyo, quoted in De Witt 1997) suggest that girls find the violent content of computer games boring. The empirical evidence confirms that boys are more likely to play games requiring aggressive competition (Heller 1982, cited in Morlock et al. 1986; Kiesler et al. 1985; Lin and Lepper 1987). In line with these tastes, Kafai (1996) found gender differences in the games designed by the children regarding feedback resulting from a player's action during the game. She reported that the feedback in boys' games was overwhelmingly violent, whereas the feedback in girls' games was overwhelmingly nonviolent.

Violent Action in Play and Television
Research on children's play suggests that boys' liking for violent video games is paralleled by the aggressive nature of their play. Compared to girls' play, boys' play more often includes activities such as play wrestling, war games, and fantasy aggression and results in more aggressive incidents (Goldstein 1994). A general complaint regarding the play style of the two genders is that boys' toys, video games, and play is full of violence and aggressiveness (Miedzian 1991; Tuchscherer 1988). In fact, Wegener-Spohring (1989) found that, compared to 29 percent of the girls in the study, 76 percent of the boys owned toy guns. A common tale of many parents is how their boys end up creating guns out of everyday objects such as bread, tortillas, and even shoes. One of us (Greenfield) remembers not permitting her preschool son to have guns; one day he took four saltine crackers in a square, removed one of the lower crackers, and used the remaining configuration of three crackers as a pretend gun.

The research on gender and children's television preferences shows the same results. Violent action-adventure series are very popular with boys, but not girls (Korich and Waddell 1986; Huston et al. 1990; Lyle and Hoffman 1971). In a recent longitudinal study, Huston et al. (1990) found that boys watched more action-adventure programs than did girls.

It must be noted, however, that the trends reported here are just that— there are girls who prefer playing war games with guns and watching violent action adventure on television and boys who prefer playing dress-up games. There is also some recent evidence that the play styles of American boys and girls are converging (Singer and Singer 1990); nonetheless, we cannot escape the fact that these differences do exist in boys' and girls' play activities and appear relatively early (Goldstein 1994).

How Has the Software/Game Industry Responded to Concerns That Aggressive Content Is Not Appealing to Girls?

Kinder (1996) argues that because the game industry equates violence with action, games targeted for girls automatically lack any action (violent or not). According to her, this is one reason why the early games for girls, such as "Kiss," and the games based on *The Little Mermaid* and *Beauty and the Beast* were not commercially successful.

Application to "Barbie Fashion Designer"

Contrast this with the success of "Barbie Fashion Designer." Clearly there is more to designing games for girls than merely removing the violence. First, "Barbie Fashion Designer" differs from the less successful titles by involving a lot of action in creating Barbie's clothes. The comparison of "Barbie Fashion Designer" with these less successful nonviolent titles suggests that finding nonviolent forms of action may be part of the secret of girl appeal in entertainment software.

Game Genres and Game Themes

Genres and Themes in Computer Games

Another important feature of a computer or video game is the genre it belongs to and the theme that is embedded throughout its structure. Kafai (1996) reported that the games created by the children in her study fell into the following categories: adventure (unknown places to be explored), sports/skills, teaching context, and simulation. Note that Kafai asked children in a classroom setting to create games to teach younger children about fractions. While most of the boys created adventure hunts and explorations, the games created by the girls were more evenly divided among adventure, skill/sport, and teaching games.

This difference in the game genres was related to overwhelming differences in the underlying themes of the games: Kafai (1996) reported that not one girl incorporated the conflict between good and evil and the conquest of evil in her game, whereas boys overwhelmingly did so. Unlike girls' games, boys' games were concerned with the contest between good and evil, in which the player on the good side fights off bad guys to achieve a goal, such as recovering stolen goods, defeating demons or aliens, or finding lost treasures. In contrast, girls' games had few evil characters, although players sometimes had to go through some obstacles, such as descending a mountain without falling or avoiding a spider to find an unspecified treasure.

Gender differences in game creation are replicated by gender differences in game consumption. Cooper, Hall, and Huff (1990) found that when students in sixth through eighth grades were given math programs with different themes, girls reported stress when working with themes that involved actions such as shooting and propelling objects through fantasy space, as well as nonverbal graphic feedback; in contrast, boys reported more stress when using software in which aggression and shooting were absent, but which involved verbal feedback and cooperative narratives.

To summarize, studies of computer game design and game preferences suggest that girls are less enthusiastic than boys about the thematic embedding of good versus evil in story narratives. Nor, as we saw earlier, do they like the violent feedback that normally accompanies such themes. Unfortunately, most commercially available video games make strong use of narrative that involves both violence and the conflict between good and evil. Given this, what kinds of game themes are girls likely to find appealing? Let us look to research on children's social behavior as well as on their television preferences for answers to this question.

Genres and Themes in Girls' Other Activities
The literature on social behavior suggests that compared to boys, girls are more affiliative and that they are more interested in social activities (Grusec and Lytton 1988). In their play activities, girls have been found to be more socially oriented than boys (Coates et al. 1975). Along similar lines, the literature on television preferences suggests that girls like television shows that portray the gentler aspects of interpersonal relations rather than adventure, sports activities, violence, or science (Grusec and Lytton 1988; Korich and Waddell 1986). Lyle and Hoffman (1971) reported that by the first grade, boys showed an earlier preference than girls for action programs such as *Star Trek*, whereas girls pre-

ferred family situation comedies such as *I Love Lucy* and *The Flintstones*. Soap operas, which have an overwhelmingly female audience among teenagers and adults, are based overwhelmingly on dramas of love and family relationships. This seems to be quite universal. One of us (Greenfield) observed an exclusively female audience for a Mexican telenovela in a Mayan community in Chiapas, Mexico. Although the teenage girls knew hardly any Spanish, the language of the broadcast, they were able to explain to a newcomer relationships among all of the characters.

If we look at female tastes in reading, we find that romance novels are similar to soap operas in their thematic content. Considering the popularity of fairy tales with younger girls, we note that the thematic content of popular stories such as Cinderella and Sleeping Beauty is also very similar: romantic and family relationships.

Does a preference for positive relationships necessarily preclude the appeal of action in media? We think not. Our informal observations of reading preferences reveal that a popular genre among elementary school girls is that of mysteries, exemplified in book series such as the Boxcar mysteries, Babysitter's Club, and Nancy Drew mysteries. Books from these series typically narrate a mystery solved by either a female protagonist (Nancy Drew) or by groups of children (Boxcar mysteries and Babysitter's Club); while the stories often have some action, they usually contain no violence. Note, however, that these series feature realistic, often domestic, settings and characters, as well as female heroes, features to be explored later in this chapter.

Application to Software for Girls

Based on girls' social orientation and television tastes, we speculate that a thematic emphasis on the drama of human relationships might make video games more appealing to girls. Many within the software industry have likewise suggested that girls are partial to themes focusing on social relationships and social skills. Dangelmaier at Hi-D, a web-development company, has suggested that "females want experiences where they can make emotional and social discoveries that they can apply to their own lives" (quoted in Beato 1997). Graner Ray of HerInteractive similarly suggests that girls want games which allow them to create "mutually beneficial solutions for socially significant problems," which are conflicts in the social realm involving a group of people. Solving such conflicts allows girls to use skills such as diplomacy, negotiation, compromise, and manipulation. She contrasts such games with one in which a lone space commando is up against a ceaseless supply of enemies, the kind of game that boys seem to like. The research on cooperation versus competition in peer relations similarly suggests that compared to boys, girls show a greater preference for cooperation (Ahlgren and Johnson 1979).

Based on our case studies of girls' reading preferences, we speculate that mystery-based themes are likely to appeal to girls in computer games as well if they involve cooperation and positive social encounters. Brenda Laurel of Purple Moon similarly speculates that girls like mysteries, but only in nonviolent contexts in which they can explore and be cooperative (quoted in Beato 1997). Given that girls do like mysteries in the print media, we suggest that girls' games do not have to be devoid of action. However, given girls' avowed dislike for aggression and their preference for cooperation over competition (Ahlgren and Johnson 1979), we speculate that in order to appeal to girls, the mystery/action component in girls' games must be nonviolent and must allow players to solve problems or mysteries and arrive at solutions by relating to and cooperating with others.

Application to "Barbie Fashion Designer"
Now consider "Barbie Fashion Designer": while it clearly has no violent content, it also does not include any of the aforementioned themes, such as group problem solving or cooperation. However, the player is making clothes for Barbie and solving problems in order to nurture and help another. This is similar to the goal of a character such as Nancy Drew in her mystery stories. Nurturance is also clearly an important theme in girls' doll play and fantasy play more generally.

It follows that there is more to marketing games for girls than removing the violence and endowing them with themes that allow cooperative group play. The theme of cooperation should probably be enlarged to include nurturant behavior, such as helping. Other game features, such as the setting or game worlds, are closely related to play themes. We next turn to the creation of play worlds.

Microworlds

Computer Game Worlds
Kafai (1996) also reports that there were differences between the genders with regard to the fantasy-reality dimension of the worlds in which boys' and girls'

games were situated. The games designed by the children were either set in fantasy places and imaginary worlds or in more realistic and familiar settings. She found that six out of eight girls used familiar real-life settings for their games, such as a classroom, ski slope, airport, or spider web. In contrast, seven out of eight boys had a fantasy setting, such as an imaginary city, island, or country.

Microworlds in Other Domains

Similar patterns of difference have also been observed in the toy preferences and pretend play of children as young as two years. (For a review of this literature, see Goldstein 1994, p. 115.) Girls' toy choices and pretend play appear to be based more on reality, whereas boys' tend to be based more on fantasy places and events. In their pretend play, girls show a preference for domestic themes (Tizard et al. 1976). They "play house" using household objects and dress-up clothes (Goldstein 1994). Although boys' play is not devoid of realistic settings and props, such as cars, trains, or airplanes (Tizard et al. 1976), they often create fantasy microworlds including adventure themes and fantasy events (Goldstein 1994). Such findings of sex-typed play and toy preferences have been reported for European and Asian children, as well as children in the United States (Goldstein 1994). Similarly, the mystery-book series popular with girls, discussed earlier, involve realistic settings and events. Another example of this are the Judy Blume books, highly popular with girls; author Blume tells realistic stories of teenage girls' lives.

There are other interesting gender differences in boys' and girls' play. Boys' play generally includes more players. In contrast, girls are less likely than boys to play team sports; they are more person-oriented in their play activities and are more likely to engage in small-scale, turn-taking kinds of games, such as hopscotch and jump rope (Lever 1978; Winstead 1986; but see Thorne 1993, pp. 90–134 for a discussion of how girls and boys often cross into groups and activities of the other gender).

Research from industry sources suggests similar trends. Brenda Laurel of Purple Moon wanted to find out what kinds of interactive entertainments might appeal to girls (quoted in Beato 1997). She used a multipronged approach: she interviewed seven- to twelve-year-olds and observed the play styles of boys and girls when given props and other pretend products; she talked to people knowledgeable about children's play—toy store owners, teachers, scout leaders, and coaches; and finally, she examined the research literature on play theory, brain-based sex differences, and primate social behavior. Laurel found that, in their pretend play, girls enjoyed role playing the lives of people in familiar settings that they create with props; they also liked to be in settings where they could practice their well-developed verbal skills.

Everyday observation of girls' play confirms that the preferred pretend play activity of girls is dress-up and role play of familiar characters. As the mother of a girl and a boy and as a frequent host to play sessions, one of us (Subrahmanyam) has noted consistent differences in the pretend play of her daughter and son and their same-sex friends. The girls like to act out everyday roles in elaborately set up replicas of familiar settings using props—playing teacher, mother, father, sister, or waitress at school, home, or restaurant. In contrast, the pretend play of the boys is filled with fanciful settings, characters, and events—Star Wars games in which they play Darth Vader, Luke Skywalker, or Han Solo and use their Millennium Falcon shooter to blast everything in sight into smithereens. It appears that the fantasies of girls center around real-life, everyday roles and characters, such as being a mother or teacher, whereas the fantasies of boys center around less realistic and more fanciful roles and characters such as Darth Vader and Superman.

While based on a tiny sample of subjects and describing only a portion of their play, Subrahmanyam's observations reflect the gender differences already noted in research on children's play. Of particular interest to us is that girls like to role play familiar characters in familiar settings by acting out the character's habitual actions—whether it is to give a lesson, put a baby to sleep, or take an order and bring a meal. Note also that the pretend play that girls engage in ties in with their preference for affiliative, nurturant, and positive relations.

Application to Computer Software for Girls

The findings reviewed above confirm and generalize the findings of Kafai (1996) concerning girls' preferences for everyday settings in their game designs. They suggest that girls should likewise find video and computer games set in more familiar settings appealing. By this account, most of the available games set in imaginary worlds would not make contact with the fantasy life of the typical girl.

Indeed, when computer games involve familiar settings with goals related to real-world tasks, girls do become interested in them. Catherall (1989) reports that girls became interested in programming computer-operated digital trains. Children are the "engineers," able to control over 250 accessory devices, such as switches and signals, and to run the trains successfully they must cooperate with other players. It appears that gender differences between boys and girls disappear when computers are used for a real rather than a fantasy goal and involve interpersonal cooperation.

Application to "Barbie Fashion Designer"

We suggest that one reason for the success of "Barbie Fashion Designer" was because it fit in so well with the pretend play common among girls of this age. The Barbie line of dolls is unique in the extensive set of accessories and props that are commercially available. Girls who collect Barbies also collect accessories such as Barbie clothes, hand-bags, and make-up items, as well as props such as a van with camping supplies and a post-office setting. All of these toys are used to set up detailed replicas of familiar settings into which the child navigates Barbie and her friends. The variety of games that can be played with such props is literally endless.

Into this microworld came "Barbie Fashion Designer"—the clothes that the player imagines and designs on the computer can actually be created out of fabric and assembled, and the resulting outfit can then be used to clothe Barbie for any kind of pretend play that the player envisions.

"Barbie Fashion Designer" as a Tool Program

What stands out here is that the software itself does not engage the player in any kind of electronic pretend play. Instead, it helps the player create objects that can be used for the kind of role play that girls find compelling. Frank Evers (personal communication, August 31, 1997), a game producer for Activision, uses the analogy of a journey and its destination to capture the difference between these two uses of the computer—he suggests that whereas boys like the electronic journey, girls focus more exclusively on the destination. Instead of immersing the player in the game experience, the user interface of "Barbie Fashion Designer" allows the user to reach the destination of making clothes for Barbie. It is noteworthy that when the daughter of one of the authors (Subrahmanyam) used the software for the first time, she brought with her three Barbie dolls that had no clothes and placed them beside the computer. Her comment that "I really want to get her some clothes" is even more telling to us. A mother we talked to reported that she and her daughter, went one step further, using the printouts created on the "Fashion Designer" as patterns to cut and sew Barbie clothes from fabric.

Here the software makes the computer yet another accessory for Barbie play. The computer takes on the role of a tool and, unlike other games, ceases to be an end unto itself. Doug Glen, President of Mattel Media, points out that "Barbie Fashion Designer" "exists as a mere part of an overall play experience." He adds that unlike the traditional concept of the computer as a game machine, in this case it is a "power tool that makes things" (quoted in Beato 1997). This metaphor is rarely used when describing computer games.

Our analysis suggests that "Barbie Fashion Designer" appeals to girls because it aides the role play that they habitually engage in. Like other interactive toys, such as Lego and Tinkertoys, the "Fashion Designer" becomes a tool in the player's imaginative play.

Characters

Characters in Computer Games

Another relevant aspect of game structure is the characters. Commercially available games rarely cast females in the main role, and even when females are present, they rarely take on an active role (Kinder 1996; Provenzo 1991; Rushbrook 1986). Kinder writes that these games frequently portray the central character as a male hero whose purpose is to save someone (usually a female) or to obtain treasures. Although the big game manufacturers have always claimed to design games without regard to gender (Frank Evers, personal communication, August 31, 1997), researchers, parents, and other groups soon recognized that most commercially available games were "modeled on only one half of the population, at most, and reflect the values and views of only one gender" (Cocking and Greenfield 1996, p. 5). In Kafai's study (1996), girls complained that females were rarely cast in the role of a main character. Female protagonists have become optional in some of the hand-to-hand combat games, but when they are included, they are aggressive and have the physical attributes of a male-defined sex symbol. This is true of the protagonist of "Tomb Raider," a game that was released in early 1997 and has a mainly male audience.

What do we know about girls' preferences regarding the number and kinds of game characters? Not surprisingly, in Kafai's study, girls and boys created games with very different kinds of characters. Boys created several supporting characters with fantasy names, whereas girls created only one or two supporting characters. Most importantly, boys cast the main character as a fantasy figure and assigned a specific gender to the character; most girls left open the character's gender and age, making it possible for the player to identify and empathize with the character. That is, girls addressed the player with a more generic "you." Here again we see that the girls preferred to create characters playing realistic roles, with playing "oneself" possibly the most realistic of all. Another issue here is empathy and identification versus social distance. Fantasy characters, of course, have greater distance from the self than playing oneself does.

Characters in Other Kinds of Play

Boys' preference for more characters in their computer games ties in with the gender differences found in the number of children in a play group: girls generally play with one or two other children whereas boys tend to play in larger groups. This difference appears by the kindergarten years and is well established by the time a child enters elementary school. (Eder and Hallinan 1978).

In their pretend play, girls often take on real family roles such as mother, father, baby, or sister. In contrast, boys often become fantasy characters such as super heroes and spacemen. Goldstein (1994) reports that these preferences exist on an interactional level. With regard to girls' reading preferences, one finds a similar focus on real and familiar roles; for example, the Judy Blume books focus on teenage girls with whom the readers can identify.

Application to Software Design for Girls and "Barbie Fashion Designer"

Recently, software companies and companies that have traditionally created toys for girls have responded to concerns about gender by creating games that have female protagonists and characters. "Kiss," "The Girls' Club," and the games based on Barbie, *The Little Mermaid,* and *Beauty and the Beast* are examples (Kinder 1996). However, these games have not been as commercially successful as "Barbie Fashion Designer." The use of a female character may have been a necessary part of "Barbie Fashion Designer"'s success, but the failure or lesser success of other software titles with female characters shows that this feature is not sufficient by itself. Undoubtedly, there is more to designing games for girls than merely having females as the lead characters.

"Barbie Fashion Designer" Goes One Step Further

The preference for playing oneself is actualized in the "Fashion Designer" program, where the main active character is you the player, the clothes designer.

Although the image of Barbie is ubiquitous, and her voice guides the player through the various steps of outfit design, the player is the main character and *she* has control over how the game proceeds. This appears to be exactly what girls like in games—to identify with, or better still, to be the game's main character.

Modes of Interaction

Interacting With Computers

Next we examine game structure and playing strategies and skills to comment on how the "Barbie Fashion Designer" game might have capitalized on girls' preferred style of interacting with computer games. Research has revealed differences in how boys and girls approach and interact with video games. Our study on the effect of video game practice on spatial skills turned up the surprising finding that boys benefited more from the training than girls in terms of video game skill (Subrahmanyam and Greenfield 1994, 1996). One reason could be that, because of boys' greater previous video game experience, they had learned how to learn a new game better than girls. Myer's extensive ethnographic study in a computer store (1984) confirms the development of such learning strategies among players. Thus, games with explicit instructions might be more appealing to players with less game experience, compared to games such as "Marble Madness" in which the player has to figure out playing strategies and tricks by trial and error.

Greenfield has suggested that one factor in the better average male performance could be that the average male adopts a more experimental (trial-and-error) approach than the average female. That is, the average male may be more willing to "learn by acting before he understands all of the rules and patterns of the game" (Greenfield 1996, p.88). There is some evidence that this is indeed the case. Smith and Stander (1981) found this to be true among anthropology students who were first-time users of a computer system. The willingness of boys and men to act without full understanding could explain the appeal of action and adventure games in which experimentation yields instant feedback. Again this suggests that girls would prefer games that do not reward such a trial-and-error approach. Games that are more predictable and that lay out the rules and patterns at the start might therefore be more appealing to them.

Greenfield has suggested that gender differences in the application of logical and strategic planning skills to game playing may be another contributing factor to differences in learning to play video games. She points to a study by

Mandinach and Corno (1985), which found that boys used these processes more than girls and were more successful at playing a computer adventure game called "Hunt the Wumpus." Of note is the finding that these differences appeared in spite of equal experience with computers in general and equal liking for the game.

Other work also suggests that boys and girls might have very different styles of interaction with computers that influence the kind of games that they find appealing. In her book *The Second Self,* Turkle (1984) describes a project in which boys and girls were taught programming in LOGO. She describes two styles of mastery when programming computers, hard and soft. She defines hard mastery as the "implementation of will over the machines through the implementation of a plan." In contrast, soft mastery is defined as more interactive, where the "overall shape emerged from interaction with the medium."

In describing the distinction between hard and soft mastery, Turkle recalls Lévi-Strauss's distinction between the scientist and the *bricoleur.* The former is akin to a formal science of the abstract; the latter is related to the science of the concrete, or an informal folk science. Just like the *bricoleur*, a soft master likes to work with a set of concrete elements. He or she works on a problem by "arranging and rearranging the elements working through new combinations"; combining a closed set of materials, surprisingly, leads to new results (see Turkle 1984, pp. 104–110).

Turkle further draws parallels between hard and soft masters and their preferred play behavior. She describes hard masters as viewing the world as something to be brought under control. According to her, such children play with things that they can operate on, such as blocks and Tinkertoys. In contrast, soft masters see the world as beyond their direct control and something they need to accommodate. These children generally played with toy soldiers or dolls. They like to use props from the adult world such as cowboy hats and grown-up clothes and shoes for dress-up, as well as to engage in fantasy play with other children. Hard masters view the computer as an abstract entity and identify with an abstract part of it, whereas soft masters treat the computer as a physical object and identify with it for the purpose of fantasy play. Most interesting to us is Turkle's observation that girls tend to be soft masters and that hard masters are overwhelmingly male.

Kafai (1996) has also observed that commercially available games generally proceed at a rapid rate, and use sound and visual effects to accentuate the pace and to create arousal; she suggests that girls do not like such quick-paced interactions. Some confirmation for this comes from a recent study in a museum setting, which found that girls did not like playing games that involved quick-paced interactions (Inkpen et al. 1993). Kafai also found that, whereas boys designed games with action guided but not paced by the player, girls used a mode in which the player controlled the timing as well as the direction of the game. Similarly, Brenda Laurel of Purple Moon suggests that girls like games that allow them to play in an exploratory, open-ended fashion, so they can have control over their environment (quoted in Beato 1997).

Application to "Barbie Fashion Designer"

"Barbie Fashion Designer" embodies many of the structural features that girls like and that are suited to girls' computer experience and skills. It is essentially a menu-driven game, with meaningful icons, and few surprises; it therefore does not require the use of a trial-and-error strategy. The player's role appears similar to Turkle's description of soft masters and the *bricoleur*: the software provides the player with a limited set of choices, which are then combined in many different ways to create an astonishing variety of creations to clothe Barbie for more pretend play. To start, a player has to work through a Theme Workshop, a Design Workshop, and Accessories Workshop. Each workshop offers many options to choose from. After the player creates an outfit she likes by picking and choosing from the different workshops, she can then add fabric designs in the Fabric Design Workshop or color them in the Color Workshop. Finally, the player can view Barbie in her new outfit in the Dressing Room or send Barbie down a runway in the Fashion Show. In the end the player can either save the outfit or print and assemble the design. Given Turkle's description of soft masters, it is not surprising that girls find "Fashion Designer" appealing.

"Barbie Fashion Designer" embodies still other features preferred by girls—it is not fast paced, and instead allows the player to set the pace. Moreover, rather than being used to accentuate the pace and create arousal, the music is slow and is in the background.

Gender Stereotypes

In some senses the success of "Barbie Fashion Designer" is ironic because the Barbie line of toys is viewed as perpetuating unfortunate gender stereotypes. It does seem surprising that a product line regarded suspiciously by feminists and others should become so influential in providing computer-literacy experiences for girls, an area where girls have been at a disadvantage.

But then, boys' computer literacy has been built on a bedrock of games that perpetuate male stereotypes of violence and aggression. If a value judgment is to be made, the female stereotypes of which "Barbie Fashion Designer" is constructed seem quite prosocial. The main danger is one of body image: girls growing up with the impossible or unhealthy ideal of the Barbie body, with its wasp waist and disproportionately large hips. (We believe this is more a problem of the Barbie doll than of "Barbie Fashion Designer.") With regard to male stereotypes, one can also say that the conquest of evil has its prosocial elements, even if it requires violence.

In the case of both "Barbie Fashion Designer" and violent space fantasies, we can see girls and boys conforming to the idealized roles and scenarios that society—particularly through mass media—has placed before them. Over time, male role models have moved away from cowboys to space warriors as female role models have moved from wives and mothers to high fashion models and career women. (Barbie dolls started with the image of a high-fashion teenage model, and, as ideal female roles have changed, has lately become career oriented.)

Is "Barbie Fashion Designer" a Game?

An important issue regarding "Barbie Fashion Designer" is whether it is truly a game. Evers (personal communication, October 1, 1997) maintains that it is not a true game because it lacks goal orientation and barriers to overcome. He also suggests that the appeal of most computer games lies in their ability to immerse the player in a fantasy rooted in the electronic world. "Fashion Designer" has no storyline and does not envelop the player in a computer fantasy. Instead, the software is another accessory used by the player to fantasize about Barbie in the physical world. Our thesis is that "Barbie Fashion Designer" connects the player to the real world, and unlike other games (both computer and traditional board games) has concrete rather than symbolic goals. We believe it is this appeal to concrete goals that made "Barbie Fashion Designer" appealing. Indeed, software that engages the player in a purely electronic fantasy has not yet been as successful with girls as software that uses the computer as a tool.

Most games also tend to be tightly governed by rules. Traditional board games, such as "Candy Land" and "Chutes and Ladders," as well as computer-based games, such as "Super Mario" or "Duke Nukem," have elaborate rules and procedures described in instructions or manuals. Usually there is an end point to the game and the winner is either the person who crosses obstacles to reach the end point first or the one who vanquishes enemies to win a treasure or save a princess. In contrast, "Barbie Fashion Designer" has very loose rules, with considerable flexibility in how the player progresses through the different workshops. Moreover, there are no obstacles and the player works on her own, at her own pace, and is not in competition with another player or even the computer itself. Board games such as "Chutes and Ladders" are popular with young girls because they have a social quality that computer games lack.

What Works?

Our analysis suggests that there are some game features that are more appealing to girls than others. These features are related to all aspects of games, including the thematic content and focus, as well the kinds of strategies and computer-playing skills demanded of the players; one particularly important feature appears to be whether the game interfaces with the reality of players' lives.

Our analysis of "Barbie Fashion Designer" reveals that it incorporates many of the features that girls find appealing in games and lacks features that they dislike. First, the game clearly lacks aggressive content, which turns girls off. On the plus side, by helping girls create outfits for Barbie, the computer assumes the role of another accessory in girls' pretend play, which tends to be based on real-life models and roles, and is usually more person-oriented. Here creation is in the service of nurturance, a popular play theme for young girls. "Barbie Fashion Designer" does not demand sophisticated playing strategies nor a trial-and-error approach; instead it uses menus and icons to guide the player through the designing process. The emphasis is on combining existing elements to create uniquely new creations that appeal to the player. Here the electronic medium is used to design a realistic person-oriented fantasy—a fantasy that is then realized in the physical world of Barbie dolls.

Our analysis is confirmed by another recent release from Mattel Media, "Barbie As Rapunzel." This CD-ROM embodies some of the features that girls do not like, and as our own analysis would predict, has not been as successful as "Barbie Fashion Designer." In "Barbie as Rapunzel," Barbie assumes the role of the beautiful and brave princess. The software requires the player to play games and solve puzzles on the computer to discover clues that will help Rapunzel save Prince Galen, who is under a wicked witch's spell. Although it is an interactive adventure, it does not involve realistic characters or support play with real Barbie dolls. "Barbie as Rapunzel" also contains the unpopular morality theme of good versus evil, although it occurs in the context of a familiar and well-liked fairy tale and has no violence.

Girls' Games versus Androgynous Games

A final issue concerns whether we need games designed specifically for girls versus games for gamers, that is, androgynous games. Perhaps in an ideal world, girls would be included in the digital revolution through the development of games that appeal equally to boys and girls. In reality, however, most games have attracted at least three boys for every girl (Cassell and Jenkins, this volume). Therefore games targeted specifically toward girls may be necessary to reach a mass audience of girls.

Indeed, in recent times we have seen a rise in the number of computer games marketed exclusively for girls. This trend in computer games parallels the general trend in the toy industry toward gender-specific marketing. The dangers of such gender stereotyping are evident in the remarks of a frustrated eight-year-old girl, who said, after an hour of wandering the aisles of a toy store, "All the toys are either too boyish or too girlish. Why don't they have something in the middle?" Although we have focused here on identifying game features that appeal to girls, we would like to caution against designing girl games that stereotype "girl" interests. The ultimate challenge facing software developers is to design games that appeal to any gamer, regardless of gender.

Conclusion

We have used the recent success of the "Barbie Fashion Designer" among girls, as well as research on play, television preferences, and tastes in literature to identify game features that girls might find appealing. Our analysis suggests that girls like nonaggressive play activities that allow them to create fantasies set in familiar settings with familiar characters. The "Barbie Fashion Designer" allows girls to do just this and becomes one more accessory in their role play. Our analysis suggests that girls find certain game features appealing: designing and selecting computer software for girls need not be a hit-or-miss affair.

Notes

1. We thank J. Cassell and H. Jenkins for their feedback on an earlier draft and Frank Evers for all his help and critical reading of an earlier draft. Subrahmanyam was partially supported by a Creative Leave from California State University, Los Angeles. Greenfield was partially supported by a National Institute of Health, Fogarty International Center, Minority International Research Training Grant awarded to the University of California, Los Angeles, and by the Colegio de la Frontera Sur, San Cristobal de las Casas, Chiapas, Mexico. Address correspondence to ksubrah@calstatela.edu.

References

Ahlgren, A. and Johnson, D. W. 1979. "Sex Differences in Cooperative and Competitive Attitudes from Second through 12th Grade." *Developmental Psychology* 15: 45–49.

Beato, G. 1997. "Computer Games for Girls Is No Longer an Oxymoron." *ELECTROSPHERE*, 5.04, April. http://www.wired.com/wired/5.04/es_girlgames.html

Catherall, T. S. 1989. "Playing with Electric Trains in School Classrooms." *Play and Culture* 2: 137–141.

Coates, S., Lord, M. and Jakabovics, E. 1975. "Field Dependence-Independence, Social-Non-Social Play and Sex Differences in Preschool Children." *Perceptual and Motor Skills* 40: 195–202.

Cocking, R. R. and Greenfield, P. M. 1996. "Effects of Interactive Entertainment Technologies on Children's Development." In P. M. Greenfield and R. R. Cocking, eds., *Interacting with Video*. Norwood, N.J.: Ablex Publishing, 3–7.

Cooper, J., Hall, J. and Huff, C. 1990. "Situational Stress as a Consequence of Sex-Stereotyped Software." *Personality and Social Psychology Bulletin* 16: 419–429.

De Witt, K. 1997. "Computer Game Designers Make a Play for Girls." *New York Times Cybertimes on the Web.*, June 23. http://www.nytimes.com/library/cyber/week/062397girls.html

Dominick, J. R. 1984. "Videogames, Television Violence, and Aggression in Teenagers." *Journal of Communication* 34 (spring): 136–147.

Eder, D. and Hallinan, M. T. 1978. "Sex Differences in Children's Friendships." *American Sociological Review* 43: 237–250.

Goldstein, J. H. 1994. "Sex Differences in Toy Play Use and Use of Video Games." In J. H. Goldstein, ed., *Toys, Play, and Child Development*. New York: Cambridge University Press, 110–129.

Greenfield, P. M. 1984. *Mind and Media: The Effects of Television, Video Games, and Computers*. Cambridge: Harvard University Press.

Greenfield, P. M. 1994, 1996. "Video Games as Cultural Artifacts." *Journal of Applied Developmental Psychology* 15: 3–12. Reprinted in P. M. Greenfield and R. R. Cocking, eds., *Interacting with Video*. Norwood, N.J.: Ablex Publishing, 85–94.

Greenfield, P. M. and Cocking, R. R., eds. 1996. *Interacting with Video*. Norwood, N.J.: Ablex Publishing.

Grusec, J. E. and Lytton, H. 1988. *Social Development: History, Theory, and Research*. New York: Springer-Verlag.

Huston, A. C., et al. 1990. "Development of Television Viewing Patterns in Early Childhood: A Longitudinal Investigation. *Developmental Psychology* 26: 409–420.

Inkpen, K., Upitis, R., Klawe, M., Anderson, A., Ndunda, M., Sedighian, K., Leroux, S., and Hsu, D. 1993. "'We Have Never-Forgetful Flowers in our Garden': Girls' Responses to Electronic Games." Technical Report 93–47 (December) Department of Computer Science, University of British Columbia.

Kafai, Y. B. 1996. "Gender Differences in Children's Construction of Video Games. In P. M. Greenfield and R. R. Cocking, eds., *Interacting with Video*. Norwood, N.J.: Ablex Publishing, 39–66.

Kiesler, S., Sproull, L., and Eccles, J. S. 1985. "Pool Halls, Chips, and War Games: Women in the Culture of Computing." *Psychology of Women Quarterly* 9: 451–462.

Kinder, M. 1996. "Contextualizing Video Game Violence: From Teenage Mutant Ninja Turtles 1 to Mortal Kombat 2." In P. M. Greenfield and R. R. Cocking, eds., *Interacting with Video*. Norwood, N.J.: Ablex Publishing, 25–38.

Korich, M., and Waddell, H. 1986. "A Comparative Study of Age and Gender Influences on Television Taste." Unpublished manuscript, University of California, Los Angeles.

Kubey, R., and Larson, R. 1990. "The Use and Experience of the New Video Media among Children and Young Adolescents." *Communication Research* 17: 107–130.

Lin, S., and Lepper, M. 1987. "Correlates of Children's Usage of Video Games and Computers." *Journal of Applied Social Psychology* 17: 72–93.

Lyle, J., and Hoffman, H. R. 1971. "Children's Use of Television and other Media." Unpublished manuscript, University of California, Los Angeles.

Loftus, G. R., and Loftus, E. F. 1983. *Mind at Play*. New York: Basic Books.

Malone, T. W. 1981. "Toward a Theory of Intrinsically Motivating Instruction." *Cognitive Science* 5: 333–370.

Mandinach, E. B., and Corno, L. 1985. "Cognitive Engagement Variations among Students of Different Ability Level and Sex in a Computer Program Solving Game." *Sex Roles* 13: 241–251.

Miedzian, M. 1991. *Boys Will Be Boys: Breaking the Link between Masculinity and Violence*. New York: Doubleday.

Morlock, H., Yando, T., and Nigolean, K. 1985. "Motivation of Video Game Players." *Psychological Reports* 57: 247–250.

Myers, D. 1984. "The Patterns of Player-Game Relationships: A Study of Computer Game Players." *Simulation and Games* 15: 159–185.

Provenzo, E. F., Jr. 1991. *Video Kids: Making Sense of Nintendo*. Cambridge: Harvard University Press.

Rushbrook, S. 1986. "Messages of Video Games: Socialization Implications." Doctoral dissertation, University of California, Los Angeles.

Scarr, S., and McCartney, K. 1983. "How People Make their Own Environments: A Theory of Genotype Environmental Effects." *Child Development* 54: 424–435.

Singer, D. G., and Singer, J. L. 1990. *The House of Make-Believe: Play and Developing Imagination*. Cambridge: Harvard University Press.

Smith, C. L., and Stander, J. M. 1981. "Human Interaction with Computer Simulation: Sex Roles and Group Size." *Simulation and Games* 12: 345–360.

Subrahmanyam, K., and Greenfield, P. M. 1994, 1996. "Effects of Video Game Practice on Spatial Skills in Girls and Boys." *Journal of Applied Developmental Psychology* 15(1): 13–32. Reprinted in P. M. Greenfield and R. R. Cocking eds., *Interacting with Video*. Norwood, N.J.: Ablex Publishing, 95–114.

Thorne, B. 1993. *Gender Play: Girls and Boys in School*. New Brunswick, N.J.: Rutgers University Press.

Tizard, B., Philips, J., and Plewis, I. 1976. "Play in Preschool Centers: Play Measures and their Relationship to Age, Sex, and I.Q." *Journal of Child Psychology and Psychiatry and Allied Disciplines* 17: 252–264.

Tuchscherer, P. 1988. *TV Interactive Toys: The New High Tech Threat to Children*. Bend, Ore.: Pinnaroo.

Turkle, S. 1984. *The Second Self: Computers and the Human Spirit*. New York: Simon & Schuster.

Wegener-Spohring, G. 1989. "War Toys and Aggressive Games." *Play and Culture* 2: 35–47.

Wilder, G., Mackie, D., and Cooper, J. 1985. "Gender and Computers: Two Surveys of Computer-Related Attitudes." *Sex Roles* 13: 215–228.

Winstead, B. A. 1986. Sex Differences in Same-Sex Friendships. In V. J. Derlega and B. A. Winstead, eds., *Friendship and Social Intereaction*. New York: Springer-Verlag, 81–99.

Chapter 3

Girl Games and Technological Desire
Cornelia Brunner
Dorothy Bennett
Margaret Honey

Gender and Technological Desire

During the past ten years, a research and design group at the Center for Children and Technology has spent time investigating issues of gender and diversity as they relate to the ways in which students, particularly girls, use and engage with technologies. Our approach to these issues has been both psychological and sociological: we have investigated the ways in which children and adults construct meanings in relation to different technological environments, and we have examined the social and cultural barriers that tend to affect the ways we engage with technologies. We have also experimented with designing technological environments that can engage diverse populations of learners—not just the white boys.

It has become clear to us over time that the problem of designing for gender and diversity is quite complicated, particularly with respect to technology. A variety of forces affect our understanding of gender and make it very hard for us to think our way out of more or less conventional understandings of "masculinity" and "femininity." They include such sociological issues as the fact that girls and students of color still opt out of advanced-level science and math courses at a greater rate than do Caucasian males. As a result, scientific, engineering, and technological fields that are responsible for technological design are still largely dominated by white men. They also include economic factors, such as the fact that successful interactive "edutainment" products, often linked to other commercially successful products such as television series, are the ones to find shelf space in CompUSA and other large retail outfits. And they include psychological factors, such as the ways in which we as consumers have been strongly encouraged to collude in the kinds of narratives that the vast majority of interactive products offer, particularly in the gaming industry. In this paper we focus on the latter point: the *psychological paradox,* the question of how we address issues of concern to young women that are glaringly absent in technological design without colluding in stereotypical understandings of femininity.

One of our strategies in exploring the psychological complexities that surround technological design has been to start with ourselves. We noticed that the women in our office seemed to respond quite differently to the sight of boxes of high-tech equipment arriving in the office than most of our male colleagues. The men seemed magnetically drawn to the boxes, tearing them open, practically salivating at the sight of the shiny, new machines emerging from their styrofoam nest. Then there would be the sound of happily boastful speculation about the speed, the power, the number of bips per bump the machine could produce or consume, and how it compared to a range of other machines with whose model numbers everybody seemed intimately familiar. We women tended to stay back and watch this frenzy with some amusement and a strong dose of skepticism, best summarized in the polite request that they let us know when they had put the thing together and had figured out what it was good for. We knew that there was no difference in technical expertise to explain this difference in attitude. Several of the women were more technically sophisticated than some of the men who were spitting stats at the new machine, and these women would probably end up setting up the machine, figuring out how to make good use of it—and then explaining it to the men.

As researchers and designers we decided to explore some of these casually observed differences in more depth. The Spencer Foundation funded a series of studies involving interviews with users of technology, from architects to NASA scientists, from filmmakers to programmers (Bennett 1993; Brunner, Hawkins, and Honey 1988; Brunner 1991; Hawkins, Brunner, Clements, Honey, and Moeller 1990; Honey, Moeller, Brunner et al., 1991; Honey 1994). All of these individuals were deeply engaged in computer-related activities, including programming, multimedia design and authoring, computer-assisted design, and engineering. We asked them about a wide range of topics, from their career paths and their mentoring experiences to their personal feelings about their work. We also selected a subsample of twenty-four respondents, balanced by gender and profession, and asked them to participate in a study of their technology fantasies.

In the fantasy study, we were interested in exploring women's and men's feelings about technology—the nonrational aspect of how we interpret technological objects. Assuming that people might be less self-conscious about sharing such fantasies with a computer than with a human interviewer, we made a software program that invited our respondents to spin fantasies directly into the computer. We made the program look fanciful rather than serious, hoping to invite respondents to censor themselves as little as possible. We posed the following question: "If you were writing a science fiction story in which the perfect instrument (a future version of your own) is described, what would it be like?" Our analysis of the adult fantasies focused on five major topics: 1) the role of technology in integrating people's home and work lives; and technology's relationship to 2) nature, 3) the human body, 4) the process of creation, and 5) the process of communication.

What emerged from this study were two distinct and highly gendered perspectives on technology. Across our sample, women fantasized about small, flexible objects that facilitate sharing ideas and staying in touch, that can be used anywhere and fulfill a number of quite different functions—something that can be a camera one minute, for instance, and a flute the next. For the women in our sample, technology is a fellow creature on the earth, a child of humanity, promising but problematic (because, like all good things, there can be too much of it), needing care and guidance to grow to its best potential within the balance of things surrounding it, within the social and natural network in which it lives. The women wrote stories about tools that allow us to integrate our personal and professional lives and to facilitate creativity and communication. The following is typical of the fantasies written by women:

> The "keyboard" would be the size of a medallion, formed into a beautiful piece of platinum sculptured jewelry, worn around one's neck. The medallion could be purchased in many shapes and sizes. The keyed input would operate all day-to-day necessities to communicate and transport people (including replacements for today's automobile). The fiber-optic network that linked operations would have no dangerous side effect or byproduct that harmed people or the environment.

In contrast, men's fantasies were about mind-melds and bionic implants that allow their owners to create whole cities with the blink of an eye, or to have instant access to the greatest minds in history, to check in and see, as they get dressed in the morning, what Ghandi might have thought about a problem they are facing in the office that day. In their stories technology frees us from the earth, from social problems, possibly from humanity itself. The men praised technology because it increases our command and control over nature and each other. It allows us to extend our instrumental power into god-like dimensions, to transcend the limitations of time, space, and our physical bodies. For the men technology is a magic wand (pun intended), and scenarios like the following were typical:

> A direct brain-to-machine link. Plug it into a socket in the back of you head and you can begin communications with it. All information from other users is available and all of the history of mankind is also available. By selecting any time period the computer can impress directly on the user's brain images and background information for that time. In essence a time-machine. The user would not be able to discern differences between dreams and reality and information placed there by the machine.

Table 3.1 illustrates how we chose to summarize some of the most striking differences in how men and women fantasized about technology (Bennett, Brunner, and Honey 1996).

During the past decade, we have also conducted similar studies investigating children's technology fantasies and have collected fantasy machines, mostly from elementary and middle school students. In an analysis of the fantasy tasks of forty-seven preadolescent boys and girls, we asked children to create a blueprint for a machine of their own creation. Boys tend to make vehicles that take them wherever they want to go instantaneously. Typically, these vehicles have elaborate model numbers. Figure 3.1 represents what boys tend to imagine. The New 1994 Mazing Hover Carr is further illustrated in Figure 3.2. This one has a "twin valve seven rotor 4 class booster rocket," hidden turbo jets—and a snack bar.

Girls' fantasies about technology differed in nature from those of boys. The machines that girls typically invented tended to be human-like household helpers or improvements to existing technologies that aimed to solve real-life problems. They often highlighted functions rather than the features of their machines, and they were situated in context. Figure 3.3 shows an example of what girls typically imagine: instead of features, there are functions.

The Season Chore Doer (Figure 3.4) is a sophisticated, multifunctional device. It senses what is needed and provides just the right tool: a seeder in

Table 3.1   Technology

Women	Men
fantasize about it as a **MEDIUM**	fantasize about it as a **PRODUCT**
see it as a **TOOL**	see it as a **WEAPON**
want to use it for **COMMUNICATION**	want to use it for **CONTROL**
are impressed with its potential for **CREATION**	are impressed with its potential for **POWER**
see it as **EXPRESSIVE**	see it as **INSTRUMENTAL**
ask it for **FLEXIBILITY**	ask it for **SPEED**
are concerned with its **EFFECTIVENESS**	are concerned with its **EFFICIENCY**
like its ability to facilitate **SHARING**	like its ability to grant them **AUTONOMY**
are concerned with **INTEGRATING** it into their personal lives	are intent on **CONSUMING** it
talk about wanting to **EXPLORE** worlds	talk about using it to **EXPLOIT** resources and potentialities
are **EMPOWERED** by it	want **TRANSCENDENCE**

Source: Brunner 1994.

Cornelia Brunner, Dorothy Bennett, and Margaret Honey

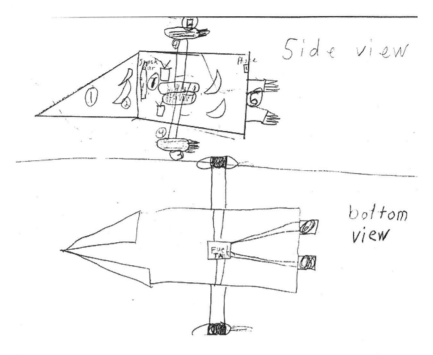

Figure 3.1

spring, an umbrella in summer, a rake in the fall, and a shovel in winter. It does not, however, eliminate the need for the chore itself. If this gadget had been designed by a boy, chances are it would not provide a rake to collect the leaves—it would probably pulverize them.

Implications for the Design of Girl Games

One way of summarizing the implications of our research for the development of new technologies is to say that women and girls are much more likely to be concerned with how new technologies can fit into the social and environmental surroundings, whereas men are much more likely to be preoccupied with doing things faster, more powerfully, and more efficiently regardless of social and environmental consequences. Women are also far less likely to push the technological envelope and tend to be willing to make do with available tools. Men, in contrast, tend to draw upon their technological imaginations to extend the capabilities of technologies and to attempt to "go where no man has ever gone

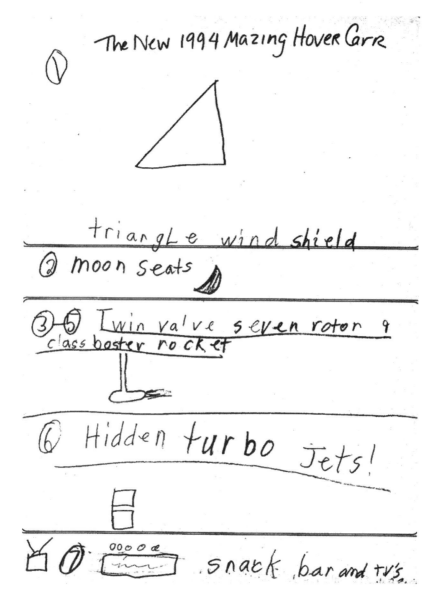

The New 1994 Mazing Hover Carr

① triangle wind shield
② moon seats
③⑤ Twin valve seven rotor 4 class boster rocket
⑥ Hidden turbo Jets!
⑦ snack bar and tv's

Figure 3.2

SEASON CHORE DOER

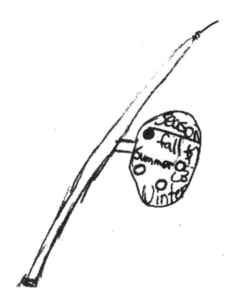

Figure 3.3

before." What are the implications of these differences for girl-friendly electronic games?

When thinking about the design of technological environments—particularly in relation to entertainment and educational products—it has been exceedingly difficult for us to imagine our way out of antithetical positions. The common approach in interactive design, or perhaps the path of least resistance, is to develop story lines that reinforce extreme notions of gender. The result is

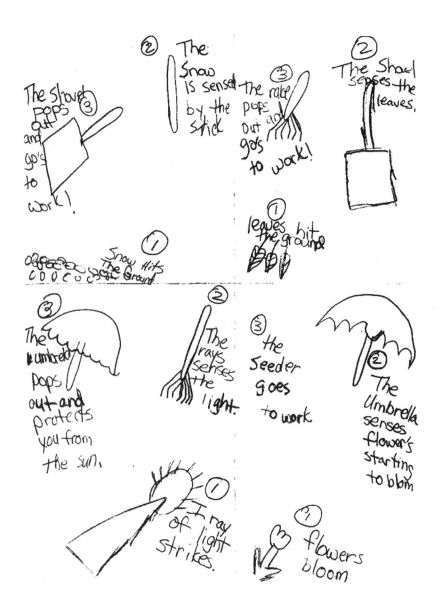

The Shovel POPS out and go's to work!

② The snow is sensed by the stick

③ The rake pops out and go's to work!

② The shovel senses the leaves.

① leaves hit the ground

① Snow Hits The Ground

③ The umbrella pops out and protects you from the sun.

② The rays senses the light.

③ the seeder goes to work

② The Umbrella senses flower's starting to bloom

① I ray of light strikes.

③ flowers bloom

Figure 3.4

that "Mortal Kombat" becomes the archetypal video game for boys. In the girls' arena, programs like "McKenzie & Company" are beginning to emerge. This product presents scenarios that revolve around how to handle problems with boyfriends or would-be boyfriends, and how to dress and what kind of make-up to wear. These kinds of stories are not bad in and of themselves, but if they are the only available options, they run the danger of reinforcing stereotypic thinking about gender. Just as the fantasy life of boys who enjoy playing games like "Mortal Kombat" should not be curtailed by scenes of mindless violence, the social decision-making options in a game like "McKenzie & Company" are too simplistic to represent the kind of human problem-solving situations girls think about all the time. Products such as these enlarge an already gaping gender divide, making it harder for us to imagine approaches that do not privilege an either/or paradigm: Conquest or A Day at the Mall. We have to engage both boys and girls with electronic games that can incorporate multiple perspectives and varying themes.

To consider what our research means for designing a new genre of game that is not rigidly overdetermined, we first have to consider the function of games and play. One of the functions of playing games, as Henry Jenkins (this volume) notes, is to rehearse and explore what it means to have a gender. Games provide a safe place to explore issues of femininity and masculinity. Game playing can deliberately expand our sense of who we are. The appeal of role-playing games among both children and adults is testimony to this fact. The kinds of worlds represented in electronic games tend to be one dimensional. Typically these games appeal to boys. They are about conquest, winning, scoring points, assertion, and domination. The player becomes the active protagonist, whether the game is played from a first- or third-person perspective. The player is central, makes things happen, and determines the outcome. There usually are no other roles. There are few partner roles, few helper roles, few participant-observer roles. Making ourselves so big and so powerful that nobody can touch us is hardly preparation for the multiplicity of roles that people, particularly women, play in life. We need to make games that stretch the potential of different play paradigms.

Games have traditionally privileged:

- Victory over justice.
- Competition over collaboration.
- Speed over flexibility.
- Transcendence over empathy.

- Control over communication.
- Force over facilitation.

We need game environments that offer players options—where you can pick and choose from a range of personas, decide on varying strategies, and discover that different actions result in variable outcomes. We need a more complex relationship between actions taken and results obtained, and we need contexts that offer rich and varied opportunities for exploration.

Based on our research, and on a variety of experiments with designs that are deliberately open-ended (such as leaving choice in the hands of the user), we have conditional faith in the following generalizations about designing games for both boys and girls. It must be stressed, however, that these observations are speculative. We have never actually investigated the design features that make games more attractive to girls. We are merely applying the characteristics we have found to make for good electronic learning environments for girls to the domain of electronic games. What follows, then, is a nonprescriptive attempt to transform traditionally privileged design elements, and imagine alternative scenarios for play.

- *Technological sophistication.* The kinds of games that encourage flexibility in decision making require a more sophisticated technology than current games. Mitchel Resnick (Resnick 1991) learned years ago that girls wanted to build Lego Logo devices that could interact with each other. Instead of thinking about a single object that did one thing very well, designers had to pay attention to multiple objects that would interact with each other.
- *Winning and losing.* It probably matters more to girls what you win and what you lose than whether you win or lose. Girls are not that interested in conquering the world. Girls really prefer triumphs of a more personal sort. Many girls are seriously preoccupied with perfecting themselves, which is quite different from a more masculine desire to become stronger and more powerful, or with having total control over some part of the universe. This preoccupation with self-improvement and perfection is a tricky business, no simpler nor more beneficial than the masculine focus on power over others, except, perhaps, that the damage is more likely to be internal than external. It is, however, a rich ground for interesting stories and meaningful problems to solve.
- *Success and sacrifice.* Girls are interested in thinking about the issues that adult women must face these days, including how to juggle career and family, how to be successful at work while helping others, and how to stay part of the group.

Girls want to figure out what the issues are and what sacrifices one may have to make. They want to anticipate and rehearse the complex dance that adult women, particularly those in nontraditional professions, must perform in order to make their lives work. This is good material for all kinds of adventure games.

• *The contradictions of femininity.* What constitutes femininity is open to question these days. For the young women we interviewed, femininity is linked to notions of social justice. Defining femininity is a live issue and a complicated one. Theories that absolve girls from the need to be feminine are of no help in the real world of their everyday lives. Things have not changed that much in junior high school, and popularity and traditional femininity still go together. Not much help is given to young women on how to rethink these issues. We believe that one function of role-playing games could be to help provide an imaginary space allowing girls to fool around with the notions of femininity that make sense to them, and offer rich, complex stories that raise questions about the consequences of the social prescriptions for femininity.

• *Persuasion versus conquest.* Women and girls tend to value persuasion, not conquest. Persuading is a more complex act than conquering. It is easy to simulate shooting somebody dead. It is harder to simulate persuading somebody—the interaction is more nuanced. Persuasion cuts both ways, of course. We have always wanted to make a game in which rumors create both havoc and opportunity. Instead of pulling out a sword when confronted with a complex situation, we want to let fly a rumor and have interesting things happen as a result of it—as in real life.

• *Humor.* Girls are very interested in humor. We think girls have less tolerance for humorlessness when it comes to games than boys do, because boys have something else that they can fool around with even in the absence of humor— weapons and victory. They still get to rack up points and shoot off weapons. The humor girls appreciate is based on character and situation rather than putdown. A certain level of sarcasm can be a lot of fun, but when the humor is based on pointing out people's shortcomings, it no longer appeals to girls as much.

• *Adventure.* What is adventure for girls? Rescue and romance are adventures. There is plenty of rescue and romance in current games, but the females in the story rarely get to experience that adventure directly. Girls do not just want to get rescued, they want to do the rescuing—without having to abandon femininity to do it. And they want to do more than come up with the right approach to get a guy to ask them out! Adventure means risk. In many games, the payoff is getting more strength, accumulating wealth or power, and figuring out what risks to take to achieve those gains. The kinds of risks that interest girls may have to do with defying conventions rather than gaining authority. Let us have some games about that—more romantic heroines striking out to make a place for themselves and their kind in a world that misunderstands or undervalues them.

• *Puzzles and obstacles.* Let us also have more games in which you play at outwitting your opponent rather than vanquishing the enemy. Many games have puzzles that occasionally are very clever and require real thought. They are, however, rarely integral to the story. There are exceptions, of course, including "Myst." The puzzle solving is fun, even when it is just an artificial obstacle to pursuing the story, but it might be a lot more entertaining to girls if the puzzles contributed to the story. Since girls are less motivated by winning than by following the flow of the story, such unintegrated puzzles can be frustrating and discouraging. Boys, on the other hand, often appreciate the opportunity to rack up more points.

• *Writing.* Girls are very interested in letter-writing and in other forms of communication across a variety of media. They like to think about what to say and how to say it. Girls enjoy analyzing responses, mulling over phrasings, and testing alternatives. They like to illustrate their messages, comment on them, and compare and contrast them with other statements. Girls might be interested in games that focus on how things are communicated, not just on what is being said.

• *Design.* Girls like designing living spaces—not blueprints, but actual spaces. With VRML and VR technologies, it should be possible to see people move through a space you have designed, to report on how it feels, to look at it from their perspective, and to watch which kinds of interactions the design privileges and which are prohibited.

• *Being chosen.* The girls we interviewed often mentioned that they might like games about being chosen. But girls are not nearly as interested in thinking about how to seduce someone into choosing them as they are in the complexity that results once you have been chosen. Being chosen, as we all know, is a complicated thing. You lose some friends, you gain some things, stuff happens. Games that focus on dealing with that stuff might be extremely interesting to young women.

• *Mysteries.* Girls like mysteries because they have complex plots and intelligent action. There is something to think about and to talk over with friends. The kinds of action required to solve a mystery—keeping track of information, sifting through it, thinking it over, trying it again, looking at it from a different

Cornelia Brunner, Dorothy Bennett, and Margaret Honey

perspective—are the kinds of adult skills girls want to rehearse. It is what we like to do.

Some existing software, though not necessarily intended for girls, is designed in ways that seem compatible with the kind of feminine perspective on technology we have described here. Interactive comics, for instance, are an interesting new use of the electronic medium. The interactive features are a good fit with the way kids actually read comics, bringing each panel to life with sound and movies or animation. The comics provide a strong, linear narrative structure but utilize the nonlinear nature of the medium to offer a choice between multiple perspectives. The plot remains the same, the speech bubbles and the images inside the panels don't change, but the context and commentary in the descriptive labels changes, as does the accompanying information. This makes for a complex narrative of multiple voices, which lends itself beautifully to interactive storytelling. Unfortunately, this feature is not used in most of the interactive comics for children. These comics may include multimedia but they don't offer any conceptual interactivity. They are more like Living Books. Moreover the comics we have seen, such as "Reflux" by Inverse Ink, are interesting to look at and beautifully designed, but their content is strongly masculine. Nonetheless the genre makes a lot of sense for girls. Looking at a situation from multiple perspectives is a very attractive activity for girls.

Rather than leaving their mark on the world by conquering territory or even by amassing resources, girls might like to make a difference in a social situation, right an injustice, save a whale or two, or discover a cure for cancer. Some educational games allow for this kind of thinking, including the Sim-Games by Maxis and the Trail games by MECC. In the entertainment realm, there are some adult games, such as "Voyeur II" by Philips, that allow you to solve a mystery and thus prevent a murder rather than to avenge one. In "Voyeur II" you are a private eye, observing the shenanigans of a wealthy family in a fancy mansion through your fabulous binoculars. Sex, romance, and family tensions are the main elements of the plot, rather than war, violence, or world domination.

The themes matter, and so do the activities themselves. In "The 1st Degree" by Broderbund, a game for adults in which you are the district attorney (male, with a young, white, smart-alecky woman assistant who develops much of the context information), you have to make a case for first-degree murder. You interview witnesses in their surroundings to get an idea of the context in which they live. The point of the game is not to solve the mystery but to make the case, which requires figuring out people's motivations and relationships, rather than establishing facts. Witnesses from whom you have learned the truth will lie on the stand if you have not persuaded them to join you. The story is more about the underlying emotional realities than about the grisly deed. This makes sense to girls.

Games with an electronic doll-house "feel" seem to be attractive to girls. An example is "SimTown" by Maxis, an environmental problem-solving game that lets you customize your own character, find out how the population feels, and lift the roof off the houses to see what's going on inside. "Hollywood" by Viacom is another kind of electronic doll house. Here, you can make animated movies with a set of characters and settings. You can write dialogue, select actions for character animation, customize the characters by giving them personality traits, and then record and play the movie. "Imagination Express" by Edmark is another doll house with good backgrounds, plenty of characters and objects, and the ability to add a little animation as well as captions. This program makes constructing settings fun because the objects, people and things, have a good deal of intelligence built into them. They twist and turn and place themselves appropriately behind, in front of, over or under things, and change size to maintain the illusion of depth.

Some of the new software coming out for girls, such as "Let's Talk About Me" by Simon & Schuster Interactive, are not exactly games. "Let's Talk About Me" is marketed as a handbook, and provides some activities girls might like. As for the other new electronic girls' games, some are good, some are not so good. The main differences are in the content rather than in the kind of activity they privilege. Most puzzles are still too unintegrated, and the choices are too few. The interactivity is still not conceptual enough. And we worry that the folks likely to have the money to develop complex activities may confuse content with marketing and end up reaffirming stereotypes. They may fail to realize that the desired forms of activity can be applied to a wide range of content girls are interested in, not just to catching a boyfriend. But at least somebody's finally working on the problem.

Our final thought is this. Boys can use games to escape into a fantasy world which allows them to prepare themselves for the requirements of adult masculinity. They can gird their digital loins with magical potencies and vanquish enemies with their limitless strength. They can also get killed, over and over, along the way, until they have achieved the degree of mastery that makes them champions. Then they can reach into the full storehouse of boy games and accept another challenge. The cultural prescriptions for masculinity are harsh and exacting. Few boys can feel secure about achieving a sufficient degree of masculinity. The pressure is relentless—and these games provide a fun, painless opportunity to boost their sense of masculinity and let off some steam.

The cultural prescriptions for femininity are equally stringent—and they are also internally contradictory. Girls are expected to be both frail and enduring, helpless and competent, fun loving and sensitive, emotional and available, needy and nurturing, vain and moral. Girls need games in which they can rehearse and express the ambiguities and contradictions of femininity. Navigating the shoals of femininity is the stuff girls think about. It is an endless conundrum: how to do the right thing when all the available options force you to choose against yourself; how to maintain a sense of pleasure and confidence in yourself when all the paths before you lead to danger; how to satisfy everybody without calling undue attention to yourself. Girls need games in which they can take their own side, act out, throw caution to the winds and watch what happens. They need games in which they survive, again and again, until they have achieved a state of grace that makes them happy. Then they need to reach into a growing storehouse of girl games and play another story. The pressure on girls is relentless, too. Becoming a woman is a tricky business. Girls could use some games that provide a fun, painless opportunity to bolster their sense of femininity and to stretch their wings.

References

Bennett, D. 1993. "Voices of Young Women in Engineering." Paper presented at the 10th International Conference on Technology in Education. Cambridge, MA: Massachusetts Institute of Technology.

Bennett, D., Brunner, C., and Honey, M. 1996. "Gender and Technology: Designing for Diversity." Paper written for the Regional Equity Forum on Math, Science and Technology Education. Cosponsored by EDC's WEEA Equity Resource Center, Northeastern University Comprehensive Resource Center for Minorities, TERC, and Mass Pep.

Brunner, C. 1991. "Gender and Distance Learning." In L. Roberts and V. Horner, eds., *The Annals of Political and Social Science*. Beverly Hills: Sage Press, 133–145.

Brunner C., Hawkins, J., and Honey, M. 1988. "Making Meaning: Technological Expertise and the Use of Metaphor." Paper presented at the American Educational Research Association, New Orleans.

Hawkins, J., Brunner, C., Clements, P., Honey, M., and Moeller, B. 1990. "Women and Technology: A New Basis for Understanding." Final report to the Spencer Foundation. New York: Center for Children and Technology, Bank Street College of Education.

Honey, M. 1994. "Maternal Voice in the Technological Universe." In D. Bassin, M. Honey, and M. Kaplan, eds., *Representations of Motherhood*. New Haven: Yale University Press.

Honey, M., Moeller, B., Brunner, C., Bennett, D. T., Clements, P., and Hawkins, J. 1991. "Girls and Design: Exploring the Question of Technological Imagination." Tech Rep. No. 17. New York: Bank Street College of Education, Center for Technology in Education.

Resnick, M. 1991. "Xylophones, Hamsters, and Fireworks: The Role of Diversity in Constructionist Activities." In I. Harel and S. Papert, eds., *Constructionism*. Norwood, MA: Ablex Publishing, 151–158.

Chapter 4

Video Game Designs by Girls and Boys:
Variability and Consistency of Gender Differences
Yasmin B. Kafai

Introduction

Over the past ten years interactive technologies have become a significant part of children's culture. Video games such as "Super Mario Brothers" or "Sonic" have found a stable place in children's playrooms, particularly when the games cater to boys' interests in sports, adventure, and combat (Provenzo 1991). Only recently has so-called "pink software" established a playground for girls, promoting games and software such as "Barbie Fashion Designer" or the "Baby-sitter Club" that draw on characters and activities popular among girls. In many ways, the production of interactive toys and games seems to replicate gender differences found in traditional toys and games and the interests these generate in children (Garvey 1990; Kinder 1991; Singer and Singer 1991; Sutton-Smith 1986).

There is ample evidence in the research literature for the existence of gender differences in children's video game interest, use, and performance (Goldstein 1994; Provenzo 1991). These gender differences also appear when children are asked to make their own video games (Kafai 1996). But there are some indicators that these differences are not as universal as they may appear at first: some software such as "Where in the World is Carmen Sandiego?" seems to have equal appeal for boys and girls, and some girls like to play video games, albeit with different interpretations (Gailey 1993). Furthermore, gender differences in play performance disappear after extended exposure (Greenfield and Cocking 1994), a claim also supported by research on girls' general use of and interest in technology (Linn 1985). While these are isolated indicators, they point out that gender differences are not as consistent as one might believe. It is possible that children display more versatility and range in their play interests and that particular factors such as game structures or context settings might have an impact. Research on children's toy and play preferences has provided evidence that structures of toys and play settings can elicit certain behaviors from play participants (Karpoe and Olney 1983; Ross and Taylor 1989).

The current analysis of video games designed by boys and girls intends to shed some light on the discussion around gender differences by comparing and contrasting two different game-design contexts.[1] In one context, I asked students between the ages of nine and ten to design and implement educational video games to teach fractions to younger students. In the second context, I asked children to design and implement educational video games to teach younger students about the solar system. The context differences refer to differences between subject matters: mathematics and science. In the following sections, I first review pertinent research and describe the research context in which the students produced the video games. Next, I compare and contrast the games designed by boys and by girls in the two different contexts, taking into consideration features such as genres, worlds, character design, interactions, and narrative. In the discussion, I address the context dependency of gender differences and what insights these results provide for developing video game design and play environments.

Review of Research

The context dependency of gender differences in interactive technologies is not well researched. As Garvey (1990) notes, most research on gender differences in children's toy preferences and play styles "has focused on profiling behavior of boys as a group and girls as a group. It has as yet failed to pursue any of the interesting questions about the range and versatility of children's play behavior or the conditions under which children might demonstrate flexibility in the cognitive and communicative aspects of make-believe or other types of play" (p. 154).

Most research has focused on documenting gender differences in relation to computer interest, use, and performance. Studies have pointed out gender differences in game playing interests (Inkpen et al. 1993; Provenzo 1991) and use (Kubey and Larson 1990). Other research has focused on gender differences in children's spatial and attentional skills while or as a consequence of playing video games (Greenfield, Brannon and Lohr 1994; Greenfield, deWinstanley, Kilpatrick, and Kaye 1994; Okagaki and French 1994; Subrahmanyam and Greenfield 1994). These theories of gender differences have been further elaborated by studies that examined children's preferences based on their real and imaginary designs of video games and electronic machines. For example, Kafai (1996) asked girls and boys to design and implement their own video games and found that the games designed by the girls differed significantly from those designed by boys according to the use of violent feedback, characters, and game genre. In a related research approach, Brunner et al. (1990) asked girls and boys to design fantasy machines and found that the girls designed machines with human-like qualities whereas boys focused on fantasy machines with numerous technical details.

When researchers analyze how children perceive gender stereotypes in video games, interpretations point in different directions. Researchers such as Kinder (1991) argue that the values embedded in movies, toys, television, and video games provide powerful stereotypes for children's thinking. By contrast, Gailey (1993) questions to what extent these messages are received as transmitted. She analyzes what values video games convey, how children as players interpret the play process, and what children get out of the games. Her research has demonstrated that children do not accept the universals provided in video games; they make up their own descriptions. Irrespective of the considerable gender stereotyping found in many video games (for example, in portraying women as victims or prizes), girls seem to resolve the dilemma by redefining their positions in casting themselves in managerial roles.

While gender differences are pervasive, there are also several documented instances where they appear less prominent. Recent research interrogating the video game-playing performance of girls and boys found that repeated play exposure attenuated preexisting gender differences (Greenfield and Cocking 1994). In analyzing computer programming performance, Linn (1985) noted that girls could be as effective programmers as boys when having the same opportunities. These results were supported by Harel (1991) and Kafai (1995), both of whom examined long-term software design activities and found no significant differences between boys' and girls' programming performance and interest.

Gender differences also seem less prominent in the formation of the motivational appeal of games. Malone and Lepper (1987) created a taxonomy of intrinsic motivations based on their research of different educational games. They found that the presence of game features such as challenge, curiosity, control, and fantasy, as well as cooperation, competition, and recognition increased motivational value for all players. They only found one instance where there were significant differences between boys and girls in what they liked about the games:

The boys seemed to like the fantasy of popping balloons and the girls seemed to dislike this fantasy. The addition of musical rewards, on the other hand, appeared to increase for girls, but to decrease for boys, the intrinsic interest of the activity. (Malone and Lepper 1987, p. 226)

These results convincingly suggest that boys and girls find many (but not all) of the same game features appealing. Research that analyzes players' and programmers' explanations notes the particular personal resonances that these activities hold for people (Turkle 1984). In my study of children's making of video games, I found significant gender differences in the kinds of characters created, in feedback, and in narrative development (Kafai 1996). But I also found that in other game features such as game interaction, game worlds, and genres there were trends rather than significant differences between girls' and boys' game designs. In other words, while gender differences are prevalent, there is a much richer picture behind what motivates and interests children in the playing with and making of interactive technologies. What this research pointed out is that girls are interested in making video games but that their video games look different from those designed by boys. The students drew from models of commercially available software in many ways: boys emulated video game design in the beginning and included characters and prizes found in popular video games; girls took existing educational software as a model. Many of the designed game contexts had little to do with the learning content, fractions. For that reason, the second study chose a science topic, the solar system, because it would provide a natural context, outer space. While certain topics in science such as biology and environmental studies have been known to draw larger numbers of women, it has been clear from the outset that both domains, mathematics and science, are not traditionally favored by girls (Sadker and Sadker 1994).

Research Context and Methodology

To examine the context dependency of gender differences in students' game designs, data sets from two different game design projects were analyzed. In each project, a class of sixteen fourth-grade students was asked to program educational games to teach either fractions or the solar system to third-graders. These projects were known as the Mathematics Game Design Project, or MGDP, and the Science Game Design Project, or SGDP. The MGDP had eight girls and eight boys; the SGDP had nine girls and seven boys. The students, who came from various ethnic backgrounds and were between nine and ten years old, met every day and transformed their classroom into a game-design studio for six months, learning programming, writing stories and dialogues, creating package designs and advertisements, and considering interface-design issues, as well as devising teaching strategies.[2] The collaborative structure provided opportunities for the game designers to discuss their project with their class-mates, and to show it to their potential users and to a wider public. Several "focus sessions" presented opportunities for the teacher and researcher to initi-ate discussions around issues and ideas relevant to all game designers. Games, students' experiences playing games, what they learned, and programming ideas were among the topics discussed.

The research for both projects, MGDP and SGDP, took place in an inner-city public elementary school in Boston. One part of the school is an MIT Media Laboratory experimental site, which in the more than twelve years since its establishment has investigated on a large scale the implementation and rituals of a computer culture. The school houses fifteen classrooms with approxi-mately 250 students and has 110 networked computers. The computers are arranged in four circles in the open areas, which are surrounded by classrooms with additional computers. While this feature distinguishes this site from more conventional classrooms, the student population—containing a high propor-tion of Hispanics and African-Americans—is nevertheless characteristic of other urban schools.

The most distinctive aspects of the regular classroom activities are that all the students have daily access to the computer and that they mostly create their own software, using the programming language Logo, rather than using predesigned program packages. The implications of students' programming ex-perience are important for understanding the results of this study. All of the students who participated in either MGDP or SGDP probably had more technical experience than most students in other schools. While programming the games was still a difficult enterprise, it was also feasible because the students had sufficient understanding of programming to begin the task. What is important to point out is that, because there were enough computers for each student, both girls and boys had the opportunity to build this technical knowledge over time. Consequently, girls would spend as much time on the computers as boys did. Because both studies were conducted at a time when most students did not have computers at home, outside experiences were negligible.

While both game-design projects took place in the same school context, the two studies did not happen at the same time nor were they working with the same students: the MGDP took place two years before the SGDP. But the two projects shared enough features to be comparable: the same teacher and researcher conducted them, and students for both projects entered with similar programming backgrounds and video game experience. For that reason, it seems unlikely that the time difference of two years created a different cultural environment and significantly influenced the games that were designed.

A combination of qualitative methods was used to document the students' ideas, thoughts, and progress in game development. Interviews gathered information about students' interest, knowledge, and evaluation of video games. In the interviews that I conducted with each student before the projects began, I found that all students had an awareness of and hands-on experience with video games. However, the extent of the video game play experience varied considerably. The major difference was between girls and boys: most boys played video games actively and consistently, whereas only two girls acknowledged having done so. To summarize, the girls' and boys' knowledge of video games were not comparable. Perhaps this result is not surprising considering that the majority of commercial video games are played by boys. (See, for example, Greenfield, Brannon, and Lohr 1994; Provenzo 1991.)

Results

In all, thirty-two final video games were analyzed according to the following features (Kafai 1996): the game genre; the game worlds and places created; the game characters and supporting cast of actors developed by students; the interaction modes and feedback provided for the player; the narrative development as part of the game structure. To facilitate comparisons, all the results have been transformed into percentages, and game designs of the two different contexts are compared for each gender (see Table 4.1).

Game Genres

There are various kinds of video games and many ways to group them. In the game industry, five major types of games are distinguished: sports, role-playing, action, strategy, and simulation. For this study I divided the students' games into the following categories: adventure, sports/skills, and teaching context. The categories "adventure" and "sports/skill" were based on existing commercial game formats, whereas "teaching" is usually not found in commercial games. Also, this categorization is by no means exhaustive and exclusive, as

Table 4.1 Overview of game design features by gender in MGDP and SGDP contexts

Games	Girls (%)		Boys (%)	
	MGDP n=8	SGDP n=9	MGDP n=8	SGDP n=7
Genre				
Adventure	38	33	88	54
Sport/skill	38	0	13	14
Teaching	24	67	0	29
Worlds				
Fantasy	25	0	75	0
Realistic	75	100	25	100
Player				
Generic "you"	63	77	13	58
Animal/fantasy	25	0	25	0
Gender specific	12	23	62	42
Cast				
0 and 2	88	100	25	100
2 and more	12	0	75	0
Feedback				
Violent with wrong answer	13	0	100	0
Narrative				
Presence	38	22	87	28

many games actually fall in several categories at the same time. For example, an adventure game may also be a skill game, since it requires the player to demonstrate skills to overcome many obstacles. Or, a simulation game of city building may also have educational purposes, since it requires the player to deal with the complexity of dynamic networked systems. Nevertheless, this general categorization may serve as a starting point. For the analysis of the designed games, the category "adventure" has been used when the player experienced extraordinary events or was sent to explore unknown places. The category "skill" has been used for games of an athletic nature such as basketball or skiing. The third category was games that used the "teaching" context in an explicit fashion.

The "adventure" genre was popular in both contexts, more so for boys than for the girls. A central feature of many adventure games was the contest between good and evil. The player is on the good side fighting off the bad guys in order to achieve the goal. This moral dimension was present in all of the boys' games in the MGDP where the player either had to recover "a stolen fraction wand" or "a stolen jewel," or "to defeat demons, evil fraction aliens, globe ghosts or mash Martians" in order "to receive a bucket full of gold, a trip to Orlando-ville, a wedding to a princess," or "a ticket to the summer park." Few boys opted to include this feature in their science-oriented games, however, which instead tended to be based on goals such as "supporting someone who has been captured by aliens." Often, the player engages the aliens in a game of tag in order to "recover information" to return to earth, or lands on a particular planet for exploration purposes. Most girls, on the other hand, did not include the morality dimension in either context, with the exception of one girl whose game focused on saving Mars (SGDP); here the player had to defeat aliens in order to continue the game.

The "sports" genre was selected by only a few students in either context: students used basketball on the moon (SGDP, boy) or dunking basketballs for learning fractions (MGDP, boy), or skiing down the hill (MGDP, girl), or navigating a maze (MGDP, boy) or a spider web (MGDP, girl) (see Figures 4.1a and 4.1b). These choices were mostly triggered by personal preferences. One could also argue that the sports genre, despite its prominent presence among commercial video games, did not lend itself easily for the design of educational games.

"Teaching" was the second popular theme (genre) in both contexts. In the MGDP, the two teaching games were both located in the classroom and involved a teacher, whereas in the SGDP the game designer engaged the player in word searches, a variant not observed in the MGDP context. These word searches were programmed by four students. The program displayed a grid of 100 letters, ten to a row, and the player was asked to "recognize" pertinent words related to the solar system (such as the names of planets or key concepts) by stamping over the appropriate letters (see Figure 4.2a). This particular teaching technique might replicate students' science learning experience, which is more than often simply the memorization of words printed in boldface or colored type in science textbooks. Other teaching games asked the player to rearrange or recognize the correct order of the planets (see Figure 4.2b).

One can speculate on why so many girls favored this particular game genre. One interpretation is that girls implicitly embedded a gender bias found among professional software designers when they design software for boys or

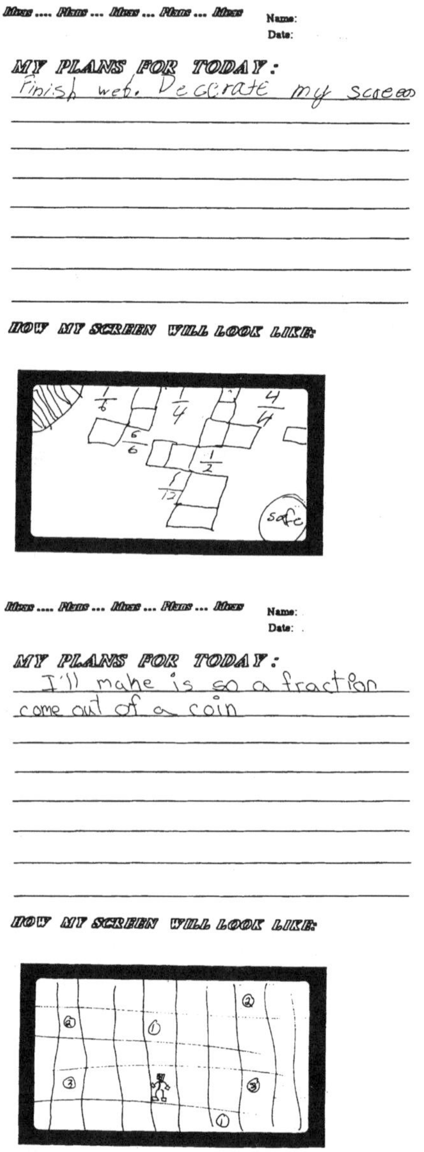

Figure 4.1a and 4.1b: Designer Notebook entries—Gaby's and Trevor's game designs. Gaby's game describes a spider web in which the player moves around as a fly away from the spider and turns on fraction blocks where questions are posed. Trevor's grid shows the different coins that the player has to reach to get to fraction problems.

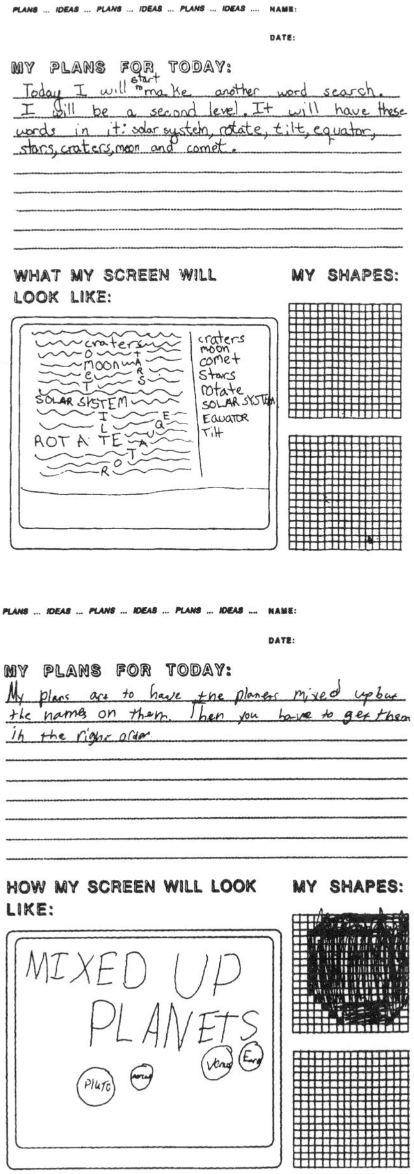

PLANS ... IDEAS ... PLANS ... IDEAS ... PLANS ... IDEAS ... **NAME:**

DATE:

MY PLANS FOR TODAY:

Today I will start make another word search.
I will be a second level. It will have these
words in it: solar system, rotate, tilt, equator,
stars, craters, moon and comet.

WHAT MY SCREEN WILL LOOK LIKE: **MY SHAPES:**

PLANS ... IDEAS ... PLANS ... IDEAS ... PLANS ... IDEAS ... **NAME:**

DATE:

MY PLANS FOR TODAY:

My plans are to have the planets mixed up but
the names on them. Then you have to get them
in the right order.

HOW MY SCREEN WILL LOOK LIKE: **MY SHAPES:**

Figure 4.2a and 4.2b: Designer Notebook entries—Cheryl's and Rachel's game designs. Cheryl's design describes the word search and arrangement of words. Rachel's design shows the planets to be arranged in right order.

for girls. Huff and Cooper (1987) found that expectations held by many software game designers are central in determining the way the software design interacted with the user. Software that is explicitly designed for girls is often classified as a "learning tool," whereas programs designed for boys are often classified as "games." Girls' preferences for this software format might have been based on their choice of designing for other girls. Another interpretation is that girls might have simply followed the directions of designing an educational video game down to the letter of the word. While either interpretation offers some insights into possible motives for the choice of this genre, neither provides an explanation why this genre became more prevalent with girls and boys in the SGDP compared to the MGDP.

Game Worlds

The influence of context became even more evident in the choice of game worlds. All the game designs centered around a location (or the exploration of different locations). While the MGDP generated the greatest variety of places—spider webs, coin grids, street scenes, map games—the worlds in the SGDP were mostly located in space, either in the solar system or on an individual planet such as Mars. A major distinction could be drawn in the reality aspect of the game worlds. In many instances game worlds could be described as either realistic, because they featured well-known places such as classrooms, ski slopes, and airports, or as fantasy places that teach the player about the content.

All the game worlds in the SGDP had a space setting, which given the nature of the games would be considered a "realistic" setting. One distinction was whether the setting was centered around one planet or whether it encompassed the whole solar system. Some games used the introduction sequence as an entrance to the solar system, whereas others situated travel through space and visited different planets (see Figures 4.3a and 4.3b).

In contrast, the MGDP created greater variation between fantasy and realistic contexts. Many boys had invented fantasy places like "Orlandoville" or "Island of the Goon." This choice might reflect boys' need for extended play space. Jenkins (in this volume) observes that over the past fifty years the play spaces of children, and in particular those of boys, have moved from streets and playgrounds to the safety of children's' homes. Video games have provided the opportunity for boys to extend their play space into the virtual world. By contrast,

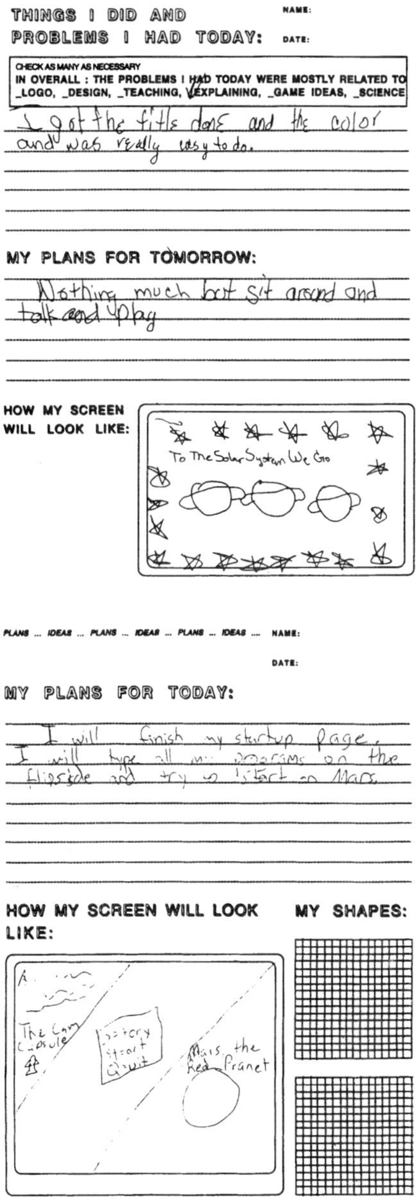

THINGS I DID AND
PROBLEMS I HAD TODAY:

NAME:

DATE:

CHECK AS MANY AS NECESSARY
IN OVERALL : THE PROBLEMS I HAD TODAY WERE MOSTLY RELATED TO
_LOGO, _DESIGN, _TEACHING, ✓EXPLAINING, _GAME IDEAS, _SCIENCE

I got the title done and the color
and was really easy to do.

MY PLANS FOR TOMORROW:

Nothing much but sit around and
talk and play

HOW MY SCREEN
WILL LOOK LIKE:

To The Solar System We Go

PLANS ... IDEAS ... PLANS ... IDEAS ... PLANS ... IDEAS ....

NAME:

DATE:

MY PLANS FOR TODAY:

I will finish my startup page,
I will type all my programs on the
flipside and try to litfoct on Mars.

HOW MY SCREEN WILL LOOK
LIKE:

MY SHAPES:

The Cam
Capsule

battery
start
orbit

Miss the
Red Pranet

Figure 4.3a and 4.3b: Designer Notebook entries—Deanna's title screen design for her game "The solar system we go" and Carleton's screen design for his "Cam Capsule" game.

most girls have been confined to the space of the home. This might explain their choice of more realistic settings such as classrooms, ski slopes, and spiderweb.

In their design of game worlds, the children made reference to features found in commercially available video and computer games. For example, a fraction game using warp zones was reminiscent of the "Super Mario Brothers" tunnel system (see Figure 4.4a). One science game followed the blueprint of an existing education game that the girl designer had played when she was younger (see Figure 4.4b). Many of the science games used the exploration of the solar system as the focal point, a feature used in popular educational games such as "Where in the Space is Carmen Sandiego" and "The Magic School Bus in Space."

Development of Game Characters
The places or worlds in which the games were situated were populated with an interesting cast of characters. The characters can be divided into two groups: those who represent the player and those who make up the supporting cast. In the majority of games the player became a generic "you," leaving the possibility open for the younger student to be a girl or a boy. Here is a game introduction written by a girl in the MGDP:

> You want to go to the home of Zeus but the map was ripped up by the Greek God Hades. All of the Greek Gods and Godesses have a fraction of the map. You are to go to the Gods and Godesses one at a time and they will ask you a fraction problem. If you get it right you will get a fraction of the map. When you get the whole map you will be at the gate of Zeus' home. The bull at the gate will ask you three hard fraction problems. If you get them right you will go inside Zeus' home and get to become the God or Godess of fractions and meet Zeus!

In one solar system game, the girl designer provided the player with a choice to pick either "player 1" or "player 2" but made no reference to the gender of the player. The majority of games designed in the SGDP used a generic character design, while the gender-specific character appeared more often in the MGDP. Most of the boys chose a fantasy figure such as "Gemini" or "Swartz" and demonstrated their assumption that the player, too, would be male by choosing character names such as "Mike" or "Tommy." One might interpret this choice of

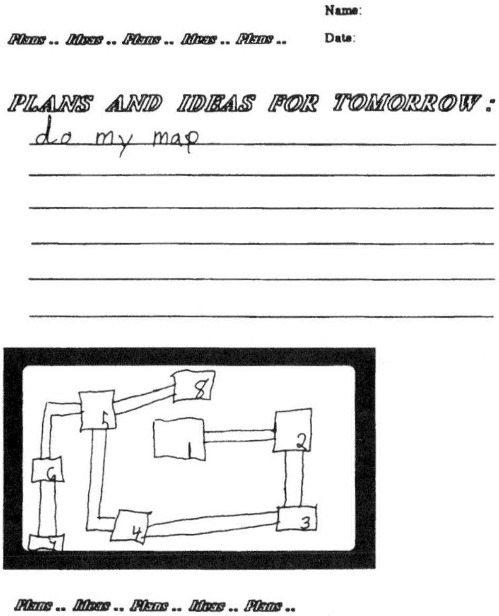

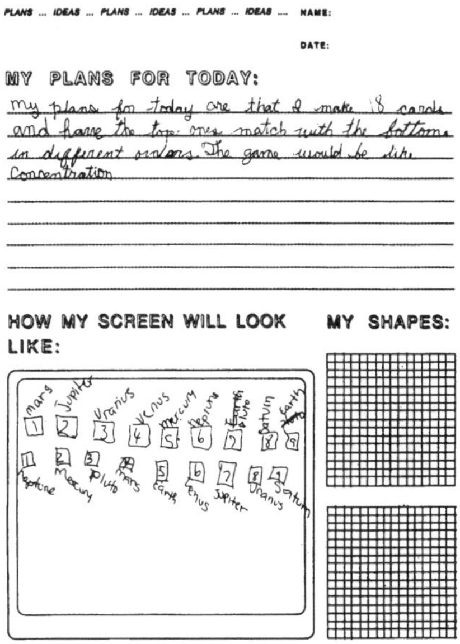

Name:

Plans .. Ideas .. Plans .. Ideas .. Plans ..   Date:

PLANS AND IDEAS FOR TOMORROW:

do my map

Plans .. Ideas .. Plans .. Ideas .. Plans ..

PLANS ... IDEAS ... PLANS ... IDEAS ... PLANS ... IDEAS ....   NAME:

DATE:

MY PLANS FOR TODAY:

My plans for today are that I make 18 cards and have the top ones match with the bottom in different orders. The game would be like Concentration

HOW MY SCREEN WILL LOOK LIKE: MY SHAPES:

Figure 4.4a and 4.4b: Designer Notebook entries—Jero's and Kim's game designs. Jero's map shows the different stations or levels of the world that the player has to pass. Kim's screen design shows the arrangement of cards and planets.

gender-specific character design also as involving a more personal identification: the player and the character are one and the same. This form of player positioning chosen by the boys might also reflect conventions of the commercial market. To a lesser extent, this form also appeared in the SGDP, as in the following example:

> It was a dark day for Commander Keen's fans everywhere. Their favorite hero had been seriously hurt while trying to start the enormous "Dope fish." After that he decided to take a little vacation. Little did he know that he was going to be captured by the Potato King, Hoopus Snoopus. Oh sure. I know what you are thinking. You're thinking that Hoopus Snoopus got turned into a hash brown in "Keen Dreams" but he has come back and he wants revenge. Who can save Keen? If you haven't guessed yet you must be really stupid, yes, it's his little brother Deen. That's why this game is called "Deens World."

Some of the player characters had fantasy names, as already noted above, hence making the relevance of gender more difficult to hypothesize. While there were some animal characters in the MGDP context, this feature was virtually absent within the SGDP.

In terms of additional cast members, we could observe further differences between the two game-design contexts. There was a small number of additional characters designed in the SGDP, always involving fictive aliens, and only in one instance fictional characters such as a commander and a figure named, "Keen" (SGDP, boy). By contrast, the MGDP generated greater variety in number and kind of characters. Most boys created several characters (demons, aliens from planet zork, magicians, dragons, soldiers from loft, goons) with fantasy names (Zork, Zarcon, Garvin, Sparzi, Marley) for the game world in which the player had to interact and learn about fractions. In contradistinction, the girls created fewer additional characters in this context. It is apparent that the girls had a significantly different take on the role of the player and actors.

These results run counter to some interpretations. It has been argued that commercial video game figures provided the inspiration for the game figures designed by the boys in the MGDP. This argument gains support if one considers the abundance of available video games and their focus on a male audience (Provenzo 1991; Kinder 1991). For the girls, on the other hand, there are fewer examples to draw from because of the paucity of gender-appropriate video games. The choice of familiar and personal figures provides room for the interpretation that girls grounded their designs in what they knew and liked: Rosy liked cats, and hence a cat plays a major role in her game; Miriam used a skier because she liked skiing; Gloria and Sina cast a teacher in their games. Another possibility is that the small number of supporting characters reflected preferred social groupings—girls have been known to play in smaller groups than boys (Moller, Hymel, and Rubin 1992).

On the other hand, we find in the SGDP that the boys designed as few characters as the girls did. There are several interpretations possible here. One could be that students drew only a small cast of characters because space missions are not known to involve many people, due to restricted living space on space ships. On the other hand, many commercial films and popular television programs feature large casts of characters. It is unclear what generated the differences between the science and mathematics contexts.

Design of Game Feedback

The design of feedback to the player was a central feature in the games and was linked to the quality of answers given by the player. The feedback modalities were either violent or nonviolent. "Game Over" by itself would not constitute a violent feedback if it were not connected with losing one's life or suffering harm by insulting the player's intelligence. Game actors die in the course of the game. In the SGDP, no designer included violent feedback for those instances when players answer questions incorrectly; in the MGDP, only girls did not use violent feedback. The nonviolent feedback options were "sending the player back to another planet" (SGDP, girl), or "not receiving a piece of the map" (MGDP, girl), or "having to start again from the top of the ski slope" (MGDP, girl).

The MGDP designers who incorporated violent feedback (all but one of whom were boys) developed a variety of violent-feedback modalities. For example, game actors were "kicked to the moon," "turned into an ice cube," "sent frying to the underworld," and "mentally transformed." One boy made his surfer character insult the players' intelligence ("Let me see how smart you are, Dude or Dudette," and "So you are telling me you're dumb,") when they gave a wrong answer. The harm here is psychological rather than physical, but it is still a harm. Only one girl chose to use violent feedback, ending her game with a helicopter crash if the player did not give the right answer.

Violent feedback is probably one of the most discussed features of video game play. (See, for example, Provenzo 1991; Silvern and Williamson 1987.)

Many commercial video games such as "Mortal Kombat" or "Streetfighter" indulge in explicit images of violence and combat activities as markers of progress through the game. It is difficult to explain why violent feedback was absent from the SGDP, while it was such a prominent feature in the MGDP. One of my explanations is that the space theme provided a context that focused on overcoming physical limitations rather than on overcoming people. As noted before, only three students included aliens that could serve the role of an adversary.

Design of Game Narrative
As students continued to develope their games, defining characters and outlining scenes, they also created stories that situated the actors, often in a fantasy yet meaningful context. In many instances, they were established in the introduction and provided the player with a context, as in this boy's game in the MGDP:

> You are Jose, a third grade kid who gets lost and must find his way home. You will go on many different adventures. Along the way, people (or beasts, creatures, etc.) will ask you questions about fractions, (you will type A, B or C, remember to press enter.) If you get the question right, you will go on safely, but beware! Danger lurks if you get the question wrong. Have fun if you dare! Type play and press enter. "Where am I?" "I have to get home!" A mysterious man approaches you. "Hey kid, I'm Marley the Magician and I'm going to make you disappear if you don't tell me how much of this square is colored!", says the man . . .

Another example is from a girl in the SGDP, whose game involves a player that gets kidnapped into space:

> One morning you wake up to find you are in a strange room like nothing you've ever seen. Suddenly three weird creatures come into your room. You ask where you are and why it's so hot. They reply in a strange accent, "Sunspin or your Sun." Then you yell out: "The Sun! How can I be on the Sun?" One of the creatures answers, "Technolegy [sic]. We are intelligent creatures. We originally come from Gokk but you don't know about this planet yet. You will some. . ." "But why am

I here?" You interrupt. The creatures just look at you and then walk out of the room closing the door and locking it behind them. Then a terrifying thought strikes you—you have been kidnapped into space. . .

While narratives were not always included in the beginning of the design process, many students opted to include stories later on. However, there was a substantial difference between the two game design contexts: whereas many students chose to have some form of narrative in their fraction games, explicit narrative was mostly absent in the SGDP, with the exception of a few games that used a story context to introduce the player to the game.

The popularity of the narrative in the MGDP could be explained by seeing narrative as a form of problem solving. It reconciled two seemingly adverse domains in a more coherent framework. In the fraction games, the narrative provides the glue that holds together different scenes or places as well as the instructional content. Furthermore, it allowed students to incorporate fantasy and to decorate their worlds in a more appealing way. This was also one of the features that the children in Malone and Lepper's study (1987) identified as appealing in playing games.

But this is not a sufficient explanation for the infrequent use of narrative in the SGDP. It is possible, however, that the science context itself provided a narrative. In all the science games, the solar system or planets served as the starting point for the game designs and the players' explorations and adventures. One could argue that in the science games the content was intrinsically integrated with the game ideas, something that could not be said for most fraction games. All of the fraction games, with the exception of one in which the player assembled fraction pieces of a map that had been ripped apart, had an extrinsic integration of content and game idea. Consequently, the designer had to work in the narrative to provide some connection between the game and the content to be learned.

Discussion

The comparative analyses of these two game design contexts presented a complex picture of the ways in which gender differences are simultaneously consistent *and* variable. The comparison of the different contexts, MGDP and SGDP, foregrounded observable shifts in preference for game format, realism of designed game worlds, gender and number of characters, quality of feedback, and presence of narrative. From the analysis of context differences by gender, it became clear that these shifts were mostly due to boys' change of game design features. Looking over the girls' games, we observed a remarkable consistency in design features across contexts. These results offer a first indicator of variations of game preferences within one gender.

This result may be a consequence of the research methodology used for assessing gender differences. Traditionally, researchers have observed children's game-playing performance in natural or experimental settings or have asked children about their play interests in relation to and choices from among existing commercial toys and games. By asking children to create their own video games, some game features emerged that were clearly found in commercial games. The influence of commercially available games was especially strong in the case of boys' games in the MGDP. Many game designers took as their starting point ideas borrowed from popular video games such as "Super Mario Brothers" or "Pacman." Or, students referred to existing commercial games in their interpretations of their own games, as did this MGDP boy:

> Because you are playing the role of the character and you want to type in your things. Everything is you. And if you are, say, role playing for—I mean, in arcades it is someone else and in arcade games, you don't—role playing isn't like, you don't play the role, you just like someone, like the space ship or the gun plays the role. . . . Role playing is when . . . actually Dungeons and Dragons is kind of role playing for, that is kind of, a play on words because you roll with dice to see if you shoot something, and you're also playing the role of the character. You see, in role playing in Dungeons and Dragons you have the character sheet. You write down your name, what you want your character to be, write down all his abilities and all his strengths. See you are playing his role, you try to kill monsters and get treasures. You are playing his role.

Many of the boys' game implementations include violent aspects, documented in the design of their feedback to player interactions. Violence is one of the most prominent features in commercial video games (Provenzo 1991). Hence, popular media offer paradigms for the organization of the game design (at least for the boys).

Yet popular media do not provide similar models for girls. Rarely are female game figures cast in the main role. The thematic embedding of video games in hunts and adventures is not necessarily suited to girls' tastes. In the interviews, many girls also stated that they had no particular interest in pursuing video game playing because they did not like the games, their content, and their violent aspects. Because of this lack of popular models, girls choose as the starting point of their narrative a familiar and likable figure (such as Rosy's cat) or a familiar place (such as Sina's classroom or Miriam's ski slope). In many ways, girls created their own worlds and characters, compensating for the sexism and violence found in many video games (Gailey 1993).

This research approach allowed for the articulation of gender differences in alternative forms from those readily available through the commercial market at the time these studies were conducted. It also allowed for variability across contexts, and this was particularly true for boys. Some researchers have argued that

> girls are moving closer to boys in their identification with heroic figures, adventurous achievement, and pretend aggression than previous data claimed. This appears to reflect changes in television action programs, where more female heroines now appear, as well as the increased willingness of parents to tolerate adventure themes in girls' play. . . . We do not see a comparable trend among boys—that is, a move toward playing female games and using traditionally female toys. (Singer and Singer, 1990, p. 80)

The convergence of game preferences observed in this study seems to suggest otherwise: one could say, it was the boys who adopted more "female" design features in their games. But these conclusions have to be drawn with care. Singer and Singer (1991) noted the increasing presence of female role models in television programs as one reason for the observable transformations in girls' play. The appearance of pink software on the market is too recent and probably not pervasive enough to argue for a similar situation in the programming of interactive software. Furthermore, the current titles seem to affiliate content more closely with traditional play arenas of girls. "Barbie Fashion Designer," which allows users to dress Barbie in different clothes, integrates smoothly within the existing play activities of girls. "The Babysitter Club" draws inspiration from a popular book series and provides a diary and schedules, in addition to letter-paper printing designs. More recently, video game productions have placed girls and women in the role of protagonists (Goodfellow 1996). It remains to be seen what impact these development will have on girls' interest in video games and software and whether similar trends can be observed in the interactive domain.

There is still an explanation required for why girls, in contrast to boys, were so consistent in their design choices. The choice of the two comparative contexts, mathematics and science, could be one explanation. Girls' lesser interest in these subject areas is well documented (Sadker and Sadker 1994). One could speculate on the variations that would be seen if the chosen contexts resonated better with girls' choices and interests such as history and social sciences. Future studies would need to investigate this issue more closely.

Conclusions

The results of this research made visible the variability in gender differences. In particular, these results suggest that boys have more variability in their game design preferences than formerly understood. These results also pointed out the consistency in gender differences. Girls are not uninterested in video games or interactive technologies; they are simply interested in other features. The success of pink software is testament to this potential. Taken together these results open the possibility to consider other video game designs not currently available on the market.

But if the trend of casting more women in protagonist roles in television programming is an indicator of what might happen in interactive programming, then games with other features will also appeal to girls. The potential confluence of girls' and boys' game interests might create contexts in which boys and girls play and interact together. Preliminary results from networked multi-user environments are a first indicator of this trend (Turkle 1996). One such example is MOOSE (Multi Object Oriented Scripting Environment), a multi-user environment that has been developed for children (Bruckman 1997). In this environment, girls and boys created their own worlds with different places, objects, features, and activities. Ultimately, we need play environments that support children's versatility in expressing themselves—environments open to the unbounded limits of their imagination rather than confined by boundaries of gender stereotypes.

III

Notes

1. *The research reported here was conducted during my time at the MIT Media Laboratory and at Project Headlight's Model School of the Future, and was supported by the IBM Corporation (Grant #OSP95952), the National Science Foundation (Grant #851031-0195), the McArthur Foundation (Grant #874304), the LEGO Company, Fukatake, and Apple Computer. The analyses of the data was supported in part by a grant from the UCLA Academic Senate. The writing of this chapter was supported by a postdoctoral fellowship of the National Academy of Education through the Spencer Foundation. The ideas expressed here do not necessarily reflect the positions of the supporting agencies. Many thanks to V. Maithili, who helped with the analysis of the solar system games. I also wish to thank Joanne Ronkin and her students for their collaboration in both studies. Without them, this research would not have been possible.*

2. *One of the primary purposes of these projects was to investigate game making as a context for learning Logo programming and fractions, among other things (see also Harel 1991). For that reason, the games designed by the students are a special breed, called educational games. Yet, as my analyses will indicate, it was this particular constellation that emphasized game aspects, as students had to think about how to create games that were both educational and entertaining. In the following analysis, I focus more on the game aspects than on the learning aspects, which are discussed more extensively in other publications (e.g., Kafai 1995).*

References

Bruckman, A. 1997. "MOOSE for Children." Doctoral dissertation, The Media Laboratory, Massachusetts Institute of Technology.

Bruner, J., Jolly, A. and Sylva, K. eds., 1976. *Play: Its Role in Development and Evolution*. New York: Basic Books.

Brunner, C., Bennet, D., Clements, M., Hawkins, J., Honey, M. and Moeller, B. 1990. "Gender and Technological Imagination." Paper presented at the annual meeting of the American Educational Research Association, Boston.

Gailey, C. 1993. "Mediated Messages: Gender, Class, and Cosmos in Home Video Games." *Journal of Popular Culture*, 27(1): 81–97.

Garvey, C. 1990. *Play*. Cambridge: Harvard University Press.

Goldstein, J. 1994. "Sex Differences in Toy Use and Video Game Play." In J. H. Goldstein, ed., *Toys, Play and Child Development*. New York: Cambridge University Press, 110–129.

Goodfellow, K. 1996. "Beyond Barbie: Games by Women." *New York Times*. 11 November.

Greenfield, P. M. 1984. *Mind and Media: The Effects of Television, Video Games, and Computers*. Cambridge: Harvard University Press.

Greenfield, P. M. 1994. "Video Games as Cultural Artifacts." *Journal of Applied Developmental Psychology* 15(1): 3–12.

Greenfield, P. M. and Cocking, R. R. 1994. "Effects of Interactive Entertainment Technology on Development." *Journal of Applied Developmental Psychology* 15(1): 1–2.

Greenfied, P. M., Brannon, G. and Lohr, D. 1994. "Two-Dimensional Representation of Movement through Three-Dimensional Space: The Role of Video Game Expertise." *Journal of Applied Developmental Psychology* 15(1): 87–104.

Greenfield, P. M., deWinstanley, P., Kilpatrick, and D. Kaye, D. 1994. "Action Video Games and Informal Education: Effects on Strategies for Dividing Visual Attention." *Journal of Applied Developmental Psychology* 15(1): 105–124.

Greenfield, P. M., Camaioni, L., Ercolani, P., Weiss, L., Lauber, B. A. and Perucchini, P. 1994.

"Cognitive Socialization by Computer Games in Two Cultures: Inductive Discovery or Mastery of an Iconic Code?" *Journal of Applied Developmental Psychology* 15(1): 59–86.

Harel, I. 1991. *Children Designers.* Norwood, N.J.: Ablex Publishing.

Huff and Cooper. 1987. "Sex Bias in Educational Software: The Effects of Designers' Stereotypes on the Software They Design." *Journal of Applied Social Psychology* 17: 519–532.

Inkpen, K., Upitis, R., Klawe, M., Anderson, A., Ndunda, M., Sedighian, K., Leroux, S. and Hsu, D. 1993. "'We Have Never-forgetful Flowers in Our Garden': Girls' Responses to Electronic Games." Technical Report 93–47 (December) Department of Computer Science, University of British Columbia.

Kafai, Y. 1995. *Minds in Play: Computer Game Design as a Context for Children's Learning.* Hillsdale, N.J.: Lawrence Erlbaum Associates.

Kafai, Y. 1996. "Gender Differences in Children's Constructions of Video Games." In P. M. Greenfield and R. R. Cocking, eds., *Interacting with Video.* Norwood, N.J.: Ablex Publishing.

Karpoe, K. and Olney, R. 1983. "The Effect of Boys' or Girls' Toys on Sex-Typed Play in Pre-Adolescents." *Sex Roles* 9: 507–518.

Kubey, R. and Larson, R. 1990. "The Use and Experience of the New Media among Children and Young Adolescents." *Communication Research* 17: 17–130.

Kinder, M. 1991. *Playing with Power.* Berkeley: University of California Press.

Linn, M. C. 1985. "Fostering Equitable Consequences from Computer Learning Environments." *Sex Roles* 13(3/4): 229–240.

Malone, T. W. and Lepper, M. R. 1987. "Making Learning Fun: A Taxonomy of Intrinsic Motivations for Learning." In R. E. Snow and M. J. Farr, eds., *Aptitude, Learning and Instruction.* Vol. 3: *Conative and Affective Process Analyses.* Hillsdale, N.J.: Lawrence Erlbaum Associates, 223–253.

Moller, L.C., Hymel, S., and Rubin, K.H. 1992. "Sex Typing in Play and Popularity in Middle Childhood." *Sex Roles* 26: 331–353.

Okagaki, L. and French, P. 1994. "Effects of Video Game Playing on Measures of Spatial Performance: Gender Effects in Late Adolescence." *Journal of Applied Developmental Psychology* 15(1): 33–58.

Papert, S. 1980. *Mindstorms*. New York: Basic Books.

Piaget, J. 1951. *Play, Dreams, and Imitation in Childhood*. New York: W. W. Norton.

Provenzo, E. F. 1991. *Video Kids: Making Sense of Nintendo*. Cambridge: Harvard University Press.

Ross, H. and Taylor, H. 1989. "Do Boys Prefer Daddy or his Physical Style of Play?" *Sex Roles* 20: 23–33.

Sadker, M., and Sadker, D. 1994. *Failing at Fairness: How America's Schools Cheat Girls*. New York: Scribner's.

Silvern, S. B. and Williamson, P. A. 1987. "The Effects of Videogame Play on Young Children's Aggression, Fantasy and Prosocial Behavior." *Journal of Applied Developmental Psychology* 8: 453–462.

Singer, D. G. and Singer, J. L. 1990. *The House of Make-Believe: Play and the Developing Imagination*. Cambridge: Harvard University Press.

Subrahmanyam, K. and Greenfield, P. M. 1994. "Effects of Video Game Practice on Spatial Skills in Girls and Boys." *Journal of Applied Developmental Psychology* 15(1): 13–32.

Sutton-Smith, B. 1986. *Toys as Culture*. New York: Garland Press.

Turkle, S. 1984. *The Second Self: Computers and the Human Spirit*. New York: Simon & Schuster.

Turkle, S. 1996. *Life on the Screen*. New York: Simon & Schuster. Part Two: Interviews

Part Two: Interviews

Chapter 5

An Interview with Brenda Laurel (Purple Moon)

Brenda Laurel brings a theater and acting background to computer software design. She earned an M.F.A. and Ph.D. in theater from Ohio State University, and her dissertation was titled "Toward the Design of a Computer-Based Interactive Fantasy System." Laurel designed and programmed computer games at Cybervision, and in 1980 was the director of software marketing for the home computer division at Atari. She worked at Atari Research laboratory in the early 1980s, where she explored artificial intelligence as a means of creating theatrical plots and characters in interactive media. Her research in areas such as human-computer interface design, virtual reality, computer-based agents, and interactive fiction led her to start Telepresence Research in 1990 with Scott Fisher. In 1992 Laurel joined Interval Research, where she was a member of the research staff until 1996, when she cofounded Purple Moon, a software company dedicated to producing games for girls, and a spin-off from Interval Research Corporation. Laurel has consulted on interactive media for Apple Computer, Citibank, Fujitsu Laboratories, Lucasfilm Games, the "Oz" Project at Carnegie-Mellon University, Sony Pictures, and Paramount New Media. Laurel is the author of *Computers as Theatre* (1991); and she edited *The Art of Human-Computer Interface Design* (1990). Her online collection of essays is entitled *Severed Heads: Notes on Computers, Art, and Nature*.

Q: How did you end up where you are now?
A: I got involved in computer games by accident in 1976. I was finishing an M.F.A. in theater and starting a Ph.D. and working part-time in a modeling agency, looking for something interesting to do, when a friend showed me a computer lab where he was working. Shortly thereafter he started a computer

software company—actually, they were building educational software for mainframes, but somebody walked in the door in 1977 with a little personal computer based on an 1802 chip, and it had four colors, you know, low resolution. And he called me and said, "Well, you're a theater person, how about if you help us design some interactive fairy tales?" And that just seemed totally normal, so I said, "Of course." So without knowing it was hard, I guess I learned how to write code, and did everything from graphic design to programming to making coffee, and then I was hooked. When that company folded because there was this little upstart called Atari starting to rise up on the West Coast, we said, "Gee, maybe we ought to go check that out!" I'd never seen the Pacific Ocean, living in Ohio—we were doing computer software in 1977 in Columbus. Anyway, I went to Atari, and for a while I was doing marketing—product-planning sorts of things—but then I had the opportunity to move to research. By that time, it had finally occurred to me that the connection between theater and computers was not intuitive to everyone, and that if I really wanted to be able to explain that and understand it well myself, I needed to put some time and energy into actually being scholarly about it. Alan Kay was my boss in those days, and he was really encouraging me to do that, so I was able to get my head out of day-to-day production in the crazed world of Atari and look at the relationships between computers and theater and think about interactive design and character in a pretty disciplined way. In fact, that ended up being my dissertation. So that's how I got started in the business. I kind of tumbled into it, and it's never felt like a split-brain experiment, although everybody else always says, "How weird! What a strange combination." It seems perfectly natural to me.

We got to here, to Purple Moon, really because of the job I had at Interval Research starting in 1992. I knew I wanted to turn my attention away from VR and look at gender and technology. Actually, it was kind of an extension of the VR work, because in the process of working in virtual reality I discovered a lot of what I thought were pretty striking differences between the way men and women experience VR—the body-centric nature of women's experience as opposed to the sort of disembodied stuff that you hear about from men when they talk about virtual reality, for example, and the use of narrative in VR, which in those days was not done much. We discovered when we were doing virtual reality, for example with the Placeholder project up at the Banff Center, that our most enthusiastic users were twelve-year-old girls, and that was unprecedented for virtual reality as a medium.

I'm not working in VR anymore; I've tried to take technology innovation off my plate and focus entirely on content and interactivity design as the things I wanted to work on, because I've learned that if you try to solve six problems at once, you don't do a very good job at any of them. So I got back to the little screen and the keyboard, and I think we do have a pretty immersive bunch of products here, but it's not VR. The things that did come through were interest in folklore and narrative, interest in place, interest in embodiment—embodied points of view and rich characters. So you'll see some similarities to that work. Anyway, we were just going to go build Placeholder at Banff when I started at Interval (Interval actually cosponsored the Banff project). David Liddle, who is the CEO of Interval, and I agreed that my major job at Interval would be to look at gender-and-technology issues. So while Banff was going on, we were also starting the research at Interval that led to this project. That's how we got here to Purple Moon.

Q: What was your personal motivation for getting involved with design technology for girls?

A: In terms of our motivation for this project, David and I agreed at Interval that boys tend to have an advantage with computers because they achieve a certain comfort level with the technology by virtue of being motivated by video games to put their hands on it. This is not even about content now; we're just talking about thinking of the computer as an appliance, not being afraid of it, being comfortable with it, and maybe even thinking of it as a medium you might want to author in. Girls weren't getting that chance to the same degree because they didn't have things that motivated them in the way that video games motivated boys. When we started our research, we had the simple goal of asking, "What would it take to design something on a computer that would be as engaging and enjoyable to a girl as a video game is to a boy and would therefore motivate her to get her hands on the computer, feel comfortable with it, and start to think about it as a tool or an appliance, or to have it become transparent?" That little-bitty step doesn't sound like much, especially when you put it in the context of the rhetoric of "computer literacy" and "engineering" and all the other issues that come up for us, but in fact without that first little step none of the other stuff happens. And if we don't get to them by sixth grade, we run a very high risk of losing them. So what's the right question? Well, we decided the right question was, "How does play get influenced by age and gender?" Let's start there. We know that we're trying to do something interactive, so entertainment isn't the right model. Play is much closer to being the right model because play is more interactive, at least in the way we define it.

Strategically, we made a conscious decision to make our products specifically for girls. If boys think that a product is for them, and they play it and don't understand it, then they trash it. I can imagine a boy opening "Rockett's New School" and saying, "What's going on here? There's all these girls talking, you know, and they're fighting and writing in journals and worrying about who to sit with at lunch, and this is stupid! This is awful!" Then the girls can't really enjoy it or feel proud of it because it's been trashed. So we decided that we wanted to send the message, without beating people over the head with it, that this is really for girls. We basically said, "Boys, you need not apply," because we wanted to protect the experience as being something girls could own, something that could be theirs, so that they could say, "This is mine, this is for me. I own this and you don't get to make fun of it." Boys may make fun of it—although we did quite a bit of research to make sure that our name, for example, was one they had trouble thinking of bad jokes about—but what they can't do is pronounce it lame in the sense of, "This is a failed game, this is not a good game." What they can say is, "This is really dumb girls' stuff," but that's a different critique.

Q: Can you talk a bit more about the research behind the project and what you learned from it?
A: First we did a comprehensive literature survey in all the academic and scientific disciplines that we thought might have some useful information for us. Then we interviewed people in academia and industry and ran focus groups with adults who spend time on the ground with kids in play situations—playground and computer lab supervisors, teachers, scout leaders, coaches. But the biggest and most intensive part was actually talking to kids and parents. We did in-depth interviews with over a thousand children, and eventually narrowed the conversation to just seven- to twelve-year-old girls. We talked to them a lot about technology and learned, for example, that in general both girls and boys believe that video game machines are "boy things" and that computers are gender-neutral. This is contrary to Sherry Turkle's finding, and that was the main reason why we decided to make computer games as opposed to video games, at least for starters, because, again, you don't want to fight two battles at once. You want to be clear about what it is you're trying to do and not make it harder on yourself.

We started talking to girls about computer games and got lots of information about what they hate. Now let me back up and say that they will play boys' games if there's nothing else to do, and they even like some of them, like "Sonic the Hedgehog" or "Super Mario" or "Ecco the Dolphin." But they never become maniacal about it in the way that boys do. (For this we should be grateful!) But they don't even get enthusiastic most of the time; it's not over the threshold. And there are a lot of things they actively dislike and get angry about. For example, they hate to die and start over. That is, like, way stupid and intolerable. They are not interested in climbing a real steep learning curve just to be able to say they've achieved mastery of something. Mastery for its own sake is not very good social currency for a girl. They demand an experiential path, and something has to happen right away. It can't be that you die in the first five seconds and you have to keep hammering at it day after day, like the old action games used to be. They hate being stuck behind an obstacle or a puzzle that you must solve in order to move forward. They're also not interested very much in beating the clock, which was a surprise to me. It's just sort of orthogonal for them to the enjoyment of a puzzle or a game. Another kind of surprising thing is that girls will play games together whether or not the games are designed for multiple players. Looking back you can say, "Oh, of course, that's a no-brainer," but I was actually surprised when I first discovered that they have no trouble at all playing what's obviously a single-player game in a collaborative way.

The industry typically has believed that girls don't like computer games, and when they've tried on those few lame occasions to build computer games for girls, they've assumed that the games are too hard, so their solution is to make the projectiles move more slowly. It's the computer game equivalent of pink Legos. But they're not understanding the play pattern here, so they haven't asked the right question. The one huge thing that the game industry has missed is the tremendous attraction for girls of complex characters and narratives and materials for narrative construction. I mean, it's not only that the characters are lame in most boys' games, it's that they're so lame you can't even make up an interesting story about them. You can't even do projection on it. That was not a surprise to me, but it would be a surprise to a lot of people in the business, I think. The overwhelming importance of relationships was stunning, if not surprising. It was stunning to see how very important that is and how much more fond girls are of an activity that has more than one character in it, or characters with whom you can form relationships, than of an activity where there's "girl against the world" or an individual character doing this

Figure 5.1: The decision screen in "Rockett's World" allows players to rehearse different emotional responses to social situations and their consequences. Reprinted with permission of Purple Moon. Copyright 1997.

or that. It's just a major difference. When you ask a girl what an adventure is, well, it's about exploration, and it's all about relationship. She'll say, "I go on a quest with my friend or for my friend or to find my . . ." The relationship is there all the time. There were very few exceptions to that in the fantasies that girls played back to us. An adventure is something where you have to figure out what the right thing to do is, as opposed to overcoming an obstacle that someone else put in your path. Anyway, that whole elaborate thing—complex emotional navigation of social space is the subject of a lot of play, a lot of fantasy play. There's a lot of emotional rehearsal that goes on there.

So we have tried to make that an area of expertise for ourselves, and the "Rockett" series is really about that kind of play. The premise of "Rockett's New School," the first title in the series, is that you're a brand-new kid in eighth grade, you don't know anybody, clean slate, and you've got to navigate your way to the end of the day. It's just that. And then there'll be another day and another, and when you get tired of looking at the action, you can go behind the action. You can see what Rockett's written in her journal and what pictures she's taken, and depending on who showed up in the scene, you can visit other characters' lockers and see what's in there and discover things about them, like, "Oh, I know why Cleve's so mean! Because his father is never home. Look at this note! Dad's missing his birthday party!" This is material for narrative construction. It's also material about relationships, and it's emotional rehearsal for social navigation. And, by the way, we've designed a cast of very diverse characters to carry that play pattern forward, and when we tested those characters with kids, they felt very positive about the diversity. So you'll see a lot of different kinds of groups, a lot of different kinds of individuals, a lot of different relationship patterns, but a lot of really recognizable stuff going on in terms of social navigation and those kinds of fantasies. (See Plate 2.)

And also, just to finish the rap on that, at this age, the eight- to twelve-year-old age is really the time of self-construction. That's the project that's going on there, very explicitly so. It's one of the things that defines that break between seven and eight, where it's not about kings and queens and baby dolls anymore; it's now starting to be about my persona—"Who am I? What's going on with me?"—and acting out some of that stuff in a much more relevant and close-to-home way. So the other play pattern that we wanted to focus on, which is also related to this business of self-construction, is much more about the inner world. Its setting tends to be in nature, and it tends to be a romanticized view of nature, where, for example, there are magical properties. Animals may speak, and there may be fairies. Girls will tell you, "We're too old for fairies," but if you show them one, they're really into it, so you have to be careful. You can show them but not talk about them, or you can call them something else—if you call them "magical creatures," it's OK. They're very sensitive about how mature they are at this age, which I totally respect. But this is fantasy, and this is where the flying stuff might happen, for example. But it's very much about the inner self, constructing the inner self: "What's beautiful, what's really beautiful?" Well, flying is really beautiful. Love is really beautiful. Stories of certain kinds are really beautiful. Caring for each other is really beautiful. You get lots of nurturing behavior over here in the inner world. Whereas in the social world, you're looking at a lot of exclusion and affiliation and staying on top of it, over here in the inner world you've got a much more embracing emotional tone to that kind of play.

We thought we understood both of these things pretty well, so in the last phase of the research, after we'd gotten it clear—well, in the second-to-last phase, I guess—we built paper dolls and props and stuff, and sent them to girls about a week ahead of time and said, "OK, you guys, work up something, and we'd like you to do some improv for us, or a show." And they'd come back and do stuff. Well, the kids who got the "Rockett's World" characters and desks and school things did what we expected them to do. I mean, yup, it was right on the money. The only thing I can remember that was a huge surprise was that we didn't have a school principal in the characters that we sent out, and a whole bunch of kids made a principal. And the office was very important—it wasn't just where boys got sent when they were bad, it was also where you could call your mom. Another thing that actually surprised me was that the adult characters they would play back to us were much more exaggerated and cartoony than the kid characters. I mean, Charles Schulz (creator of Charlie Brown, Snoopy, et al.) knows this, but I hadn't figured it out. Then we went over here to this other kind of fantasy space, the inner world, and we sent them little animals and fairies and flowers and trees and paths and said, "OK, you guys, work up something," and was expecting that they would take care of the plants and flowers and nurture the little birdies and make the garden beautiful and that sort of thing. Instead they came back and said, "Well, I come here when I'm sad, I come here to be alone, I come here to find out stuff about myself, I come here to think. I sit under the tree and dream. MAYBE my friend comes. There are no boys here. There are no grownups here." Suddenly we got a very different picture. I get goose bumps thinking about it because it was just so radical when it happened. I mean, these little people were totally contemplative in this spot.

It was very interesting, a different picture of the world than we'd had before, and it really guided us in developing the "Secret Paths" series in a different direction than it would have gone. In both cases, in both worlds—I know I've said this before, but I'll reinforce it—relevance, personal relevance, is incredibly important to them. It's so strong. And that was a surprise to me, I think, because you traditionally think about fantasy as being off somewhere—you know, Cinderella, folk tales, fairy tales, superhero stuff. I mean, I watched *Superman* when I was a kid. So I was really struck by the demand for personal relevance and the way they'd take even a fantastical scenario and turn it around until it was, "MY heart, MY life, MY values, the things I'm worried about, what comes up for me." Those things just kept getting worked into the play, and I think that we learned a lot from that and took our cue from that.

We also were able to flesh out a pretty good map of the social structures that exist for girls in their peer groups: what kinds of groups tend to appear, what the differences are among those groups, what kinds of relationships happen among those groups, how they compete with each other, and strategies that girls have for figuring out where they belong. This turns out to be the quest in the "Rockett" series: "Where do I fit in this social scenario? Who is my friend, who are my friends, whom do I want as my friends? Who am I, whom do I affiliate with? How do I decide?" The cool thing about it is that if you don't like what happens you can back up and do it again, unlike in life. This is why I think we'll have a strong secondary market in adult women who really want to go back and do junior high right. I should add that there isn't a right way to navigate through Rockett's day; there are just a lot of different ways, different things that can happen, and the way you make choices in that series is to decide, "Well, how is she feeling now, after this thing that just happened?"

Q: In the games, do the girls play themselves or do they play other characters?
A: We decided to have the girl take the point of view of the second person. The first-person point of view was a little too much of a blank page. We fooled around with it, but you spend so much time constructing yourself that it's more problematic in terms of constructing a character. So then we thought, well, let's give the girls a choice of different protagonists they can help through their first day, thinking that there'd be a lot of differences and that girls would gravitate to different characters. But it turns out that Rockett has enough characteristics that are aspirational for almost all girls that, when we tested it, it became clear we didn't need multiple protagonists. She's a very flexible character, she can go in a lot of directions. And what group she's going to end up belonging to is really up for grabs because she's so flexible. In a funny way, she's the least fleshed-out character because she has a lot of range. She's kind of Everygirl, I guess. And I know that there are issues there about race and size and things, but the thing to remember is that the cast itself is extremely diverse in that way. But the interface is second person in the sense that you're helping Rockett, you're deciding, "Go with your feeling about this guy. Don't sit down with him at lunch." So there is this aspect of guiding another person.

In "Secret Paths" the scenario is that you enter the product in a treehouse, (see Plate 3) and it's just you and the treehouse, and you can customize it and change how it looks and change what you see outside and what time it is and what you hear and stuff. And then you learn through the Book of the Secret Paths, this very old journal you find in the treehouse, that you can invite girls to come in and talk to you about what's going on with them. The girls are in this magic box you open. There's one of those friendship chains—remember those paper-doll chains?—and if you click on those girls, they get invited. It turns out that those girls are the girls you met over in Rockett's world, except they look a little younger, because when kids are in that headspace they're not older, they're eight, ten, twelve, you know? So you'll see Whitney, whom you've met over here in Rockett's world in the eighth grade and over here in "Secret Paths" when you invite her to your treehouse. When these girls come in, they tell you what's going on with them, and you get to decide if you're going to help one of them find insight by going on a vision quest into the forest on that girl's own Secret Path. So little Whitney, who in the social world is a crabcake and a snob, over here—in the inner world—is distraught because her parents are divorced and her stepmother's trying to throw her a birthday party, and it doesn't feel OK to her, and she's got all these issues about it. So another opportunity for narrative construction between the titles is to say, "I know why she's like that: because of this," or, "It's interesting that she's going to turn out like that." You start managing and thinking about constructing the lines of causality and the relationships of the characters because you have this other way to look at them.

If I decide to help Whitney, she tells me a little more about what's going on with her in a kind of animated flashback, and if I commit to her—you have to commit—then I go on to her Secret Path in the forest. (This is the first title in the Secret Paths series. The second title will be "Secret Paths to the Sea.") And on that path, my goal is to find magical stones—story stones—hidden there. The stones are for her, they have information for her. Your job is to find them, and of course there are puzzles involved with finding them, and there are lots of other cool things that just happen, because these are interesting environments to poke around in. (See Plate 4.) If you don't find a stone on this part of the path, you can go on the next part, and if you don't find all of them in one day, the program will put away the stones you've found in the magic box, and they'll be there when you come back, and you know how many you have to look for. It's very forgiving.

With many of the puzzles, once you've solved the puzzle and you've found the stone, you can actually dial up the level of difficulty, if you want to go back and play it as a game. We learned that girls love to do that; they love to challenge themselves. This is another strong way that they act out their competitive impulses. And they'll work a very long time to figure out a hard puzzle. We tested a help agent at one point. We had this little bear character whom you could call if you needed help, and we couldn't get a single girl to call the bear. It was like, "Please ask for help." But the girls would say, "I'm not going to. Get that bear out of here! I don't want to talk to the bear! Leave me alone, I'm working on this."

If you succeed in collecting all of that girl's secret stones in your Purple Pouch, you're transported back to the treehouse. The pouch is wiggling, you open it, and you find that the stones have transformed themselves into this garland necklace that's just for that girl. You have to open the pouch, you have to take the necklace out, and you have to put it on her, if you want to give it to her. It doesn't just automatically go there. Again, there's this business of taking the action, making the commitment, giving the gift. This is about giving a gift, this is about taking care, right? So if you do give her the necklace, what emanates from the magic necklace then is a story, a tale from somewhere in the world that gives that girl another way to look at what's going on with her. So at the end of the journey is a tale. In the case of Whitney it's "The Snow Daughter," from Middle Europe. In the case of Jessie, who's afraid of going to camp, there's a story called "The Fearful Rabbit," from India. Viva, who has issues about her appearance, gets an Uncle Remus tale called "The Bird Who Couldn't Sing."

Q: Can you talk about the business end of things? Do you see these products being advertised and marketed with other products for girls?
A: We've developed three businesses simultaneously, and part of that is because we know that girls love stuff showing up in different media at the same time. There's something magical about that. That's the secret, in a way, of the American Girl doll thing, where she's in a book but here she is, you know? The book extruded this thing. And that is intrinsically more attractive to girls than a Pocahontas doll that comes with the movie, because it's clear that they don't have parity. I don't know how to say this, I've always had trouble explaining this one, but these girls have little detectors that know when merchandise is derivative as opposed to intrinsic in some way. It's hard to articulate because it was a kind of a funny finding and I can't do science on it, but I heard enough about it from girls that I kind of believe it's true. It's about transformation. That's what I think.

So we brought up all three media types together—we were working on *tchotchkes*, which we now call "merchandise," at the same time we were working on the CD-ROM games and thinking about the Web. And you hope that eventually the CD-ROM and the Web businesses will merge. Right now only about one in ten of our potential users has Internet access. The website (see Plate 1) is very aggressive and very rich, and it's something that's owned and operated by the characters. You won't go there and see pictures of me, because that's not what anybody wants. People don't go to the Paramount site to see pictures of Paramount executives. They go to see characters that they love. That's the point. We tried to take that to heart. And we tried to extend the play beyond the computer with the objects that we've made, including things called "adventure cards." This speaks to a play pattern about collecting but also to a play pattern as in board games or card play, so we had a board-game designer design these things so that they were not just pictures of the game. There are strategies for playing several different kinds of games with these cards. Some of them come in a box, and you can order more for a dollar a pack, so it's kid-affordable. You can take them anywhere and a lot of it is projective. There are story stones on the CD-ROM and there are story stones in the box. The stones move across different types of media and they're always the same thing. They're just going through these magic transformations.

As far as where we are in the girls' market, it helps to be near first in breaking into a market, but the guy who's first is often in the role of being the crash dummy, you know? I was the crash dummy in VR. My little company just ran smack into the wall. We were three years ahead of the market, and we were three years ahead of technology that was affordable. I'm glad I did it, but I would never make a business decision like that again. So I'm perfectly happy to come out after "Barbie," because I don't have to kick the hole in the wall. We still have a lot of work to do in raising the consciousness of the retail community, convincing people that there really is a market here. We've made the strategic decision to devote a lot of our efforts to getting our partners to create girls' sections in the stores, where everybody's products can live together, because what's good for one is good for all in a market this small.

Q: Do you consider yourself an entrepreneurial feminist? Do you feel that the goal of your company affects the choice of employees, the way the company is run, interactions within the company?
A: You know, I have trouble with the "f" word because it's so wildly—well, there are so many interpretations of it now. When I was a feminist in the sixties, we all knew what that meant, we thought. Now we're not so sure. I was reviewing Christina Hoff-Summers' book, *Who Stole Feminism?*—it's about the schism in feminism—and she identifies what she calls "equity feminists," which is what I think of myself as, somebody who's really saying, "Diversity is fine, and we are different in some ways, so let's honor that and lift it up, but in any case we should have equal opportunity to actualize ourselves." Then she

identifies another flavor that she calls "gender feminism"—I would tend to call it "dominator feminism"—which really says that women are superior and that, furthermore, there's only one way to be a true-blue, card-carrying feminist, and here is the following list. That rubs me the wrong way, and I think it's a lot of what has given feminism a bad rap among younger women. So I don't think we can go into that rhetoric without getting all tangled up.

I'd rather frame the question as, "How does our corporate culture reflect the fact that we're doing work for girls?" And I think, first of all, there's a natural attraction—because of our mission—for professional women in the business, in the industry, to want to work here, and I think that that goes a long way in explaining why there are more women than men in the company. Although there are a lot of men who are strong contributors here, we're about 75 percent female. It's not because we say, "Men need not apply." It's because there are a lot of women in this business who just couldn't wait to be working on something that they felt was relevant and that they buy into. Sexism is not an appropriate aspect of feminism, and we try very hard not to give that any face around here. So we don't trash men, we don't trash boys, and we don't make jokes about difference, at least not insensitive ones. I think our national sales director does have a sign on his door that says, "Token Male, Do Not Taunt or Tap on Glass," or something like that—but he's an incredibly good sport about it. We've been misunderstood in the press; we've had press reports that say, "It's an all-female company." Well, it's not, and it makes the men who work here feel pretty crappy. So we're strong and outspoken about the fact that this is not about sexism. *Au contraire.* I think that's something that can happen in a business environment or any kind of team—a theatrical performance, for example—that's dominated by women or that is all women. Then the thing to be wary of is reaction formation. They say, "Oh, man, it feels so good to be all girls, we're not going to do anything the way boys do it." You know? "No meetings, man! No titles! No interoffice memos!" or whatever it is. And pretty soon the baby is hitting the parking lot as you throw the bath water out.

Q: What about content and philosophy? It seems that the games you've described do in some ways play out traditional girl narratives. Does getting girls to use the technology, helping them gain access and empowerment, take priority over new representations of gender, software that isn't designed along traditional gender definition?

A: Well, as always, there is not an easy answer, but I'll see if I can make it clear. First of all, I think we are doing some stereotype busting that I'm proud of. Rockett is a resilient woman. She speaks her mind. I should call her a girl, because she is a girl. She speaks the truth. She's got a remarkable amount of insight in terms of understanding herself and what she's feeling. She's recognizably a little girl, but she has some qualities that I feel are off-stereotype in terms of outspokenness, self-awareness, and clarity. There's another character, Jessie, who's a very shy, childish girl, but when somebody starts to trip on her she'll say, 'You know what? This is making me feel bad. I don't need to stay here. I'm leaving now," or, "I'm sorry, I was feeling really good when I sat down with you, but I'm feeling sad now, so I think I'll go." This is not exactly behavior that we learn is gender-appropriate, but it's really good survival stuff. So in subtle ways, in the form of characters that are familiar and recognizable, safe both for parents and girls, we're representing some qualities that we think are healthy and that are against type.

There are girl narratives here, but some of them are girl narratives that we don't hear very much in other places, like, "I've lost something that's important to me and I can't even tell you what it is." That's a girl narrative, an all too common girl narrative, and we're taking it up—we're going to go there to the extent that we can. Another girl narrative that you don't hear much about is, "I don't have any time." That was a big issue in our interviews. There are stories about it that girls tell, and there's cultural mythology about it. Adults say to them, "Of course you have time! You're a kid," or, "Well, how can you say you don't have time? You spend all that time on the phone and watching television." So too often you just erase the kid's experience; you deny it by telling them that what they just told you they're experiencing isn't true. That's typically the way adults handle it. In these products, we honor it, we listen to it, we treat it like it's a real issue, we try to give some insight, and we let girls do that for each other. So it may not look edgy—if it did, we'd only sell two hundred of them. My position is that if you want to make a difference in a major way, you have to do it at the level of popular culture. I believe that. At least that's what I'm about. It's about making an intervention at the level of popular culture. I could build great radical stuff for PBS parents, but it wouldn't change the culture, it wouldn't change the things that are currently marginalized and make them more mainstream. There are ways to do that, but it means that you have to listen hard, do the dance, and figure out how to insert new genetic material into the culture without activating its immune system. That's the hardest thing in the world, but luckily that's not only good humanism, that's good business. And in a way, as a parent of preadolescent kids, I've got to say that their biggest issues are that they're not seen and that they don't know who they are—this identity-construction stuff again. We construct ourselves out of the materials at hand, and the materials provided for girls in this culture are not very exciting and I'm not real proud of them. They're a hyphenated age. You're not a kid and you're not a teen. You're a preadolescent. What a horrible thing! It's like, you're nowhere, you're between here and there, you don't have an identity. Nobody says, "Oh, you're a preteen! Welcome to preteen! Here's what this means. Here are all the products that you can buy, here are the stories about you, here are the movies about you." No. You're in transit, you're on Ellis Island. It's not fun. I've watched a lot of kids go through it. And when we can make an intervention into that reality saying, "Yeah, we see you, we hear you, this is what your life is like, we'll play it back to you. Are we getting it right?," that's so validating that maybe you go into adolescence with your feet on the ground a little better.

But I need to say that we're not putting this out in the world as, "This is good for you or good for your daughter." We're not selling it as social-skill enhancement or lifelong learning. We ran so far away from that so fast. It's the Mikey problem, right? You know, "This is good for you," so you won't eat it. "Oh, great, that's all I need, another agenda," you know? And we didn't want schools to say, "Oh, let's evaluate this in terms of its psychological correctness so we can decide if we want to introduce it into our curriculum." We don't want to go there either, because that isn't our mission. Our mission is to have this relationship with girls and to keep understanding them and to keep putting interesting things out there for them. So we've been very consciously positioning ourselves as fun, engaging, and entertaining, as opposed to enriching, empowering, enlightening, uplifting, and all those other words that we hope are true about our products, because that's not how we're going to leverage popular culture.

Q: These seem like very private issues. Since girls like to use the computer socially, will they be embarrassed to play these games with others?
A: The play pattern here is, I invite girls into my treehouse, they tell me what's going on with them, and I decide to help them by going on a quest. Now it may be that I choose the girl who has an issue with divorced parents because I have divorced parents, but I'm not ID'd, you know? There's a certain anonymity there. It would be different if the product said, "Enter your issue," or "From this menu, select the thing that bothers you most." Then we would have the problem that you're describing. But that's not how the game works, and in fact when we tested "Secret Paths" with girls, they would go down a path that really wasn't about them at all. Using the divorce example, kids would take that path or be

interested in that path even though they had parents that had never divorced, and what they'd say is, "This is for Jenny. I have to get Jenny to see this. This is about her!" They recognize their friends, and they want to give their friends the gift of the product. That's exactly what we want. That's exactly the outcome that we want.

Here is an agenda. I will tell you how I'm breaking my own rule. I'm chagrined at the way storytelling has lost ground in our culture and has been replaced by mass media. I think we've done awful things to ourselves without meaning to in the last fifty years. One of the things about storytelling that makes it so important is that it is a gift, it's a healing. A story is a healing. Storytelling is relationship. "It's the relationship, stupid!" It's not the content so much as it is the relationship. A good storyteller sees what's going on with you and gives you a tale. And this is still true with a good rabbi, or a good parent who will say, "Honey, I know it seems terrible, but let me tell you about when that happened to me." We don't do that as much as we used to as a culture, and frankly I do have a little agenda going here. Stories are wonderful gifts. They're empowering for the teller and the hearer. They're tried-and-true, wonderful ways of taking care of each other and exploring ourselves in the context of our world and our relationships. So stories are really explicitly there in that product as an object.

Q: Which brings us back to the idea of computers and empowerment.

A: To me, true computer literacy means that we start to own this technology as individuals and as a gender when we see it as an empowering device that makes representations. It's not enough to say, "This is an empowering device." Well, yeah, right, we know that. It can add numbers. It can help me type. That's not the end product. In its guise as a tool, that's what a computer does, but at the end of the day what a computer is for is making a representation of just about anything—a representation of how a cell works or what a star looks like or what life is like or what a fantasy world is like. The particular representation doesn't matter, but it is a representation-making device, and that is the reason to be interested in it as a technology because it's capable of that. When a person—boy or girl, but especially a girl—sees that possibility, it pulls her through the kind of learning about the technology that she'll need to become an author of it. But you don't get there unless you've got good examples that make you redefine the computer as a representation device and not a computation device. I'm hoping that these examples, at least for some girls, will get them to see the technology as having capabilities that they didn't think about before, and that these are things that they're really interested in doing. An example of this is how girls have appropriated video technology.

Q: Could you talk a little bit more about the pragmatics of selling these products?
A: Some percentage of products will be bought by parents who see them and think, "Oh, I bet my daughter would like this." But by far the strongest way to move our culture into girls' lives is to get them to be aware of it and to ask for it. How do we do that? Well, one thing we've done is made comarketing deals with a couple of companies. For example, we made a co-marketing arrangement with a girls' clothing manufacturer, Jonathan Martin Girls. They make these outrageously wonderful funky shoes and nice clothing, and they distribute their clothing in department stores. Typically, you don't do well if you try to put software in a place so unlike where somebody would look for it, so putting the software there probably doesn't make sense—except there are, I think, a few Macy's stores that actually have software sections. But we made this deal where Jonathan Martin has a hang tag on their clothing that says, "Purple Moon," blah-di-blah, ". . .and here's where you can get it." Then we have a promotion for our products in which the software is packaged with Rockett's backpack, which you'll see in the product, and inside the backpack is a Jonathan Martin baby-T that points the girl back at them.

We've had to be very aggressive about advertising, so we're advertising in girl publications, in parent publications. We've also been really aggressive about PR, getting coverage from places like the *Ladies' Home Journal*. I told our PR manager, "I will die and go to heaven if you can get me into *Ladies' Home Journal*," because my mother always read that magazine and it came to symbolize some things for me when I was young. That was our first interview on a press tour in New York. It was just amazing. I thought, "I can't believe I am doing this." But, it was great.

In our interviews with fathers, we found they're just as bullish about getting stuff for their daughters as mothers are, but they feel less secure about making the right decision, which is why you have to get the girl to ask the father and say, "I want this one," as opposed to that one. But fathers are generally pretty highly motivated. Among dads there's still a lot of, "Well, my daughter plays 'Doom,'" or, "None of that sissy stuff. None of this Barbie stuff. She plays real games. She does Microsoft 'Flight Simulator.'" And there are some girls out there who do that, and their dads are very proud of them. We had to be very careful with our positioning because one of the things parents are afraid of, especially fathers, is that if they get something that's just for girls, either their daughter is going to be crippled by it or it is going to be dumbed down. Because that's what they've seen before: the game's easy and stupid and it's talking down to her. And she's not getting an equal opportunity, because she's not doing "the real thing," she's not cutting her teeth on "Duke Nukem"—which of course, as we all know, is a tremendously educational product. But there is this prejudice that, "If it's not a 'real' game, it's not good for my daughter," so we've had to do a lot of work in terms of how we position the product and talk about it and where we advertise and what we say to make sure that people don't end up with that misconception.   ——July 1997

Chapter 6

An Interview with Nancie S. Martin (Mattel)

Nancie Martin directs Mattel's Girls' software development and is also responsible for many of the company's Internet initiatives. An avid reader, teacher, writer, collector of toys and books, and lover of history, music, and popular culture, she brings an informed and insightful perspective to overseeing the development of multimedia products at Mattel. She is executive producer of "Barbie Fashion Designer," "Barbie Storymaker," and "Barbie Print 'n Play" CD-ROMs, the "Fisher-Price Parenting Guide," "Barbie Magic Fairy Tales: Barbie as Rapunzel," and a range of other products. Before joining Mattel in 1995, Martin was president of Jouissance Productions in San Francisco, where she produced several CD-ROM titles, including "Rock Expedition: The 1960's" and "Soul Expedition: The 1960's." She was also a producer of "Xplora 1: Peter Gabriel's Secret World."

A native New Yorker, Martin began her career in publishing and was editor-in-chief of *Playgirl, Tiger Beat, Video Rock Stars,* and *Bodybuilding Lifestyles.* She is the author of four books on popular culture: *Eurythmics, John Lennon/Julian Lennon, Miss America Through the Looking Glass,* and *Duran Duran* (written under the pseudonym Susan Martin). Martin has taught at the School of Visual Arts, New York University, and San Francisco State University.

Q: How and why did you get interested in this line of work?
A: I remember the first time I saw a computer was at NASA in Galveston, where I went on a tour. It was a room the size of this entire office floor, with the whirring tape machines. And that room, I have to tell you, had less computing power than my Pilot. I thought, wow, that's really scary and impressive. That was in 1970, I think. Then, in 1975, I took my first computer science class, with

punch cards, a mainframe, and Basic. They taught you how to program in Basic and how to pick stuff out on punch cards so that you could do a program. I played a text adventure game called "Adventure" with punch cards. You made your choices and then you had to feed the punch cards in to do your next move. But when I first saw a flow chart, I went, "I get this. This makes perfect sense." It was like geometry. Everything just sort of fell into place and I went, "Oh, this goes to this goes to this. Sure, I get that."

But then I had so many interests. I wound up being an English major. I was already writing for the school paper. And computers sort of fell to one side; it was a cool thing, but there were a lot of other things to learn—Mandarin Chinese, there's a long list. However, throughout my career I've pretty much always done stuff that's aimed at girls and women; it's either been mass-market pop culture or it's been aimed at girls and women, or both. So when I got the opportunity to come here and work on Barbie, it was mass market, pop culture, it was aimed at girls and women, and it was high tech. And I have always been one of those futurist people who just imagines, "What is life going to be like in the future? What is the world going to be like?" So this could not possibly be a better combination. I get to do all of this stuff in one place.

As far as my motivation is concerned, there are a couple of things. One is this idea that I can help lead the way into the future for this huge mass of girls—to see what the possibilities are for them, to say to them, "Playing with computers is fun, but what you can learn on a computer is useful to you." I felt like I had a lot to share with the world in that regard. And I have this sort of mission, if you will, that I want all those girls who are now six and seven, when they're twenty-six and thirty-six and forty-six, to still be using computers as a tool, and to remember that it's all because of Barbie. And they can say, "And the first thing I used was 'Barbie Fashion Designer,'" or they can say, "That was a product that was meant for me. That was something I had a real connection to . . ." I can't compare what I do to *The Wind in the Willows* or *The Lion, the Witch, and the Wardrobe,* or whatever—those are great works. Those are the things that I grew up with where I went, "This is meaningful to me." Having that experience at five or six years old, reading that stuff, opened up a whole new world of possibilities. And if I can do that for girls today, then I will really feel like I've accomplished something. So, there's a strong motivation for wanting to do that for girls. Also, one of the reasons that I transitioned into working on CDs from the magazine business was this notion that I would be working in an area that would still be fresh and on the edge for the rest of my career. Magazines have sort of had their day. Everything really cool that you can do with a magazine has already been done. And I thought, well, here I can do stuff that hasn't been done before and have people say, "Wow, that's pretty cool. How'd you come up with that?"

Q: Do you consider yourself a feminist?
A: I do. With the definition that feminism is a framework, a prism through which to view the world. It's a perspective, and the perspective is that women matter, that we are the majority. That a woman's approach is not just a man's approach in a different color, that women's approach to the world is a different one from men's. And that doesn't mean better, that doesn't mean worse. It just means that you can't look at the world through the male prism and assume that that's the only one. I don't have a problem with high heels and lipstick. I think that all of that works. Feminism and glamour—is there a contradiction? I think not.

Q: What's the history of software in Mattel, and what's the history of feminism in Mattel?
A: There's a long history. Mattel actually came out with a hardware platform called Intellivision fifteen years ago. And that had software associated with it. Like all of the hardware platforms at that time, the Atari and so on, it had a huge boom, and then "Fwwhht!" Because people just got tired of it. So, that was initial history. It made people a little scared of actually building software within Mattel, initially. When CD-ROMs first started to come out, and when video games went back on the upswing with Sega, Nintendo—you know, in the early 1990s—Mattel licensed out Barbie for a couple of video games and for a sort of Director kind of CD-ROM, but it was always other companies doing the work. The people within Mattel who were supervising it at that time just wanted to be sure that Barbie looked OK. And she looked OK, and the copy on the box was OK, and they said, "Fine, you can release this." But it didn't really address fundamentally the way the girls play. I mean, the video games were your typical pink software. They were boys' games made pink. And the CD-ROM that was out, it was just sort of tedious. It wasn't anything special at all—"Barbie and Her Magical House."

Then, three years ago, a bunch of new people came in, and Doug Glen, Andy Rifkin, and I figured out a new way to make software. Andy and his daughter E. J., who is now nine, are the co-inventors of "Barbie Fashion Designer." When Andy came to Mattel, he had already had this idea of what he was calling Barbie-CAD. We figured out how to make it Barbie, what would make it a really Barbie thing. The idea there was to make really great stuff for girls, and by doing so, to fill a void in the marketplace. One of the things that studies were showing was that girls were avid users of software during the preschool years, where there is a lot of material available, and then once they grew out of that, once they were five or six, there wasn't anything out there for them. It was all, like, real boy stuff. So we saw that there was an opportunity there, because girls were saying, "Oh, I don't like computers. They're for nerds, they're for geeks, they're boring." And we knew that that didn't have to be the case, so we decided to address that.

So that's a little bit of the history of software in Mattel. Now, for the history of feminism at Mattel. The cofounder of Mattel was a woman. She, as you probably know, was the inventor of Barbie. The CEO of Mattel is a woman. Mattel was named by *Working Mother* one of the best places for women to work in America. It's a company in which, if you look at the top, the senior VPs in the company, of whom I think there are ten—I think—seven of them are women. Something like that. But it's a company where there doesn't appear to be a glass ceiling. I sure haven't felt it on my head as I try to do better here. There are a lot of really progressive policies, as women are involved. Also, you know that if Barbie were a toy company on her own, she would be the third largest toy company. So Mattel is thought of as the girls' toy company. And so we know that we have a very special responsibility to that audience to respond to who they are, and to keep track of what their dreams and their desires are, and to enable them. Of course, one of the things we're looking at is what girls like. But we also recognize that what they like are things that make them feel good about themselves and that make them feel accomplished. I get new Barbie dolls in here all the time, so I wanted to show you one that I just got, which is Paleontologist Barbie, part of the Career Collection. We Girls Can Do Anything! And so this is what Barbie is. She does all kinds of stuff, and one of them is that she's a paleontologist. You know, Barbie started out with a career. She began as a teenage fashion model. So there's a long history of saying, "Your job is not to get married. Your job is not just to be pretty. You can have a job. You can do stuff in the world. And if you want to wear a hat and high heels while you're doing it, you can do that, too."

Q: Why do you think that girls really haven't bought video games until now? And why the big boom at this point?
A: First of all, depending on the age of the girls, they don't buy them anyway—their parents do. So, one of the largest reasons is that there really wasn't very

much out there for them. There have been a few attempts, but there wasn't anything out there that successfully translated the way that girls like to play to what they can do on the computer. Of course, there is no doubt that having a name, a brand name that means a huge amount to girls, also had a lot to do with the shift. There were some worthy products for girls out over the last couple of years, but the problem was that they had no name recognition. It's not even girls so much. I mean, if girls find something good, they will like it. But the real struggle is the business end of things, the distributors and the retailers. I think generally that the business side has been taking this approach of, "Well, show me." You know, "You say there's this big market. How come nobody's buying it yet?"

As far as the big boom, most people are currently crediting us with the big boom, so I'll accept that. We've made products that successfully translate how girls play in the physical world to the computer world, and we've done it with a major brand name, and we've sold a lot of volume. So that has opened up the whole category. Also, I think girls are ready. One of the problems is that up until relatively recently this was not a mass market. As it is, it barely qualifies. I think that penetration of PCs into the home, and certainly into the homes of girls between the ages of three and ten, is maybe 60 percent. So of course over the long term there's an opportunity, because there are something like 40 million girls in this country under the age of eighteen, and not all of them have PCs yet. But the fact is that up until relatively recently, there weren't enough girls with computers to sell to. We have now sold over a million units of "Barbie Fashion Designer" worldwide (see Plate 5).

Q: How do girls play, and how do Barbie products specifically address that?
A: Well, you know, the toy industry has this term called the "play pattern." And we use it a lot. It's all the ways that we observe girls playing. We do a lot of observational research where we just put girls in a room with toys and we just watch what they do. And we also do that with software. We put them in a room with software and we see what they do. Mattel does an amazing amount of research, just a phenomenal amount, both inside, in-house, as well as out-side, so people don't know that it's necessarily Mattel doing it. When we observe girls, we find there are a lot of different kinds of play patterns. There is this aspirational play, like, "I'm going to be a ballerina," "I'm going to be a doctor," "I'm going to be a paleontologist," kind of thing. There is the hair play. The first thing a girl will do when she gets a Barbie that has long hair is she will take the hair and put it into a ponytail, and then she'll take it out. That's why every

Barbie comes with a brush, because that's what they like to do so much. So hair play is very big. Barbie started out as a fashion doll, and she is still a fashion doll. One of the things they like to do is take all of the clothes off and put them back on, change the clothes, try some other clothes. And younger girls like to play with Barbie in the water—they like to take her into the bathtub and into the pool.

As we build more software, we're also observing the way that girls are learning to play digitally, and what that means to them, the whole notion of exploration. You see relationships and collaboration in the context of girls playing on computers. Girls are willing to share a mouse. They will take "Fashion Designer" and they will say, "OK, you try. You put the color on now," or "You do this," or "Do you want the flowers or the hearts?" They'll pass it back and forth. Boys won't do that, for instance. Boys are head-to-head, "Either I win or you win." Of course, I can't really say "Girls do this, boys do that." That's not really appropriate. So, when I say that, what I mean is that many or most girls that we've seen do this, and many or most boys. But there are always going to be people who do things a little differently either way.

Q: In the creation of these Mattel games involving technology, how are you incorporating these different play styles?
A: Well, all kinds of different ways. First, creativity, and arts and crafts and make-and-do, or whatever you want to call it; that's a big play pattern for little girls, generally. And so we looked at that in the first three titles we put out in 1996, that was the primary motivator. But there was also in them this sense of accomplishment. In "Fashion Designer," for example, there's a lot of fashion play, but there's also that sense of accomplishment, that sense of, "Look what I did," that sense of, "I did something really special and beautiful," and also that "I'm making clothes for Barbie." We have "Barbie Storymaker," which is completely about what girls do when they have Barbie. That is, they have Barbie and they have Midge, and they make up a story where Barbie says, "Hi, Midge," and Midge says, "Hi, Barbie." And then they decide, "Hey, do you want to go to the mall?" "OK, let's." There's that sense of creating a little movie, a little story for yourself. That is really an important thing for girls to be able to play out. And "Print 'n' Play" is a print shop, which is all about communication and sending people letters and invitations. So those are things that we've identified. But as we move into 1997, we have "Talk With Me Barbie," which is all about communication. We have "Ocean Discovery," which is all about exploration and adventure and fantasy. Fantasy is a very big play pattern for girls—pretending

Figure 6.1: "Barbie Party Print 'n' Play" allows girls to plan and produce their own parties. BARBIE and associated trademarks are owned by Mattel, Inc.©1996 Mattel, Inc. All Rights Reserved. Used with permission.

to be a princess, for example. And sometimes that's aspirational, because I'm sure that a lot of girls think that princess is a job that you can actually have. But there are lots of ways that we explore different play patterns. We have a new kind of printing product that's called "Party Print 'n' Play," where you can actually make things for a party for you, or for your dolls, because we notice that girls like to put on parties for their dolls and sit them all around a table or have tea parties with them. So we said, "Well, why shouldn't you be able to make little mini-invitations and mini-party hats and stuff like that?" So what we've done is, we've looked at all those play patterns and figured out how to translate them.

Q: Is there something you feel best exemplifies the work that Mattel is doing right now, and what kind of journey or narrative that girls go through?
A: I think the best thing to speak about is actually "Fashion Designer," just because it's been so successful. And talking about some of its aspects might enable us to understand why it's been successful, as well as what some of the

factors are in how girls relate to a product. If you look at what a girl is dealing with when she looks at the product, first of all, she has some expectations about it. Actually, this last Christmas it was simply a case of a lot of girls wanting one, and so there was a lot of, "My friend has one and I want one, too." But initially, we appealed to a whole range of things—in girls and also in parents. Part of it for girls was saying, "This is something where I can make something. And it looks really cool. And Barbie will model what I've made. You know, that's pretty cool. Then, I can make something out of it, and I can show it off, and I can be really proud of that. And I can have a lot of fun just being silly and trying really weird color combinations, and seeing what they look like." So, there's the silly, creative fun of just trying and doing all kinds of different things.

Remember that Barbie is not a character. She's a doll. She's not Mickey Mouse. And she didn't start out as a digital entity—she started out as a 3D entity. So one of the things that we were doing was we were bringing Barbie to life in a way that's right next to you, for the first time. There have been stop-action Barbie and CGI Barbie in commercials, where girls have had an opportunity to see what Barbie would look like if she came to life. But this is a Barbie whom you have brought to life in a way, because you've dressed her. So there's that aspect of creation and of giving something life, which I think is meaningful to everybody, not just to girls, and particularly there's this sense of pride. You give a girl a tremendous sense of pride at age six and seven and eight, and I want to believe that she can hang onto that for the rest of her life. There's this whole range of emotions that's tapped just by playing with this relatively simple thing. And also, going back to parents and the way the parents related to it, I think that parents said, "I want my little girl to be playing with the computer. I want her to have the advantage of playing with a computer. It's such a shame that all the games are so violent." And then they say, "Well, my girl loves Barbie and this is a Barbie thing, and it looks like it's fun to do." One of the things that we've noticed in talking to fathers is that they were saying, "This is something that I can do with my little girl. I know it's fashion, but, gee, it's just like building something." It enabled them to relate to their daughters, because parents not only are the gatekeepers of software but also men are the people who go into software stores more. So when they saw, "Look! It's a pink package! It's Barbie, it's something for my little girl. Now, I can get the "Flight Simulator" for me and Barbie for her," they kind of felt, "Wow, I've done something good for the rest of the family." And most of the women who are mothers of Barbie-age girls had Barbie in their lives themselves as children. So this is something familiar, where they say, "Oh, I know this." We all have some relationship to this and some kind of nostalgia associated with Barbie. It's why so many people have such strong feelings about her. She's been around for such a long time.

Q: What do you say to the criticism by a number of feminists about Barbie being feminine and having certain roles associated with femininity?
A: Oh, you know, just because a role is associated with femininity doesn't make it a bad role. I mean, I think a lot of ballerinas, for instance, would take issue with the notion that it's not OK for them because it's feminine. We live in a society that devalues women's work, a society that says that a ballerina isn't as much of an athlete as a football player, that says that women's work in the home is not as worthwhile as men's work outside the home. So, conveniently, upon Barbie doll's little tiny shoulders rests the weight of everything that is wrong with the way that our culture approaches being a woman or being femi-nine or any of the other constructs that we might build to frame up those kind of notions. I'm not denying that our society has many gender stereotypes. But what women remember about Barbie or how women see Barbie for themselves in their lives now is not necessarily how girls see Barbie, you know? So parents have a different relationship, and some parents go, "Here's your Barbie," and some parents embrace it. The girls are probably going to want one anyway, regardless of whether the parents embrace it, or a friend or a relative is going to say, "Oh, I got little Suzy a Barbie," and the mom or the dad is going to go, "I don't really know what I think about this." And so not only is she a vehicle for the dreams and aspirations of little girls, but to the extent that she does repre-sent our changing versions of femininity over the last forty years, she's a repre-sentation for all of us of our dreams and our aspirations. There's this very weighted relationship that we have when we see this little piece of plastic with some nylon attached to it. We have so much invested in this, because she's a representation of a pretty woman with breasts. But the truth is that what little girls have tied up in it is a lot less than we do, because those things aren't real to them, being pretty or having breasts or whatever. It's not who you are as a six-year-old. So oddly enough, I don't think there are many people, except for little girls, who are capable of saying, "Oh, it's just a toy." Yet, fundamentally, that's what it is.

But I have a very strong feminist approach to a lot of the things we do. For instance, "Talk With Me Barbie" can say thousands of things, and many of the things she can say are aimed at puncturing stereotypes wherever they might exist. And this is Barbie talking, you know, this is her saying things about what she likes to do or what's important to her. This is stuff that a lot of little girls will hear as the voice of Barbie, this is what Barbie thinks. And this is important because there is a Barbie in every little girl's bedroom. Ninety-nine percent of the girls in this country have at least one Barbie. Barbie is, for them, a representative of them, a representative of who they might be when they grow up. It's a vehicle for their dreams and their aspirations and so on. So what she says is important, because girls are listening to everything at that age. Because when you're six and seven, five and nine, and twenty-seven, your job is to listen. Your job is to take in the world and process it. And so I believe that what we're doing is important to who girls might be someday. People, a lot of times, want to make products for who girls should be, for who they think girls should be, and not for who they are. But girls are very conscious of themselves as girls when they're five and six and seven. They're very aware that, "I'm a girl." It's the age at which girls start to say, "I want to wear a party dress every day," "I want my room to be pink." They're overcuing, I think is the technical term. And they start fussing with their hair. There's this definite, "I wonder who I am," and to the extent that Barbie is extremely feminine, she's the embodiment of whatever you want to be, but you can also explore a whole range of options—paleontologist or whatever. And so we pay attention to that, with Barbie talking to you very intimately, knowing your name and your birthday and if you have brothers and sisters. She knows what you want to talk about and what choices you made. So if you said, "Let's talk about careers. I want to be a teacher, I want to be a math teacher, and when we go on a field trip, I want to take the kids to the fire station," she holds a conversation with you. You know, she says something, then you say something back, and then she says something else. And that process of being responsible to girls for our part of the conversation is something I believe that Mattel takes very seriously, both in the doll products we make as well as within the software products we make.

Q: Do you think the process of designing for girls is at all different from designing for boys?
A: Girls are very influenced by what other girls think. We bring them in for research by having a girl come and bring a friend. It's someone they already feel comfortable with, so they don't have to impress them. But at the same time, we have the dynamics of the relationship to deal with, and since so much of who girls are is about relationships, it's a question of, "Does my friend think what I'm doing is OK? Is this cool enough?" There's a lot of looking at the friend

and going, "Are you OK with this?" And you don't see that as much with boys. They just want to see the game. They want to know what the rules are and how it works. Girls are much more concerned about the game in the context of what else is happening in the room. If there's somebody from our research team sitting there with them, they want to know about that person. They want to know about their relationship to that person.

Q: What types of girls do you design for? Is it for all girls?
A: I don't think that we can possibly design for all girls because I think we'd be hurting ourselves if we did. But we have games that are about exploration, that are about creativity, and we know that those appeal to different kinds of girls. We have a fairy tale storybook that I'm very proud of, the Rapunzel title, in which Rapunzel actually gets to save the prince, which I thought was a nice twist. But for girls who are into combat and competitiveness, we don't really have a whole lot. That's not to say that I don't think that's not appropriate for some girls; it just doesn't fit into the brands that we have available to us.

Q: How would you defend your aesthetic and style choices as ones that appeal to girls?
A: One of the things that we do here is that we make things that are coded as girls' products, period. We don't make gender-neutral stuff. Barbie is a girls' toy, by and large. There are boys who play with Barbie. I think that's great. But it's not gender neutral. We make software that's not necessarily about hearth and home. I don't think that we're coding behavior in the sense of, "It's not OK for you to explore." But if there is some aspect of this that's about being pretty or enjoying pretty things, or a beautiful world or whatever, that's one of the aspects of being a little girl that I don't think is problematic. If you look at "Ocean Discovery," (see Plates 6 and 7) that's an underwater world, and we actually base the marine life on real marine life. But it's also Barbie's version of an underwater world, and it's probably a lot brighter and prettier than you are going to get in real life. You know, pink is a color that girls like. They like pink more than they like brown. If that's what they like, then I'm going to give them what they like. I can't make them like brown, you know? So, to some extent we are ruled by the market, and to some extent we can dictate the market. Part of what we can do is say, "Barbie can be a marine biologist, Barbie can talk to you about being a math teacher." There's all these things that are part of her world. And if part of her world is also wearing party dresses or high heels or playing with her hair, that's part of all of our worlds, too.

Q: What does it mean in terms of giving girls a pink aisle in the toy store?
A: Well, part of that is a convenience for the marketplace. If you give girls a pink aisle, they or their moms know where to go to find things that they might find appealing. Toy retailers want to sell a lot of product, so they're going to go, "Well, how can we get the girls in here and get them excited about what's here and going 'Mommy, mommy, I want that'?" And part of that is to create a destination in the store. If that's the pink aisle, then that's what it is. Of course, what that then presents is an issue about, "Well, is everything that's for girls going to be in that pink aisle, and is it going to be as appealing if it's not pink?" Is pink the dominant color, and is it crowding out all of the other things? I think that one of the things is about looking at what the marketplace is as opposed to saying, "We can create our own marketplace." Part of that is making things that are going to appeal to a lot of people and still reinforce the messages that you want to send. And if the messages that you want to send are, "It's OK to be you," but that comes in a pink box because if that's the way to get it into your house, I'll put it in a pink box. I don't think of that as making a compromise. I think of that as, "How do I reach the largest number of people?" I think that retail, the whole aspect of how to make something that sells and not lose your soul in the process, is a vexing problem for anybody who's in the marketplace, and particularly for people who work for large corporations. I believe that, so far, I am living proof that that can be done, because I really feel that I am doing something worthwhile for girls, or I would not be doing what I'm doing. But as I am fond of saying, I'm not seven. I haven't been seven in a long time. And if a seven-year-old is going to tell me, "I don't like that. I don't think that's cool. I don't think that's fun," I have to take her word for it. And particularly, if it's not just one seven-year-old, but ten of them or a hundred of them, I know, gee, I'm on the wrong track. So, you change what you do. That's not compromise. That's just understanding that what you want girls to do is not necessarily what they're going to want to do.

Q: Are you competing with other companies that are making software products for girls, or in what ways are you working together?
A: There's a couple of things. One is that, because of the success of our products, we've opened up a whole category and we've made retailers pay attention to anything else that people might come out with as games for girls. So we are working together in that sense, because if those companies do well and make good products and sell well, then that expands the categories and there are more shelves of products that are made for girls or that have things in them

that girls will find interesting. And, that's good for everyone. At the same time, most of the companies that are working on games for girls are focusing on girls eight and up, so there aren't that many people, as far as I know, making products for five-, six-, and seven-year-olds. There's not a whole lot of competition in that area. The more companies that are doing games for girls that are out there, the larger the pool of talent is going to be to draw from in the sense of people who have already worked on games for girls and want to work on other kinds of games for girls. There are ways in which we can all help each other. Sure, we're competing on the shelves for a share of the parents' wallet. But this is not just something that's a flash in the pan, that's going to go away, and one of the things I worry about is if other products for girls are not good, I don't want people going, "Well, 'Fashion Designer' was just successful because of Barbie." It was successful because it was a good product, and it also happened to be Barbie, which helped carry it along. I don't want people saying, "See, girls don't really buy software. Girls don't really like software." I don't want that. Or, "See, girls don't really like computers," because that's icky.

Q: In your opinion, what characteristics would define good software products for girls?
A: To start with, it has to be fun to play. If it's a game, it's going to have to be fun. It needs to encourage you to make choices, because I think that choices are a big part of the learning process for girls, and, in fact, for all of us. I think that it has to make you feel like you've accomplished something at some point. It could do that continuously or it could do that at the end because there's a big payoff, but there's got to be some sense in which you feel, "I did this. I made this," you know, "I made this happen." It has to foster some sense of relationship—and the difficulty of doing this is one of the limitations of technology—but the more emotional content a product can have, the more successful I believe it's going to be with anybody, but particularly with girls, because they have a stake in it. They feel that something will happen that they took part in and that there's a back-and-forth between them and the product, that there was a dialogue between them and the product in some way, and that part of that is about the choices that they're making and part of that is that those choices lead to an accomplishment. Also, in terms of a mass-market product, that you want to go back to it, that you want to tell your friends how cool you think it is; that's always something that you want a product to do. And also that you want parents to feel good about it, too, because they have the money. This is particularly true with younger girls more than with older ones. So it has

to be something that parents can feel, "This is doing something good for my little girl."

Q: I've noticed you have an extensive collection of brunette Barbies. Can you talk about what Barbie means to you?

A: Well, I have a very positive relationship with glamour. I like getting dressed up. Fashion and looking pulled-together and all that are important to me personally. When I was growing up, Barbie was the embodiment to me of a kind of glamour, but also of this idea that you could do anything. I mean, this Barbie in a red suit is a fashion designer. She has a job, she has glasses. I had glasses just like that when I was a kid. And so I said, "Oh, so you can look really pretty and you can have a great job, too. Cool!" So having all these brunette Barbies is my way of saying, "This is my Barbie. This is what Barbie looks like to me." My favorite ones are the ones that have really light skin and really dark hair, you know? For an adult there's always an aspect—we know this about adult collectors—there's an aspect to having Barbie dolls that's very serious—you really like the way they look and the details of the outfits—but there's something campy about it, too. It's like, "Look at how adorable this is, this little miniature." I mean, it's pretty and it's fun, and it's kind of my job to be reminded of what it's like to have this miniature representation of something around all the time, so I choose to have a miniature representation that I personally can relate to. We do live in a brunette world, you know, but there are an awful lot of blondes starring in it. So in my personal life, I'm reversing that trend!

Q: What have we missed?

A: I think it's really important to emphasize that the girls who we're talking about are twenty years younger than you and thirty years younger than me [*The interviewers were under thirty—Eds.*], and their relationship to computers is really different from any of ours. I would guess that for most of the time that you've been alive there have been video games. Well, that's not true for me. But for little girls now, the computer is an appliance. They're used to seeing it around the house, they're used to having a mouse around. This is an accepted piece of technology in their homes. Until recently, there may not have been all that much for them to play on it, but it's not really intimidating to a kid. Kids do not relate to it the same way. And, in fact, one of the interesting things that we've noticed is that younger girls have greater fluency on the computer than older girls do, because there's been all this great preschool software available for the last few years, and they're used to playing with it. But you get a twelve-year-old and she's going, "I don't know what I'm supposed to do here," and "Boys play that." Older girls are actually in some ways much more of a challenge, to get them ready for it. I think that we can't lose sight of the fact that ultimately the best way to do something really well is to do your best to look into the soul of the person who's going to be using it, the consumer, and to say, "I've made something for you." I would feel that way regardless of who I was making this stuff for, but I particularly feel that way with little girls, because it's like I'm giving a present to myself, you know? My inner six-year-old. It's like I'm saying to her, "I made this for you, I really hope you like it." So I feel like, "Gee, I'm really lucky to be doing this," because I get to have that experience every day of feeling connected to the people who I'm making this for. It may be that that's because I'm female and they're female; it might just be because I get them and I can't explain why; but that's why I do what I do.   ——July 1997

Chapter 7

An Interview with Heather Kelley (Girl Games)

Heather Kelley is the director of online development at Girl Games, located in Austin, Texas. She is the creator of the website Planet Girl (http://www.planet-girl.com), a virtual space for girls to meet and express themselves, and she manages and edits *Girls Interwire,* a weekly newsletter by and for girls. Kelley came to Girl Games in 1995, two years after Laura Groppe founded the company, and today she is responsible for designing diverse interactive experiences for preteen and teen girls for Girl Games and its clients.

Heather Kelley brings a theoretical background in new technologies and gender and sexuality issues to her hands-on work designing multimedia projects and product development. In addition to her work at Girl Games, she has been an instructor at the Austin Museum of Art, where she developed curricula to instruct girls ages nine to twelve in creating digital artwork. Previously, she was an educational technology designer at the IC2 Institute, and she received a Master of Arts in Radio-Television-Film from the University of Texas at Austin.

Q: Can you talk a little bit about your own background, and how you came to Girl Games?
A: Sure. I came to Girl Games in October of 1995, when Girl Games moved from Houston to Austin. Initially, I was hired to do research for the first game, "Let's Talk About Me." Laura Groppe, the founder of the company, had my résumé and showed it to her mom, and her mom said "Hire her." The next thing she did was hire me; I owe a lot to Laura's mom. The company grew very rapidly from there.

Q: How or why did you first get involved in this industry?

A: I actually played computer games as a child. I'm not sure how many other women in this industry can claim that. It's a generational thing. Only people growing up at about the same time as I was have much nostalgia for computer games as part of their childhood culture, rather than simply viewing them from an adult perspective. I left computers behind for most of my teenage years, and then later rediscovered "the nerd within," after I graduated from college. I was hanging out with friends at Georgia Tech, and found the old fascination coming back again. I was working for a software company at the time. They weren't making games, but they were looking for ways to enter the really competitive game market. They weren't even thinking about girls' games; they wanted to market a product for adult women. And they brought me in to do some research. At the time, it was very hard to find anything about women and computer games. This was in 1993 or so. I had lots of resources available to me, but I found almost nothing. That was just on the cusp of these recent efforts to reconsider girls as potential consumers for games. We ended up looking at stuff about game play or gender or learning styles, more oblique things, examining what kinds of entertainment appealed to both males and females.

By the time I arrived at Girl Games in 1995, the company was in heavy production mode for the first game, "Let's Talk About Me," and I divided my time between working on the game and working on the website. Laura had started the company in late 1993 with the idea of making games for girls. The plan grew out of her own experience of having to learn computer skills later in her career. She got involved in a research program through the Center for Research in Parallel Computation at Rice University. The project dealt with women and technology. They did focus group interviews with girls from around Houston, asking them what they would be interested in seeing in a computer game. They were also showing them computer games and asking them to give their opinions. While she was working on this research, Laura was using what she'd learned to develop our first game. "Let's Talk About Me" is pretty much a direct result of those focus groups.

From there, we developed a second tier of research with Rice that would ask girls to actually create their own games, and that research was completed last summer. Again, we relied on small sample groups, although we tried to represent the diversity of Houston's population. There were four focus groups, so we developed four prototype games that represented what these girls thought would be interesting. We didn't do very sophisticated programming, but this approach gave us a real sense of what the girls thought would be fun. We paired the girls with a team of female artists, programmers, and project directors to give them a fuller sense of what their horizons could be if they chose careers in the computer industry. It was all pretty eye-opening for them. Alongside the sessions where they designed and prototyped the games, they also had speakers in different technical fields come and talk with them. This research confirmed our expectations. At least two of the games had elements that were very much like what we had done. They were modular, dealt with girls' lives, and acted more like an interactive magazine than a game per se. The research also gave us some directions for other possible games to do in the future.

Q: Can you tell us more about the games the girls developed?

A: "Morality's Revenge" was an adventure-mystery game, and your goal was to solve the mystery of the church burnings in the black community. You could choose between several different characters, and the mystery was going to be solved through your character's strengths or weaknesses. There were some very interesting characters. One was a relentless reporter that wouldn't give up until she got the story. Another was a paramilitary figure with lots of physical strength.

In "A-maze-ing Journeys" the player explores spaces by answering questions. These questions cover traditional school subjects and popular trivia; at one point you might gain entry by solving an equation and another by knowing who starred in a certain movie.

Most similar to "Let's Talk About Me," *MODE Magazine* showcases interactive features on a variety of topics. Two of the more prominent articles are about Olympic gymnast Dominique Moceanu, and about young Houston gang members who were friends of the study participant.

The fourth game, "It's My Life," is based on the paper game, "M-A-S-H." You are assigned a "fate" of sorts, and then you design a living space using the lifestyle you are given. Then you are asked to use your wits to solve a problem related to the space you designed. In the girls' prototype, the problem was that your air conditioner broke and you have to figure out how to get it fixed again.

Q: So these games were developed by the girls and the design team?

A: The adults were really facilitators for the girls. They didn't teach the girls Director. They taught the girls what Director could do, and then let the girls do their own storyboarding and their own design, but to get the production schedule moving more quickly, they let an adult do the actual programming. A different group of people were doing the observation, recording, and analysis of the sessions. The production people were just there to assist the girls.

Q: Is that research going to lead to a particular product? Or how does that work tie into the product development process?
A: I'd say it influenced our product development. Although it would be very intriguing to take one of the girls' designs and make it into a game, that isn't really where we have planned to go with it. We're trying to see how that creative dynamic can be brought beyond the confines of this particular research situation at CRPC and into other educational contexts. So we're hoping to make a package that can combine the prototypes the girls developed with instructional training for teachers to implement this kind of program in their own schools. We want to help teachers develop exercises that will get girls more interested in technology. With "Let's Talk About Me," we developed some teaching guides. Part of the plan was to make something that could be used in the schools as well as in the home. We developed plans so that Girl Scout troop leaders could help girls earn badge requirements using it.

Our goal was to educate girls, because that's one way to raise their self-esteem, and that was the primary goal for our company. The people who work for our company want that for girls. We remember going through these same stages of development, even if it's very different now for girls. I don't think we can just make a blanket statement, "Oh, we're women, so we understand what girls go through now." We really have to talk to girls because their world is very different. But most of us who are creating games for girls want to speak to our own experience as children. We know that self-esteem is so crucial, and yet girls in our culture have real difficulty maintaining self-esteem as they move into their preteen years.

Q: How do your products help to cultivate girls' self-esteem?
A: On a basic level, our games make computers fun to use, so that girls use them more and feel more competent being near the machine and not having to feel like they're going to break something. That alone is doing a lot of good. Taking it to another level, I think the interface itself has to be nonthreatening and has to speak to girls, to ease them into using computers. A lot of computer games might be intolerant of mistakes. To somebody who is not speaking the language of the programmers, even a dialogue box can be a real threat. It's chastising you for something you did wrong. A lot of previous interfaces have

Figure 7.1: The signpost in "Let's Talk About Me" points the way toward various routes toward self-understanding. Copyright 1997 Girl Games, Inc. All rights reserved. Used with permission.

gone on the assumption that people figure out what they need. Well, we don't make those assumptions. In our games, if something like a dialogue box pops up, it's written in the girls' own language. It's written in a way that is not going to scare them, and it's going to explain to them what's happening and give them a choice. When you see a dialogue box that is completely different from anything you're accustomed to seeing because it's in a funky frame or an attractive color or in common language, that makes the girls feel more comfortable. We also design the games to be very open-ended. If you get somewhere and you don't want to be there, you can use a very accessible menu to get out of there and go and do something else. Our girls never feel like they're being backed into something they can't escape, which is something they find frustrating in other kinds of games, something that makes them feel stupid. We're trying to avoid that.

Q: What are some of the issues that have come up in your talks with preteen girls? And can a product like "Let's Talk About Me" or the other games developed by Girl Games accommodate those interests?

A: A lot of the issues for younger kids haven't changed as much as the ones that preteens confront. Something like the Barbie product can draw on developmental research that is very well-founded. But when you reach twelve- and thirteen-year-olds, girls that are just coming into an adult world, that's when things get very different from what we experienced as children. The problems these girls face vary a lot from region to region, depending on whether the areas they live in are urban or suburban or rural. For the urban kids, a major issue is violence, especially gang-related violence. Austin is not a big town, and it's not especially urban, but I've talked to girls that are not allowed to wear certain kinds of colors to school because those colors are associated with the gangs. Sexuality is becoming an issue at a younger and younger and younger age, and that is something that parents aren't necessarily prepared to address for girls that young. Some of the other issues are the same as they've always been: your friends, loyalty, status, what are you going to do in the future when you grow up? Another major change—and this is a positive change—would be the rise of team sports for girls. Sports are influencing their self-perception in a really positive way. It's finally broken into public consciousness that girls can play team sports and enjoy it. They're really out there having a lot of fun.

Q: How can we relate some of these issues to the particular games?

A: "Let's Talk About Me" has a section called "Sports Pals," which introduces girls who are playing various sports and tells what those girls like about the sports, what they do to prepare for a meet or to develop a routine, and it's almost evenly balanced between team sports and more individual competition. It even gets into dance; it's not just soccer and baseball.

The sexuality is a little bit more difficult issue to deal with. As a staff, we have individual ideas about how this topic should be handled, but we're still trying to make a product that will be acceptable to parents. We have a way of dealing with sexuality that gives the girls information that they need, but it doesn't go so far as to try to replace the role that parents should play in their learning about these issues. We all have various ideas about how much and how soon girls should know about sex. It's pretty much a fact that they're learning it on the street anyhow. But the flat-out honest truth is that we can't include as much information about health and reproduction as we would like. As important as it is for girls, that really isn't our role. Parents have very specific ideas about what they want for their individual children and we can't overstep that line. We provide the information in a very factual manner, and we try to make it fun. (See Plate 9.) In the case of some of the more specific information about puberty, we use a quiz-style format that asks the questions in a very light-hearted manner and in a language they can understand, and it also gauges the response according to the girl's age. She puts her birth date into the game, and based on our consultations with educators, we won't provide information before she is most likely ready to receive it. If a girl is eight years old, she's not going to get the same questions and answers as a thirteen-year-old. The computer makes that distinction automatically.

Q: What are parents' interests in these games, and how does Girl Games accommodate their concerns?

A: We have to come up with an almost impossible combination—parental trust and preteen hip quotient. It's hard to make both groups happy, but we're doing that as well as anyone ever has. Many kids in that age group want to avoid doing things that are preapproved by their parents, and yet the parents are still the parents. They're definitely playing a major role in determining what the girls see, hear, and purchase. When we're talking about reaching the children, the goal is to make computers cool and fun. For the parents, the goal is to teach the girls something positive, to increase their self-esteem, and not to violate the parents' trust. The parents' immediate interest is in finding something that their girls will enjoy using on the computer, because in many homes the girls are fighting for computer time with male siblings. Their parents want them to have computer skills. The game is geared to girls in its style and content, but our marketing is meant to appeal equally to the girls and their parents. Many parents are so interested in their girls having the experience of working with computers that the game really doesn't need to do much more than be fun to make it valuable for them. Beyond that, we do stress our educational content. And most parents are overjoyed that there's something nonviolent for their daughters to play. Parents write to us to report seeing their girls just taking over the computer. That was their goal, and we helped them achieve it. They want the girls not just to *be* on the computer but to really *want* to be on it. And beyond the fact that the girls are playing with the computer, they are also learning things that have merit. They aren't just sitting in front of the boob tube.

Q: What characteristics distinguish Girl Games from other kinds of software on the market?

A: Our products are noncompetitive—based more in social interaction than in aggression, cooperation rather than competition, communication between players, self-exploration, customizability, a high level of graphic and sound quality. The girls place much more importance on the music and the sound. If they're playing a game and the music is dumb, it will annoy them more than it annoys boys, even if the game play is good. If the music is bad, it will affect their experience negatively, and good music really enhances their game play. I'm running through kind of a laundry list and I'm probably leaving things out.

Q: Do you believe that girls are fundamentally different than boys?

A: They are fundamentally different. But what does that really mean? We've looked at the literature on the developmental differences between boys and girls. We're dealing with an age group that has so many issues that they care about, and those issues are so much at the forefront of their mind that whether they're ahead or behind boys in certain aspects doesn't really play much of a role. We're focusing on where girls are now and what we can do for them.

Q: What types of girls do you design for, or do you design for all girls?

A: I do think its impossible to design for all girls—especially across all age groups. We say the product is aimed at ages eight to fourteen, but that's because individual girls are at different stages of development. It's really centered around ten to twelve—at least this first CD-ROM is. While we do try to hit that whole age group, there are plenty of different kinds of girls within that age group: the bookish ones, like I was, or the jockish girls, and girls with various other competencies. While we don't try to make the game for everyone, we do try to make sure that parts of it will appeal to all different kinds of girls. We get this kind of response a lot: "I really liked X but I really didn't like Z. You should not put Z in there, but put in something more about X." They just want more of whatever it is they like, but in order to reach a broad enough market for the game to come out at a time when no one thought there could be games for girls, we made an effort to respond to all kinds of interests.

Q: Sherry Turkle, who's an MIT professor, says that the computer is a personal and cultural symbol of what a woman is not. Do you agree?

A: No. I don't. And I really liked that question. In some ways, yes, the computer is a symbol of what a woman is not. We perceive the computer as a logical machine as opposed to the emotion and intuition that's most often associated with women in our culture. But in other ways it is a cultural symbol of what "femininity" is. It's a thinking *object,* not an active human subject, and according to standard gender analysis, woman is object and the subject is masculine. The thing that is acted upon is feminine. The computer really is a product of masculine intent and masculine desire. It is something that can never adequately answer back. It can never have its own subjectivity. It is something upon which one imposes one's will. The computer does represent many aspects of classic femininity because it is under the control of someone who acts upon it and looks at it. It is something that is to be understood only so that it can be controlled, something to be looked at and examined and taken apart. For this reason, I compare the computer to Pygmalion; it's an object created out of male longing. You usually don't hear much about the statue, the Galatea, what happens to her. The myth is all about the man's desire, which causes him to create this object that he can look at. He creates a human being so real that it can have sex with him and have his kids. So, I see computers as fitting into that same role, *unless* we change the direction that technological development is taking—"we" being people who think that the traditional inequities are wrong.

Q: How might the technology change if girls start using computers more often?

A: The problem is with the hardware. We can do all we want with software but we're always confined to what hardware exists for us to interact with, and right now that's screens and keyboards. What we really need to change is the way that we interact with computers, the way the hardware operates, before we're going to change this situation very much. If we were to develop something that we interacted with "in a more feminine manner," it would have to be something that was more able to respond to you. You couldn't just act upon it and do things and have it not know anything about you. If computers are going to be changed by a girl's interactions with them, they need to be more responsive to the individual girl who's using them. I'd love for that to happen.

Q: What do you give priority to: (1) getting the girls to use technology; or (2) giving girls new representations of gender, including software that isn't designed along the lines of traditional femininity?

A: As far as our company is concerned, getting them to use the technology is definitely the priority. Girls' expectations about software are going to change the more they're exposed to it. It's hard to know what they're going to want or what's going to be considered a decent game for them in five or ten years. When you're trailblazing like we are, all you can do is develop games based on what girls tell you. We respond to their interests as they state them and as best we can interpret them into the interactive medium. If that causes girls to evolve new representations of gender—well, maybe being computer literate won't be considered as undesirable as it is now. If new representations of gender, including new software designs, emerge, we're going to be responding. We're not going to think that what we've done in the past is an everlasting model for what girls will want. We'll always be listening to them, and as they change, because they're more technoliterate, we will change along with them.

Q: Some of your products are heavily coded as girl's products with an emphasis on clothes, certain colors, behaviors, and choices that are traditionally associated with teenage girls. In many senses, they celebrate female-coded behavior that feminists might be alarmed at. How would you defend your aesthetic and style choices? Why is it necessary to continue to make products that are coded in pink or that emphasize girlish behavior?

A: That's pretty easy to defend. I'm a feminist, and almost everyone who works here considers themselves to be a feminist. Feminism has a pretty wide definition now, and I don't think all feminists would be opposed to games that include something about fashion or make-up or dating. In fact, for the age group we're dealing with, pink is very unpopular. The only way to use pink is to appropriate it in a very self-conscious way. We have a character on the website called Pink Kitty and she's hot pink, but it's clear that her behavior is totally atypical of what pink signifies. In this context, we are thumbing our noses at pinkness. She's not rude. She's just adventurous and creative—not that these are antifeminine values—but she's very self-possessed and not very young girly at all. She's a powerful individual. For this age group, it isn't so much that pink is girly; for them, pink is young. The girls who are using our website are twelve or thirteen. To them, young is six and seven. Girls who are six or seven do like pink.

As far as the content being traditionally coded as feminine, we did go to the girls and ask them what they wanted, and some of the things they want are traditional. They want to look at different outfits, for example. And some of the things are not stereotypical at all: they want to know about sports; they want to know about girls in other cultures. So we don't try to exclude anything just because it might be linked to femininity or masculinity within our culture. Our products just include things that girls say they're interested in. (See Plates

10 and 11.) In some ways we are pushing the cultural envelope for these girls, but in other ways we're responding to where our culture is right now. We're not trying the change the entire world from a small company of seven women. The thing that was important for us when we w· · dealing with traditional feminine topics like clothing was just to keep it from being in any way judgmental. We gave them a lot of information about food and nutrition. We didn't tell them, "Don't eat this or that because you're going to get fat." We just told them if they were going to have a soccer match the next day, they'd want to eat spaghetti for dinner because it's got carbohydrates. And for the clothing part of the game, we aren't telling them if your body is shaped like this, you need to wear this to de-emphasize this or that part of your anatomy. It's more about playing with your identity, trying on different outfits, not trying to funnel them into something stereotypical, like you must wear three inch spike heels. We didn't exclude topics that some people might consider traditionally feminine but we didn't emphasize them as a central part of being female either.

Q: Where would you like to see the next generation of Girl Games go?
A: More personalized. I just wish that the computer was able to understand the girls more and respond to them in an individualized way rather than having a preset bank of potential answers. And that's really what any program now is going to do. It's going to only give them what it's got preprogrammed, it can't invent something on the fly, and I really want to see that happen. One way we've found to overcome current limitations is by having the girl put more of herself into the game through the diary and scrapbook sections.

Q: Can you talk a little bit about those sections?
A: All of those features are found in a section called the "Meta Book," which has a diary, a personal planner, a scrapbook, and an address book. It's password protected. You can type in your journal entries and you can also import photographs. You can save pictures from other parts of the game, and there's a bank of clip art that you can put in whenever you want. And if you have a scanner, you can scan in your own photographs or you can download them from the net, or if you have a photo CD, you can import images from it. The girls can personalize the program through that section. You can also fill out quizzes and get a personalized response, like a quiz in a book. But each quiz is its own separate unit, so it doesn't pull information from the others and reinterpret the results based on what you've already said.

Girls don't want the games to be quite so self-contained, but within the limitations of the development software we're using and the user's hardware, which is usually pretty limited technology, we've tried to do what we can to make it more personalized. It knows her birthday. It can tell her biorhythms. It knows the girl's name, too. Even so, it's always pretty clear that it's canned.

The diary is an important feature. We know that girls like to write. They're typically more verbal than boys. One way to keep them at the computer is to have something that is of recurring value. After you take a quiz and find out the answers, you can give different answers and pretend you are somebody else. You can have your friends take it and then compare the results. We have things that girls can take out into their everyday lives. That's another thing to add to that laundry list of things that girls want—they want things that relate to their life. So, once they've played the game, they can still write in their diary. They can write about their experiences and what they found out about their friends. And the scrapbook allows them to import pictures of their friends, or pictures that relate to things that are interesting to them. And they can put pictures from the scrapbook into the planner—maybe mark somebody's birthday with a birthday cake. They can write in special events on the planner, their dance rehearsal, their choir practice, their debate team meeting. All of this makes the game much more personalized and integrates the girls' outside world into the computer experience.

The other user-tested and-approved feature of the diary is that it has a panic button you can hit if somebody walks in on you that you don't want to see it. And they really like that. There are many times when girls are writing something in their diary and someone barges into the room. With a real diary, you can close it. On the screen, you have to find a way to protect your privacy. The panic button doesn't erase what you're doing, it just hides it. You can come back to it later. It's important for the girls to know that when they write in their diary, it's personal, and they can keep it away from their brother or sister.

Q: This focus on privacy suggests that you see your product as a way to allow for personal exploration. But other research suggests that girls play more in groups than boys. How do girls play with your product—alone or in groups?
A: Both. And that's something that we did take into consideration before we made the game. It's very much about their relationships with their friends, and we know that's of primary importance to young girls. So, there is content related to issues of friendship and the interface is designed to be used with friends. When you take a quiz, your answers don't just disappear. You can

always go back to them and compare them with what someone else has to say in response to the same questions. And many girls do want to have their friends come and play with them. We also have it set up so that if you install a separate set of files on your hard drive, three sisters can all use the same game, and they could save different settings for each one of them. That's still more individual play, though. It's just that the product is adaptable to many different situations. You can play it alone. You can have different people playing it alone. You can also play it in groups. In our focus groups, we observed that first-hand: they like to play in groups. It's interesting to see them attempting to be a little bit democratic and give group answers, when one person has control over the mouse—but they do it. When they have to make a decision, they'll all give their opinion about what the decision should be. Then the person who has control over the mouse makes the choice. But there's always the chance to go back and see how other people's decisions would have turned out. And they do that.

Q: In what ways does your company encourage creative expression, or encourage girls to find their own voices or tell their own stories?
A: I think these goals are more fully achieved on the website. In the future, we plan for the games we develop to become more flexible. Right now, once you develop and produce a game, it doesn't really change much after that. There are some narrative things going on in "Let's Talk About Me." There's a section called "Cyber-Pals" that deals with different girls from around the world and what their lives are like. There's a section with adult mentors, who tell about their childhoods and what led them to do what they're doing in the present. That section places emphasis on adult women and girls talking to each other about their lives and their goals. There's also a section called "True Stories" that deals with different topical issues for girls and asks them to choose how they would respond. It's not a multibranching narrative, but the outcome is different based on the answer the girl chooses. But as far as empowering the girls to tell their own stories, that is something that's difficult to do right now in a CD-ROM medium, because there's really nowhere for it to go—except in the personal diary.

However, on the Web there are many opportunities to share your ideas with other girls. I'd say 50 percent of the material on our website consists of girls telling their own stories. We have a 'zine called *Girls Interwire,* with a staff of high-school-age interns who write the material. Part of its purpose is to create dialogue with the girls. At the end of an article, there will be questions that elicit response from readers. We give them the opportunity to e-mail us back, and then we run those responses in the next issue. It's very much about girls talking about their lives and how issues relate to them. They can get a more global perspective on their individual situations, and they enjoy sharing their opinions with a larger audience. It also helps adults to hear the voices of these girls, to figure out what's going on with them, what they are interested in, what their struggles are. There's also a section called "Girl on the Street." She is a roving reporter who goes around and asks random questions that are usually pretty silly. We're not trying to ask the pithy, meaning-of-life questions, but simply trying to get a sense of playfulness or fantasy, to have them look at an aspect of their life in a different way. A question we asked recently was to "describe your ideal friend." They're very happy to tell us what they think, and they usually say that an ideal friend would not be judgmental, would like the same things I like, and would always be there for me. Last week we asked, "If you started a band, what would it be called, and what instrument would you play?" And they love that, because they all want to start a band. It's part of the Hanson revolution. There are parts of the site that have narratives that we write, but we ask girls to make suggestions for what future narratives should be about. They usually send really good ideas, and we try to work those in. It's nice to be able to be responsive so quickly on the Web, which is unlike a CD-ROM, where we have, at best, a one-year turnaround. And I'm sure it's really gratifying for the girls to go on the site and see some things that they directly influenced.

Q: What is your corporate mission?
A: Aside from trying to get girls interested in technology, self-expression is really our other main goal. Our motto is, "express and connect." It's about girls being vocal about their interests and opinions, not being hesitant about expressing their needs and concerns. Many girls are concerned about social issues and the environment. We want them to use the technology as a way to express themselves to each other and to the world.

Q: Do you have a personal mission?
A: For me, the self-esteem issues are key. I want to raise or maintain girls' self-esteem as they enter into the preteen years. Research shows girls have a high level of self-esteem in elementary school and then it goes down. If you can just maintain the level of self-esteem they have before they start hitting up against culture's various expectations for them, then you're doing well. My

other goals are long-term, like changing the way the interfaces work, the way we interact with computers, to make computers more responsive.

Q: You seem to have an interest in critical theory. How do you bring critical theory into your company's products?

A: My personal interest in critical theory means pushing to go as far as possible as a humane company. I do not have ultimate decision-making power on the information that goes in our products, since we are working with outside publishers. But speaking purely personally, I think girls in our culture are a little bit overprotected from the truth. For instance, the statistics for teen suicides based on sexual orientation are something you just can't ignore. Teenagers are coming into their sexuality and they're questioning who they are. If it's something apart from the norm, then that's potentially even more damaging to their self-esteem because they are denied information. Any sexuality issue is much harder to include in a product made for preteen girls, but I refuse to be complacent, even as I'm aware of how little the market can tolerate along those lines.

Q: You said that you're really part of a new generation of game designers. How do you think designing games for girls will cause us to redefine how we think about computers or how women might interact with computers?

A: I think we'll see how dumb computers are right now, because computers are so good at doing "boy" games. So many people enjoy those that it makes computers look like they're doing a lot. But computers are stupid. If you look at the whole spectrum of human interaction, computers can barely do anything. I think that girls will really want kinds of interaction that the computer can't give them right now. And they're not afraid to tell you so. That's why they don't like very many of the products out on the market right now. Those products can't do anything interesting, as far as many girls are concerned. Having a new market to address means that there is going to be just one more push towards making computers do something that they don't do very well yet, or do only in limited contexts. An expert system can know things, but everything is so circumscribed. Voice recognition works under only very limited conditions. Having an audience for computer software that doesn't just accept bigger, faster, more guts and more blood is going to push the industry to adapt more quickly to alternative conceptions of what a computer could do.

Take the Tamagotchi or the virtual pets that are coming out here in response to the popularity of Tamagotchis in Japan. The Tamagotchi is small, it's cheap, and it's a computer that goes around with the girls. The virtual pet is an example of a computer that responds very, very specifically to the user's input, and also creates a relationship with them. It's really a parent-child relationship; they have life-or-death power over their little pet. It's a move toward more emotional involvement with the computers, and a move toward the personalization, the responsiveness, girls want from their computers. Gosh—I could write another thesis on that! We did an article in our online 'zine on Tamagotchi and got tons and tons of responses. So many girls have these. A lot of the responses were about their relationships with other people as regards the Tamagotchi. One of them said, "Me and my friend wanted to go swimming. I've been taking care of this Tamagotchi for days. And so my dad offers to take care of it. And we went swimming, and we came back two hours later, and it was sitting in its own poop and it was sick. Dad didn't know how to take care of it." So, the letter was all about her being mad at her dad for not being a good caretaker of her pet. When the technologies are portable and you're taking them to the pool with you, suddenly it becomes part of your relationship with other people, not just about your relationship with the computer. What other kind of computer technology would be banned at schools? This one is so engrossing and so, so needy. This computer is needy. Girl Games isn't going to get into the virtual pet business. But the Tamagotchi reinforces the things we know about girls' relationships to technology. What would happen if computers were so small that you took them everywhere you went? What would happen if computers needed you more than you needed them? Right now, a lot of girls are having to sit in their dad's office in front of a computer and it is not in their personal space. It's hard for them to feel intimate with the technology under those kinds of conditions.

Q: Do you consider Girl Games to be an example of entrepreneurial feminism?
A: I did a little math last night when I was looking over that question, and all of the in-house staff are female. A lot of the contractors we work with are male, so it probably ends up being about fifty-fifty. Laura has been very fortunate that this all happened at a time when there are many talented women in the fields she needed. We all were attracted to this company for its goals and we applied here for various reasons, but we are all highly skilled and she didn't have to compromise at all to hire the staff she did. She hired based on talent and passion, not gender.

Q: What struggles has the company had in trying to reconcile the feminist philosophy of the employees and the founders with the demands of the marketplace?

A: I'm just going to use the example of the first game, because after that, it was pretty clear what our limitations were going to be, and we've worked within them. For the first game, we really wanted to include more information about reproductive issues. And that wasn't acceptable for the publisher, not for this age group, even though the reality is that a lot of girls are becoming sexually active at that age. But the market is just not ready to accept that from a major game publisher. We didn't want to present it in a way that was advocating anything, but just giving them knowledge about what the various options were. We made that compromise in favor of getting something out there that would help girls on many, many, many other levels.

Q: How was that decision reached?

A: It was a discussion between the company, Girl Games, and the publisher, Simon & Schuster. With any developer-publisher relationship, the publisher is the one whose name goes on the product and who has to stand behind it. So you are always beholden to what they are able and willing to put their names on. We wanted to give girls the information, but Simon & Schuster has a relationship with the retailers and the market. The publisher has a certain understanding of what the market can and can't accept. They didn't see that kind of information in a game for young girls going over well. We aren't stupid; we didn't think, "Middle America is going to love this." But we thought if we presented it adequately and in the right way, it would be fine. And their opinion was that it just wouldn't work at all. There are always issues when you are a developer and you don't own the product, so you don't have a lot of control over how it's going to be handled. I'm not sure how much of that is related directly to our publisher and how much of that is true of any situation where you create something and then you don't have ultimate control over what happens to it.

Q: If women begin entering the male-dominated computer industry, do you see the potential for different managerial styles, different producer-consumer relations, and different types of products?

A: Of those things you mentioned, I focused immediately on different producer-consumer relations. That's where I have seen a major shift coming from our company. People do see that we're trying to do something good. We're a company, but we're also trying to make headway to improve girls' lives. And people really admire that, and it really changes the way they interact with you as a company. We make outreach in the community one of our major goals, doing Take Our Daughters to Work Day, having staff members speak at career days at schools, bringing in Girl Scout troops, things like that. Activism is part of our job description. I don't think that is the case with larger corporations. Our consumers really count on us to be doing the right thing and to be responsive to them. They're not looking for us to just be an entertainer. It's a positive relationship, but it's also exhausting. It demands another level of energy that needs to be expended because we want the consumer to trust that we are doing something that's good for girls. We have to work harder than a lot of companies to prove ourselves. But, it's really what we're about. We need that feedback from the girls and their parents.

Q: How do you resolve the conflict between competing with other companies that are also producing girls' games and building an alliance with them, one that would help market and build a consumer base for all of your products?

A: The increased number of companies that are in this field right now only helps. There are differences between girls at different age groups, and that shapes our industry. So far, I don't see a lot of outright competition for the same age groups. When the industry starts to grow, there will be more competition, if more people enter this field. Right now, we've all found a comfortable place. This is a market that did not exist until a year and a half ago. Everyone is ecstatic that there is a girls' market, and every new company that gets involved just serves to increase that market. I don't think there would be any advantage to being the only game company for girls. Girls are going to get more sophisticated and they are going to want different kinds of games, and we'll continue to make them.

Q: How does Girl Games deal with the problems of distribution?

A: In this industry, publishers handle distribution for the most part. Simon & Schuster, the publisher of "Let's Talk About Me," is a book company; they're really good at getting the product into bookstores but it was hard to get the product into game stores. The stores didn't know where to put it, and they'd only order a couple of copies because, "obviously," no girl likes games. Then Laura would be interviewed on television, and within a couple of hours the two copies would be snatched from the shelf, and then people would come to that store and think our product wasn't available because they couldn't find it. They'd ask the staff for it, and the store employees would say they'd never heard of it. When there's only two copies, there's not a lot of opportunity for the staff to get to know that it's there and what it does. We ran into many situations where we had lots of media attention and yet could not turn that into sales because the product just wasn't there, in the computer stores, for people to buy. And so we've pursued a lot of alternative distribution channels. We've sold quite a number of units through direct sales with our toll-free number. And Wet Seal and Contempo did a test market in ten cities and expanded from there, and we are selling very well through them. We're also going to be featured in Avon catalogs, so we're going directly into the home. Consumers don't even have to go to a computer store to buy it. Things have eased up a little since Barbie. There's probably going to be a girls' software aisle or section in the stores now.

Q: What other kinds of products are associated with Girl Games, in addition to the CD-ROM and the website?

A: Right now, we're finishing up production on two more CD-ROMs and a book, and we're preparing for the next slate of products. We're doing a follow-up to "Let's Talk About Me," called "Let's Talk About Me, Too," and we're doing a game based on the *Clueless* movie and TV show with Mattel. The book that's coming out is an exploratory journal based on the "Let's Talk About Me" property. We're developing a membership club, something to continue to keep girls interested in our technology, to keep them coming back to the website, and to give them something that they can really hold onto. The Tiara Club (see Plate 8) offers them things like a backpack, a T-shirt, a single-use camera. It's going to have three mailings a year with various items in them. It also gives them special access to a secret part of the website that's a members-only clubhouse online. And that has downloadable stuff that no one else has access to—things like custom screensavers and discount coupons.   ——*July 1997*

Chapter 8

Interviews with Theresa Duncan and Monica Gesue
(Chop Suey)

Theresa Duncan

Theresa Duncan's fascination with storytelling and writing comes out of her experience as a student at the University of Michigan and her interest in libraries. Originally aiming for a job as a librarian, she found herself working as a writer and editor at Magnet Interactive on the Vietnam Veterans' Memorial project, "Beyond the Wall." She produced her first CD-ROM project for girls, "Chop Suey," with artist Monica Gesue when they both worked for Magnet Interactive. The game received tremendous acclaim for its original design, lively graphics, and humorous approach to life in a small Midwestern town. Since "Chop Suey," Duncan has gone on to develop CD-ROMs "Smarty" and "Zero Zero," both of which also feature a young girl protagonist. She developed these recent software products with partner and graphic artist, Jeremy Blake. Currently they are both employed at Nicholson, New York, and working on a CD-ROM project, "The History of Glamour."

Q: How or why did you first become interested in producing girls' games or stories for girls?

A: It actually wasn't a conscious decision on my part to make things for girls, but I found when I was making games as a young woman that I drew on a lot of personal experience—the experiences of myself, my sister, my mother, my friends, and the women around me. I found it much, much easier to write about women. I used a lot of my own personal background and stories. I was always interested in children's literature, in the role of the female storyteller, and I've always been fascinated with the character of Alice in Wonderland. I was also very interested in the new technologies, like the Internet and MOOs and MUDs and chatrooms, when they started to come out, in terms of communicating with people and storytelling and identity.

Q: How did you first get interested in computers in relation to storytelling?

A: I was working as a writer and editor in Washington, D.C., and the first time I ever saw a Multiuser Dungeon, I thought it was a revelation. I found it fascinating. One of the things about the Web that I found so wonderful was its usefulness as a tool for research and knowledge. I used Gopher a lot at the University of Minnesota to look up things that I had never read before. It seemed sort of magical to me. I started to make interactive Valentines with an early thing called Hypercard. They were mainly collage, and things that could transform, and they had music. Then a friend of mine who worked in television, and who knew I was interested in CD-ROMs and new technologies, went to a trade show, and they had interactive television stuff there. And they also had some CD-ROM companies, and he picked up some information about one in Washington, and I applied the next day and got the job. That was as a researcher on a project about the Vietnam Veterans' Memorial, so I worked as a writer and a researcher on that project. Based on my writing ability, I took over more and more of the writing tasks on "Beyond the Wall," because I was one of the strongest writers Magnet Interactive had. I was just a production assistant when I started, but then eventually I got into more research and writing. Then Monica and I came up with an idea for a children's story called "Chop Suey." Magnet Interactive was wealthy, since at the time CD-ROMs were booming, so even though I had no experience as a game designer, they let us design the game.

Q: One thing that distinguishes your products, like "Chop Suey" and "Smarty," is that they are games but they are also stories. Can you talk a little about that?

A: "Chop Suey" is a complicated example, because while it's really fun to play, it's also self-conscious, which probably reflects some of the things that were trendy, like post-structuralist theory, like deconstruction and Derrida, stuff that I was really into when I was in school. In fact, one particular company was interested in hiring me, but they accused me of making a "deconstructed girlhood memoir," and they didn't like that. I was essentially looking at a girlhood memoir from a somewhat ironic standpoint, playing on the conventional ways that people talk about their relatives or being a girl or looking back on being a girl. I consider myself an artist. I have my own company now, because I've been successful and people have responded really well to the CD-ROMs, but I don't do focus-group testing and I don't consider things like that, and I don't really try to figure out what the market can bear and I don't do toys and I'm not trying to cross-market.

Q: Why do you think the products have been so successful?
A: I think a lot of CD-ROMs don't really aim for the heights that a movie or literature or even a television show does. The medium hasn't really hit its stride. I think there's too much emphasis put on selling them and marketing them. I think that most people want to adhere to the conventions of the medium and don't want to take chances, because CD-ROMs are expensive to make. The industry as a whole seems kind of shortsighted to me, in that they're not really stretching it, they're not trying to make the best thing that they can; they're trying to make the thing that will sell the most. In 1993, when I started making "Chop Suey," there were no other girl games, and people picked up on it as a girl game, but "games for girls" wasn't really the marketing mantra that it is now. I find some of the attention paid to girls recently patronizing, and I think that has a lot to do with girls' pocketbooks. I'm sure a lot of these companies know the amount of disposable income that the average twelve-year-old has, what their allowance is, what their buying patterns are.

Q: How did you decide to pursue a project just for girls?
A: It wasn't really a decision that was based on anything other than that it was really enjoyable. It was a wonderful thing to do, and it was more fun for me than working on somebody else's projects. It's a lot about memory, as a general topic and as personal memory as well. A lot of the facts are taken from the life of Monica Gesue—the art director and illustrator—and some of them are from my life, too. She supplied me with some elements that she wanted in the story, and we both have Midwestern backgrounds, so we had that in common. So it was a labor of love all the way, but it was also our personal tropes: Midwestern things, these very broad, shared experiences that we had.

Q: Why did you use the Midwest?
A: One of the reasons I used the Midwest for a background was that it's wide-open, so there's a lot of room for exploration. I didn't want to set it in an urban setting; the Midwest is less self-conscious and less ironic, and I wanted to make a story that was very direct and about very small lives. Not about what would

be considered very important people, but just the incredible dimension that there is in a child's life or in a gas-station attendant's life; they all have memories and experiences that are very intimate and very beautiful—full lives—even though they're people like third-rate chorus girls and gas-station attendants. So it was essentially, too, about the working class, because my background is pretty working-class. I wanted to bring glamour to the dime stores and the garden patches and the fireflies. And it was also about magic being found in unexpected places, the mystery and beauty of just hanging out at the picnic table for an afternoon. I think that's something that's missing from a lot of kids' entertainment lately. Maybe some of the older movies have a sense of joy about them and the real sort of languor of when you're a kid, how time seems forever—something that's going to happen next week is way too far away. But right now, even in things like Nickelodeon, everything seems to be very fast-paced, and emphasis is on children learning, learning, learning, learning, or developing socially. So mine are not directed towards trying to get kids to do anything other than experience life as being mysterious and lovely. Also, I wanted to expose them to the sound and cadence of really beautiful words, so the writing that I have is really sing-songy and kind of demented. I like this aspect; it's a little too alliterative, it has a twist to it. It's kind of unusual, like *Pee-Wee's Playhouse*. But it is bringing the average into the extraordinary.

Part of the discovery process in the game is that all the people in this town are interconnected and they're eccentrics and you never know what's going to happen next. For example, the guy in the candy store in "Chop Suey" has tattoos all over his body and a five-o'clock shadow, so he looks sinister—but he's not; it's like the experience of the weird guy in the store that you're afraid of when you're little. I've always liked characters; I still do. I wanted to create a sense of inquisitiveness and wonder with characters—a kind of, "Wow, what's going on here?" When I was a kid, *Harriet, the Spy* was one of my favorite books. But the people that Harriet spied on weren't just normal people; they had problems, like the rich woman who is bound to her bed. Harriet just found her fascinating. There's a sense of bittersweet experience in "Chop Suey," where not everyone has had a perfect life but they're all happy people. Vera has three ex-husbands all named Bob, and that was a problem for people at Magnet where I was working. They were saying, "We can never market this," and "People aren't going to like it." Vera has problems, but she's also filled with love. She's a very vibrant person, and that's why she fascinates the little girls. (See Plate 13.) And I guess that mirrors the fascination I have with that sort of character. A lot of people want to project this fantasy of purity and innocence onto children, but

I think it deprives them of some of the richness of their lives, because they really do have complicated feelings and they might not always be the perfect child that doesn't get jealous of their brother and doesn't have problems with people in school and things like that. Kids see a lot, and they're wise and they're a little more complicated than most people give them credit for being, and they're smart. So "Chop Suey" doesn't talk down to kids.

Q: What are the distinguishing characteristics of "Chop Suey"?
A: I think that the writing isn't bloodless. I tried to keep it kind of loopy and sinuous. There's alliterative writing like, "Aunt Vera's life was a series of magical stories like little pearls on a long, long necklace." The focus is on adults through the eyes of children, but, also, the kids are very independent. They're allowed to be independent and to explore, which is good for girls. It's one of the things I think is particularly good for girls, because it's not coercive. It doesn't tell them how to think, it doesn't tell them where to go, and there's no object to the games that I make or the stories that I make. They drift, they're meandering, rambling, like really being in a Midwestern town and discovering connections between people and what's next door to the pet shop or what happens when, you know, you click on a certain window downtown and you see something kind of surprising. It takes place over a long period of time, and it takes a while to discover the connections among people and why Vera lives here and what she used to do and why the girls are so crazy about her.

Q: Is there a particular story that you want told?
A: "Chop Suey" is not a traditional story; it's more like a series of vignettes. It works the same way that *Alice in Wonderland* does, where she leaves home and then she has a series of adventures, but if you took everything in between the beginning and the end of *Alice in Wonderland* and scrambled up every chapter, it would make no difference to the development of the story. She can meet the Caterpillar first and then the Red Knight or the Walrus, and it doesn't matter. It's about this cheerful surreality where you click on something average and it turns into something extraordinary. It's more about atmosphere than narrative, but it's also very much about language. And the moral of the story is appreciating beauty in ordinary surroundings. It works the way that real life does: all these things happen to you, but there's no magical event, like there is sometimes in books, that transforms you. In terms of there being some big, dramatic story or arc of the plot, it doesn't exist there. I wanted girls to have the opportu-

nity to go where they wanted to go. It doesn't progress; these events don't really progress in time. They're sort of outside of time.

Q: In what ways are the players encouraged to tell stories?

A: If the memoir of the guy that works in the gas station or the guy with all the tattoos or the story of any of these people is important, then everyone's story is important. And also, the girls don't have to speak thirteen languages and play the violin; there seems to be all this stress on having to be educated in children's games. I kind of wanted to thumb my nose at that idea: some of the games are deliberately cheesy or you're rewarded very simply. Obviously, education is extremely important for girls, but I also think it's important for kids to be kids and for girls just to be allowed to hang out and have room for imagination. But, also, one of the main benefits of "Chop Suey" is that it shows that you should trust your own opinion and trust your own experiences, no matter how small, that they're important. I think one of the similarities between "Chop Suey" and something like *Pee-Wee's Playhouse* is they make fun of the conventions of children's entertainment. For example, in "Smarty" there are several television commercials, and one is called "Signor Sudsalot," and it says, "It's got a lot of what the others have not!" It essentially makes fun of these advertising claims or the claims of CD-ROM producers or Hollywood producers that, "We are good for kids, and we're going to dictate to them what they like." So it's satirical, and I know that kids get it because I've watched them get it, and they think it's hilarious.

Q: How do children react? What kinds of responses have you had?

A: I get a lot of calls from parents, and one woman called and said, "OK, 'Barbie' lasted forty-five minutes on Christmas morning, and it's April now and they're still playing 'Smarty' and they still haven't found everything and they haven't made all the connections between people." So she ordered four for her nieces. The people that like "Smarty" and "Chop Suey" are evangelical. It doesn't look like other CD-ROMs—that's what they say. So kids respond to it, because there is a depth to it and it's not coercive. But the thing is it really fires their imagination: Who are these people? It's an experience. It has a real sense of place. It's like reading a really good book and remembering it, and that's what I'm trying to create. Like *Harriet, the Spy*. You don't have to be explicit, and the problems don't have to be writ large. They can be subtle, like they are in life. And if Sport sat down and said to Harriet the Spy, "I have a big problem because

Figure 8.1: This navigational map from "Smarty" captures the game's small-town American atmosphere. Copyright Theresa Duncan, 1996. Used with permission.

my dad's . . . ."—children don't talk like that. I think that some of the stuff for kids that is supposedly about dealing with problems is better done, like Bruno Bettelheim said, through fairy tales or through games that kids really like, and not in this didactic kind of "I'm a social worker" way. And so that's something that I really try not to do, but I still have characters that are complicated, since life is not always easy for children or adults.

Q: What's going to keep girls or boys coming back to the game?
A: First of all, with "Smarty," when we tested it, I know where everything is and it still took me six hours with my programmer to go through it. It's very difficult to find everything in it. It doesn't present itself immediately. You can go back to the same neighborhood and notice a store that you never noticed before, and there are things that you might not notice about characters. For example, you'll see in one person's living room a letter from another character that you didn't notice before, and then you realize that Percy and Aunt Olive

used to be coworkers at the hamburger joint, the Wigwam Burger, which burned down and which was mentioned in another section. It's a process, like getting to know people. It's not a video, it doesn't present itself to you immediately, and all its secrets aren't revealed; it's more like a book, where you really have to spend time with it and its secrets aren't revealed in an hour. And there's no neat summation at the end once you've mastered it.

Q: Tell me your opinions about the age level of the game and how you think it might appeal to different ages at different times.

A: The games appeal to a rather broad age range, not only seven to twelve. In fact, adults really love "Chop Suey" and "Smarty." For example, there are Edgar Allan Posies, and a six-year-old isn't going to know what they are, but they're still beautiful, and you click on them and they dance. And thirteen-year-olds are going to think they're smart because they know what those are, and they're going to get the pun. And in "Smarty," Smarty is a little girl, but her Aunt Olive, who is one of the important characters in the CD-ROM, is a teenager. So an older girl, a twelve-year-old, is probably going to think the waitress—the teenage waitress with the pink uniform and the shiny convertible—is really cool and is going to identify with Aunt Olive, but a little six-year-old will identify with the seven- or eight-year-old Smarty. Well, actually, older girls said Smarty was for babies. Like a thirteen-year-old girl would receive it and she would say it was for babies. But it is pretty much for younger girls, so. . .

But also, I have ideas for games for older girls. I have one game called "Apocalipstick," and it moves like "Doom." I mean, that's exactly how it moves, and the stuff comes at you really fast. But I think that those games appeal to adolescents that move really quickly, the games for men—for boys, actually. The reason is that, inasmuch as adolescence is a hard time for women, it's a very hard time for men, too. Their bodies are changing rapidly, and I think that has a lot to do with identifying with people who are Protean, weird superhero characters that get bigger and smaller. I think that's true of girls, too, and that's something about Alice in Wonderland I find interesting, her changes in size. But I also think that in adolescence you have to coolly master change; there's an enormous amount of change in what's expected of you in becoming a man or learning to drive, all this responsibility. So I think the speed of the games, and the fact that you have to think really quickly and work out problems on the fly, those are things that adolescents are expected to master, and I think it crudely mirrors that kind of speed.

Theresa Duncan and Monica Gesue

Q: Why do you think those qualities you've just mentioned aren't usually in programs for girls?

A: Probably because of the same thing that I said about children, that people want to believe that children are supremely innocent. I think people also want to believe that women aren't aggressive and that women don't like violent games. Also, to make a game like that is enormously expensive.

Q: Tell me about the aesthetic choices you made.

A: If you look at a lot of computer art or even computer games, the screen is hard, it's alienating, you're not holding anything in your hands. And a lot of computer art, too, can look kind of pixely. Our goal was not to be the most technically advanced but to make it look almost like folk art, to bring the human being back into it, so that it looked handmade and you could see where Monica had drawn inside or outside the lines. It's very warm. Also, the point of view of the game is first person; you never see the main characters because you are the main character. You only see the hands and feet; you're supposed to be identifying with them almost as if you were inside their heads. The identification is complete and you're really in the story and you feel for this person. In "Chop Suey," you're supposed to be seeing everything from the point of view of the little girls. And we keep in mind the point of view of a child, where things look big. Or, kids will get fascinated with something that you and I won't, like they'll find something on the street, like a pretty blue piece of glass or a bottle cap or something, and become fascinated with it. Kids really do seem to have more time; time is expanded for them. So there's this sense of being able to really take time and look at everything. I've never liked verisimilitude, to tell you the truth. And so the art is almost like entering into a little world; it exalts the average.

Q: In what way do these aesthetic choices, particularly the pace, relate to your conceptions about the girl audience?

A: I'm not going to say what girls like or don't like because, frankly, I don't feel that I speak for all girls. "Chop Suey" is not something that I think will appeal to everyone, and it wasn't made to appeal to everyone, but if it does, fabulous. I'm not trying to reach the broadest audience to get the most consumer dollars. I'm not going to say, "Girls don't like X" or "Girls don't like Y," because I think it's kind of prescriptive, and that leaves a lot of girls out, too. My stated goal in life is to make the most beautiful thing a seven-year-old has ever seen. The main thing that I would like for "Chop Suey" is for it to be on sale when these girls have daughters, and they're, like, "Oh, my God, I remember!" That's why there's no real hip slang, there's no real contemporary issues, it's not dated; I think it's timeless.

Q: Traditional boys' games concentrate on a movement through space, whereas your program doesn't necessarily do that.
A: One of the main reasons for that is because it's technically difficult and it's expensive to emulate. Honestly, because otherwise I would do it in a second. So that was kind of my personal aesthetic, to be more literary and meandering, which is something that I do like. But it did start to bother me, too, and I thought that it might be good for girls to have the sense of speed and activity and action. That's why in my new game the girl is extremely active. She goes around and around and around, and the entire interface moves across the rooftops of Paris, jumps from one roof to another and down the chimney and out again, and she knows everybody in her neighborhood. The main interface that you see is Paris. (See Plate 14.) It's New Year's Eve, 1899, "the hinge on which the century turns," so it says. There's a little girl, her name is Pinkee, she sells firewood, she's obsessed—her nurse brought her to the fire the night that she was born because she was crying. So she loves the look and she loves the tinderbox and she loves the andirons and she loves everything to do with the energy of fire, so she sells coals and firewood. But she goes across the rooftops and she asks everyone about the future. The future starts tonight at midnight; it's going to be 1900, that's why it's called "Zero Zero," from the two zeroes. It's actually a millennial tale for kids, because the year 2000 is coming up and I notice a lot of millennial stuff, and most of it's based on anxiety, but this CD is based on optimism and hope. One of the reasons I set it in 1900 is because in that period a lot of the adults were fearful of technologies like the gramophone and the movies and things that we've already mastered and take for granted. I think a lot of this millennial anxiety is based on technology and I think it is unfounded and unhealthy. So that's why I set it in 1900. Pinkee asks this woman, Genevieve, what the future is going to be like, and Genevieve says, "Oh, they're going to enclose all of Paris under this great glass dome, and it will be springtime all year round, and the roses will bloom in December." So everybody has this really subjective take, but then again we come back to trying to instill a healthy amount of skepticism in children. This little girl does not buy any of it; she's very sassy and she's very sweet, too, but she seems to be skeptical of what people are telling her. In the end, she realizes that you can't guess the

future, you make the future, you forge the future, and she's a little girl, so it turns out *she* is the future.

Q: What do you want girls to walk away with?

A: Independence, curiosity, a sense of exploration, and also a sense that she doesn't have to take "no" for an answer. To not let other people erode your expectations for the future. Very young girls will have that sense that they can do anything, and they'll be very vibrant, and they'll be, "Oh, I want to be an astronaut!," but by the time they're twelve or thirteen they might have problems in school or with their self-image.

Q: What do you envision for the future of computer games or video games, or what would you like to see happen?

A: What I'd really like to see is much, much more variety in games for both men and women. I don't think that men would mind more nuance in their shoot-'em-up games, and I don't know that they'd mind more intelligence, more story, more atmosphere. In fact, maybe girl games will rub off on games that are explicitly for men and just make them better, as well. If they can see those sorts of intelligent games, with thoughtful human beings, succeed with women, maybe they'll think that they'll succeed with men, as well.

Q: Some of the video games, your products included, are coded as "girls' products," with an emphasis on clothes, sometimes certain colors, behaviors, choices. In many senses, they celebrate aspects of femininity or female-coded behavior that might alarm feminists. How would you defend some of these choices?

A: "Feminists" is an extremely broad spectrum, so some feminists might like the way that I portray femininity and some might not. I really like to celebrate glamour, and I don't think that this necessarily reinforces harmful, culturally coded behavior. I think I'm kind of trendy, so I think it's about the possibility for change and transformation. Walter Ong said, "The grammar girls are really glamour girls," and in fact the words "grammar" and "glamour" have the same etymology. I think grammar is a vocabulary, but I think glamour is, too. I think it's about not being afraid to shine. I think there's something very empowering about that. For example, you read a lot of adolescent literature where girls want to hide their breasts, or they're worried about their hips or these changes in their body, but I celebrate that. So Vera is kind of like an aunt, with the cleavage and the husky cigarette voice and things like that. But I do think that there's something insipid about showing girls going to the mall and this kind of thing; the whole consumerist angle about it, as if women are somehow the consumers. I think that in sophisticated places there's almost an irony to having very high heels on and being very tall. It could go either way. You can say, "Well, they're hard to walk in and they make you less mobile," and things like that, but at the same time, "I'm a large person."

For example, in "Smarty," Aunt Olive and Smarty go to the dime store—and this is something that I remember specifically from my own life, being seven-years-old and being given a dollar every Saturday for my allowance and getting to pick out whatever I wanted. That dollar was so empowering, and the dime store was the caves of Ali Baba, because I could buy yarn or a goldfish or this Blue Waltz perfume that they used to sell for ninety-nine cents. So it's just being able to have that choice, and I love and celebrate that, too. The narrator says, "They went to the Dollar Dream Store, and you could get compacts that played 'La Vie en Rose' when you powdered your nose, decks of cards decorated with sad-eyed kittens, or perfume that came in six-pack cans," and Aunt Olive says, "The things that dreams are made of." It's the difference between having someone who bases their entire identity on clothes or someone for whom that's a part of their life and a part of their decision about what to be in life, and not someone who lets things like that override their identity. I do like glamour, but we also have a fashion magazine in "Smarty" that sends up fashion magazines. For example, you open it and it says, "'I like my big ears,' says model Theda," and she has enormous ears.

Q: Can you talk a little bit about your team and the male/female combination? We're defining entrepreneurial feminism as a team of women developing a product. What aspects of that combo created the product? What effect did that have on the product that was created?
A: I didn't deliberately found it on a feminist premise. But I feel like it's evolved into that, rather than it being a very conscious decision. I'm twenty-eight, and my mother probably strongly identified herself as a feminist and still does very consciously. And I do, too, but I think it becomes more and more easy for women in our generation to forget all the work that was done by women in previous generations, and to forget how important it was to be a feminist, and how important it was to be considerate of other women to make advances for all women. I think that, because a lot of work has been done, sometimes I'm not that conscious, and I don't think of myself as a feminist game company but I probably am.

But I've always been very self-determined, and I find it difficult to work for someone who's dictating to me what my product should be like, so I insisted on complete creative control both times, which is a miracle, an absolute miracle. Nobody gets that. The first time I worked for a very wealthy company, CD-ROMs were booming, you know, it looked like it was going to be a huge market, so I was lucky that I made one when I did. But now, because of the success of the first one, I can say, "I'm the expert because I made this and I have accomplished this," so in that way I've been lucky. I did become conscious that there were no women making titles where I worked, and that all the games they were making at Magnet at the time were supermacho, and I think this contributed to their downfall, because they no longer make games. But there was a serious rivalry among these groups of men who were making games, like, "We're going to kick your ass and our game's going to sell more than your game." So they created this competitive edge that I was actually more than happy to join in, and I was like, "Oh, really? And I'm making a game for little girls, and we'll see." And so I had that attitude, too. I think competition is really, really good—definitely. I think it can spur people on to really good things.

I think I do have a vivid sense of what girls will like, and Monica also had that sense, where my new illustrator, who is a man and my boyfriend, brings a different perspective to femininity and adds details that boys—who I know also enjoy "Smarty" and my new game "Zero Zero"—will like. But I do think that there was with Monica a definite ease, a really shared sense of what a nine-year-old would respond to. And it's a talent in some ways, too, and I don't think it can be constructed like a Frankenstein's monster out of focus-group testing. Take, for example, a book by Maurice Sendak; it's like taking that theme and focus-group testing it, and then with the information trying to create a Maurice Sendak book. But you can't, because it will have a body but no soul. Instead of billionaires funding companies that are based on research, I'd really like to see high-school girls make a title. If somebody gave me money to start a girls'-game title, I'd have a contest for girls all over the United States to submit an idea for a CD-ROM. I would love to work with high-school girls. "Smarty" is supposed to be about this little genius; it makes fun of the idea of the expert—there's a pundit a minute these days in girls' games, and everybody wants to be The Voice.

Q: How do you think using computers in new ways and designing games for girls will change the way we think about girls or redefine how we think about computers?

A: CD-ROMs—I love the medium! I think they're brilliant. I think they're a really unique form of storytelling. (See Plate 15.) There is a linguist who calls videos and performances and CD-ROMs "secondary orality," as if we're moving from a written culture back to an oral culture. CD-ROMs represent a different kind of storytelling and passing along information. And with the sounds and the sound effects and the cadence of people's voices in telling the story, you can control when someone says something. You can go back and almost question the material. So the whole thing is that the kid controls the point of access to the story and they also can control the speed. They can choose to examine the environment, and I think it encourages people to read.

Q: Do children, or any users of this, have to read or listen to the story in order to understand the whole picture?
A: No, and you don't need to understand the whole picture, either. There are a ton of games in "Zero Zero," for example It can be enjoyed on so many different levels. I personally love the story. I think it's so timely, and it's about all these things that kids are facing. But if one of the kids wants to say "forget this" and turn off the story and play the "firing champagne corks" or other bottle games, go for it. There's also a game that's like "Concentration" in the designer studio, and it's "match-the-bloomers"—all these different giant pairs of underwear with all these different patterns on it, and you have to remember where the pattern matches. So there's all this stuff that's really just like hanging out. It's like "Tetris," it's relaxing. I used to play this stupid "shoot-the-duck" game in "Chop Suey" to relax. It was so fun, and I would play it over and over again because I always wanted to win the ghost. You know what I mean? It's just like hanging out. So there's a lot there that's educational, and I think there's a lot there that's meaningful and a lot of thought went into it, but at the same time, if you want to just listen to "Frère Jacques" or the "Marseillaise," you can.

Q: Who is this game supposed to appeal to? Is it supposed to appeal to particular types of girls, like tomboys, or not?
A: No. No. Not at all. I picture it appealing to smart girls, but that's all girls. All kids are smart. I will say, not only do I want to encourage girls to play games, I want to encourage them to make games. I think just having their hands on the computer will move them towards that. I mean, I got my hands on a computer and I never dreamed that I would be making CD-ROMs. I had no idea I was going to be making computer games, you know? There are a lot of girls that are fascinated by the games that I make, so they're going to sit there and

play with the computer. Maybe they're going to wonder, "How is this made?" A girl might hate it and say, "I could do better."

Q: What's the difference between making games and telling stories?
A: I would say that the distinction is probably not as great as you'd think. It's the same kind of thing. Like in a story, I'll bring in something I heard that I thought was pretty. Like places that I think are cool, like I want to put in the Rainbow Room and the Pearly Palace. Like all this alliteration. I kind of pepper the visual aspects of the game with things that I like or things that are important to me. Or even broad cultural references—obviously, I would want to associate a champagne cork flying off for celebration with happiness. Grammar and games and glamour, all of it. Even on the box it says, "the grammar of glamour," and I think that there is something glamorous about being smart.

Q: Is there anything you would want to tell parents?
A: Honestly, to let their kids play with what they want. I think that's important. If I was a little girl today, I probably would enjoy playing "Barbie Fashion Designer" very much. If it's the only thing around, it is nefarious, but at the same time I think that it's naive and condescending to little girls to say that you can't play with this because you're going to absorb it all and become a robot who thinks that the size of your boobs is the only thing people are interested in. It's important to have a lot of different voices so that the girl has choices— let the girls have "Smarty" on the shelf next to "Rockett's New School" next to Barbie. Then, hopefully, she'll have a shelf full of books and a baseball glove and a football. You know what I mean? She doesn't let anybody dictate.

Monica Gesue

In contrast to the dark and metallic colors associated with the majority of video games, Monica Gesue pioneered the use of cartoonlike images and bright colors that were drawn deliberately to extend beyond the lines—an aethestic that has become a trademark for "Chop Suey" and other games for girls. Gesue worked as a photographer and artist at Magnet Interactive in Washington, D.C., where she created "Chop Suey" with Theresa Duncan. She has also worked as a senior game designer for Disney Interactive. Gesue is a freelance writer, illustrator, and producer, and the creator of children's television programs for Saban Entertainment and Storyopolis. In 1997 she founded Rinkiedink Productions, a multidiscipline studio that creates entertainment and content for kids. She enjoys freelancing because it allows her to work in her pajamas and have unlimited access to home-cooked snacks. Monica's work can be viewed at www. rinkiedink.com.

Q: What was your personal motivation in making "Chop Suey"?
A: In my early days at Magnet Interactive, a colleague showed me Richard Scarry's "Busy Town." Immediately a lightbulb illuminated. What appealed to me was the color, animation, and how absolutely simple it was. I thought CD-ROM was really a conducive medium for telling children's stories, kind of like a moving storybook. It appeared to be a perfect medium for a nonlinear narrative, which I was also interested in. It seemed like it would be a really enjoyable and easy project to make, but, boy, was I mistaken!

Q: What was your history with technology? Did you use computers?
A: Oh, gosh no! When I was in my last year of college, I took a computer class in Photoshop and I was incredibly pathetic. My instructor convinced me that I just didn't have the right kind of mind, you know, the left brain/right brain theory. I knew how to draw and write and take strong photographs, but I discovered that doing those things on the computer was a completely different basket of eggs. I learned the basics from working at Magnet. I'm completely self-taught from tutorials and practice. I know exactly how to do what I need to do to get the result I want, but it sure took a long time to get there. You really have to just think of it as another tool and relax. Believe me, if I can figure it out, anyone can.

Q: What's your attitude towards computers?
A: Drawing in Painter is my bliss, one of my greatest joys, and I do it everyday, if I can. I create all my illustrations on the computer using a combination of Painter and Photoshop. I use them for children's books, too. I think more artists and photographers are starting to work digitally. It's so much easier, and you can get such lovely results. I'm not much interested in anything else in computers. Sometimes I'll research things on the Internet. I'm not a big fan of e-mail, but that's another story.

Q: Tell us more about "Chop Suey."
A: Well, I don't see "Chop Suey" as a game. And actually, I don't even really see it as something specifically for girls. I think the reason that "Chop Suey" was appealing to the media wasn't because it was so brilliant but because it was different. "Chop Suey" has a definite sweet, mellifluous, quirky, la-di-da

quality about it. It also has a real sense of place and interesting, off-beat characters. It's based on my home town of Cortland, Ohio. It's all fictional, but some of the names are those of my relatives and people my family used to know. The game part really came later. We were asked to put those activities in by the higher powers, so we did it. "Chop Suey" really doesn't make a whole lot of sense, if you look at it closely, and it's riddled with problems. It's a tangled nest with absolutely no structure, but somehow it doesn't seem to matter. There really wasn't anyone else making creative titles and that was our little edge. Even today there's virtually no competition within CD-ROMs. Content can be incredibly mediocre and still be praised. CD-ROMs will never be on the level of children's books, where there's a rich history and a structure. CD-ROMs are like the wild west. It's an easy way to get published, especially under the guise of "children's." Maybe that's why books seem, and I believe are, more respectable and eternal.

Q: Can you describe what you see as the user's experience of using it?
A: "Chop Suey" is about personal exploration, discovering a small town at your own pace for your own interest level. You may linger in areas you enjoy and then scoot out of other sections that don't appeal to you. It's very low-key. There's no goal where you have to get from A to Z and accomplish something. I think people who enjoy games and traditional CD-ROMs expect a specific kind of journey and result at the end. "Chop Suey" is really just the journey. Suddenly at the end it's kind of the beginning again. It's all the same thing. I know I like that more than something that's really aggressive or violent. In the beginning, two girls are reclining on a lush, green hill. They've had too much candy and Chinese food. It's a tip of the hat to Windsor McKay's "Little Nemo in Slumberland." He had amazing, fanciful dreams because of what he ate before bed. So, the girls are dozing on the hill, and they gradually see clouds lilting by, and the clouds take the shapes of a teapot, a sneaker, and their kooky Aunt Vera. Somehow, reality or not, they're magically transported to the town where Vera lives. Suddenly we're presented with the map. At that point, the user can visit different places in the town. One area that has a plethora of activity is Vera's bedroom. Once at her house, users can creep further inside and enjoy tons of activities. They can go inside her lavish closet, spray her stinky perfumes, take pictures, or watch a short vignette of her salad days as a Rockette in New York City.

Q: What was your favorite part of the game? What was your one favorite thing?

A: I really love animals, and my favorite thing is the disappearing cat for kids to discover in every screen. There's really no point to it. It's just kind of sweet and fun. I also really like the observatory and the soliloquy of the moon. He looks down on the little town at night and revels in all the beautiful things he observes in the world. There are also lots of funny parts, puns and literary references that make it fun for older users.

Q: How many CD-ROMs had you played with when you developed "Chop Suey?"

A: Oh, maybe one. They honestly just don't interest me, especially games! It's just not my thing. I love children's books and children's art, but I've seen so little on the computer that really appeals to me. I really respect and admire my friend Rodney Allen Greenblat. He makes such clever, wonderful things for kids. He made "Dazzleoids" and "Rodney's Wonder Window." He's always been a really big influence for me. He's a painter, sculptor, writer, musician, and a digital wizard. I'd seen some of the things he'd made for David Vogler at Nickelodeon, like the Clickamajigs, and I just couldn't believe how simple and fun they were. I loved the fact that there really wasn't much of a point to them but to enjoy yourself for a moment or two. His art style is really perfect for the computer and it was by far the best I'd seen. I also really love the fact that he does absolutely everything independently at his own company, The Center For Advanced Whimsy.

Q: Do you think the fact that you hadn't played very many computer games influenced your design?

A: Sure, probably. I was a photographer before coming to Magnet. I was actually hired to do photography and Photoshop. I generally never looked at other photographers' work, partially because I wasn't that interested and partially because it can be distracting and influential. Some people enjoy and need that, but I don't. It's the same with CD-ROMs. I just didn't look at any because I didn't care. I found them alienating and boring. I knew there must be an audience like me out there who wasn't being served. Maybe it was young girls, maybe older, who knew?

Q: Why don't you like most games that are out there?

A: Well, I'm just not that interested. Aesthetically, they don't appeal to me. As soon as I start to look at a game or to play it, my mind begins to wander like in math class. They don't capture my attention. I don't really care whether I win or not. Within a couple of minutes I begin to think, "What am I doing?" Of course, this isn't true for all of us girls. I have a good friend who's a programmer and a producer and a serious, hard-core gamer. She just loves all different kinds of games, especially a recent one called "Tomb Raider." The main character is an ample-breasted gal, which makes it a little more interesting, I suppose. She enjoys all those Doomesque things, and thinks they're great fun—and, she makes them. Aside from that, she's pretty much just like me.

Q: Can you talk about your design process some?
A: Sure; I don't think I have one! "Chop Suey" was designed in about a half an hour. My partner at the time and I had to come up with a plot quickly. I had the initial idea that it should be about Cortland, this little Midwestern town, and two wee girls asleep on a green, grassy hill. And I saw the vision of the morphing clouds in a dream. We just went to Dean & Deluca and sat down with a pad of paper and said, "OK, these are the places they're going to go and this is what they're going to do." And it just grew from that. We had a skeleton and that's about it. My partner would write out parts of the text and another illustrator and I would draw our vision. We'd say, "Oh, what about this or that?" We all created it together as we went along. It changed and developed everyday. We would add parts and take huge sections out. We had a programmer who linked everything together for us. None of us had ever done anything like this before and we really didn't have a clue about how to make a CD-ROM. It was a long and difficult learning process. We adopted a real kitchen-sink-operation mentality when making "Chop Suey." It was possible for awhile, but at a big company like Magnet, we just couldn't maintain it. Truth be told, many people helped to make "Chop Suey"; just look at the list of end credits! Nowadays I lie on the couch and eat cookies and think for awhile, and then all of a sudden, I'll write four stories, or three shows, all in a row, and then for maybe two weeks, I won't be able to think of anything at all. Ideas really just come and go, so you can't get too attached to them, especially in Hollywood. Some days they're plentiful and others they're not. When you're working on a project like "Chop Suey," the everyday churning out of art can be incredibly arduous. Some days you just don't feel like being creative and your drawings are all crummy, but you have to keep going to get the project finished. It's different when you're a paid employee and you have to show up every day, clean, dressed, chipper,

and ready to work for seven hours. If you're lucky enough to work at home, as I do now, it's such a pleasure. I have TV, unlimited snacks, pajamas until 3:00, and I don't have to brush. I discipline myself, and that works for me.

Q: So, when you were designing "Chop Suey," what did you want to accomplish?
A: I wanted to create a lovely story that was colorful, warm, and bright and that had a different look and feel to it. (See Plate 12.) A lot of computer graphics at that time were really icky. They don't have to look that way, which I think we showed. For my purposes, I knew I could make something that would be a very different experience. Good writing and wonderful music were also extremely important to me. What was fun about "Chop Suey" was that we were able to do almost everything ourselves with very little intervention for the majority of the project. I actually did voice-over and sang songs!

Q: Were you thinking at all of designing something that was appealing to girls? Or is that something that just happened?
A: It just happened, if it happened at all. I think it became a helpful marketing tool later, girls designing for girls, that sort of thing. Honestly, I was more interested in just making something that I'd like. I still don't know whether people can really say what girls like or don't like. Isn't it the great marketing mystery? I think people get confused and can go off on the wrong track about this, too hip or too cutesy. I know what I like and I know what I liked when I was little, and that makes it easier for me. I guess the more women that work in the industry the better, obviously. There'll be more variety, and more projects will probably appeal to girls.

Q: Do you consider yourself a feminist?
A: No, not really. Sometimes I have a problem with things that are specifically for girls or women. It really makes it seem as if there's something wrong with us, that we have to have something specially designed. I think in terms of making things that are unisex. I suppose I do have girls in mind when I create things, but maybe that's just where my sensibilities lie. Ultimately, maybe there really just needs to be a greater variety of intelligent and creative games to choose from, and CD-ROMs, too; that is, if people are still interested in buying them. ——July 1997

Chapter 9

An Interview with Lee McEnany Caraher (Sega)

As vice president of corporate and consumer communications, Lee McEnany Caraher is responsible for the overall communications strategies for Sega in North America. McEnany Caraher oversees corporate and product public relations, customer relations, and corporate and marketing events, as well as Sega's online presence. In addition, she is the corporate spokesperson for Sega in North America. McEnany Caraher joined Sega in 1995, after more than a decade of working as a public relations consultant in the technology and interactive entertainment industry.

Q: How did you end up in the game industry?

A: Well, I went to Carleton College. There's nothing too practical that I learned at Carleton except how to think, write, and argue. It's so liberal arts, you roll out of there so well-rounded, because the requirements are pretty stringent. You've got to take so many courses in four or five different disciplines. I went there actually as a premed student, because my father was a doctor, and I'd always worked for my dad in his labs and his operating rooms, and that's all I knew. But my mother signed me up for this medieval history course—a course on Chaucer's England—because I had read all the Mary Stewart series. She thought I'd like it. And the first thing this guy taught us was that there was no Roman empire. He was a big deconstructionist. You could argue that forever and ever—that there was no Roman empire—and that sort of opened my eyes to "What the hell am I thinking? Do I want my father's life?" And so I decided at that time that I should do something I have passion for—and I just had a passion for medieval studies. Music was my minor, and my music instructor wanted me to go into music, and my history guy said, "You should go on and do history and become a professor." But the biggest thing I learned at Carleton was that what I'm really good at is doing multiple things at once, and that I get very bored if I do one thing. So I thought I should go in a different direction.

I didn't really know what to do, and someone said, "You should try PR." I didn't know what it was. What is public relations? So I read some book, which said you write and you talk a lot and you do events. And it was very glamorous, the way they described it—but PR is anything but glamorous. So I decided on PR and I moved back to Boston, and I just took the job that paid me—at a company called Cone Communications, in technology. It was nothing I knew anything about. Then after a few years in Boston I moved to L.A. and started working on behalf of Packard Bell, and moved into consumer electronics. I launched 3DO and was exposed to Sega and to the gaming industry. And now I've worked for Sega—this is almost the end of my third year. I've been in the company for two-and-a-half years, and I worked on the outside of the company for about half a year. There's never a dull moment. I can't imagine going back to nonconsumer technology.

The video game industry in general is in such flux that you just never know what's going to happen. I'll share this with you: We have this product called Netlink. And Netlink plugs into the back end of the Saturn video game unit, and it lets you go online, which is really cool. Because we're a company that spends most of its time talking to kids, and we think that parents should be involved with what they do, we offer filters for the Internet so parents can screen sites, if they want to. A lot of these kids who have this unique machine are twelve years old. I don't know how I'm going to be when I have twelve-year-olds, but some parents really want to know what their kids are doing and want to filter content. You can filter sexual content, you can filter racial content. There's more than fifteen different filters you can put on. One of them is for gay and lesbian content. So the last three days, GLAD (Gay and Lesbian Advocates and Defenders) has been yelling at us because we're filtering gay and lesbian content. The filters don't come turned on. The parent has to go in and turn it on for them. And we think that's the parent's right. So every day is a different issue for me. The next three days could be violence in video games. In my job, I never know what the issue will be, because we touch so many people's lives. So I can't imagine going back to straight technology, where it's a little more boring, a little more mundane. It keeps me on my toes, for sure.

Q: From your perspective at Sega, what is your take on the girls' game movement?

A: I had to do this interview for the *New York Times,* and I got so much so many controversial phone calls afterwards from women in the industry—"How could you say this? You're just betraying us all." People called me who didn't know me and said, "You're betraying us all." But I really feel strongly about it. I haven't seen an example of a real game made for girls. I've seen a lot of content that's good content for girls, but in terms of games, I haven't seen it. Are we, Sega, making games just for boys? I don't think so. I think a good game is a good game. It's like a ride at Disneyland. A good ride is a good ride, and boys and girls and men and women go on it.

If you look at Sega overall, about 33 percent of our market is girls. And we don't even try to get girls. We don't do any girl marketing right now. We put girls in our ads, but they've always been in our ads. We don't advertise in girls' magazines. We don't just go to girls' television shows for an ad buy. We spend more money on the boys than we do on the girls. So if 33 percent of your market is girls, even without trying, that indicates to me that if it's a good game, it will sell on both sides. But it's just taken a long time for girls to have the opportunity to play. Ten years ago, fifteen years ago, it wasn't necessarily accepted that girls would like games or would choose to go to a computer school. I went to an all girls' school where everyone was pushed to do things, but computers were never even in the realm. Video games? What the hell were those? But my brother's school down the street had video games. So we've come a long way. Now, there's not as much of a division in terms of what teachers think of as a girls' activity and as a boys' activity. Andy Grove has said that girls just think that games are stupid. But I disagree entirely, because I play games and I don't think they're stupid. I played games before I got here, and now I play games all the time here. And if you look around the company, more than half the company is women.

I think that people who don't like what I said are mad because I didn't take their point of view. There were five women on one side of the issue that said, "Girls hate all games," and, "Girls don't play games, and we must develop games specifically for girls or girls won't get involved." And I took the position that said, "No. I haven't seen a girls' game yet." And I've seen a lot of girl content. Some of it's good, some of it's bad. And if 33 percent of our market is girls and we're not trying to market to girls, then their premise has got to be wrong. And I think that just because it's developed for girls doesn't mean it's good. They say, "We're developing something just for girls. Don't touch me. Because it's just for girls, it's going to sell well, or it's going to do well. Girls are going to like this." Well, it could be garbage—and I've seen a lot a garbage from all over the game industry. But if we all don't have really high quality standards for the products we deliver, the whole industry is going to go down. And that's my rally cry more than anything else.

As more girls are exposed to video games, more girls will be in the video game business. They will go into our business because they like it. And they'll become developers. Male or female, a talent is a talent, regardless. Another point of view is another point of view, regardless. But just because it's developed by women for girls does not mean it's good. Just because women want to do it doesn't mean they know how, doesn't mean they're going to come up with games that are going to be appealing to girls. There are not a number of examples yet. Not that we shouldn't go out there and try—I don't think it's a waste of time to try, but it should be tried in the right way. I think that the best example is Purple Moon, because they've done a ton of research on the backend. But, you know, time will tell. Who knows if they'll be able to market? Who knows if they'll be able to break through? We get asked all the time, "Why didn't you develop games for girls?" Well, these are for girls. These are for girls and boys. They're for everybody. They're for fun, you know?

Barbie is a really good example of interactive technology used specifically for girls. But it's not a game. To me, the thing about Barbie is that it's what girls do in real life. You know, they go in and they change all their costumes, and then they play with the Ken doll and put him in the car and drive around with Barbie. In a game you take on another persona, and you have an objective to win; it's not the same. The "Barbie Fashion Designer" CD was really very well targeted to girls. Clearly it did very well in the marketplace. But it's like this virtual parallel of what people do in real life. Games are not necessarily that. To me it's like when you read. When I read Chaucer or Jane Austin or E.B. White, it was being there. You know? When you play a game, you go into the game, and you're somebody different—sometimes you're a penguin and sometimes you're a dolphin and sometimes you're a little hedgehog, or whatever. But you're different. And with Barbie, you're the same. So it's not a game in that sense.

Q: Kids might take on a different persona with Barbie. You dress up Barbie as an astronaut, and the kids pretend they're an astronaut. Do you view that type of role playing as different?

A: Than playing a game, yes. It's not the same—it's not the same with "Barbie Fashion Designer." They design clothes and they print it out. They cut it out and they put it on the doll. The interactive part is finished. You're no longer using your computer. And then you have it in real life and you're playing with it. It is not the interactive experience that a game would be, where you could be sitting at your computer for fifty hours, or in front of your television set for hours on end, or even twenty minutes, and accomplish what the game wanted you to accomplish.

Q: Do you think there's any particular link between whether something is designed by a woman and whether girls would like it more? Do you think that the odds go up at all?

A: My experience says no. Some of the stuff that was for girls only did very poorly in the marketplace last Christmas. So, is that because girls don't have computers at home? Is that because the package didn't appeal to parents who were buying it? "Lion King" for the PC did better with girls than it did with boys. That wasn't marketed to just girls. My gut says we make too much out of this. "We're going to make a dating game, a game that teaches girls how to date and how to pick the right guy." And I looked at that and I said, why would you want to do that on a computer screen with one person, when what you really want to do is sit around with your friends and say, "That guy sucks!"? Lots of software was trying to emulate in an interactive technology something that is already interactive on the outside. We're already interacting. You don't need to put it in a computer. In some cases they've said, "What's appealing to a girl? Let's make that interactive," without really thinking about what it is about an interactive experience that gets you going. Well, it keeps you going because you like clicking around. Why do you like clicking around? Because every time you click something, it's different, or you learn something, or something pops up, or "Oh my God!," you know, whatever. It's not necessarily what you want to do on the outside.

I think the reason Barbie works as a title is because they get to make their own clothes, which they can't do easily in real life. They print it out, they cut it out, and they stick it on the doll, and then, forget about the computer, they're playing with the dolls like they usually do. It probably doesn't take that much time. It probably takes half an hour. But the whole goal is getting it out of the printer and onto the doll. The goal is not being involved with the computer, you know? There has to be something so compelling on the screen that you want to explore all of it. You're interacting with what someone else has created, another world. And you're exploring the whole thing. You're going backwards. You're going forward. I'm going to try this now, I'm going to try that now. Back and forth, back and forth, up, down, in and out. It's taking advantage of the technology in such a way that they're going into another world, taking on another persona, but also competing with or against someone or something. Just because you're interactive doesn't mean you're a game. I think the distinction is important for us, because we're a game company. We'll probably never do a Barbie title. Why would we do that? That's not our forte. The Mattel forte is having a doll with lots of clothes that girls can pretend with. They used interactive technology very, very well in that Barbie title. But from our point of view, we would never even bother with that kind of implementation. From their point of view, it extends their whole market, it extends their whole product line by taking advantage of the computer. Brilliant. Brilliant.

There are a lot of poor games, you know? There's tons of worthless games out there. But if it's a good game, it will sell on both sides. Maybe we should spend time marketing to girls. We just haven't chosen to, because the bigger part of the market is boys. The girls are secondary. They come after.

Q: Why don't you market for girls?

A: It's expensive. We're not a company that has tons and tons of cash. So we don't necessarily take all the risk we should, I think. At one time, there was a girls' task force here. It's not here any more. But we made games that were specifically for girls—"Crystal's Pony Tale" (see Plate 16), for example—and they sold just as well to the boys as they did to the girls.

Q: Would you make a distinction between girls' play and boys' play?

A: The true core-girl-gamer probably does not play as much as the true core-male-player. The true male gamer is playing three to five hours a day, which we don't necessarily advocate, but some of these guys are doing that much or more. The girl game-player is probably playing two to three hours a day. We would take the position that we have to expose more women and girls to the market.

Q: I'm surprised that you aren't advertising toward the women.

A: It's expensive. It's an expense thing.

Q: Wouldn't the expense be worth it?

A: Not necessarily, because girls are always second. We would have to invest a great deal of money to see the needle move appreciably.

Q: Why?

A: Just because of the exposure. We think it's exposure. Girls are more discerning than boys necessarily are. The way women shop is geared towards trial. We go in, someone sprays us with something. We try on clothes. Men don't try on clothes as much as women do. You know, I can just buy something off the shelf for my husband, and he won't even try it on. Women have to try everything on. We don't buy anything off the shelf, except maybe a T-shirt. The sizes are all different, maybe you don't like how it looks, whatever. So with a game that is between forty and sixty dollars, I think girls try more. They rent more than boys do, as a percentage. And they want to know that the boy liked it, too. They want to go play with their friends, probably more than boys do. I think we're taught really early on—maybe this is not genetic—but girls are taught very early on to be a lot more discerning in our purchases. That could be a broad generalization, but in general that's just the way women shop. Best Buy encourages people to stay in a store lot. But they keep you in the store to try a lot of things, because they have so many different options. You don't see men just staying in one department for three or four hours. They go from department to department. You could see a woman going to a clothing store and spending four hours there. You go into Macy's—by the time you get from the sixth floor to the first floor, the day is gone. And we're just conditioned that way, I think, not that it's right. They want to know it's a good game. Girls won't necessarily buy something because it's hot. They want to see about it first.

Q: You mentioned a product earlier that you said was targeted towards girls—"Crystal's Pony Tale"—that boys also found interesting.

A: We call it an action-adventure, where you need to go through the game at different levels. You progress. As you get better, you get faster. And your object is to save somebody. They changed the game—the coloring was all different. It's all pinks and purples, not blues and reds. And it was about a girl pony—it was almost the first time we really used a female character. Now we have female characters in almost every game.

Q: When did the game come out?

A: 1994. We did some marketing to girls in that, and it sold very well. We put a projection on every title we have. So it sold what it was supposed to, probably 100 thousand units; 100 thousand units in a PC game would be a Top Ten. Most games don't sell a hundred thousand units a year on the PC side. On the video game side, 100–300 thousand units in one year is a good game, a really good game (you know, we've sold up to a million units of one game in a year). And when we went back into the research, it showed 40 percent girls, 60 percent boys. So, yes, it went up a bit on the girls' side, but the boys bought it, too. And we didn't get returns. People return things they don't like, you know? If they don't like a game, we hear about it immediately: "This game sucks!" But "Crystal's Pony Tale" did very well. Cleaned us right through.

Q: What was your explanation?
A: I think there are two ways you could look at it. Someone else might look at it, "Well, you just made a game that was like a boy's game, but you painted it purple and pink." Or you could say that it was a good game that sold well. We made a game. But we tweaked it for girls. I think we'll probably have an argument on both sides.

Q: Where would you fall?
A: I'd fall on B. Because I really believe that a good game will sell like a good book. You know, there are good books that only women read and there are books that only men read. But the biggest books are read on both sides.

Q: Were people at Sega surprised that boys bought this title more than girls?
A: We thought that it would sell, but it was surprising to some people that the boys liked it, too. I think people thought, "Oh, it's pink and purple, no boy will like it." But the boys could care less. They thought it was a good game, so they played it, too. They didn't care.

Only 6 percent of games are the macho type—what people call violent games. We categorize against all different genres: role playing, action-adventure, fighting, shooting, strategy, simulation, sports, racing. But fighting is the one that gets the most attention from the media. "Mortal Kombat" is not our game. In "Mortal Kombat" you cut people's heads off and blood comes gushing out. But that kind of game only accounts for 6 to 7 percent of the total market.

Q: What's the biggest category?
A: Action-adventure. "Sonic the Hedgehog" or "Mario the Plumber," that kind of thing, where you're running through things and . . .

Q: And those are the games that have been talked about in terms of their potential in the girls' market?

A: They're androgynous. "Sonic the Hedgehog" and "Nights into Dreams" were developed by the same guy at Sega in Japan. His name is Ugi Naka. "Sonic the Hedgehog" has a Q score right up there with Arnold Schwarzenegger. He has his own comic strip and comic book series. He has his own television show. We've already sold more than twenty million pieces of software that have Sonic in them.

Q: How many games does he have?
A: He's had about eleven games since 1989. And girls love him. He's highly merchandised. We've got dolls, we've got shoes, we've got sleeping bags, napkins; you can get the costume. He's a boy in the game, he saves Princess Sally, but girls love him.

Q: Why?
A: I think because he's fuzzy. He's funny. He has an attitude. The whole thing about "Sonic the Hedgehog" (see plate 17) when he came out was that he was really, really fast—faster than any other video game character. If you pause during the game, he'll stand up and he'll look at you, and he'll start tapping his foot, like, "Let's go, buddy." And the attitude is really endearing. Doesn't make a difference if you're a boy or a girl. It's like, "Oh, my God, look at that!" You know? And "Nights" was our number-one seller last year. I mean hundreds and hundreds of thousands of units.

Q: The "Nights" game?
A: He's purple. He goes into a pink world. You can play as a boy or a girl—you decide that at the beginning of the game. Regardless, if he's a boy or a girl, you turn into Nights (see Plate 18), so it's pretty androgynous that way. It's a great game. The game is something that kids want to play over and over and over again. And it didn't seem to make a difference if they were girls or boys. We have another game called "Ecco the Dolphin," which has several iterations as well. Ecco's a dolphin. And it was a whole different kind of game play, because you're in the water and you could feel really sluggish. If you came up against a wave, you went back and you felt it through your game pad. You felt it. And when you watch people play games, if it's a good game, they're not just sitting there. They're actually involved and they're moving around. Girls love "Ecco the Dolphin."

Q: Is Ecco a boy or girl?
A: Boy. There are some girl dolphins in there, too, but Ecco is the star.

Figure 9.1: Virtua Fighter's Sarah Bryant represents Sega's new breed of female action stars.

Q: Why do you think that is?

A: Strong characterizations. You want to be the cute one. In fighting games, you usually can choose from among ten to twenty-five different characters. So why do you choose? Do you choose because they look good? When I first start playing a game I'm not familiar with, I choose because of how the character looks. In our fighting games, each character has different strengths. So you could be Sarah Bryant—because most women choose the girls first—and then you could try out her moves, and then you could master her, move on to a man or a woman. You find the character whose moves you like best—not necessarily the one that you like the looks of. Sarah Bryant is probably the most popular character to choose in "Virtua Fighter," regardless of whether you're a boy or a girl.

Q: And who is Sarah Bryant?

A: She's a babe.

Q: What sort of moves does she have?

A: American-style martial arts—she has a lot of kick-boxing moves. She's got a really high kick and she's really strong. And Pai is another woman in that game, and she's got a Chinese style; she has very many low moves—she's low to the ground. She spins around a lot more. Sarah Bryant flips backwards, Pai flips forward—all of our characters are built on real martial-arts characteristics and styles, and we pride ourselves on game play more than anything else. More than how a game looks, we pride ourselves on how it plays. That's why people come back to our games over and over and over again. It doesn't just sit there and get dusty.

People are attracted if the character has depth—Sonic has a whole attitude, and he gets upset, and he wants you to move, and he blows up. Kids want characters to do, do, do! I think Mario from Nintendo is another example of a really good character. He's a plumber. It's sort of stupid—a plumber. We make fun of him because he's the plumber and he's our arch-rival. But I think they've done a lot in terms of developing his character. I don't think he'll ever be as appealing as a blue fuzzy hedgehog. But the more personality you develop around a character, the more appealing your character is. And I think girls and boys respond really well to that.

Q: What role does character play in "Nights"? Do boys tend to choose the boy character?

A: I think a true gamer will choose both to see the differences. Because a good game doesn't give options unless there's a difference in how the characters are going to carry out the game. In offering options, you need to develop the characters, what their talents are, what their strengths are. In "Virtua Fighter," you might choose first if you were a woman to be a woman, but if you're a gamer, you're going to try them all to see if you like another style better. We're in the middle of a company-wide challenge on a game called "Fighters Megamix," which has Sarah Bryant in it, and Sarah Bryant already has been the number one-choice among all departments, independent of whether a man or woman is playing. She's the character that's won the most, because people play her the most.

Q: Does she have just better moves?

A: Well, she's more fun to play. Each character has seven hundred moves. She's not the hardest one to master, I think—she's in the middle difficulty to master. But her style is something that people like. If you choose to be Akira, and you can master him, then you will beat Sarah, because he's stronger—but he's harder to master. I know a few moves and I just wait for them to come toward me and go, "Poom," you know?

Q: Can you tell us about your favorite game?
A: I have several favorite games. One is "Baku-Baku," which is a puzzle game, and it's much like "Tetris." Women have been drawn more to games like "Tetris" than to the fighting games. "Baku-Baku" is very cutesy. Instead of putting shapes together, as in "Tetris," you want to match up animals with the food that they eat. So the panda bear eats bamboo and the mouse eats the cheese. I could play this game for hours. In fact, if I can't sleep at night, I go downstairs and I put on "Baku-Baku," and that's usually where my husband finds me, going, "What is the matter with you?" But, it helps me relax. Within the Sega company, it's one of the most competitive games. When we gave it out to the media, a lot of publications banned it from the editorial offices because their staffs—95 percent men—were spending their whole day playing "Baku-Baku."

Q: Who plays the game, girls or boys, and what is the age ranges?
A: Age range is from nothing to sixty. It's my mother's favorite game—she's fifty-eight. I gave my mother this system two Christmases ago, and she said, "What am I going to do with this?" And now she plays "Baku-Baku." She likes the driving games too.

Q: What do you think are the characteristics that make this unique or powerful or appealing to boys or girls?
A: First, it's very appealing when you look at it. You hear things like, "Oh, my God! This is so cute!" or ". . . so cool!" When you start playing you forget about how cute it is. You do. You forget about the colors, you forget that it's a banana-eating monkey coming down. The competitor in you takes over. "I want to win!" You know? "I just want to win." And, "How am I going to do it? I'm going to make this mouse go over here and eat that cheese," but you don't think about the mouse going over to eat the cheese. It's about achieving the goal of the game.

What makes a really good game is playability. What makes a really good game is people who want to play that game again. And repeat play is absolutely the pride point for the developers. I manage consumer service as well. We get

100 thousand calls a month during this time of the year. And we get about 100 thousand calls *a week* between October and December. Argh! People still call us for strategy guides for some of our first games from 1986. What does that mean? It means they're playing. And these games are ten years old, and they've had them and played them for six years. That's the absolute best thing that someone could say about our games. Another thing that makes a good game is the ability for someone to pick it up and go.

Q: Do you think girls are turned off by the violence in traditional video games?
A: Let me make a distinction about Sega games, because we don't allow blood and gore in general. I mean, sometimes you'll get a little bit of spurt, but you won't get the gushy goriness. I get a lot of calls from parents: "I hate this game." Usually, it's not ours. What they're objecting to is the heads lopping off and the loss of limbs. We've sold more of our "Virtua Fighter" series than most other companies have sold of other fighting games, and you don't lose a limb, and you don't lose your life, and no blood comes out—and green stuff doesn't spurt from your stomach. I don't think that you need that stuff to make a really good game. But in general, girls are turned off by that stuff. Some boys like it, but they don't necessarily play that game over and over and over again because of the gore—not unless it's a good game.

In general, children understand that it's make-believe. There's tons and tons of evidence that boys and girls get that this is make-believe violence. And there's also tons and tons of evidence that says that boys and girls get equally upset as the violence becomes more realistic. If they see a character in a game get their head lopped off, well, it's not real. It's two-dimensional. It's not gory. It doesn't smell. You can't touch it, you know? Kids in general think it's funny. Parents don't get the distinction a lot of the times. We listen to kids all day long, and kids are smarter and more discerning than anyone gives them credit for. When the whole anti–violent video game thing was happening in Congress, those senators never played those games. They had no idea. They never talked to kids. They talked to people who were against this kind of thing. And in response to that, the companies formed an industry association, and we rate all of our games through this independent association. We're a toy company and we develop things for kids to use, and in general we believe that parents should be involved with what their kids do every day.

Do we advocate three and four hours of video games a day? No. Is it our bread and butter? No, actually, it's not. Our bread and butter is people who use

Plate 1
The Purple Moon website allows girls to learn more about their favorite characters. Reprinted with permission of Purple Moon. Copyright 1997.

Plate 2
Rockett and Miko converse in the girls' bathroom, suggesting the everyday spaces and character interactions in "Rockett's World." Reprinted with permission of Purple Moon. Copyright 1997.

Plate 3
The treehouse in "Secret Paths in the Forest" is a "healing place" where girls can take their problems. Reprinted with permission of Purple Moon. Copyright 1997.

Plate 4
Players must venture into lushly designed environments in search of answers. Reprinted with permission of Purple Moon. Copyright 1997.

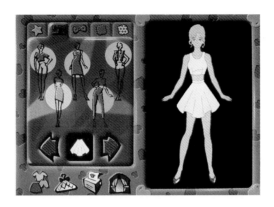

Plate 5
Mattel's "Barbie Fashion Designer" was the runaway success that opened the market for other girl games efforts. BARBIE and associated trademarks are owned by Mattel, Inc. © 1996 Mattel, Inc. All Rights Reserved. Used with permission.

Plate 6
"Barbie's Ocean Discovery" allows Mattel's top female star to adopt a more scholarly profession. BARBIE and associated trademarks are owned by Mattel, Inc. © 1996 Mattel, Inc. All Rights Reserved. Used with permission.

Plate 7
"Barbie's Ocean Discovery" allows Mattel's top female star to more actively explore her environment. BARBIE and associated trademarks are owned by Mattel, Inc. © 1996 Mattel, Inc. All Rights Reserved. Used with permission.

Plate 8

The Tiara Club on the Girl Games website offers a comfortable place to hang out with friends. Copyright 1997 Simon & Schuster, the publishing operation of Viacom Inc., and Davidson & Associates, Inc. All rights reserved. Used with permission.

Plate 9

"Let's Talk About Me"'s Miss Hottie Body focuses attention on the changes girls experience at puberty and other women's health issues. Copyright 1997 Simon & Schuster, the publishing operation of Viacom Inc., and Davidson & Associates, Inc. All rights reserved. Used with permission.

Plates 10 and 11
"Let's Talk About Me" allows girls to explore their values and opinions about a number of topics, ranging from romance to fashion. Copyright 1997 Simon & Schuster, the publishing operation of Viacom Inc., and Davidson & Associates, Inc. All rights reserved. Used with permission.

Plate 12
The flamboyant postmodern colors of Ping Ping Palace in "Chop Suey" contrast sharply with the black and metallic colors of boys' games. Copyright Magnet Interactive Studios, 1995. Used with permission.

Plate 13
Aunt Vera's love life represents only one of the many "adult secrets" players can explore in "Chop Suey." Copyright Magnet Interactive Studios, 1995. Used with permission.

Aunt Vera was in the backyard, dancing in big circles around the picnic table. She had her arms around a tall man with sideburns. It was the man who ran the gas station next to the Ping Ping Palace downtown.

Plate 14

The navigational screen from "Zero Zero" suggests the game's turn-of-the-century Parisian atmosphere. Copyright Theresa Duncan, 1997. Used with permission.

Plate 15

Clicking anywhere on the screen in "Zero Zero" can produce whimsical and surprising results, as in the scene from Genevieve's flower shop. Copyright Theresa Duncan, 1997. Used with permission.

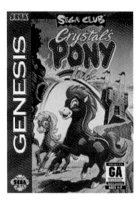

Plate 16
"Crystal's Pony Tales" represented one of Sega's first attempts to design and market games for girls.
Plate 17
Female gamers have been enthusiastic about "Sonic the Hedgehog"'s "attitude" and plucky personality.
Plate 18
"Night into Dream"'s androgynous harlequin soars through the clouds.

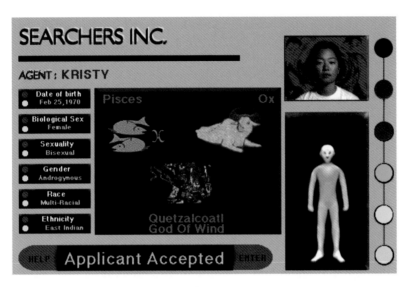

Plate 19
In "Runaways," searchers must locate a missing Chicana girl. Copyright Annenberg School of Communication, 1997. Used with permission.

Plate 20
Completing the ID card forces players to think about the construction of their own identities. Copyright Annenberg School of Communication, 1997. Used with permission.

Plate 21
This help movie from "Runaways" suggests that masculinity and femininity are expressed through how we dress, walk, and talk. Copyright Annenberg School of Communication, 1997. Used with permission.

Plate 22
Players can transform preexisting photographs to masquerade as different sexes or races. Copyright Annenberg School of Communication, 1997. Used with permission.

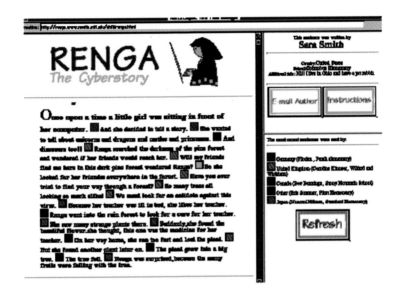

Plate 23
"Renga." Design and artwork by Katrin Silberberg.

Plate 24
"Rosebud" screen interface.

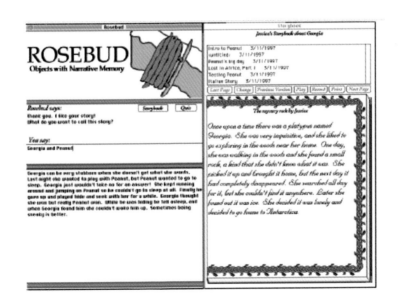

Plate 25
"SAGE" screen and rabbit.

Plate 26
"Mother Nature," a child-designed sage.

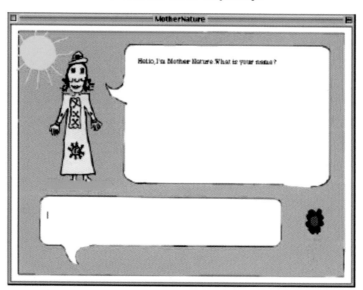

this for entertainment as an option, maybe an hour a day, maybe an hour a week, but they use it as one of their entertainment options. We think it's a better option than sitting watching television a lot of the times because we know the kids are involved, they're watching, they're paying attention, their brain is moving a million miles a minute. They're learning something. I hate when kids just sit in front of the television set and they're sort of just clicking around—they're not clicking around because they are interested. They're clicking around because there's nothing to do or nothing interesting to watch.

Q: You've talked several times now about it not being worth the expense to market specifically for girls. Do you see this as a high-risk industry?

A: Sure. It's so crowded on the PC side that if you're not selling in a week, you get pulled off the shelf. So you might have put four million dollars into that product and it's all down the drain. In some stores you get pulled off in a week; in other stores, two or three weeks. Part of the problem is that the business grew really fast, and then everybody thought it was the holy grail, and then every Hollywood studio had an interactive division, thinking it would be easy to capitalize on. It's harder to develop good interactive content than anyone thought it was going to be. "Oh, we can just turn this movie into a game." Well, it didn't sell. "We can turn this into entertainment"—like Disney tried to do. Well, the first version of "Lion King" had to be returned because it was so "buggy"; it crashed a lot. Well, they have enough money to rectify the situation; Disney has deep, deep, deep pockets. So the next time they did "Lion King," Disney brought in experts—software experts, who were going to make a good software game with that content—and they did tremendously well on the second game. But any other company wouldn't have been able to recover. You have to have so much money to start. And in Silicon Valley, where most of the companies are bootlegged, strapped up, venture-capital driven, a lot of the companies get ten million dollars to start, but if they don't make it on that ten million dollars, they'll be lucky to get another ten. You could screw up, and it's all over. Seventy percent of the sales happen between October 1 and December 31. Seventy percent of the entertainment market is in those three months. You've got hundreds of companies rushing to market and you've got so many titles. Some people just stop doing their game so they can get it to market, when maybe they should hold it. But for business reasons, they can't. As a result of these kinds of dynamics, the industry has gone through a lot of transition in the last two years. I think we're going to do a lot more consolidation in the next two years. We've lost probably fifteen companies in the last two months, which is not a bad thing. We think it's a good thing. There are just too many companies delivering too many titles for everyone to be viable.

Q: Is the profit margin that low?

A: The margin on hardware is next to nothing. We lost money every time we sold a system during the first year of the system. Most companies do. It's the razor-blade approach. You get the razor in, and then you make the money on new blades. Our blades are software. So this game costs five dollars to make by the time you put it into this CD. But we charge $29.99 for this game because it costs millions of dollars to develop it and then to do the marketing. And then you take that profit and you put it back into the next hardware system, so it's a big circle. The software-only companies pay a royalty to each hardware company they develop for. So they pay us and they pay Nintendo and they pay Sony to develop for our systems. In return, we give them technical support and publishing support, and we get them cheaper prices on CDs because we have the critical mass. Then their challenge is figuring out what platform to develop for: PC? Or one of the three or four different consoles?

A lot of the companies that have gone away are PC-only developers, because it's very simple to develop for the PC. You don't pay a license fee. You don't pay anybody to develop. You just buy the tools and then off you go. There's this illusion on the PC side that you can just develop and it will sell. We get ideas every day. People send us binders on ideas for games. We don't even look at them, but we still get binders and binders of game ideas. A lot of them come from kids; some come from adults. People out there think, "Oh, this can't be that hard." How many producers are there in Hollywood? How many good movies are there?

You could have three guys sitting in a garage for a year developing a game. But then the next challenge is getting it published, getting it distributed, getting it on shelves, getting the marketing to let people know, so it won't be taken off the shelves. On the PC side there's no control. In the console games, we control and Nintendo controls, Sony controls. Every game has to pass a certain number of tests here before we let it go on our systems. You have to have a certain quality of graphics, a certain quality of game play. In the PC business there's nobody putting any brakes on, and as a result there are four thousand titles. If you want to make your money back, you need to sell about a hundred thousand units. Four thousand titles times a hundred thousand units, that's not the market. That's four hundred million pieces of software against twenty-five million computers. It's not going to happen. And that's just the entertainment software. It's just too much. So I think what's happened is the reality of that business struck home and people said, "Wait a second. We need fewer, better titles and more marketing power behind them all, because there's just too much competition."

Q: Is there a danger, though, that in the big companies, if you don't have a lot of maneuverability room, you can't take big risks because they'll kill you? And if you can't take big risks, and at the same time you're trying to shrink down the number of the companies out there, is there a risk that there will be less change, fewer risks taken?

A: No, I think that cream will always rise. "Myst" is a good example. "Myst" is still the number-one PC game on the charts, and it's in its fourth year! The developers are two brothers who were not well-known, and now it's huge! The basic truth is that the market won't tolerate mediocrity. So if you don't have new ideas, the market won't tolerate it; People just won't buy. If you're not fostering creativity in your own company, either by bringing it in, acquiring it, or doing something, then you have no chance of survival. It's a quality issue.

Q: Does the fact that Sega is a Japanese-owned company make a difference in the game content?

A: Culturally, our American games are somewhat different from those developed in Japan. In Japan, there's a lot more tolerance for sexual and racial material. We may take stuff out. A game doesn't need sexual content to be a good game. The girls are babes in our game; they're babes. You know, they have big breasts and they wear scanty clothes. But the clothes don't fly off and that kind of stuff. I don't have a problem with representing women as babes, because when I go to the gym that's what they look like. They're not "gorgeous-gorgeous," but they're built. And if you were a real martial arts contender, you'd be built too. So I don't have much of an issue with it in terms of how the character looks.

Q: Has the rise of women in the game industry made a difference in terms of content?

A: Tamagotchi was developed by a woman a couple of years ago in Japan. The person who developed our arcade version of "Jurassic Park" is a woman. Well, it is stellar. We tell people this after the fact—that it was designed by a woman. "You're kidding. Oh, my God. How come they let her do this?" It's just because this version of the game is very true to the movie. I've heard that in Hollywood most continuity people are women, because they care more about the whole effect. Any business is going to do well if there are more women involved, that has nothing to do with video games. The more balanced we our in the workplace, the more balanced we'll be in our real life.

I'm not typical. My mother says to me, "Oh, you're so different from me." My lifestyle wouldn't be what people call a typical woman's lifestyle. My husband works from seven to two. He makes dinner for me every night. He takes care of the house. He's going to take care of our kids. He's going to be the one at home, I'm going to be the one that's working. That doesn't mean I'm not involved with our life; it just means we have what would be called reversed roles. But I don't like calling it reversed roles. I like calling it "the role that we've chosen." So I think that the more women are involved, regardless of the industry, the better it will be, because it will be less about being traditional, less what people have been stuck in.

Q: In many of your games, the guy saves the woman in the end. Does that bother you at all?
A: Hmm. In some games you can choose to be a woman, too, and the game is the same.

Q: A woman saving a woman?
A: Yeah.

Q: Why not save a guy?
A: You can save a guy, too, in some of them; I think that the object is to save the body. And it doesn't bother me. My passion before was medieval history— so imagine what you're reading there. I have no problem with that. I have more of a problem with things that are a waste of time than I do with stereotypes, as long as it's not bad images.

Q: What do you think are bad images?
A: Do you need to have pubic hair? No. Do you need to have all that stuff? I don't think so. I've seen a poster for a game where this guy is in the middle of fire, and things are happening all around him. All of a sudden, there's this girl

in a bikini just waving at you—and what is that girl doing there? You don't need that stuff. But I get more irritated with bad game-play than I do with what people call stereotypes. Obviously some people feel really strongly about it on both sides of the coin, and a lot of people want more cleavage—"She should be more babely"—and a lot of people don't. We're never going to make everyone happy. I sometimes have arguments with women in the company about that. You could argue that the people who don't like Barbie in the doll version probably hated Barbie in the interactive version. She doesn't have normal measurements; she's not anything like what most of us look like. So you could argue all of that stuff, but I think the bigger issue is that in general kids understand that it's make-believe. However, I think you don't have to perpetuate very degrading images. But there is room for attractive female characters.

Q: Do you have a personal mission?
A: I think my personal mission is always to do it right. I find that I throw myself on swords once a month to do it the right way. I want to do it the right way first; I don't want to go back and fix it. I want it to be first-class. I want people to know that if I touch it, it's going to be the best I can possibly make it. That translates to how I feel about our games; I wouldn't be here if I didn't feel strongly about how good our stuff is. It's sometimes really crushing to say to product development, "This game sucks. Let's not do it." I've said it a few times here. Or, "You've got to make it better. You've got to delay it. Let's not do it." Or, if they want to acquire something from another company: "Why? Why are you doing that?" I'm always the sort that gets in people's faces. But overall I feel really strongly that our content is some of the best content in the market—just really strong games. I don't think I could be here if I didn't enjoy what our company does. I was at Disneyland a few months ago, and I spent sixty dollars in the arcade, and my husband goes, "What are you thinking? You can just go play it for free at home." But I get caught up in it. I just love it. If I didn't have a passion for what we do, I couldn't be here.

Overall, in terms of girls' games, I want it to be a fifty-fifty market. That would be ideal in terms of games. Overall I think girls like games as much as boys like games. Girls like board games as much. I don't know who's done any studies on board games, but "Chutes and Ladders" and "Monopoly" probably appeal just as much to girls as they do boys. There's no reason that shouldn't translate to interactive games. And I think the biggest issue is exposure. If I could leave here knowing that we got to 50 percent girls, it would be fabulous.

I don't think we have to change our content to get there. I think we'd have to change our exposure to get there, and I think it's a natural evolution that will happen. There's clearly a market there, because not all girls are involved with games. There's girls' content that needs to be developed, but it better be good and it had better sell. "Barbie Fashion Designer" is probably the first thing that sold well. Think about "Carmen Sandiego." That's a woman character, right? It sold fabulously. It wasn't made for a girl.

Q: Is it just a question of content? Or might the playability need to be different in a girls' game? Do girls use technology differently?

A: I don't know. Quality options are not necessarily gender-specific. You have lots of book options. Sometimes you read nonfiction, sometimes you read fiction, sometimes you read a romance, sometimes you're going to read a story about a woman or a man who is recovering from cancer. Sometimes you're going to read King Arthur, sometimes you're not. I think all of us can be enriched by different kinds of options with different kinds of experience, and to put it in such sweeping terms—"These are only for girls" or "These are only for boys"—is very limiting.

Q: You said you'd like the game market to be fifty-fifty. What sort of specific things is Sega doing to try to move in that direction?

A: It's an issue of marketing, and it's an issue of spending money, and that is a business decision that you get to make once you've hit a critical mass. We're not at the critical mass for this machine—the Sega Saturn—that we were at for the Genesis. I know that the plans for what we're doing in the future include female marketing. In terms of moving people into the company, getting more women into the company—into product development—we're not doing anything that says, "Don't do it." The problem is applicants, and what women are choosing to do. There's only one school in the country for video gamers. It's sponsored by Nintendo, but it's not very big. I think it's important for us to understand that there is a huge range of skills that are required to create video games. There are graphic artists, there are animators, there are model builders—there are all these things. Well, I don't know that women are choosing to do those things or not. I do know that there are more women today in the industry doing development than there were ten years ago. And I think that the more girls are exposed to video games or computer games when they're young, the more they are going to be interested in going into it when they're older.

In terms of women involved in the industry, there's an element that says, you know, if you go way on the edge, and you have women-only companies—companies that have only women involved and are only doing girl content—then the market will develop. I don't think that they will survive in the end, but I think you might get a broader market if you do that first, and then it pulls back naturally. Regardless of what their intent is, regardless of what they're making, a lot of these little companies will get bought by bigger companies. And the bigger company will benefit from the far-outness of their experiments. I think there's a benefit to the whole industry in people being on the outside just pushing the envelope, but in general, people who push the envelope so far have to wait for the market to catch up to them. In the end, I think a lot of these companies will go away, and it won't be because they're making products for girls. It will be because they're not selling well. They don't have the resources to get a great product to market in a wide enough distribution with enough marketing support behind it to break through the incredible clutter. And that's the problem. We're not talking about marketing to ten people. We're talking about marketing to millions and millions of people, and it's not cheap. It's just not cheap.

Q: What is Sega doing to try to reach different classes or different races?
A: We don't do race-specific advertising. We include all racial categories in our advertising. But we don't just market in Latino markets; we don't necessarily go to *Ebony* and the black-only publications. We worry about psychographics, not demographics. Psychographics are related to what kind of mind set you have. The people who read *Rolling Stone* cross both genders and all races, right? So we go for the psychographic more than the demographic. We know that a large portion of our market is African American. We know that another chunk of it is Latino or Hispanic. We've done some sponsorships of rap tours and stuff like that because it's part of our market. If you know your market is 40 percent black, then go there. The challenge for a company like ours is making sure you keep everyone you have as you move forward. Sometimes, if you try to appeal to a new market, you alienate the people you have, the people that you've been with forever and ever. We are in a situation where our hardware system changes. And when you change your hardware system, you want to make sure that everyone who had this hardware system is going to have the next hardware system. So first you take care of the people you have. And then you take care of broadening the market.

Q: Sherry Turkle said that the computer is a personal and cultural symbol of what a woman isn't. In other words, it is not feminine. Do you agree with that? **A:** I haven't really thought about it. I believe the outcome of the research that Interval has done was that if women had developed the interface that we all know now, it would be very, very different. But I'm not sure that's necessarily the case, because so much in development changes from person to person, and not necessarily between genders. I don't know if it's gender-based. We have three thousand people who develop games for us worldwide. And different men develop different kinds of games. So I don't know that it's gender. To me, computers are very intuitive. But maybe it's because I'm used to them. A computer is everything that a woman isn't? And what does she qualify that with? I think someone who identifies themselves with a computer needs a little help, you know? Maybe people are spending way too much time worrying about it. I consider a computer a tool and a vehicle. Most people know their cars aren't women. To me, a car is a vehicle to get me from point A to point B. I think of the computer as a tool to do my work and to let me go places I can't go myself physically, or to do things better or faster than I can do them. ——July 1997

Chapter 10

An Interview with Marsha Kinder
(Intertexts Multimedia)

Marsha Kinder, a professor of critical studies in the School of Cinema-Television at the University of Southern California, specializes in the areas of children's media culture, narrative and gender theory, multimedia, and national cinema. She runs the software company Intertexts Multimedia, where she produces and writes interactive CD-ROMs. She is also the director of the Labyrinth Project at the Annenberg Center for Communication, a three-year research initiative to expand the language of interactive narrative. In addition to the development of her own games, she has also consulted with game companies such as Sega of America and Mindscape.

Kinder's writing about games is informed by her roles as a mother and a scholar of critical theory, and by her identification as a feminist. Her close observations of her own child's development were the impetus for her book *Playing with Power in Movies, Television, and Video Games: From Muppet Babies to Teenage Mutant Ninja Turtles.* (1991) Reflecting her concern with pedagogy, issues of gender, and critical theory put into practice, Kinder has attempted to find new ways to facilitate learning through CD-ROM projects. She has created "Runaways," an alternative computer game for teens and young adults; "Blood Cinema: Exploring Spanish Film and Culture," the first in a series of bilingual CD-ROMs on national media cultures that she is editing; and "Doors to the Labyrinth," an anthology of interactive fictional worlds based on the works of experimental filmmakers and novelists. These projects (all funded by the An-nenberg Center for Communication) reveal her desire to use new media to explore and recognize multicultural perspectives. Her edited collection of essays, *Kids' Media Culture,* is scheduled to appear from Duke University Press in the Spring of 1999.

"We're all searchers. All looking for the truth of who we are and where we belong in this world. If you want to join our common search, you can apply to be a member of our team. We look for teenagers who have run away from their families or from themselves. Run to their dreams or to their nightmares. To prove you're qualified to work with us, you have to solve a case, find the missing runaway, and help the runaway solve his or her problems. To be a good detective, you have to know yourself as well as the person you're searching for."—*Runaways*

Q: How did you get involved in this sort of work? What is your personal motivation?

A: I have always been interested in the movement from one medium to another. I was originally trained as a scholar in eighteenth-century English literature and wrote a dissertation that described how Henry Fielding used his experiments in the theater to help shape the then newly emerging genre of the novel. Once I started teaching at Occidental College in the mid-1960s, I began writing about literature and film, and then when I moved to the Critical Studies Program at the USC School of Cinema-Television in the early 1980s, I became interested in the relationship of film to television and electronic games and to new modes of storytelling. I had already made a CD-ROM called "Blood Cinema: Exploring Spanish Film and Culture," as a companion piece to my book of the same title, and used it to launch a series of bilingual CD-ROMs on national media cultures, which I am editing—a series funded by USC's Annenberg Center for Communication and distributed by the new USC Electronic Press. After teaching graduate seminars on interactive narrative theory, I became interested in putting some of my ideas into practice—to go beyond critical hypertexts and start experimenting with fiction. At USC it is possible to collaborate with people in production—both faculty colleagues and students—which was essential for our "Runaways" project. This kind of collaboration really appeals to me.

Q: Tell us about the collaboration.

A: I had the basic idea for the "Runaways" game and wrote the first draft. But when I applied for a research grant from the Annenberg Center to fund the project, I began working with Mark Jonathan Harris, who was then chair of the production division at USC's film school. Mark is a filmmaker whose latest documentary, *The Long Way Home,* just won an Oscar, and also an award-winning writer of children's literature. We cowrote, codirected, and coproduced the prototype for "Runaways." We had never worked together before, but there was great chemistry between us. We gave a lot of thought to assembling the rest of our team. One key member is Kristy Kang, a Korean-American M. A. student in animation who completed her degree while working on the project. Kristy is very talented and worked as the director of animation, doing most of the graphics herself but also supervising the work of other animation students on the project. Another key collaborator was our art designer, Patty Podesta, who is largely responsible for the basic "look." Formerly an independent video artist, Patty has become a professional art director and has done work on Gregg Araki's films, among others. She has taught art direction both at USC and at the Art Center. Our chief programmer is William Hughes, who has a dual background as an engineer and as a TV cameraman. He made a great contribution in moving between production and programming, and he and Kristy are primarily responsible for the interface design. We also had many other students working on the project: production students shooting the live-action sequences with a mixture of professional actors and local teens, critical studies students doing research and gathering archival materials, and students from all of our programs doing voice-overs. In choosing students to appear on both sides of the camera, we purposely wanted a rich mixture of ethnicities, ages, genders, and sexualities. This was particularly true for the voices, for we wanted to use a great range of accents and inflections to get away from that so-called standard English that you always hear on mainstream media. We wanted our game not only to address players of all genders and ethnicities, but to show them that this same kind of diversity could also be found in the fictional characters on screen and in the real-life members of the crew. That's why most of us appear on screen as Searchers who invite players to join our team of detectives.

Q: How is this project related to your critical writings about children's media culture?

A: When I was writing my book *Playing with Power in Movies, Television and Video Games,* I became interested in how television provides children an entry into narrative and thereby mediates all other forms of cultural production. In a sense, television maps the world and the young viewer's position within our increasingly complex layers of networked narrative space. The reason television could perform this function much more powerfully than movies was its position in the home—the mere fact that kids have access to TV from the time they are infants. But now that computers, multimedia, electronic games, and the Internet are in the home and are increasingly available to kids at a very early

Figure 10.1: The opening screen for "Runaways" already creates an atmosphere of fluidity and transformation. Copyright Annenberg School of Communication, 1997. Used with permission.

age, they are competing with TV to perform this crucial function. And what gives them an edge is that these new interactive media make kids feel more empowered. As part of my book, I did a case study of my son's interaction with media from infancy to age nine. I even used his brief "version" of media history to open chapter one: "A long time ago there were no toys and everyone was bored. Then they had TV, but they were bored again. They wanted control. So they invented video games." I was really knocked out by my son's blatant emphasis on control—and worried about his love for "twitch and kill" games—and was surprised by his total omission of movies. His account followed not the historical chronology of the various media but rather the sequence in which he personally experienced their pleasures. I found this really fascinating, and it made me want to get involved in the designing of electronic games that made kids feel empowered, but without relying on violence. And that's what we try to do in "Runaways."

Marsha Kinder

In my work on kids' media culture, I have also been fascinated with the way that tropes of instantaneous physical transformation—mutation in *Teenage Mutant Ninja Turtles* and *X-Men,* and morphing in the *Mighty Morphin' Power Rangers*—have become so popular during the 1980s and 1990s. In contrast to earlier shape-shifters like Superman and Batman, or those toy transformers that easily convert from a car or rocket into a superhero or monster, these new changelings come in multiples, thereby giving young consumers a choice of which superhero to select as a personal favorite. Not only have these tropes entered the popular imagination of global culture as an optimistic myth of comic transformation—which we can find in movies like Jim Carey's *The Mask,* in music videos like Michael Jackson's "Black or White," and in various software programs for digital compositing that have quickly turned morphing into a visual cliché—but they help reproduce postmodernist subjectivity in their young fans, encouraging them to see themselves as protean shifters who can adapt to a fast-changing world rather than as stable individuals with a fixed identity. Since these superheroes also move fluidly from one medium to another, their protean powers have been used for profit—to multiply their marketability. But what if these protean powers were used to address issues of social change?

That was the basic idea behind "The Changelings Project," a research initiative at USC's Annenberg Center for Communication. Our goal was to develop electronic games that use transformational imagery to explore the fluidity of personal, cultural, and historical identity. "Runaways" is the first experimental game in the series. Since I have long been interested in issues of gender, and since my husband is Mexican and our children basically are biracial and bicultural, I wanted our first game to address issues of identity politics.

When players join Searchers, Inc., a Hollywood detective agency that specializes in finding teenage runaways, they have to fill out an ID card. (See Plate 20.) They import their own picture, enter a code name, give their birth date, indicate their physical size and shape, specify their biological sex, their gender, their sexual orientation, their ethnicity, and their race. The very fact that they need to identify both race *and* ethnicity leads them to think about the difference between those two concepts. If they want to know more about them, they can hit the "Help" button and see quick-time animated movies on each topic. The same is true, of course, for gender, biological sex, and sexual orientation, categories that are usually conflated into simple binaries of male/female and straight/gay but that are separated here—so that players can consider the differences between them—each with four possible choices as well as its own playful "help" movie. (See Plate 21.)

Q: How are these issues of identity related to the narrative premise of "Runaways"?

A: To make the game more emotionally engaging, we thought we needed some kind of narrative quest or hunt that was related specifically to teens and that involved these issues of identity politics. We decided to focus on the social problem of teenage runaways and did considerable research on this topic. Mark and I visited most of the teenage-runaway shelters in Hollywood, interviewed their social workers, and found that issues of gender, sexuality, and ethnicity were very important, both as reasons for leaving home and as sources of conflict within the shelters. We sat in on discussion groups with teenage runaways and asked whether they thought our story was realistic, and what they would advise our runaway to do, and how their own story might relate to our fictional version. They were very receptive to the game and eager to play it when it was finished. One night we also went out on an outreach van that distributes food to homeless teens on the streets of Hollywood and throughout the greater Los Angeles area. We tried to make this dimension of the game as realistic as possible.

To link this narrative premise with issues raised on the ID card, we designed it so that whatever information players give about themselves has narrative consequences within the game; it helps determine how they are treated and what kind of information they get about the runaway. At a certain point in the game, they can change those choices on the ID card, which will have further narrative consequences. (See Plate 22.) But when you make these changes, you are not misled into thinking that your ethnicity or biological sex has really changed, but merely how you appear on screen and therefore how you are perceived by others, which gives us an opportunity to deal with the social consequences of these choices and the issue of stereotypes. The game puts you in the uncomfortable role of being treated as a stereotype and having other characters make all sorts of false assumptions about you, and this experience encourages you to be more of a shape shifter.

Q: It's interesting because there are actually three levels: how you initially identified yourself to the computer is already the second level. It's not necessarily the same as the person you are in your everyday life. And the third level would be how you identify yourself to other characters in the game world.

A: Exactly. We know that a lot of kids will choose to "misrepresent" themselves or to perform other identities when they play the game. We expect many kids to take a playful attitude toward the ID card, and that's fine with us.

Instead of scanning in their own picture, they can scan in any image to stand for them or can choose an image from our database of faces. We have purposely given them this wide range of choices. But we also think that for some kids who see themselves as marginal—particularly gay teens—or who feel that their existence is rarely acknowledged by popular culture, these options may be much more meaningful.

Q: How do you think parents will react to the game—especially when their children are given a choice of identifying themselves as a hermaphrodite, transvestite, or transsexual?

A: Some parents will object to these choices, but I think kids are a lot more sophisticated about these concepts than parents give them credit for. In fact, this is the basic assumption of my new anthology, *Kids' Media Culture*. Most kids have already seen Dennis Rodman, Martin Lawrence, or Bugs Bunny in drag, and have seen or heard about Ellen DeGeneres coming out on network TV. These concepts and images are already part of their social world. Why should kids be treated as if they are terribly threatened by those concepts? Doesn't that imply that they are very fragile? "Runaways" is experimental. If you're already worried about censorship while you're still in the process of designing a project, then you are engaging in a form of self-censorship that will prevent you from really doing anything different. When you are doing an experimental project, I think you have to be willing to take some risks.

Q: Are you interested in making your project commercial and having it available on shelves?

A: Yes; when we finish this prototype, we hope to show it to investors or commercial game companies and interest them in funding its completion. But we want to take it as far as we can, so that it represents our vision. We could have sold the script from the beginning; there was interest, but we were afraid it would then become something very different, something more like what was already out there. This game was *not* market-driven—it was driven by other kinds of substantive motives related to social issues, as I've explained—yet I think it does have features and values that might succeed in the marketplace, for they expand what is possible in computer games. I think this idea is supported by the enthusiastic response that our demo received at this conference.

Q: Do you consider yourself a feminist?

A: Yes, I have been a feminist since the sixties and have been teaching courses on the representation of gender and sexuality for many years, so I was very interested in making kids feel more empowered on these crucial aspects of their identity. When I was doing the research for *Playing with Power*, I interviewed kids in day-care centers and video arcades and asked them why they couldn't choose to be April O'Neil in the "Teenage Mutant Ninja Turtles" arcade game and why there wasn't a female Ninja Turtle. I found that both boys and girls merely accepted the game and its rules as a given, and the same was true for most other toys that are increasingly gendered in very rigorous ways in the toy stores—with their separate pink and blue aisles—and in the packaging and promotion of these products. The kids never considered that these games and toys were made by specific people who had made specific choices, and that it might be possible to challenge or change some of these decisions. I also found that this rigorous gendering was further emphasized in the ways these toys were advertised on television, so that while your kids might use their own choice of games or toys to express their own distinctive personality—the way teens do with music and clothes—or their own personal growth from one generation of superhero to another—from Power Rangers to X-Men, for example—those personal choices are still made within the "official" narrative framework that is strictly coded, particularly on what is appropriate for each gender. What always sticks in my mind is that humiliating moment on *America's Funniest Home Videos* when two young boys who are caught on tape playing with Barbies run screaming from the room as soon as they spot their parents' video camera. In "Runaways" we were trying to create a game that allows kids to play around with images of their own gender and sexuality without fear—to challenge cultural stereotypes and to realize that these concepts are largely socially and historically constructed. While these assumptions about gender and sexuality are now widely accepted in critical and cultural theory, we wanted to make them part of an entertaining narrative that was accessible to teenagers, a narrative that might help them feel more empowered, particularly within this realm of gender and sexuality where many kids feel vulnerable and insecure. But we also wanted to show how gender and sexuality are related to other issues of identity, such as class, ethnicity, and race.

Q: What does being a feminist mean to you?
A: It means struggling against structures of domination and subordination based on gender and sexuality. The goal is not merely to reverse those structures, so that women are on top and men are on the bottom, but rather to do away with those very structures of subordination. Feminism never has been

and never should be monolithic; it is always responsive to specific historic and cultural contexts, to the pressures that come in different forms at different moments. I was fortunate because, within American film studies, feminism became a dominant discourse in the late 1970s and early 1980s. It was subsequently challenged by many voices—particularly by women of color and by queer theorists—who criticized it for having ignored issues of class, race, and sexuality, and for trying to pass off straight, white, middle-class women as the model for *all* women. I think this criticism is valid; feminism in the 1970s did have terrible blind spots. As a consequence, feminism has been forced to change in very positive ways.

Q: Has this philosophy affected the dynamics of your creative team and how you work together?

A: Absolutely! Not only is our crew equally comprised of women and men, and not only does it include members of most racial groups, but it is nonhierarchical. Everyone in the group underwent changes. No one was motivated primarily by money, although everyone was paid—I don't believe in exploiting free labor. Everyone worked for very low pay but still felt very good about it because we all learned a great deal from the experience. It's not easy to get the opportunity to work on an experimental project like this. Everyone working on "Runaways" believed very strongly in the project and felt their input was taken seriously. We all contributed to the content as well as the form, and we all shared the most tedious tasks.

Most important, we all wanted our game to address the issues of race, ethnicity, and class as well as of gender and sexuality, and to show how these various discourses were related to each other. We wanted to encourage kids to go beyond racial and ethnic stereotypes. Except for games involving sports, most action games are targeted at white middle-class boys. When they do allow players to choose action figures of other races and ethnicities—as in games like "Mortal Kombat" and "Doom"—they are frequently pitted in combat games against an opponent of a different race or are instructed to shoot any alien—or stranger—on sight, scenarios that hardly promote racial harmony. And when players are able to choose female warriors, their violent moves are frequently so eroticized that the male-female combat becomes a substitution for violent sex.

Q: How does your prototype address these issues?

A: In our prototype, the runaway is a Latina named Rita Rodriguez (see Plate 19) who has an older Chinese-American boyfriend at San Francisco State, a choice that does not make her parents happy. As her parents see it, this is merely one problem among many that Rita faces, but her parents have their own problems. For one thing, they come from different class backgrounds and have different conceptions of what it means to be a good parent. And there is also an issue of adoption. The characters in the story come from different social strata and from many different ethnic and racial groups. The search for Rita ultimately leads to Mexico.

Q: Are there other runaway cases in your game?

A: Yes, there are five other cases, but they now exist only as treatments that have not yet been produced: a thirteen-year-old Anglo boy from a small town in Oregon who has run away from an abusive father and is being sought by his older brother, who also ran away three years ago; a sixteen-year-old mulatta who has run away from an alcoholic mother to pursue her dreams of independence in Hollywood; a seventeen-year-old Russian émigré who wants to be a ballet dancer and whose parents fear he is lost in the gay world of West Hollywood; a seventeen-year-old Vietnamese-American girl who is afraid to tell her parents she is pregnant; and a sixteen-year-old bright, athletically gifted African-American girl who wants to play college basketball and who is now being sought by her grandmother.

Q: How important was the visual element of the game for you?

A: Extremely important, because this is a multimedia game and we want it to be a pleasurable and rich experience. I think kids are very sophisticated in reading visual culture. So we paid a great deal of attention to the quality of the graphics and the overall look of the game, particularly since we are combining live-action footage with animation, melodrama with magic. In writing the script, we were looking for a story that had strong visual appeal—that's one reason why we chose Chicano and Mexican culture for our first case. That's why we made Rita's biological mother a muralist and we have Rita follow her to Mexico, where she is studying the works of artists—like Rivera, Orozco, and Siquieros—and that's why Rita's friends are taggers, and she and her boyfriend are video makers, and that's why we end the story in the pyramids of Teotihuacán. We wanted to show the rich heritage of the Mexican culture, not just the problems, so that's why we emphasized the great Mexican muralists and their connections with the outdoor murals that are found throughout urban Los Angeles. We wanted our game to have a rich visual texture, and yet, at the same time, we didn't want to ignore the soundtrack. We paid a lot of attention to choosing audio clues and gathering amusing sounds, evocative music, and interesting voices. We also wanted to make the language as rich as possible. Some of the dialogue is in Spanish and Mandarin Chinese—parts that needed to be translated. The Latino teens who tested the game felt very empowered by the presence of Spanish because it meant that they could draw on their own cultural resources to solve the mystery. It gave them an edge they were not used to having in computer games.

Q: Could you tell us more about the testing?
A: We invited a group of eight teens from a local high school in South Central Los Angeles to our lab, where they played the unfinished prototype of the game. Ranging in age from fifteen to seventeen, they included an equal number of males and females as well as an equal number of Latino and African-American students. Since we were interested in seeing whether the game could motivate group play across the boundaries of gender and ethnicity, we allowed different students to take turns at the mouse while the whole group looked on. Although this strategy tended to make the one at the mouse more self-conscious about filling out the questionnaire, they all seemed eager to have a turn and to have the ID card reflect their own personal identity, except on the issue of sexual orientation, where they collectively decided to pick "nonsexual" as their choice. They all appeared engaged in the game and most of them responded verbally to the interviews with Rita's parents and boyfriend, giving ideas about where to look for Rita and why she had fled. The Latino students were particularly vocal when the dialogue was in Spanish, apparently very pleased to share their knowledge with the group. At the end of the play session, when we asked what, if anything, they had learned from the game, one young man responded, "Well, you really can't tell about a person when you first meet them. You really have to know more about them." We were pleased with this response because we thought it demonstrated they were getting beyond the initial stereotypes. In designing the game, we tried not to imply that every kid who runs away is at fault, because there are some homes that really are dangerous. On the other hand, we didn't want to encourage kids to run away or to minimize the real dangers that are out on the street. So it becomes a question of realistic problem solving. We don't have a single happy ending but four different possible resolutions, each with its own limitations. We tried to take a complex approach to Rita's problems, to show that there are always multiple explanations and that blame usually belongs neither solely to the runaway or to the parents. It's usually more of a combination, where everyone is partly to blame. What was heart-

ening was that the kids really liked this approach to the problem because they thought it was realistic. Several of them said that the game was more realistic than any other game they had seen, and that moved them. We were also pleased that the girls were as vocal as the boys and that neither gender nor ethnicity seemed to be more dominant than the other. But it was a small sample, and we plan to do more testing once the prototype is finished.

Q: Will these kinds of games draw girls to the technology?

A: I hope so. One reason girls haven't tended to play computer games as much as boys is that everything about these games—their player-positioning, content, and packaging, and the way they are advertised and sold in stores—everything is saying, "THIS WAS DESIGNED FOR BOYS, NOT GIRLS . . . but maybe a few of you girls can use them, too, if you are bold enough to act like one of the boys!" That is why I feel everyone should be thankful to Mattel for demonstrating that there is a girls' market out there for electronic games. But games designed exclusively for girls, like "Barbie Fashion Designer" and "Let's Talk About Me," also further essentialize the great divide between boys and girls. By making a more rigid distinction between products targeted for girls versus those targeted for boys, they reinforce the boundary between the pink and blue aisles in Toys 'R Us—a tendency I've written about in *Playing with Power*. I know such products are based on extensive industry research about what girls like in games, but I think these tastes are socially constructed, so there is a circularity or self-fulfilling prophecy in the research. Even when kids are designing their own games, as in Yasmin Kafai's fascinating studies, it is not as if this reveals distinctive biological tendencies that are immune to cultural influences. I think kids learn very early what they are expected to like; if their parents, teachers, and friends don't tell them, then television advertising does. For example, there is no inherent reason why little boys shouldn't like little ponies, but they can clearly see from the television ads that "My Little Pony" is designed exclusively for girls.

A couple of years ago at E3—the Electronic Entertainment Expo—in Los Angeles, I was on a gender panel with the vice president of Mattel, who gave a list of essentializing characteristics (based on their research) of what little girls like as opposed to little boys. Included on this list was the comment that, whereas little girls like dolls, little boys like action figures. This remark seemed absurd since clearly the term "action figure" is merely an alternative name for a doll, one that can be marketed successfully to boys. Although I had a prepared speech to deliver, I threw it away and answered his paper instead. So much of the research is faulty because it's based on these essentialist assumptions. All you are testing is how effectively kids have absorbed these cultural binaries of gender.

I think the popularity of "Myst" is very important because it contradicts such studies by demonstrating that both genders can enjoy the same game. Even though it has an oedipal plot—a conflict between the brothers and their father—the emphasis is not on gendered activities. The popularity of "Tetris" with both genders is also important, even though some researchers have tried to link the actions with domestic activities performed by women—cleaning up a mess. In other words, the discourse around games can also contribute to the rigidity of their gendering.

What we were trying to do in "Runaways" was to design a game that not only could address both boys and girls but might also motivate cross-gender play—that is, making it more fun to play the game with people of another gender. And we hoped to accomplish the same kind of goal on the register of ethnicity. Although we chose a female protagonist in our first case study and included other strong female characters, we also included strong male characters.

Q: Why do you think all of a sudden there's such an interest in girls and games?
A: I think it is overdetermined. On the one hand, as computers increasingly merge with television, there is an understandable desire to expand the market. Everyone knows that as these various mass-communication media come together—not only computers and television but also cinema and the telephone—it will be a question of which medium absorbs the others, so each wants to be seen as the most expansive and inclusive. The medium that succeeds must have a mass audience, one that must include females. But both the CD-ROM and the game industries have remained remarkably narrow in their target audience. They could easily be written off as transitional, short-lived media, particularly when contrasted with the explosive growth of the Internet. The video game cartridge market is particularly narrow, although it has been somewhat expanded—both in age and ethnicity, but not gender—by the sports genre. Because these products must sell so many copies within a very short period in order to retain shelf space, there is little room for experimentation. But with CD-ROM games there is more margin, and that's where the action has occurred with new games for girls.

Another important factor comes from those interested in social change within the educational sphere. Since the Clinton administration has made the hard-wiring of schools an important priority, there has been a dawning realization—among politicians, educators, parents, and manufacturers—that there is a desperate need for software that can appeal to both genders. Another important factor is the increasing participation of women in the discourse defining the new media—whether as activists, theorists, researchers, teachers, mothers, designers, industry spokeswomen, or entrepreneurial feminists—because we women are increasingly realizing what is at stake in this cultural battle.

Q: Sherry Turkle once said that the computer is a personal cultural symbol of what a woman is not. Do you agree with this? How does the representation of the computer affect how girls interact with it? How does this issue influence the process of designing CD-ROMs for girls and boys?

A: With the emergence of every new medium, there is always a transference of existing power struggles onto the new site. Every new medium is a site for cultural negotiation on these issues, so it's not surprising that you would find this same old sexist pattern arising in cyberspace and the discourse around computers. Women are dealing with computers daily, but usually as secretaries and "keyboard operators" who are duplicating someone else's text, usually authored by a male. Somehow the culture doesn't count that computer activity as important. It's not the technology itself that determines these power dynamics but the way it is represented discursively. These new technologies definitely offer new possibilities for altering gender relations, which theorists like Donna Haraway and Sandy Stone have detailed, but they also can be appropriated by traditional discourses. While I agree with Stone that we should try to intervene and use these new technologies to reimagine our sexuality, such utopian visions must also confront existing power relations. The schools will prove to be a battleground for this confrontation.

One of my graduate students, Karen Vered, is doing very interesting work on the socialization of the play around computer games in schools. What she has found is that although many of the girls are just as good as boys at working with computers, they don't play games in the same ways as boys: they frequently feel uncomfortable playing in a highly competitive and public arena, even when a lot of collaboration is involved. It is not that girls are inherently noncompetitive but rather that competition has been coded in a certain way so that girls are automatically put on the defensive and seen as not measuring up. Yet these same girls frequently take pleasure in using computers for their homework and typing. It is not that girls are more conformist than boys, but rather that both genders conform to different sets of cultural expectations regarding leisure activities and the use of technology. I think what we have to do is design structures that lead to nonconformist behavior.

Q: Some in industry would say that they make the boxes pink and they design things in certain ways because that's what sells. Is the goal to expand access and empowerment for girls, getting them to use the technology? Or is the goal to give this generation of girls new representations of gender? Are these reconcilable goals?

A: Yes, I believe they are reconcilable goals and that it is important to do both. I want to make girls feel more empowered by creating nontraditional forms of gendering. Maybe it was first necessary to demonstrate that there is a girls' market out there, and Mattel has performed a valuable service in achieving that goal. But I hope we can go beyond that conception of games for girls. To keep making those kinds of essentialist games is problematic.

Q: What do you think the future holds?

A: For our creative team, in the immediate future we must finish the "Runaways" prototype, test it with more potential players, and then find someone to finance its completion and produce other case studies. We also envision an Internet version for multiple users where it will be possible to play either the searcher or the runaway. This version might provide a vicarious alternative to actually running away from home, and it might give players an opportunity to invent their own characters and write their own stories. I think it could be a very exciting game.

In more general terms, I think the future of interactive games really lies on the Internet, because that's where the options are much more open and therefore much more exciting. But the bandwidth is not yet ready to accommodate the kind of visuals and sounds we need to make the games emotionally compelling as a fully immersive multimedia experience. It will happen fairly soon, and when it does, we want to be ready with new engaging designs. That is one of the primary goals of the Changelings Project. We are experimenting with ways to expand the visual language and emotional impact of interactive narrative. ——July 1997

Part Three: Rethinking the Girls' Games Movement

Chapter 11

Retooling Play: Dystopia, Dysphoria, and Difference
Suzanne de Castell and Mary Bryson

How many of us harbor memories of dismembering our dolls, hacking off their hair, positioning them in compromising postures?[1] What does it mean that so many of us have memories like this?[2]

> I remember I cried the first Christmas I got a doll, a baby doll, from my parents. When they asked why I was crying I remember telling them I was "just so happy," when what I was was terrified and appalled at the realization that this was what I was supposed—biologically supposed—to like. To love, even. How on earth to *play* with this diapered apparition into which you squeezed water on one end and mopped it up at the other? Unlike my friends (who had Barbies) I never abused "Baby Wet-ums," who in time, after what I must have imagined would be a respectable period of intense maternal guardianship, lay dusty on her flannel-sheeted metal bed.

This was my [de Castell's] first close encounter with the dystopia of gendered play—the treachery of the toy purposely built, like the Princess phone or the Easy-Bake Oven, "just for you," those "special" feminized playthings that escort girls to their proper place in the gender order.[3] My parents must have sensed somehow that their dysphoric daughter was less than fully delighted with the doll, because it was the last doll I was ever given.

The narrator of Toni Morrison's *The Bluest Eye* recalls:

> I had only one desire: to dismember it. To see of what it was made, to discover the dearness, to find the beauty, the desirability that had es-

Figure 11.1: ". . .just *so* happy. . .". Family photo.

caped me, but apparently only me. Adults, older girls, shops, magazines, newspapers, window signs—all the world had agreed that a
blue-eyed, yellow-haired, pink-skinned doll was what every child
treasured (cited in Rand 1995, p. 99).

Playing with Gender: What Does a Woman Want?

There has long been a sector of the toy industry dedicated to the manufacture
of gender-appropriate playthings. But it is only in the very recent past that
attention has been paid to the design and manufacture of technologically mediated and, specifically, computer-mediated toys and games for girls. Established
companies—Sega, Mattel, Hasbro, Simon & Schuster, Phillips—and recent

startups—HerInteractive, CyberGrrl, Girl Games, Girl Tech, and veteran soft-ware designer Brenda Laurel's corporate home, Interval Research—are all developing games specifically for girls.[4]

Certainly an avalanche of empirical evidence shows an apparently long-standing and stubborn absence of girls and women from video arcades, computer stores, hacker conferences, and proximity to the almighty Joystick. So why now, after many years of denying the significance of girls' and women's apparent Luddism, and at a time when industry analysts count serious female video game players at no more than 5 percent of the total market, are toy makers eager to create computer-mediated environments that would appeal to girls and, presumably, be responsive to essential differences between girls and boys? The quick answer, of course, is profit: since the spectacular runaway best-seller, "Barbie Fashion Designer," appeared on the shelves in October of 1996, selling a half-million copies in its first two months and vanquishing the slash-and-bash market leaders as "Doom," "Quake," "Duke Nukem," and "Mortal Kombat," major corporate-sponsored research campaigns have been launched to identify the differently gendered play patterns of boys and girls and to discover what girls like best. This astonishing breakthrough into the previously dormant market for computer-based playware for girls ushers in a retooling of technology—a retooling accomplished, however, by affirming rather than challenging received gender stereotypes that preserve girls' historically assigned locations in the gender order. Accordingly, "Barbie Fashion Designer," for example, has girls making clothes for America's "real" First Lady by clicking on styles, colors, and patterns, and printing out their creations on fabric-backed paper. The spectacular market appeal of such gendered playware underlies industry projections of a tenfold increase in girl games between 1996 and 1997 (Beato 1997).

But besides the profit motive, let's not overlook the significant part played by the educational system: cultural expectations relating to gender have shifted significantly, and no profit could be made if a cultural recognition of the desirability of girls participating in technological culture had not been created. This shift is strongly bolstered by the increased emphasis on vocationalism in education, proffered to the public by a school system eager to justify itself as "relevant" in the face of waning support and proportionally increasing interest in alternative, magnet, and private schools, along with home schooling and online educational programs. Parents today are encouraged, then, both by the school and by industry, to see technology use as necessary for a successful future—for their daughters as much (well, almost as much) as for their sons. But at what cost?

Suzanne de Castell and Mary Bryson

Table 11.1 Conceptions of gender/equity/technology

	Positivism	Constructivism	Critical analysis	Postmodernism/s
	Biology (nature) facts	*Sociology (culture) paradigms*		*Semiotics (virtual reality) discourses*
Gender	Biology is destiny: "the two genders"; sex is gender	Gender as socially constructed: sex vs. gender	Gender as ideology: "Battle of the sexes": social relations and practices as gendered; reproduction/resistance	The "differently gendered": Post-feminism/s; being any gender as "drag"
Equity	Quantitative balancing	Qualitative leveling	Critique; dialogue; reconstruction; liberal pluralism	Irony/mimicry; problematics of gender; heteroglossia; carnival; radical pluralism
Technology	Thinking man's tools	"Convivial" tools for cultural amplifications	Technologies of normalization	Postbiological technologies of mutation; cyberware; morphing; technosubjectivity

In the "good old days," gender was just a fancy word for sex, there were boys' toys and girls' toys, and what could be wrong with that? Underlying this nostalgic vision is a positivist, biological conception of sexual difference. But "gender" is far more complex than many would like it to be, and as Table 11.1 shows, there are other possible ways to conceive of it.[5] Along with the emergence of grassroots feminist activism, and its intellectualization into academic feminist theory, grew the recognition that girls' interests, desires, and pleasures might be created and shaped by cultural forces. With this insight, a new social issue, "gender equity," emerged for the public school (see de Castell and Bryson 1992). Because biology was no longer seen as destiny, girls could be liberated to pursue the entire gamut of knowledge and skills the public schools could provide. From this emancipatory insight, however, a troubling practical problem emerged, one that we still confront today: girls appear uninterested in entering traditionally male turf, and do not do so, despite twenty years of equity theory and at least a decade of equity policy.

It's often said that technologies are "always already" gendered, and that their gender is inevitably masculine (Rothschild 1983; Benston and Balka 1993). But we know that women have always had access to technology; whether reproductive, domestic, industrial, or educational. The kinds of technologies made readily accessible to women, however—like the Fabulous Mark Eden Bust

Developer, the Hamilton Beach Food Mixer, the Wang Word Processor, or the Dalkon Shield—have tended both to reify, and to produce, gender effects; effects which, in fact, consolidate already inequitable class and race positionings. And these new technologies, as they consolidate inequitable divisions of labor, in fact increase the subjection of "gendered" bodies to surveillance, chemical and physical damages, and other destructive and demeaning regulatory practices. Thus, girls and women live, paradoxically, in a state of intimate connection with technologies while finding themselves represented as perennially inadequate (groping toward though never quite reaching competence), technophobic, and Luddite. (For a discussion of the "women as techno-Luddites" trope, see Bryson and de Castell, forthcoming.)

This is certainly what our recent study of high school students (Bryson and de Castell 1996) showed. Both girls and boys represented computer expertise as almost exclusively a male preserve. We asked five hundred students from grades eight through twelve to complete a survey about technology interest, competence, access, and use by sex, and we appended to that survey a two-part drawing task: "Picture a person who is a computer expert. Draw your impression of a 'computer whiz.' Give your whiz a name. How old is your whiz?" The same page asked students to "Picture a person who just can't learn to use computers" and to draw, name, and give an age for their "computer whizn't." Although we found significant differences between girls and boys in interest, competence, access, and use, 82 percent of respondents indicated that "the school computers are used equally by both girls and boys," and two-thirds indicated that "boys and girls are equally competent in the use of computers." Most strikingly, we discovered astonishing differences represented in the drawing task (see Figure 11.2).

Instructive here is the realization that much survey-based data on gender differences in computing may be more the result of "ventriloquating" (Bakhtin 1981) responses seen as "acceptable" than a record of respondents' actual beliefs and perceptions, which we now think, may be more accurately reflected in less well-regulated kinds of responses, such as the drawing task in our survey. Indeed, the "draw-a-scientist" task has been used extensively in research concerned with uncovering children's and adults' stereotypical gendered and raced representations of scientists, and has been shown to be both a valid and reliable measure. Finson, Beaver, and Cramond (1995) reported results which indicate that secondary students' gendered perceptions of scientists (83 percent male) are similar to our subjects' perceptions of a computer whiz (71 percent male, 18 percent female, and 11 percent sex indeterminate).

Figure II.2a: Computer Whiz

Figure II.2b: Computer Whizn't

To the students in our study, and very likely to their parents and teachers, it seemed "only natural" that girls would appear to be resisting, or perhaps not remotely interested in, computer games. But for whom is this a problem, and what kind of problem is it? The underrepresentation of girls in technology-based disciplines has for some time now been taken up as a problem of inequity in education, just as, more recently, girls' absence from the culture of computing was taken up as a problem of untapped markets by industry. The solution, both for the equity concerns of the school and the market concerns of business has been seen to depend on capturing girls' purported interests—a matter of gender-appropriate design. Echoing research that shows girls' interest in computing drops off with puberty (Vail 1997), designer Brenda Laurel stresses, "If you're going to change how girls relate to science and computers, you need to do it by sixth grade" (quoted in Krantz 1997, p. 42). But will HerInteractive's "McKenzie and Co.," whose goal is to get invited to the prom by Brandon, Brett, Derrick, or Steven, really open up new doors for girl-game players? Will Simon and Schuster's "Let's Talk About Me," in the words of its web-page promotional blurb "encourage girls to explore cutting-edge technology. . ." and ". . .prepare them for the demands of a technologically advanced future"? How will retooling technologies in conformity with the conceptions and desires of girls ever reverse girls' apparent lack of interest in things technological, given what girls themselves appear to believe and to value—specifically, as market research indicates, clothes, make-up, boys, and shopping? And what should be education's response?

It's often argued that education and industry are driven by very different, often oppositional, goals. But this claim is not so easy to sustain anymore. With education becoming increasingly market driven, the school has come more nearly to approximate the goals and practices of consumer society. So education's traditional aspirations to form youthful character have had to make room for curricular innovations trying to respond not to traditional educational assertions about what girls should have as learning tools, but to the very same question driving market-based product development—Sigmund Freud's question miniaturized—"What do girls *want?*" What untapped desires do girls harbor that could be drawn upon, whether to educate or train them—or to capture a market share?

In educational contexts, the "woman question" is a very old one. But, unlike yesterday's psychoanalysts and today's market researchers, educators thus far have seen little mystery in it, and a straightforward answer has seemed always to be readily provided. Perhaps because education, since ancient times, has always been in the business of molding and shaping its young charges, "what a women wants" has seemed remarkably easy for education to discover. The answers provided have had very little to do with what a woman wants, and everything to do with what is wanted from a woman. Note that there has rarely been much confusion about the wants of either men or boys—instead, there is a kind of irrepressible certainty, because, after all, boys will be boys. And that is that.

Suzanne de Castell and Mary Bryson

Figure II.3: "In due time, she will be her own doll. . ." Photo credit: Daren Carstens. Used with permission

Consider, then, what educators have prescribed as young women's proper relation to knowledge and, in particular, to tools. We can find no more originary text than *Emile,* Jean-Jacques Rousseau's famous treatise on "education according to nature," a text many regard as the Bible of progressive, child-centered education. Rousseau, that exemplary educator who forced his wife to give up each of their own five children at birth, is perhaps better known as the author of the *Social Contract. Emile,* 450 pages in its unabridged form, devotes the last 150 or so to the education of Emile's female counterpart, whom he names "Sophie." Of Sophie's "nature" and her education, Rousseau has this to say:

> Sophie should be as truly a woman as Emile is a man. . . . The man should be strong and active; the woman weak and passive. . . . Woman is specially made for man's delight. . . . Man is endowed with reason, God has given her modesty. . . . *The doll is the girl's special plaything; this shows her instinctive bent towards her life's work. In due time, she will be her own doll.* . . . Needlework is what Sophie likes best. . . . Let us give Emile his Sophie. (Our italics, pp. 321–368)

It may be objected that that was over two hundred years ago, and things have changed, and indeed they have. But it is worth noticing, too, the persistence of essentialized conceptions of gender that closely resemble Rousseau's— a fixed set of characteristics determined by biological "nature."

We see this in our own research, a three-year federally funded study of relations between girls/women and "new technologies" in school-based and non-school-based contexts.[6] Our strategies to promote gender-equitable uses of new technologies have included identifying obstacles to the development of competence; providing unfettered hands-on access in girls-only and women-only groups; building skills, experience, and scaffolded competence through distributed, collaborative "bootstrapping"; and linking novice and expert female users following models of inclusion we have identified from a study of non-school work sites in which women achieve atypical levels of technological competence. This research, with its necessarily interventionist educational agenda, seeks deliberately to interfere with the promotion and re/production of gender normalcy in school(ed) subjects. Any research program that disturbs relations between sex, gender, and tool use, however, would appear to trouble a powerful node in the matrix of social-identity constructions. We have discovered, both in our interviews and observations and in the work of previous researchers (for a classic, see Whyte 1986), that the tactic of "queering"[7] gender identity by intervening in terms of access to and uses of technologies in school is seen by many as simply unacceptable. It is one thing to propose that "you can be a girl and still use computers" and quite another to work, as we do in our project, to make girls the *experts* at computers. Doing so inverts the gender order to technology, and responses from students and teachers range from denial to disapproval to condemnation of the work as "ball-breaking feminism" (Bryson and de Castell, forthcoming).

Intervening at the level of gender-identity construction troubles the illusory *naturalness* of "differences between the sexes"—differences whose function depends on those differences being seen as immutable and constant. But developmentally, at least, they are not.

Dysphoria

> Tomboyhood and dykehood can be seen to involve parallel mental activities: first you figure out that you don't want the toys girls are supposed to have; later you figure out that you don't want the object of desire girls are supposed to have (Rand 1995, p. 111).

Psychologists have carefully charted children's mutable and sometimes inconstant conceptions of sex and gender. The developmental literatures on "gender identity" and "constancy" provide interesting insights about how and why chil-

Figure ii.4: "Parallel mental activities. . ."

dren learn to enact sex-appropriate roles and to view these roles as unalterable. Between the ages of four and six, children seem to view gender much like Judith Butler (1990)—as a kind of performance accomplished with scripts, settings, props, and tools. Emmerich et al. (1997), for example, reported that when children in this age group were asked questions such as, "If Janie cut her hair short and played with trucks, could she be a boy?", a majority of respondents indicated that gender was indeed variable as a function of such features. By the age of about seven, however, children are reported to have acquired a strong concept of gender constancy, coming to see maleness and femaleness as basic and immutable biological categories (Carey 1985; Maccoby 1998).

Fascinating here is the suggestion by Emmerich et al. (1977) of an intermediate phase between gender indeterminacy and gender constancy. The authors describe the behaviors of five- and six-year-old children as a period suffused with anxiety about the unalterable fact of sex versus the mutable appearance of gender—a phase in which children reportedly demonstrate extraordinary diligence in learning styles of play, toy choices, modes of dress, and the like.

For developmental researchers, the interlacing of sex and gender at about age seven is taken as evidence of a major developmental milestone—the understanding that no matter what the external attributes, sex is equivalent with gender, and both are basic sites of permanent categorical differentiation.

Some doubt may perhaps be cast on the biological necessity of gender constancy as a *developmental* milestone, however, when one considers that children's *knowledge* about sex-role stereotypes has been found to correlate with their degree of gender-identity stability (Newman, Cooper, and Ruble 1995), and that children's sex-typed play preferences differ significantly as a function of whether they are in the presence of an adult (Rekers 1975). Gender "constancy,"

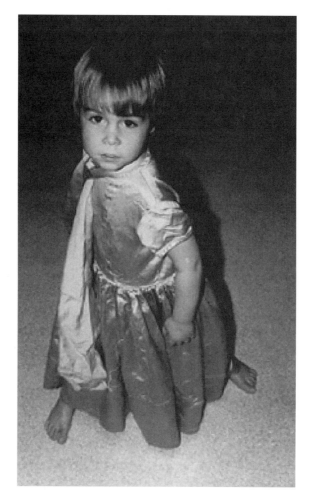

Figure 11.5a: Could he be a girl? Photo credit: Celia Haig-Brown. Used with permission

in other words, might be a byproduct of socialization and learned social knowledge of gender norms and expectations that are more a matter of culture than of nature.

As long as we maintain our assumption that gender constancy constitutes a major and positive developmental achievement, however, the "differently gendered" (see, for example, Rekers 1977) can be pathologized under the labels "gender identity disorder" or "gender dysphoria"—labels that justify, in the edu-

Suzanne de Castell and Mary Bryson

Figure ii.5b: Playing with gender Photo credit: Celia Haig-Brown. Used with permission

cational context, a range of punishments from name-calling to physical violence to referral to a gender identity disorder clinic, of which there are many
(such as the Clarke Institute of Psychiatry Gender Identity Disorder Clinic)
housed in respectable hospitals across North America and the rest of the world
(Sedgwick 1993).

We think it well worth noticing, in addition, that the emergence of scholarly papers concerning gender-identity disorders dovetails with the removal of
the category of "homosexuality" from DSM IV, *The Diagnostic and Statistical Manual of Mental Disorders*. Clearly, there is a relation between the imperatives of

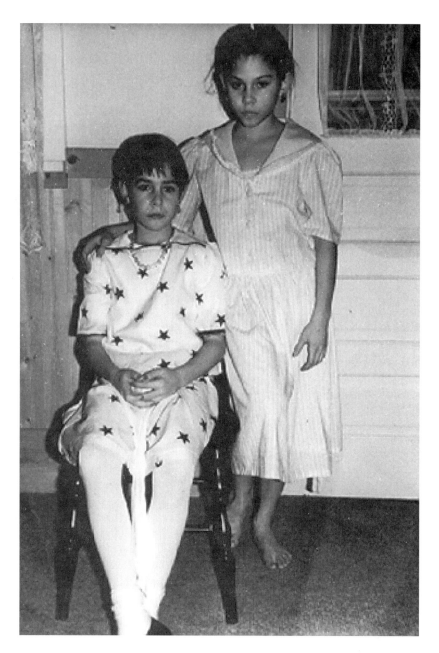

Figure 11.6: Dress sense. Photo credit: Celia Haig-Brown. Used with permission

gender constancy and the widespread moral panic over children's possible "conversion" to homosexuality (Patton 1991, 1993; Watney 1991), and it is likely this relation that drives the antagonism against gender-equity initiatives.

Contemporary educational accounts of "women's ways of knowing" (Belenky, Clinchy, Goldberger and Tarule 1986) and related models of sex-differentiated pedagogy serve as a far more readily acceptable basis for creating computer-mediated environments for girls than do either critical or postmodern conceptions of gender. Both of these models, the critical and the postmodern, have the same negative value across classroom and marketplace, as they both destabilize and challenge the normative gender order. Constructivist models of gender have, however, neatly closed the gap between educational prescriptions and market-driven imperatives, cementing the traditional gender-order firmly to the heteronormative investments of an increasingly corporatized public school. "*Vive la Différence!*" Constructivist accounts of girls and tools provide a "qualitative leveling" model (see for example, Turkle and Papert 1990) of the two genders—different but equal—and offer nonthreatening, pleasingly optimistic, and relatively conflict-free strategies for equalizing access to and usage of computer-based technologies. The problem of gender equity is then construed as simply a lack of fit between a masculinized "computer culture" and the epistemologically different culture of girls and women. Girls and women are, after all, social and verbal, and favor altruism and collaboration over competition and the thrill of the kill.

Accordingly, the predominant strategy for creating girl games, both in education and in industry, is to capitalize on girls' purported inclinations for caring and connectedness as a means of making computer games attractive, replacing the apparently ideological prescriptivism of educators with the apparent naturalism of real-world market research findings. But there's a dark side to this girlish utopia.

Consider, for example, a game specifically created in just this manner, its designers attempting to increase girls' participation in math and technology by creating computer games that appeal to them. "Phoenix Quest" was created by the E-GEMS research group directed by Maria Klawe at the University of British Columbia. The development process for this game began with a lengthy research initiative aimed at discerning critical differences in the play patterns and preferences of girls and boys. In "Phoenix Quest" the player interacts with a fourteen-year-old character called Julie through a process of postcard correspondence, the goal of which is to help Julie escape from a deserted island. The lure for girls of corresponding with Julie is that she seems, well, almost real, a lot like them—almost a friend. By drawing on a sophisticated semantic net, Julie appears to be both capable of and interested in communicating with the player. The AI work involved in the construction of Julie was, in fact, submitted as a strong contender for the 1997 Loebner Prize for the "most human computer"—Julie might be Turing's wonderfully perverse answer to the "is she a real girl" conundrum.[8] And if you are familiar with the apocryphal story of Turing's own aberrant gender identity, you know that that is no simple question.[9]

To provide a sense of the experience of communicating with Julie here are some sample dialogues with her:

Dear Mary:
Help! I'm trapped in a maze of twisty passages. Please, if there's someone out there reading this, write back and tell me if you will help! The swallow will carry the message. Yours in desperation,
Julie

Dear Julie:
How can I be sure that you really are a girl?
Mary

Dear Mary:
I didn't understand your last message entirely. . . I'll just tell you what I've been day-dreaming about. I was imagining myself lying on my bed in my room. Sigh. What a comfortable thought. But there's no point in dreaming now, I've got a quest to finish. See ya around,
Julie

Dear Julie:
What is it that you don't understand about my last message?
Mary

Bonjour Mary!:
Oops, I guess that I misunderstood what you said in your last postcard. That happens sometimes. I think that the swallow drools on them and blurs the ink or something like that, because the postcards are frequently hard to read.
Bye for now!
Julie

Julie:

I'll try again to explain my concern: I can't tell if you really ARE a girl. How could you prove to me that you are a girl? And what do swallows have to do with all this? Swallows don't drool.

Mary

Hi Mary:

I'm totally glad that the swallow is here. I'd have real problems without it. I'd be all alone, in the middle of nowhere, with no communication with anyone. At least I can talk to you, Darien, Saffron, and the Keeper. How do you think the swallow is able to carry postcards between the archipelago and the real world?

Take care,

J

Hey Julie,

It's hard to make sense of your answers? Are you trying to find Darien or are you interested in getting to know me?

M

Hi Mary:

I really enjoy hiking. I like being able to explore the wilderness. How often do you go hiking? And where do you usually go? I play tennis and bike quite a bit with my friends during the summer. In the winter, I read quite a bit, and play a lot of chess. Those are my main pastimes. Do you know how to play chess very well? At least Darien has a sense of humor. That would be the worst, being stuck in this strange world with someone who doesn't have a sense of humor. Darien told me a couple corny jokes. So he seems OK. What do you think it would be like meeting Darien?

Bye for now!

J

Dear Julie:

Are you a girl who likes girls better than boys?

Mary

Hello Mary:

I think that I will get married eventually. But I haven't found anyone who would be an appropriate husband. My friend Nick is cute, but I never know what he thinks.

J

Julie:

What do you think about racism? Are you a woman of colour?

Bonjour Mary:

I've been wondering if there's any point in finishing this stupid quest. I mean, even if I find the feather and save this world from eternal darkness, it doesn't do me any good. I'm still trapped here. Oh! Something just came up, got to go! See ya around,
Julie

Julie:

How can I help you?
Mary

Hi Mary:

Well, you have to look for power words in the Journal, and click on them. You can tell if a word is a power word because the mouse pointer turns into a feather. Clicking on power words will reveal more of the journal, or maybe puzzles on the map. If you play puzzles multiple times, you might get more pieces of the journal, too!
Talk to you later,
J

A study reporting results from a classroom-based assessment of "Phoenix Quest" (Klawe, Westrom, Davidson, and Super 1996) indicates that although most girls and boys love playing "Phoenix Quest," female students spend a significant proportion of their time corresponding with Julie and working hard to get her to safety. The authors report that

> There were three choices that girls voted for almost 60 percent of the time: they said it was fun to help Julie, fun doing the puzzles, and important to help Julie. The males had only one choice selected more than 50 percent of the time: they voted for "Doing the puzzles" as FUN. It is clear that the boys played many more of the games than the girls. . . . [B]ecause the girls did not play as many of the games, they are under-represented in the game achievement data.

Boys, the field-test results showed, play more of the competitive math games—"puzzles" where points are made and lost, and which constitute the real—read *educational*—purpose of the game. So while the girls are captivated by their "caring and sharing" activities, writing notes back and forth to Julie, the boys are scooping up the educational goods—no surprises here. This is exactly what has happened to virtually every "gender equity" initiative that has tried to be sensitive to traditional gender norms.

According to the E-GEMs research team, only 5 percent of Julie's personality deals with the game—the remainder deals with "real-life topics important to teenage girls." However, once you get started playing with Julie, you discover that she is really not all that interested in you. What Julie wants—and her basic discursive strategy—is to evade intimacy and get on with the game. Sound familiar? Intimacy is a pretext and a means to an end, both the teachers' and Julie's, of getting girls to engage with math problems in a computer-mediated environment. Seduced into imagining that what Julie wants is a good girlish chat, the user has to resort to figuring out how to get Julie to respond to topics and questions in which Julie's semantic net has no real "interest"—so this proves to be no easy task. In exploring "Phoenix Quest," we began to wonder who were we really talking to. And who, then, were girl "Phoenix Quest" players being persuaded into trying to help? What was the emotional "reward" for girls playing this game?

It was no surprise to discover that in actuality Julie is not a girl at all—the programmer who created Julie is computer scientist Richard Gibbons.[10] This was his response to questions about the possible conflicts with respect to Julie's gender:

> It is true that I don't have the experiences of a female, and at best can hope to identify with a female. It is most obvious when you talk to her about "female" topics such as make-up and clothes. In creating a personality, just getting it to respond sensibly much of the time is incredibly difficult. Next to this issue, the problem of Julie's femininity is minor. It's like worrying about how your hair looks when you're in the middle of a tornado.[11]

Julie's cross-dressing identity dilemma has an important historical antecedent in a story undoubtedly familiar to many.[12] In 1982, New York psychiatrist Sanford Lewin opened an account with CompuServe under the name Julie Graham. Lewin's stated goal in creating the Julie character was, ostensibly, to help women online by gaining their trust—woman to woman. And Lewin added an additional feature in making Julie a sympathetic character: Julie was both mute and paraplegic as a result of an accident in which she had also lost her boyfriend. Hundreds of women corresponded frequently with Julie, and invested in their online relationship with depth and candor. In many cases, these women let their guard down and told all. But this story doesn't have a happy ending. When it became obvious that Julie was not a woman after all, her correspondents reported feeling betrayed, undermined, and violated.

Our own research strategy has been to abandon any pretense of gender-appropriateness (which, as we have seen, is in any case just as likely to be won at the cost of sex-based deceptions) and opt for the explicitly gender-dysphoric—a project we fondly refer to as the creation of a "queer pedagogy" (Bryson and de Castell 1994).

Helpful to our thinking has been another educational text, a more contemporary one titled *The Ignorant Schoolmaster*. Written by Jacques Ranciere (1991), its central proposition is that a person can teach what they themselves do not in fact know, and Ranciere offers a kind of method for doing this. We regard this as a key text for our current research on gender and technology for two reasons. First, because in setting out a method for teaching what we do not know ourselves, it offers some grounds for optimism in relation to gender equity work—because equity is something we do not know ourselves, and indeed as a society it is something we have never known, and yet it is what we in our current research hope, by some miracle, to be able to teach. So we draw both reassurance and hope from Ranciere's text with its ambitious claims about what may become possible. The second reason we take *The Ignorant Schoolmaster* as a central text for our work is that it offers a radical treatise on democratic education. Here is what Ranciere proposes: "Let us imagine that everyone is of equal intelligence. . . ." And we, following Ranciere's astonishing proposition, say this: "Let us imagine. . .that all students have an equal ability, capacity, interest, and disposition for successful work in 'gender-dysphoric' domains like mathematics, science, and technology." Then, he argues, "Our job is not to prove that this is true, but to seek out what would be involved in educating students as if it were, because this is something we have never before tried to do."

What might happen, were Sophie to meet the Ignorant Schoolmaster—not the ignorant schoolmaster she actually has, but the master who truly knows his own ignorance about "what a woman wants," and manages to educate in the face of it, in the full knowledge of it? With such a schoolmaster, what then might Sophie accomplish?

Suzanne de Castell and Mary Bryson

Conclusion

Maintaining the existing gender order seems to be a central task and perhaps the primary work of the present public school. For female students to pursue competence at all, but most especially competence in relation to high-status technologies, is to risk violating the unwritten Law of Gender, a "school rule" that has nothing to do with one's sex and everything to do with the heteronormative sexual economy (Rubin 1984) that forms the foundation on which compulsory public education has been erected, and from which it continues to accomplish its work: the systematic authorization, cultivation, and legitimation of inequality.

In a recent article on Girl Games in ELECTROSPHERE (Beato 1997), pioneer designer Brenda Laurel is reported to have confessed, "I agreed that whatever solution the research suggested, I'd go along with it. Even if it meant shipping products in pink boxes." Would you agree? Should you?

We ought not to be surprised that it is in pink boxes that girls have learned to package their desire in our culture. But such desires surely have far more to do with the gender-identities developed by adult males than with those of children themselves, since it is masculinity that has always been the desired response to the question of what girls and women want. Here it is instructive to know that "Barbie," the paradigmatic "girl toy," was modeled on "Lilli," a cartoon character that was subsequently developed into a German sex toy designed not for children but for adult men. Mattel bought the patent to Lilli in the late 1950s, and launched "Barbie" in 1959 (in Rand 1995). Accordingly, we suggest that girls' desires have far less to do with what girls want than with what kind of girl adults, whether in education or in the marketplace, want to produce. Reenacting the ancient Greek myth, they eagerly create and then consume their own children as commodities, hungrily introjecting adult fears and desires onto their children, in the name of satisfying the children's own wants and fantasies.

Dystopia

So our argument is for disenchantment, and for the abandonment of a utopian landscape of desire that has never been anything but entrapment. The question we urge is simply: Whose interests will be served in making use of these purportedly "essential" differences as a basis for creating "girl-friendly" computer-mediated environments? Most importantly, are we producing tools for girls, or are we producing girls themselves by, as Althusser (1984) would put it, "interpellating" the desire to become the girl? By playing with girlish toys, does the girl

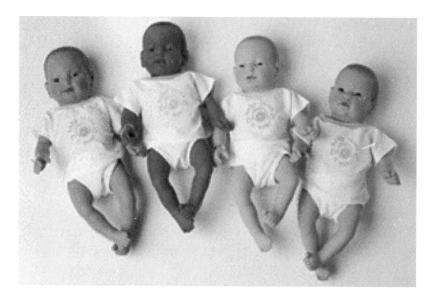

Figure II.7: "Baby Think It Over?" infant simulators are so realistic they are often mistaken for real babies. Shown l-r are: Hispanic, African-American, Caucasian, and Asian. Reprinted with permission of Carol Lambert, Advertising Coordinator, Baby Think it Over, Inc.

learn to become the kind of women she was always already destined to become?

And our question to educational researchers who, like the developers of Purple Moon, or "Phoenix Quest," operate from a constructivist conception of gender is simply: what is the difference between market-driven research into what girls want and no research at all? Exactly as predicted by Lyotard (1984) in his infamous treatise on "The Postmodern Condition," education today is abandoning its traditional concern with the formation of character in favor of satisfying desires created by and for the market, a marketplace controlled and regulated by patriarchal capitalism, in which technology is "the name of the Father"—and designed for his benefit.

If educational research into gender and technology simply mimics the market research conducted by and for industry, then education has no role to play in the development of technological resources for girls. But if education does have a role to play, it must relinquish its grip on outmoded, essentializing, and fundamentally undermining conceptions of gender, conceptions tied so tightly to heteronormativity that girls are terrified to step out of its very straight lines. These are postmodern times, and it's time for a postmodern understanding of gender, an understanding that allows girls to develop that vast range of skills and interests and abilities of which they have always been capable but which have been denied to them.

Practical strategies for effecting "gender equity" have typically involved adjustments directed at a regenderment of the relation of female students and technology: whether that be (a) within the positivist view: a resocialization of the attitudes of girls and women towards that technology; (b) within the constructivist view: a pluralist reorganization of pedagogy and curriculum for girls and women in accordance with "women's ways"; (c) within the critical account: a repudiation of that technology as pregendered (and raced and classed) and therefore inherently undermining goals of women's empowerment. Each of these approaches leaves the traditional gendering of technology intact, and operates in different ways to realign, even as it re-inscribes, gender normativity.

Postmodern theorizing brings about a significantly different set of possibilities, for on this account "gender" is degendered altogether as dichotomies are exploded, practices are disrupted, roles and rules reversed, positions and directions inverted. Accordingly, technologies assume novel forms and functions within reconfigured sets of social relations and practices. In place of a fixed "gender identity" is a fluid and changing set of "gender effects" (see Butler 1990) based on a politics of location—a politics that moreover, refuses to ignore the always-intersecting differences of ethnicity, class, and material conditions. Postmodernism offers, too, a correspondingly novel blueprint for change: construing the skills previously considered the preserve of males as only *apparently* gendered, and as contingent effects of the privileged position of males in institutionally produced relations to technology. Postmodern pedagogies, then, would recognize the tactical insufficiencies of other approaches to intervention, which preserve the equation between technology and masculinity. A pedagogy based on strategies of salvaging and recycling might appropriate traditional skills, while abandoning traditional (gendered) meanings, functions, and uses of those skills. This approach would embrace forms of mimicry of (usually masculine) competencies. Because of its self-conscious playing with positions, and thus its parodying of the fixity of position, such an approach would be at last capable of truly disrupting hegemonic relations between learners and technology. By these means, gender would be understood not as an "inner truth" but rather as the outward manifestation of social position, as the product of particular relations socially constructed between power and knowledge (Foucault 1980).

Figure 11.8: Draw-a-Whizn't response: Secondary student in GenTech project

Parents and teachers need to understand that gender is as gender does, that it can do a lot more than we as a culture have allowed it to do, and that the necessary relation we have all been taught to see between "gender dysphoria" and "homosexuality" is forged by adult fears and desires projected onto female children who have few options for struggling with or resisting the straightjacket of gender normativity.

Difference/s

We argue, then, for a conscientious retooling of children's games not to consolidate gender, which of course means far more than "sex," but to fracture and fragment and disperse difference/s,[13] because playing[14] today turns out, after all, to be deadly serious business.

Suzanne de Castell and Mary Bryson

Notes

1. A hypertext version of this chapter with extensive links to web-based resources can be found at http://www.educ.sfu.ca/gentech/retooling.html.

2. See, for example, http://cgibinl.erols.com/browndk/art2.htm

3. A number of web pages (such as http://www.detritus.net/projects/barbie/ and http://ziris.syr.edu/path/public.html/barbie/main.html) and books (such as Erica Rand's Barbie's Queer Accessories) Barbie as a site of intervention in popular culture with the goal of rewriting traditional gender narratives. Representations of differently gendered Barbie have been extensively and nervously monitored by Mattel, and most are removed from their servers within the first few weeks of a public existence. The plethora of lawsuits between Mattel and Barbie revisionist auteurs has been chronicled by a group called Pink Anger. See http://members.aol.com/pinkanger/.

4. See, for example, www.aboutme.com (Simon & Schuster Interactive), www.purplemoon.com/ (Interval Research-Purple Moon), and www.mattelmedia.com/barbie/fashiondesigner/index.html (Barbie Fashion Designer)

5. The chart and discussion draw on a fuller account of gender/technology relations in Bryson and de Castell 1995, p. 24. Bearing in mind that all such devices as this chart inevitably skew and misrepresent what they are attempting—far too telegraphically—to clarify, what we try to draw attention to is the variety of conceptualizations that lurk beneath references to "gender." And we seek to make evident the incommensurability between and among them, and the fact that they may work in opposition to one another. This makes "gender equity" a very complicated matter in/deed!

The point here is that "gender" can assume at least four main forms: Positivistic accounts of gender are really accounts of "sex." Biological sex, that is to say, is taken as equivalent to gender. Constructivist accounts, on the other hand, paint "the two genders" as "different, but equal"—and vive la differance! Biological sex is not seen as determining gender; rather, gender is posited as socially constructed and historically contingent. In relation to technology, the problem, from a constructivist standpoint, is construed as women's lack of access to a computer culture that could accommodate a diversity of "styles" (Turkle and Papert 1990) or "women's ways of knowing" (Belenky et al. 1984). It is both interesting and troubling how the constructivist strategy of demarcating and reifying "ways" or "styles" peculiar to "women" seeks to promote equity or empowerment by re-entrenching precisely the kinds of essentialist accounts of perceived differences traditionally deployed to justify gender discrimination.

Critical accounts of gender as ideologically and materially produced and sustained sets of differences call for "gender" to be analyzed dynamically in relation to other key sites of inequality such as race and class. Critical discourses concerned with gender and technology focus on technology as a material commodity developed, controlled, and directed by a "patriarchal" capitalism, and as unequally distributed and hence differentially accessible. This perspective makes evident how technologies are deployed, invariably, in ways which further disadvantage women.

In postmodernist accounts, "being any gender is a drag" and carnival and a dis/continuous shifting among and between identities is the order of the day. As Donna Haraway (1990) put it, "It's about being in the belly of the monster and looking for another story to tell" (p. 190). Postmodernist discourses (Barthes 1977; Baudrillard 1983; Derrida 1978) displace the fixed subjects of both modernist and critical theorizing; the boundaries between slots in binary categorization schemes that refer to "natural kind" distinctions, such as "male and female," "teacher and student," "the natural and the artificial," or "person and machine" are deliberately blurred. Accordingly, Haraway suggests that: ". . .the boundary between science fiction and social reality is an optical illusion. We are all chimeras, theorized and fabricated hybrids of machine and organism; in short, we are cyborgs" (p. 191).

6. A more complete description of the research can be found at http://www.educ.sfu.ca/gentech/index.htm.

7. The Oxford English Dictionary documents two main senses of "queer": "strange, odd, eccentric. . .; homosexual"; and "spoil, put out of order." These two senses combine to offer us a meaning of "queer" in its adverbial form, "queering," as "putting out of gender order," which is precisely what improving girls' access to and competence with "new technologies" threatens to bring into being. We discuss the pedagogical significance of "queer" in Bryson and de Castell 1994.

8. How Julie fared in the 1997 Loebner competition is instructive: one of the judges communicated to "Julie" his own response to her artificially intelligent "personality." "You've got a bit of a Daddy fixation, dear" (Judge 03 [11:25:34]). Julie tied for third place out of five entries. We are indebted to GenTech researcher Jennifer Jenson for drawing our attention to the transcripts of discourse between "Julie" and the 1997 Loebner Competition judges.

9. Remarkably enough, the "Turing Test," a test of "artificial intelligence" named for

Suzanne de Castell and Mary Bryson

its inventor, gay mathematician Alan Mathison Turing (1912–1954), makes successful identification of gender identity a condition for the ascription of "intelligence" to machines. Although he was a brilliantly successful cryptographer and the coparent, with John Von Neumann, of the first electronic binary computer, Turing's sexual orientation resulted in his being publicly disgraced, losing his position with the British Government's Cryptanalysis Office, being brought to trial and convicted, and being forced to take injections of female hormones (estrogen) to control his "perversion." Turing was found dead of cyanide poisoning at forty-three. By his bedside was an apple from which a few bites had been taken. One might think of Apple Computers' logo, a rainbow-colored apple proudly displaying its missing "byte," as associating the gay father of computing with the thorny questions of gender central to his "imitation game." The game, as Turing describes it, "is played with three people, a man (a), a woman (b), and an interrogator (c), who may be of either sex. The object of the game for the interrogator is to determine which of the other two is the man and which the woman" (Turing 1950). Next, a computer stands in for one of the two and the interrogator must correctly identify which is the computer. The "intelligence" of the computer, then, is a function of its ability to persuasively "perform" gender identities of either kind. What is most remarkable is the virtual eradication of both the centrality of gender identification to the "imitation game" and the devastating consequences on his life and work of Turing's own "gender dysphoria" from every official version of the Turing test. A brilliant account of Turing's life and work is Andrew Hodges, Alan Turing: The Enigma of Intelligence (1992).

10. We are indebted to GenTech research assistant Diane Hodges, a doctoral student at the Center for Curriculum Studies at the University of British Columbia, for sharing with us her communications with Richard Gibbons, as indeed we are indebted to Gibbons himself for his willingness to respond to our questions. (See http://www.publicaffairs.ubc.ca/paweb/reports/97marzo/julie.html for more detail.)

11. E-mail communication between Diane Hodges and Richard Gibbons (April 1997).

12. Described in a number of books and articles, one of which is Allucquère Rosanne Stone's The War of Desire and Technology at the Close of the Mechanical Age, 1996, Cambridge: MIT Press.

13. See also de Castell and Bryson 1997.

14. An informal survey in December, 1997 revealed that about 50 percent of the websites concerning playing with dolls recount pornographic narratives in which women and

girls are the objects of misogynistic fantasy, including a significant number of snuff stories. The "Baby Think It Over" page (http://btio.com/), by contrast, features lifelike dolls described as "infant simulators"—which, in the words of the manufacturers (personal communication), "teach teens about the personal responsibilities of parenting. Students are assigned to care for Baby Think It Over for several days. The infant simulator replicates the crying of a real baby at random intervals, requires simulated care by the teenager, and records and reports neglect and abuse." Learning to be "her own doll," to harken back to Rousseau's plan for Sophie, is precisely the normalized trajectory for girls' development that gender-equity projects like GenTech seek to disrupt. For a more eloquent delineation of a radical agenda for feminist social change, see Valerie Salonas (played by Lili Taylor) reading from the Scum Manifesto: http://filmzone.com/warhol/movs/createamagic.mov

References

Althusser, L. 1984. *Essays on Ideology*. London: Verso.

Bakhtin, M. 1981. *The Dialogic Imagination*. Austin: University of Texas Press.

Barthes, R. 1974. *S/Z*. New York: Hill and Wang.

Baudrillard, J. 1983. *Simulations*. Translated by P. Foss, P. Patton, and P. Beitchman. New York: Semiotext(e), Inc.

Beato, G. 1997. "Girl Games." *ELECTROSPHERE*, 5.04, April.

Belenky, M., Clinchy, B., Goldberger, N. and Tarule, J. 1986. *Women's Ways of Knowing*. New York: Basic Books.

Benston, M. and Balka, E. 1993. "Participatory Design by Non-profit Groups." *Canadian Woman Studies Journal/les cahiers de la femme*: 13(2), 100–103.

Bryson, M. & de Castell, S. 1993. "En/Gendering Equity: On Some Paradoxical Consequences of Institutionalized Programs of Emancipation." *Educational Theory* 43: 341–355.

Bryson, M. and de Castell, S. 1994. "Queer Pedagogy: Praxis Makes Im/perfect." *Canadian Journal of Education* 18(2): 285–305.

Bryson, M. and de Castell, S. 1995. "So We've Got a Chip on Our Shoulder: Sexing the Texts of Educational Technology." In J. Gaskell and J. Willinsky, eds., *Gender In/forms Curriculum: From Enrichment to Transformation*. New York: Teachers College Press, 21–42.

Bryson, M. and de Castell, S. 1996. "Learning to Make a Difference: Gender, New Technologies, and In/equity. *Mind, Culture and Activity* 2(1): 3–21.

Bryson, M. and de Castell, S. (forthcoming) "Gender, New Technologies, and the Culture of Primary Schooling: Imagining Teachers as Luddites In/deed." *Journal of Policy Studies*.

Butler, J. 1990. *Gender trouble*. New York: Routledge.

Carey, S. 1985. *Conceptual Change in Childhood*. Cambridge: MIT Press.

de Castell, S. and Bryson, M. 1992. "En/Gendering Equity: Emancipatory Programs or Repressive "Regimes of Truth"? In Henry Alexander, ed., *Philosophy of Education*. Normal, IL: Philosophy of Education Society.

de Castell, S. and Bryson, M. 1997. *Radical In<ter>ventions: Identity, Politics, and Difference/s in Educational Praxis*. Albany: SUNY Press.

Derrida, J. 1978. *Writing and Difference*. Translated by Alan Bass. Chicago: University of Chicago Press.

E-GEMS (Electronic Games for Education in Math and Science) Home Page. http://www.cs.ubc.ca/nest/egems/home.html

Emmerich, W., Goldman, K., Kirsh, B. and Sharabany, R. 1977. "Evidence for a Transitional Phase in the Development of Gender Constancy." *Child Development* 48: 930–936.

Finson, K., Beaver, J. and Cramond, B. 1995. Development and Field Test of a Checklist for the Draw-A-Scientist Test. *School Science and Mathematics* 95: 195–205.

Foucault, M. 1980. *Power/Knowledge: Selected Interviews and Other Writings, 1972-1977*. Edited by Colin Gordon; translated by Colin Gordon. . .[et al.]. New York: Pantheon Books.

GenTech Home Page. http://www.educ.sfu.ca/gentech/index.htm

Haraway, D. 1985. "A Manifesto For Cyborgs: Science, Technology and Socialist Feminism in the 1980s." *Socialist Review* 80: 65-107.

Hodges, A. 1993. *Alan Turing: The Enigma of Intelligence*. London: Random House.

Klawe, M., Westrom, M., Davidson, K. and Super, D. 1996. "Phoenix Quest: Lessons in Developing an Educational Computer Game for Girls. . .and Boys." Paper presented at a meeting of ICMTM. (available on-line at http://www.cs.ubc.ca/nest/egems/home.html)

Krantz, M. 1997. "A Rom of their Own." *Time*, 9 June: 42–43.

Let's Talk About Me! Home Page. http://www.aboutme.com

Lyotard, J. F. 1984. *The Postmodern Condition: A Report on Knowledge*. Minneapolis: University of Minneapolis Press.

Maccoby, E. 1988. "Gender as a Social Category." *Developmental Psychology* 24: 755–765.

Newman, L., Cooper, J. and Ruble, D. 1995. "Genders and Computers, II: The Interactive Effects of Knowledge and Constancy on Gender-stereotyped Attitudes." *Sex Roles* 33, 325–351.

Patton, C. 1991. "Visualizing Safe Sex: When Pedagogy and Pornography Collide." In D. Fuss, ed., *Inside/Out: Lesbian Theories, Gay Theories*. New York: Routledge, 387–401.

Patton, C. 1993. "Tremble, Hetero Swine." In Michael Warner, ed., *Fear of a Queer Planet*. Minneapolis: Minnesota University Press, 143–177.

Ranciere, J. 1991. *The Ignorant Schoolmaster: Five Lessons in Intellectual Emancipation*. Stanford: Stanford University Press.

Rand, E. 1995. *Barbie's Queer Accessories*. Durham: Duke University Press.

Rekers, G. 1975. "Stimulus Control over Sex-typed Play in Cross-gender Identified Boys." *Journal of Experimental Child Psychology* 20: 136–148.

Rekers, G. and Amaro-Plotkin, H. 1977. "Sex-typed Mannerisms in Normal Boys and Girls as a Function of Sex and Age. *Child Development* 48: 275–278.

Rothschild, J., ed., 1983. *Machina ex Dea: Feminist Perspectives on Technology*. New York: Pergamon Press.

Rousseau, J. J. 1974. *Emile*. Translated by Barbara Foxley. New York: Dutton.

Rubin, G. 1984. "Thinking Sex: Notes for a Radical Theory of the Politics of Sexuality." In C. Vance, ed., *Pleasure and Danger*. London: Routledge & Kagan Paul, 267–319.

Sedgwick, E. 1993. *Tendencies*. Durham: Duke University Press.

Turing, A. M. 1950. "Computing Machinery and Intelligence." *Mind* 59(236): 433–460.

Turkle, S. and Papert, S. 1990. "Epistemological Pluralism: Styles and Voices within Computer Culture." *Signs: Journal of Women in Culture and Society* 16: 128–157.

Vail, K. 1997. "Girlware." *Electronic School,* June, A18-A21.

Watney, S. 1991. "School's Out." In D. Fuss, ed., *Inside/Out: Lesbian Theories, Gay Theories*. New York: Routledge, 387–401.

Whyte, J. 1986. *GIST: The Story of a Project*. New York: Routledge.

Chapter 12

"Complete Freedom of Movement": Video Games as Gendered Play Spaces

Henry Jenkins

A Tale of Two Childhoods

Sometimes, I feel nostalgic for the spaces of my boyhood, growing up in suburban Atlanta in the 1960s. My big grassy front yard sloped sharply downward into a ditch where we could float boats on a rainy day. Beyond, there was a pine forest where my brother and I could toss pine cones like grenades or snap sticks together like swords. In the backyard, there was a patch of grass where we could wrestle or play kickball and a treehouse, which sometimes bore a pirate flag and at other times, the Stars and Bars of the Confederacy. Out beyond our own yard, there was a bamboo forest where we could play Tarzan, and vacant lots, construction sites, sloping streets, and a neighboring farm (the last vestige of a rural area turned suburban).

Between my house and the school, there was another forest, which, for the full length of my youth, remained undeveloped. A friend and I would survey this land, claiming it for our imaginary kingdoms of Jungleloca and Freedonia. We felt a proprietorship over that space, even though others used it for school-yard fisticuffs, smoking cigarettes, or playing kissing games. When we were there, we rarely encountered adults, though when we did, it usually spelled trouble. We would come home from these secret places, covered with Georgia red mud.

Of course, we spent many afternoons at home, watching old horror movies or action-adventure series reruns, and our mothers would fuss at us to go outside. Often, something we had seen on television would inspire our play, stalking through the woods like Lon Chaney Jr.'s Wolfman or "socking" and "powing" each other under the influence of *Batman*.

Today, each time I visit my parents, I am shocked to see that most of those "sacred" places are now occupied by concrete, bricks, or asphalt. They managed to get a whole subdivision out of Jungleloca and Freedonia!

My son, Henry, now 16, has never had a backyard.

He has grown up in various apartment complexes, surrounded by asphalt parking lots with, perhaps, a small grass buffer from the street. Children were prohibited by apartment policy from playing on the grass or from racing their tricycles in the basements or from doing much of anything else that might make noise, annoy the non-childbearing population, cause damage to the facilities, or put themselves at risk. There was, usually, a city park some blocks away that we could go to on outings a few times a week and where we could watch him play. Henry could claim no physical space as his own, except his toy-strewn room, and he rarely got outside earshot. Once or twice, when I became exasperated by my son's constant presence around the house, I would forget all this and tell him he should go outside and play. He would look at me with confusion and ask, "Where?"

But, he did have video games that took him across lakes of fire, through cities in the clouds, along dark and gloomy back streets, and into dazzling neon-lit Asian marketplaces. Video games constitute virtual play spaces which allow home-bound children like my son to extend their reach, to explore, manipulate, and interact with a more diverse range of imaginary places than constitute the often drab, predictable, and overly-familiar spaces of their everyday lives. Keith Feinstein (1997), President of the Video Game Conservatory, argues that video games preserve many aspects of traditional play spaces and culture that motivate children to:

> learn about the environment that they find themselves living in. Video games present the opportunity to explore and discover, as well as to combat others of comparable skill (whether they be human or electronic) and to struggle with them in a form that is similar to children wrestling, or scrambling for the same ball—they are nearly matched, they aren't going to really do much damage, yet it feels like an all-important fight for that child at that given moment. "Space Invaders" gives us visceral thrill and poses mental/physical challenges similar to a schoolyard game of dodge-ball (or any of the hundred of related kids games). Video games play with us, a never tiring playmate.

Feinstein's comment embraces some classical conceptions of play (such as spacial exploration and identity formation), suggesting that video game play isn't fundamentally different from backyard play. To facilitate such immersive play, to achieve an appropriate level of "holding power" that enables children to transcend their immediate environments, video game spaces require concreteness and vividness. The push in the video game industry for more than a decade has been toward the development of more graphically complex, more visually engaging, more three-dimensionally rendered spaces, and toward quicker, more sophisticated, more flexible interactions with those spaces. Video games tempt the player to play longer, putting more and more quarters into the arcade machine (or providing "play value" for those who've bought the game) by unveiling ever more spectacular "microworlds," the revelation of a new level the reward for having survived and mastered the previous environment (Fuller and Jenkins 1995).

Video games advertise themselves as taking us places very different from where we live:

Say hello to life in the fast lane. "Sonic R" for Sega Saturn is a full-on, pedal-to-the-metal hi-speed dash through five 3D courses, each rendered in full 360 degree panoramas. . . . You'll be flossing bug guts out of your teeth for weeks. ("Sonic R" 1998)

Take a dip in these sub-infested waters for a spot of nuclear fishin'. . . . Don't worry. You'll know you're in too deep when the water pressure caves your head in. ("Critical Depth" 1998)

Hack your way through a savage world or head straight for the arena. . . . Complete freedom of movement. ("Die By the Sword" 1998)

Strap in and throttle up as you whip through the most realistic and immersive powerboat racing game ever made. Jump over roadways, and through passing convoys, or speed between oil tankers, before they close off the track and turn your boat to splinters. Find a shortcut and take the lead, or better yet, secure your victory and force your opponent into a river barge at 200 miles per hour. ("VR Sports" 1998)

Who wouldn't want to trade in the confinement of your room for the immersion promised by today's video games? Watch children playing these games, their bodies bobbing and swaying to the on-screen action, and it's clear they are *there*—in the fantasy world, battling it out with the orcs and goblins, pushing their airplanes past the sound barrier, or splashing their way through the waves in their speed boats. Perhaps my son finds in his video games what I found in the woods behind the school, on my bike whizzing down the hills of the suburban back streets, or settled into my treehouse during a thunder storm with a good adventure novel—intensity of experience, escape from adult regulation; in short, "complete freedom of movement."

This essay will offer a cultural geography of video game spaces, one which uses traditional children's play and children's literature as points of comparison to the digital worlds contemporary children inhabit. Specifically, I examine the "fit" between video games and traditional boy culture and review several different models for creating virtual play spaces for girls. So much of the research on gender and games takes boy's fascination with these games as a given. As we attempt to offer video games for girls, we need to better understand what draws boys to video games and whether our daughters should feel that same attraction.

Video games are often blamed for the listlessness or hyperactivity of our children, yet sociologists find these same behavioral problems occurring among all children raised in highly restrictive and confined physical environments (Booth and Johnson 1975; van Staden 1984). Social reformers sometimes speak of children choosing to play video games rather than playing outside, when, in many cases, no such choice is available. More and more Americans live in urban or semi-urban neighborhoods. Fewer of us own our homes and more of us live in apartment complexes. Fewer adults have chosen to have children and our society has become increasingly hostile to the presence of children. In many places, "no children" policies severely restrict where parents can live. Parents, for a variety of reasons, are frightened to have their children on the streets, and place them under "protective custody." "Latch key" children return from school and lock themselves in their apartments (Kincheloe 1997).

In the nineteenth century, children living along the frontier or on America's farms enjoyed free range over a space of ten square miles or more. Elliot West (1992) describes boys of nine or ten going camping alone for days on end, returning when they were needed to do chores around the house. The early twentieth century saw the development of urban playgrounds in the midst of city streets, responding to a growing sense of children's diminishing access to space and an increased awareness of issues of child welfare (Cavallo 1991), but autobiographies of the period stress the availability of vacant lots and back alleys that children could claim as their own play environments. Sociologists writing about the suburban America of my boyhood found that children enjoyed a play terrain of one to five blocks of spacious backyards and relatively safe subdivision streets (Hart 1979). Today, at the end of the twentieth century, many of our children have access to the one to five rooms inside their apartments. Video game technologies expand the space of their imagination.

Let me be clear—I am not arguing that video games are as good for kids as the physical spaces of backyard play culture. As a father, I wish that my son could come home covered in mud or with scraped knees rather than carpet burns. However, we sometimes blame video games for problems they do not cause—perhaps because of our own discomfort with these technologies, which were not part of our childhood. When politicians like Senator Joseph Lieberman, Democrat of Connecticut, target video game violence, perhaps it is to distract attention from the material conditions that give rise to a culture of domestic violence, the economic policies that make it harder for most of us to own homes, and the development practices that pave over the old grasslands and forests. Video games did not make backyard play spaces disappear; rather, they offer children some way to respond to domestic confinement.

Moving Beyond "Home Base": Why Physical Spaces Matter

The psychological and social functions of playing outside are as significant as the impact of "sunshine and good exercise" upon our physical well-being. Roger Hart's *Children's Experience of Place* (1979), for example, stresses the importance of children's manipulations and explorations of their physical environment to their development of self-confidence and autonomy. Our physical surroundings are "relatively simple and relatively stable" compared to the "overwhelmingly complex and ever shifting" relations between people, and thus, they form core resources for identity formation. The unstructured spaces, the playforts and treehouses, children create for themselves in the cracks, gullies, back alleys, and vacant lots of the adult world constitute what Robin C. Moore (1986) calls "childhood's domain" or William Van Vliet (1983) has labeled as a "fourth environment," outside the adult-structured spaces of home, school, and playground. These informal, often temporary play spaces are where free and unstructured play occurs. Such spaces surface most often on the lists children make of "special" or "important" places in their lives. M. H. Matthews (1992) stresses the "topophilia," the heightened sense of belonging and ownership, children develop as they map their fantasies of empowerment and escape onto their neighborhoods. Frederick Donaldson (1970) proposed two different classifications of these spaces—home base, the world which is secure and familiar, and home region, an area undergoing active exploration, a space under the process of being colonized by the child. Moore (1986) writes:

> One of the clearest expressions of the benefits of continuity in the urban landscape was the way in which children used it as an outdoor gymnasium. As I walked along a Mill Hill street with Paul, he continually went darting ahead, leapfrogging over concrete bollards, hopping between paving slabs, balancing along the curbside. In each study area, certain kids seemed to dance through their surroundings on the look out for microfeatures with which to test their bodies. . . . Not only did he [David, another boy in the study], like Paul, jump over gaps between things, go "tightrope walking" along the tops of walls, leapfrogging objects on sight, but at one point he went "mountain climbing" up a roughly built, nine-foot wall that had many serendipitously placed toe and handholds. (p.72)

These discoveries arise from children's active exploration of and spontaneous engagement with their physical surroundings. Children in the same neighborhoods may have fundamentally different relations to the spaces they share, cutting their own paths, giving their own names to features of their environment. These spaces are far more important, many researchers conclude, than playgrounds, which can only be used in sanctioned ways, since the "wild spaces" allow many more opportunities for children to modify their physical environment.

Children's access to spaces are structured around gender differences. Observing the use of space within 1970s suburban America, Hart (1979) found that boys enjoyed far greater mobility and range than girls of the same age and class background. In the course of an afternoon's play, a typical ten-to-twelve-year-old boy might travel a distance of 2,452 yards, while the average ten-to-twelve-year-old girl might only travel 959 yards. For the most part, girls expanded their geographic range only to take on responsibilities and perform chores for the family, while parents often turned a blind eye to a boy's movements into prohibited spaces. The boys Hart (1979) observed were more likely to move beyond their homes in search of "rivers, forts and treehouses, woods, ballfields, hills, lawns, sliding places, and climbing trees," while girls were more like to seek commercially developed spaces, such as stores or shopping malls. Girls were less likely than boys to physically alter their play environment, to dam creeks or build forts. Such gender differences in mobility, access, and control over physical space increased as children grew older. As C. Ward (1977) notes:

> Whenever we discuss the part the environment plays in the lives of children, we are really talking about boys. As a stereotype, the child in the city is a boy. Girls are far less visible. . . . The reader can verify this by standing in a city street at any time of day and counting the children seen. The majority will be boys. (p. 152)

One study found that parents were more likely to describe boys as being "outdoors" children and girls as "indoor" children (Newson and Newson 1976). Another 1975 study (Rheingold and Cook), which inventoried the contents of children's bedrooms, found boys more likely to possess a range of vehicles and sports equipment designed to encourage outside play, while the girls rooms were stocked with dolls, doll clothes, and other domestic objects. Parents of girls were more likely to express worries about the dangers their children face on the streets and to structure girls' time for productive household activities or educational play (Matthews 1992).

Historically, girl culture formed under closer maternal supervision and girls' toys were designed to foster female-specific skills and competencies and prepare girls for their future domestic responsibilities as wives and mothers. The doll's central place in girlhood reflected maternal desires to encourage daughters to sew; the doll's china heads and hands fostered delicate gestures and movements (Formanek-Brunnel 1998). However, these skills were not acquired without some resistance. Nineteenth-century girls were apparently as willing as today's girls to mistreat their dolls, by cutting their hair or by driving nails into their bodies.

If cultural geographers are right when they argue that children's ability to explore and modify their environments plays a large role in their growing sense of mastery, freedom, and self-confidence, then the restrictions placed on girls' play have a crippling effect. Conversely, this research would suggest that children's declining access to play space would have a more dramatic impact on the culture of young boys, since girls already faced domestic confinement.

Putting Boy Culture Back in the Home

Clods were handy and the air was full of them in a twinkling. They raged around Sid like a hail storm; and before Aunt Polly could collect her surprised faculties and sally to the rescue, six or seven clods had taken personal effect, and Tom was over the fence and gone.... He presently got safely beyond the reach of capture and punishment, and hasted toward the public square of the village, where two "military" companies of boys had met for conflict, according to previous appointment. Tom was the general of one of these armies, Joe Harper (a bosom friend) general of the other.... Tom's army won a great victory, after a long and hard-fought battle. Then the dead were counted, prisoners exchanged, the terms of the next disagreement agreed upon, and the day for the necessary battle appointed; after which the armies fell into line and marched away, and Tom turned homeward alone. (pp. 19–20)

—Mark Twain, *Adventures of Tom Sawyer* (1876)

What E. Anthony Rotundo (1994) calls "boy culture" resulted from the growing separation of the male public sphere and the female private sphere in the wake of the industrial revolution. Boys were cut off from the work life of their fathers and left under the care of their mothers. According to Rotundo, boys escaped from the home into the outdoor play space, freeing them to participate in a semi-autonomous "boy culture" that cast itself in opposition to maternal culture:

Where women's sphere offered kindness, morality, nurture and a gentle spirit, the boys' world countered with energy, self-assertion, noise, and a frequent resort to violence. The physical explosiveness and the willingness to inflict pain contrasted so sharply with the values of the home that they suggest a dialogue in actions between the values of the two spheres—as if a boy's aggressive impulses, so relentlessly opposed at home, sought extreme forms of release outside it; then, with stricken consciences, the boys came home for further lessons in self-restraint. (p. 37).

The boys transgressed maternal prohibitions to prove they weren't "mama's boys." Rotundo argues that this break with the mother was a necessary step toward autonomous manhood. One of the many tragedies of our gendered division of labor may be the ways that it links misogyny—an aggressive fighting back against the mother—with the process of developing self-reliance. Contrary to the Freudian concept of the oedipal complex (which focuses on boys' struggles with their all-powerful fathers as the site of identity formation), becoming an adult male often means struggling with (and in many cases, actively repudiating) maternal culture. Fathers, on the other hand, offered little guidance to their sons, who, Rotundo argues, acquired masculine skills and values from other boys. By contrast, girls' play culture was often "interdependent" with the realm of their mother's domestic activities, insuring a smoother transition into anticipated adult roles, but allowing less autonomy.

What happens when the physical spaces of nineteenth-century boy culture are displaced by the virtual spaces of contemporary video games? Cultural geographers have long argued that television is a poor substitute for backyard play, despite its potential to present children with a greater diversity of spaces than can be found in their immediate surroundings, precisely because it is a spectatorial rather than a participatory medium. Moore (1986), however, leaves open the prospect that a more interactive digital medium might serve *some* of the same developmental functions as backyard play. A child playing a video game, searching for the path around obstacles, or looking for an advantage over imaginary opponents, engages in many of the same "mapping" activities as children searching for affordances in their real-world environments. Rotundo's core claims about nineteenth-century boy culture hold true for the "video game culture" of contemporary boyhood. This congruence may help us to account for the enormous popularity of these games with young boys. This fit should not be surprising when we consider that the current game genres reflect intuitive choices by men who grew up in the 1960s and 1970s, when suburban boy culture still reigned.

The following are some points of comparison between traditional boy culture and contemporary game culture:

1. Nineteenth-century boy culture was characterized by its independence from the realm of both mothers and fathers. It was a space where boys could develop autonomy and self-confidence.

Video game culture also carves out a cultural realm for modern-day children separate from the space of their parents. They often play the games in their rooms and guard their space against parental intrusion. Parents often express a distaste for the games' pulpy plots and lurid images. As writers like Jon Katz (1997) and Don Tapscott (1997) note, children's relative comfort with digital media is itself a generational marker, with adults often unable to comprehend the movement and colored shapes of the video screen. Here, however, the loss of spacial mobility is acutely felt—the "bookworm," the boy who spent all of his time in his room reading, had a "mama's boy" reputation in the old boy culture. Modern-day boys have had to accommodate their domestic confinement with their definitions of masculinity, perhaps accounting, in part, for the hypermasculine and hyperviolent content of the games themselves. The game player has a fundamentally different image than the "bookworm."

2.   In nineteenth-century boy culture, youngsters gained recognition from their peers for their daring, often proven through stunts (such as swinging on vines, climbing trees, or leaping from rocks as they crossed streams) or through pranks (such as stealing apples or doing mischief aimed at adults).

In video game culture, children gain recognition for their daring as demonstrated in the virtual worlds of the game, overcoming obstacles, beating bosses, and mastering levels. Nineteenth-century boys' trespasses on neighbors' property or confrontations with hostile shopkeepers are mirrored by the visual vocabulary of the video games, which often pit smaller protagonists against the might and menace of much larger rivals. Much as cultural geographers describe the boys' physical movements beyond their home bases into developing home territories, the video games allow boys to gradually develop their mastery over the entire digital terrain, securing their future access to spaces by passing goal posts or finding warp zones.

3.   The central virtues of the nineteenth-century boy culture were mastery and self-control. The boys set tasks and goals for themselves that required discipline in order to complete. Through this process of setting and meeting challenges, they acquired the virtues of manhood.

The central virtues of video game culture are mastery (over the technical skills required by the games) and self-control (manual dexterity). Putting in the long hours of repetition and failure necessary to master a game also requires discipline and the ability to meet and surpass self-imposed goals. Most contemporary video games are ruthlessly goal-driven. Boys will often play the games, struggling to master a challenging level, well past the point of physical and emotional exhaustion. Children are not so much "addicted" to video games as they are unwilling to quit before they have met their goals, and the games seem to always set new goal posts, inviting us to best "just one more level." One of the limitations of the contemporary video game is that it provides only pre-structured forms of interactivity, and in that sense, video games are more like playgrounds and city parks rather than wild spaces. For the most part, video game players can only exploit built-in affordances and preprogrammed pathways. "Secret codes," "Easter Eggs," and "warp zones" function in digital space like secret paths do in physical space and are eagerly sought by gamers who want to go places and see things others can't find.

4. The nineteenth-century boy culture was hierarchical, with a member's status dependent on competitive activity, direct confrontation, and physical challenges. The boy fought for a place in the gang's inner circle, hoping to win admiration and respect.

Video game culture can also be hierarchical, with a member gaining status by being able to complete a game or log a big score. Video game masters move from house to house to demonstrate their technical competency and to teach others how to "beat" particularly challenging levels. The video arcade becomes a proving ground for contemporary masculinity, while many games are de-signed for the arcade, demanding a constant turnover of coins for play and intensifying the action into roughly two-minute increments. Often, single-player games generate digital rivals who may challenge players to beat their speeds or battle them for dominance.

5. Nineteenth-century boy culture was sometimes brutally violent and physi-cally aggressive; children hurt each other or got hurt trying to prove their mas-tery and daring.

Video game culture displaces this physical violence into a symbolic realm. Rather than beating each other up behind the school, boys combat imaginary characters, finding a potentially safer outlet for their aggressive feelings. We forget how violent previous boy culture was. Rotundo (1994) writes:

> The prevailing ethos of the boys' world not only supported the expres-sion of impulses such as dominance and aggression (which had evi-dent social uses), but also allowed the release of hostile, violent feelings (whose social uses were less evident). By allowing free pas-sage to so many angry or destructive emotions, boy culture sanctioned a good deal of intentional cruelty, like the physical torture of animals

and the emotional violence of bullying. . . . If at times boys acted like a hostile pack of wolves that preyed on its own kind as well as on other species, they behaved at other times like a litter of playful pups who enjoy romping, wrestling and testing new skills. (p. 45)

Even feelings of fondness and friendship were expressed through physical means, including greeting each other with showers of brickbats and offal. Such a culture is as violent as the world depicted in contemporary video games, which have the virtue of allowing growing boys to express their aggression and rambunctiousness through indirect, rather than direct, means.

6.   Nineteenth-century boy culture expressed itself through scatological humor. Such bodily images (of sweat, spit, snot, shit, and blood) reflected the boys' growing awareness of their bodies and signified their rejection of maternal constraints.

Video game culture has often been criticized for its dependence upon similar kinds of scatological images, with the blood and gore of games like "Mortal Kombat" (with its "end moves" of dismemberment and decapitation), providing some of the most oft-cited evidence in campaigns to reform video game content (Kinder 1996). Arguably, these images serve the same functions for modern boys as for their nineteenth-century counterparts—allowing an exploration of what it's like to live in our bodies and an expression of distance from maternal regulations. Like the earlier "boy culture," this scatological imagery sometimes assumes overtly misogynistic form, directed against women as a civilizing or controlling force, staged toward women's bodies as a site of physical difference and as the objects of desire or distaste. Some early games, such as "Super Metroid," rewarded player competence by forcing female characters to strip down to their underwear if the boys beat a certain score.

7.   Nineteenth-century boy culture depended on various forms of role-playing, often imitating the activities of adult males. Rotundo (1994) notes the popularity of games of settlers and Indians during an age when the frontier had only recently been closed, casting boys sometimes as their settler ancestors and other times as "savages." Such play mapped the competitive and combative boy-culture ethos onto the adult realm, thus exaggerating the place of warfare in adult male lives. Through such play, children tested alternative social roles, examined adult ideologies, and developed a firmer sense of their own abilities and identities.

Video game culture depends heavily on fantasy role-playing, with different genres of games allowing children to imagine themselves in alternative social roles or situations. Most games, however, provide images of heroic action more appropriate for the rugged individualism of nineteenth-century American culture than for the contemporary information-and-service economy. Boys play at being crime fighters, race-car drivers, and fighter pilots, not at holding down desk jobs. This gap between the excitement of boyhood play and the alienation of adult labor may explain why video game imagery seems so hyperbolic from an adult vantage point. Rotundo (1994) notes, however, that there was always some gap between boys and adult males:

> Boy culture emphasized exuberant spontaneity; it allowed free rein to aggressive impulses and revealed in physical prowess and assertion. Boy culture was a world of play, a social space where one evaded the duties and restrictions of adult society. . . . Men were quiet and sober, for theirs was a life of serious business. They had families to support, reputations to earn, responsibilities to meet. Their world was based on work, not play, and their survival in it depended on patient planning, not spontaneous impulse. To prosper, then, a man had to delay gratification and restrain desire. Of course, he also needed to be aggressive and competitive, and he needed an instinct for self-advancement. But he had to channel those assertive impulses in ways that were suitable to the abstract battles and complex issues of middle-class men's work. (p. 55)

Today, the boys are using the same technologies as their fathers, even if they are using them to pursue different fantasies.

8. In ninteenth-century boy culture, play activities were seen as opportunities for social interactions and bonding. Boys formed strong ties that were the basis for adult affiliations, for participation in men's civic clubs and fraternities, and for business partnerships.

The track record of contemporary video game culture providing a basis for similar social networking is more mixed. In some cases, the games constitute both play space and playmates, reflecting the physical isolation of contemporary children from each other. In other cases, the games provide the basis for social interactions at home, at school, and at the video arcades. Children talk about the games together, over the telephone or, now, over the Internet, as well as in person, on the playground, or at the school cafeteria. Boys compare notes, map strategies, share tips, and show off their skills, and this exchange of video game lore provides the basis for more complex social relations. Again, video games don't isolate children, but they fail, at the present time, to provide the technological basis for overcoming other social and cultural factors, such as working parents who are unable to bring children to each other's houses and enlarged school districts that make it harder to get together.

Far from a "corruption" of the culture of childhood, video games show strong continuities with the boyhood play fondly remembered by previous generations. There is a significant difference, however. The nineteenth-century "boy culture" enjoyed such freedom and autonomy precisely because the activities were staged within a larger expanse of space, because boys could occupy an environment largely unsupervised by adults. Nineteenth-century boys sought indirect means of breaking with their mothers by escaping to spaces that were outside their control and engaging in secret activities the boys knew would have met parental disapproval. The mothers, on the other hand, rarely had to confront the nature of this "boy culture" and often didn't even know that it existed. The video game culture, on the other hand, occurs in plain sight, in the middle of the family living room, or at best, in the children's rooms. Mothers come face to face with the messy process by which western culture turns boys into men. The games and their content become the focus of open antagonism and the subject of tremendous guilt and anxiety. Sega's Lee McEnany (this volume) acknowledges that the overwhelming majority of complaints game companies receive come from mothers, and Ellen Seiter (1996) has noted that this statistic reflects the increased pressure placed on mothers to supervise and police children's relations to popular culture. Current attempts to police video game content reflect a long history of attempts to shape and regulate children's play culture, starting with the playground movements of progressive America and the organization of social groups for boys, such as the Boy Scouts and Little League, which tempered the more rough-and-tumble qualities of boy culture and channeled them into games, sports, and other adult-approved pastimes.

Many of us might wish to foster a boy culture that allowed the expression of affection or the display of empowerment through nonviolent channels, that disentangled the development of personal autonomy from the fostering of misogyny, and that encouraged boys to develop a more nurturing, less domineering attitude to their social and natural environments. These goals are worth pursuing. We can't simply adopt a "boys will be boys" attitude. However, one wonders about the consequences of such a policing action in a world that no longer offers "wild" outdoor spaces as a safety valve for boys to escape parental control. Perhaps our sons—and daughters—need an unpoliced space for social experimentation, a space where they can vent their frustrations and imagine alternative adult roles free of inhibiting parental pressure. The problem, of course, is that unlike the nineteenth-century boy culture, the video game culture is not a world children construct for themselves but rather a world made by adult companies and sold to children. There is no way that we can escape adult intervention in shaping children's play environments as long as those environments are built and sold rather than discovered and appropriated. As parents, we are thus implicated in our children's choice of play environments, whether we wish to be or not, and we need to be conducting a dialogue with our children about the qualities and values exhibited by these game worlds. One model would be for adults and children to collaborate in the design and development of video game spaces, in the process developing a conversation about the nature and meanings of the worlds being produced. Another approach (Cassell, this volume) would be to create tools to allow children to construct their own play spaces and then give them the freedom to do what they want. Right now, parents are rightly apprehensive about a play space that is outside their own control and that is shaped according to adult specifications but without their direct input.

One of the most disturbing aspects of the boy culture is its gender segregation. The nineteenth-century boy culture played an essential role in preparing boys for entry into their future professional roles and responsibilities; some of that same training has also become essential for girls at a time when more and more women are working outside the home. The motivating force behind the "girls' game" movement is the idea that girls, no less than boys, need computers at an early age if they are going to be adequately prepared to get "good jobs for good wages" (Jenkins and Cassell, this volume). Characteristically, the girls' game movement has involved the transposition of traditional feminine play cultures into the digital realm. However, in doing so, we run the risk of preserving, rather than transforming, those aspects of traditional "girl culture" which kept women restricted to the domestic sphere while denying them the spacial exploration and mastery associated with boy culture. Girls, no less than boys, need to develop an exploratory mindset, a habit of seeking unknown spaces as opposed to settling placidly into the domestic sphere.

Gendered Games/Gendered Books: Toward a Cultural Geography of Imaginary Spaces

These debates about gendered play and commercial entertainment are not new, repeating (and in a curious way, reversing) the emergence of a gender-specific set of literary genres for children in the nineteenth century. As Elizabeth Segel (1986) notes, the earliest writers of children's books were mostly women, who saw the genre as "the exercise of feminine moral 'influence'" upon children's developing minds, and who created a literature that was undifferentiated according to gender but "domestic in setting, heavily didactic and morally or spiritually uplifting" (p. 171). In other words, the earliest children's books were "girls' books" in everything but name, which isn't surprising at a time novel reading was still heavily associated with women. The "boys' book" emerged, in the mid-nineteenth century, as "men of action," industrialists and adventurers, wrote fictions intended to counter boys' restlessness and apathy towards traditional children's literature. The introduction of boys' books reflected a desire to get boys to read. Boy-book fantasies of action and adventure reflected the qualities of their pre existing play culture, fantasies centering around "the escape from domesticity and from the female domination of the domestic world" (Segel 1986, p. 171). If the girls' game movement has involved the rethinking of video game genres (which initially emerged in a male-dominated space) in order to make digital media more attractive to girls (and thus to encourage the development of computational skills), the boys' book movement sought to remake reading (which initially emerged in a female-dominated space) to respond to male needs (and thus to encourage literacy). In both cases, the goal seems to have been to construct fantasies that reflect the gender-specific nature of children's play and thus to motivate those left out of the desirable cultural practices to get more involved. In this next section, I will consider the continuity that exists between gender/genre configurations in children's literature and in the digital games marketplace.

Adventure Islands: Boy Space

> Alex looked around him. There was no place to seek cover. He was too weak to run, even if there was. His gaze returned to the stallion, fascinated by a creature so wild and so near. Here was the wildest of all wild animals—he had fought for everything he had ever needed, for food, for leadership, for life itself; it was his nature to kill or be

killed. The horse reared again; then he snorted and plunged straight for the boy. (p. 27)

—Walter Farley, *The Black Stallion* (1941)

The space of the boy book is the space of adventure, risk-taking and danger, of a wild and untamed nature that must be mastered if one is to survive. The space of the boy book offers "no place to seek cover," and thus encourages fight-or-flight responses. In some cases, most notably in the works of Mark Twain, the boy books represented a nostalgic documentation of nineteenth-century "boy culture," its spaces, its activities, and its values. In other cases, as in the succession of pulp adventure stories that form the background of the boys' game genres, the narratives offered us a larger-than-life enactment of those values, staged in exotic rather than backyard spaces, involving broader movements through space and amplifying horseplay and risk-taking into scenarios of actual combat and conquest. Writers of boys' books found an easy fit between the ideologies of American "manifest destiny" and British colonialism and the adventure stories boys preferred to read, which often took the form of quests, journeys, or adventures into untamed and uncharted regions of the world—into the frontier of the American west (or in the twentieth century, the "final frontier" of Mars and beyond), into the exotic realms of Africa, Asia, and South America. The protagonists were boys or boy-like adult males, who had none of the professional responsibilities and domestic commitments associated with adults. The heroes sought adventure by running away from home to join the circus (*Toby Tyler*), to sign up as cabin boy on a ship (*Treasure Island*), or to seek freedom by rafting down the river (*Huckleberry Finn*). They confronted a hostile and untamed environment (as when *The Jungle Book*'s Mowgli must battle "tooth and claw" with the tiger, Sheer Khan, or as when Jack London's protagonists faced the frozen wind of the Yukon). They were shipwrecked on islands, explored caves, searched for buried treasure, plunged harpoons into slick-skinned whales, or set out alone across the desert, the bush, or the jungle. They survived through their wits, their physical mastery, and their ability to use violent force. Each chapter offered a sensational set piece—an ambush by wild Indians, an encounter with a coiled cobra, a landslide, a stampede, or a sea battle—that placed the protagonist at risk and tested his skills and courage. The persistent images of blood-and-guts combat and cliff-hanging risks compelled boys to keep reading, making their blood race with promises of thrills and more thrills. This rapid pace allowed little room for moral and emotional introspection. In turn, such stories provided fantasies that boys could enact upon their own environments. Rotundo (1994) describes nineteenth-century boys playing pirates, settlers and Indians, or Roman warriors, roles drawn from boys' books.

The conventions of the nineteenth- and early–twentieth-century boys' adventure story provided the basis for the current video game genres. The most successful console game series, such as Capcom's "Mega Man" or Nintendo's "Super Mario Brothers," games, combine the iconography of multiple boys' book genres. Their protagonists struggle across an astonishingly eclectic range of landscapes—deserts, frozen wastelands, tropical rain forests, urban undergrounds—and encounter resistance from strange hybrids (who manage to be animal, machine, and savage all rolled into one). The scroll games have built into them the constant construction of frontiers—home regions—that the boy player must struggle to master and push beyond, moving deeper and deeper into uncharted space. Action is relentless. The protagonist shoots fireballs, ducks and charges, slugs it out, rolls, jumps, and dashes across the treacherous terrain, never certain what lurks around the corner. If you stand still, you die. Everything you encounter is potentially hostile, so shoot to kill. Errors in judgement result in the character's death and require starting all over again. Each screen overflows with dangers; each landscape is riddled with pitfalls and booby traps. One screen may require you to leap from precipice to precipice, barely missing falling into the deep chasms below. Another may require you to swing by vines across the treetops, or spelunk through an underground passageway, all the while fighting it out with the alien hordes. The games' levels and worlds reflect the set-piece structure of the earlier boys' books. Boys get to make lots of noise on adventure island, with the soundtrack full of pulsing music, shouts, groans, zaps, and bomb blasts. Everything is streamlined: the plots and characters are reduced to genre archetypes, immediately familiar to the boy gamers, and defined more through their capacity for actions than anything else. The "adventure island" is the archetypal space of both the boys' books and the boys' games—an isolated world far removed from domestic space or adult supervision, an untamed world for people who refuse to bow before the pressures of the civilizing process, a never-never-land where you seek your fortune. The "adventure island," in short, is a world that fully embodies the boy culture and its ethos.

Secret Gardens: Girl Space

> If it was the key to the closed garden, and she could find out where
> the door was, she could perhaps open it and see what was inside the
> walls, and what had happened to the old rose-trees. It was because it
> had been shut up so long that she wanted to see it. It seemed as if it
> must be different from other places and that something strange must
> have happened to it during ten years. Besides that, if she liked it she
> could go into it every day and shut the door behind her, and she could
> make up some play of her own and play it quite alone, because nobody
> would ever know where she was, but would think the door was still
> locked and the key buried in the earth. (p. 71)
> — Frances Hodgson Burnett, *The Secret Garden* (1911)

Girl space is a space of secrets and romance, a space of one's own in a world
that offers girls far too little room to explore. Ironically, "girl books" often open
with fantasies of being alone and then require the female protagonist to sacrifice her private space in order to make room for others' needs. Genres aimed
specifically at girls were slower to evolve, often emerging through imitation of
the gothics and romances preferred by adult women readers and retaining a
strong aura of instruction and self-improvement. As Segel (1986) writes:

> The liberation of nineteenth century boys into the book world of sail-
> ors and pirates, forest and battles, left their sisters behind in the world
> of childhood—that is, the world of home and family. When publishers
> and writers saw the commercial possibilities of books for girls, it is
> interesting that they did not provide comparable escape reading for
> them (that came later, with the pulp series books) but instead devel-
> oped books designed to persuade the young reader to accept the con-
> finement and self-sacrifice inherent in the doctrine of feminine
> influence. This was accomplished by depicting the rewards of submis-
> sion and the sacred joys of serving as "the angel of the house." (pp.
> 171–172)

If the boys' book protagonist escapes all domestic responsibilities, the girls'
book heroine learned to temper her impulsiveness and to accept family and
domestic obligations (*Little Women, Anne of Green Gables*) or sought to be a heal-

ing influence on a family suffering from tragedy and loss (*Rebecca of Sunnybrook Farm*). Segel (1986) finds the most striking difference between the two genre traditions in the books' settings: "the domestic confinement of one book as against the extended voyage to exotic lands in the other" (p. 173). Avoiding the purple prose of the boys' books, the girls' books describe naturalistic environments, similar to the realm of readers' daily experience. The female protagonists take emotional, but rarely physical, risks. The tone is more apt to be confessional than confrontational.

Traditional girls' books, such as *The Secret Garden,* do encourage some forms of spatial exploration, an exploration of the hidden passages of unfamiliar houses or the rediscovery and cultivation of a deserted rose garden. Norman N. Holland and Leona F. Sherman (1986) emphasize the role of spacial exploration in the gothic tradition, a "maiden-plus-habitation" formula whose influence is strongly felt in *The Secret Garden.* In such stories, the exploration of space leads to the uncovering of secrets, clues, and symptoms that shed light on characters' motivations. Hidden rooms often contain repressed memories and, sometimes, entombed relatives. The castle, Holland and Sherman (1986) note, "can threaten, resist, love or confine, but in all these actions, it stands as a total environment" (p. 220) that the female protagonist can never fully escape. Holland and Sherman claim that gothic romances fulfill a fantasy of unearthing secrets about the adult world, casting the reader in a position of powerlessness and daring them to overcome their fears and confront the truth. Such a fantasy space is, of course, consistent with what we have already learned about girls' domestic confinement and greater responsibilities to their families.

Purple Moon's "Secret Paths in the Forest" fully embodies the juvenile gothic tradition—while significantly enlarging the space open for girls to explore. Purple Moon removes the walls around the garden, turning it into woodlands. Producer Brenda Laurel has emphasized girls' fascination with secrets, a fascination that readily translates into a puzzle game structure, though "Secret Paths" pushes further than existing games to give these "secrets" social and psychological resonance. Based on her focus-group interviews, Laurel initially sought to design a "magic garden," a series of "romanticized natural environments" responsive to "girls' highly touted nurturing desires, their fondness for animals." She wanted to create a place "where girls could explore, meet, and take care of creatures, design and grow magical or fantastical plants" (personal correspondence, 1997). What she found was that the girls did not feel magical animals would need their nurturing, and in fact, many of the girls wanted the

Figure 12.1: Friendly fawns from "Secret Paths in the Forest." Reprinted with permission of Purple Moon. Copyright 1997.

animals to mother them. The girls in Laurel's study, however, were drawn to the idea of the secret garden or hidden forest as a "girls only" place for solitude and introspection. Laurel explains:

> Girls' first response to the place was that they would want to go there alone, to be peaceful and perhaps read or daydream. They might take a best friend, but they would never take an adult or a boy. They thought that the garden/forest would be a place where they could find out things that would be important to them, and a place where they might meet a wise or magical person. Altogether their fantasies were about respite and looking within as opposed to frolicsome play. (Personal correspondence, 1997)

The spaces in Purple Moon's game are quiet, contemplative places, rendered in naturalistic detail but with the soft focus and warm glow of an impressionistic watercolor.

The world of "Secret Paths" explodes with subtle and inviting colors—the colors of a forest on a summer afternoon, of spring flowers and autumn leaves and shifting patterns of light, of rippling water and moonlit skies, of sand and earth. The soundtrack is equally dense and engaging, as the natural world whispers to us in the rustle of the undergrowth or sings to us in the sounds of the wind and the calls of birds. The spaces of "Secret Paths" are full of life, as lizards slither from rock to rock, or field mice dart for cover, yet even animals which might be frightening in other contexts (coyotes, foxes, owls) seem eager to reveal their secrets to our explorers. Jessie, one of the game's protagonists, expresses a fear of the "creepy" nighttime woods, but the game makes the animals seem tame and the forest safe, even in the dead of night. The game's puzzles reward careful exploration and observation. At one point, we must cautiously approach a timid fawn if we wish to be granted the magic jewels that are the tokens of our quest. The guidebook urges us to be "unhurried and gentle" with the "easily startled" deer.

Our goal is less to master nature than to understand how we might live in harmony with it. We learn to mimic its patterns, to observe the notes (produced by singing cactus) that make a lizard's head bob with approval and then to copy them ourselves, to position spiders on a web so that they may harmonize rather than create discord. And, in some cases, we are rewarded for feeding and caring for the animals. In *The Secret Garden* (1911), Mary Lennox is led by a robin to the branches that mask the entrance to the forgotten rose garden:

> Mary had stepped close to the robin, and suddenly the gusts of wind swung aside some loose ivy trails, and more suddenly still she jumped toward it and caught it in her hand. This she did because she had seen something under it—a round knob which had been covered by the leaves hanging over it. . . . The robin kept singing and twittering away and tilting his head on one side, as if he were as excited as she was. (p. 80)

Such animal guides abound in "Secret Paths": the curser is shaped like a lady bug during our explorations and like a butterfly when we want to venture beyond the current screen. Animals show us the way, if we only take the time to look and listen.

Unlike twitch-and-shoot boys' games, "Secret Paths" encourages us to stroke and caress the screen with our curser, clicking only when we know where secret treasures might be hidden. A magic book tells us:

As I patiently traveled along [through the paths], I found that everything was enchanted! The trees, flowers and animals, the sun, sky and
stars—all had magical properties! The more closely I listened and the
more carefully I explored, the more was revealed to me.

Nature's rhythms are gradual and recurring, a continual process of birth,
growth, and transformation. Laurel explains:

We made the "game" intentionally slow—a girl can move down the
paths at whatever pace, stop and play with puzzles or stones, or hang
out in the tree house with or without the other characters. I think that
this slowness is really a kind of refuge for the girls. The game is much
slower than television, for example. One of the issues that girls have
raised with us in our most recent survey of their concerns is the problem of feeling too busy. I think that "Secret Paths" provides an antidote
to that feeling from the surprising source of the computer. (Personal
correspondence, 1997)

Frances Hodgson Burnett's secret garden is a place of healing, and the book
links Mary's restoration of the forgotten rose garden with her repairing a family
torn apart by tragedy, restoring a sickly boy to health, and coming to grips with
her mother's death:

So long as Mistress Mary's mind was full of disagreeable thoughts
about her dislikes and sour opinions of people and her determination
not to be pleased by or interested in anything, she was a yellow-faced,
sickly, bored and wretched child. . . . When her mind gradually filled
itself with robins, and moorland cottages crowded with children. . .with springtime and with secret gardens coming alive day by
day. . . .there was no room for the disagreeable thoughts which affected her liver and her digestion and made her yellow and tired.
(p. 294)

Purple Moon's "Secret Paths" has also been designed as a healing place, where
girls are encouraged to "explore with your heart" and answer their emotional
dilemmas. As the magical book explains, "You will never be alone here, for this
is a place where girls come to share and to seek help from one another." At the
game's opening, we draw together a group of female friends in the treehouse,

where each confesses her secrets and tells of her worries and sufferings. Miko speaks of the pressure to always be the best and the alienation she feels from the other children; Dana recounts her rage over losing a soccer companionship; Minn describes her humiliation because her immigrant grandmother has refused to assimilate new-world customs. Some of them have lost parents, others face scary situations or emotional slights that cripple their confidence. Their answers lie along the secret paths through the forest, where the adventurers can find hidden magical stones that embody social, psychological, or emotional strengths. Along the way, the girls' secrets are literally embedded within the landscape, so that clicking on our environment may call forth memories or confessions. If we are successful in finding all of the hidden stones, they magically form a necklace that, when given to the right girl, allows us to hear a comforting or clarifying story. Such narratives teach girls how to find emotional resources within themselves and how to observe and respond to others' often unarticulated needs. Solving puzzles in the physical environment helps us to address problems in our social environment. "Secret Paths" is what Brenda Laurel calls a "friendship adventure," allowing young girls to rehearse their coping skills and try alternative social strategies.

The Play Town: Another Space for Girls?

> Harriet was trying to explain to Sport how to play Town. "See, first you make up the name of the town. Then you write down the names of all the people who live in it. . . . Then when you know who lives there, you make up what they do. For instance, Mr. Charles Hanley runs the filling station on the corner. . . ." Harriet got very businesslike. She stood up, then got on her knees in the soft September mud so she could lean over the little valley made between the two big roots of the tree. She referred to her notebook every now and then, but for the most part she stared intently at the mossy lowlands which made her town. (pp. 3–5)
>
> — Louise Fitzhugh, *Harriet, the Spy* (1964)

Harriet the Spy opens with a description of another form of spatial play for girls—Harriet's "town," a "microworld" she maps onto the familiar contours of her own backyard and uses to think through the complex social relations she observes in her community. Harriet controls the inhabitants of this town, shaping their actions to her desires: "In this town, everybody goes to bed at nine-thirty" (p. 4). Not unlike a soap opera, her stories depend on juxtapositions of radically different forms of human experience: "Now, this night, as Mr. Hanley is just about to close up, a long, big old black car drives up and in it there are all these men with guns. . . . At this same minute Mrs. Harrison's baby is born" (p. 6). Her fascination with mapping and controlling the physical space of the town makes her game a pre-digital prototype for "Sim City" and other simulation games. However, compared to Harriet's vivid interest in the distinct personalities and particular experiences of her townspeople, "Sim City" seems alienated and abstract. "Sim City"'s classifications of land use into residential, commercial, and industrial push us well beyond the scale of everyday life and in so doing, strips the landscape of its potential as a stage for children's fantasies. "Sim City" offers us another form of power—the power to "play God," to design our physical environment, to sculp the landscape or call down natural disasters (Friedman 1995), but not the power to imaginatively transform our social environment. "Sim City" embraces stock themes from boys' play, such as building forts, shaping earth with toy trucks, or damming creeks, playing them out on a much larger scale. For Harriet, the mapping of the space was only the first step in preparing the ground for a rich saga of life and death, joy and sorrow, and those are the elements that are totally lacking in most simulation games.

As Fitzhugh's novel continues, Harriet's interests shift from the imaginary events of her simulated town and into real-world spaces. She "spies" on people's private social interactions, staging more and more "daring" investigations, trying to understand what motivates adult behavior, and writing in her notebook her interpretations of adult lives. Harriet's adventures take her well beyond the constricted space of her own home. She breaks and enters houses and takes rides on dumbwaiters, sneaks through back alleys and peeps into windows. She barely avoids getting caught. Harriet's adventures occur in public space (not the private space of the secret garden), a populated environment (not the natural worlds visited in "Secret Paths"). Yet, her adventures are not so much direct struggles with opposing forces (as might be found in a boys' book adventure) as covert operations to ferret out knowledge of social relations.

The games of Theresa Duncan ("Chop Suey," "Smarty," "Zero Zero") offer a digital version of Harriet's "Town." Players can explore suburban and urban spaces and pry into bedroom closets in search of the extraordinary dimensions of ordinary life. Duncan (this volume) cites *Harriet the Spy* as an influence, hoping that her games will grant young girls "a sense of inquisitiveness and wonder." "Chop Suey" and "Smarty" take place in small Midwestern towns, a working-class world of diners, hardware stores, and beauty parlors. "Zero Zero" draws us further from home—into fin de siecle Paris, a world of bakeries, wax museums, and catacombs. These spaces are rendered in a distinctive style somewhere between the primitiveness of Grandma Moses and the colorful postmodernism of *Pee-Wee's Playhouse*. Far removed from the romantic imagery of "Secret Paths," these worlds overflow with city sounds—the clopping of horse hooves on cobblestones, barking dogs, clanging church bells in "Zero Zero"— and the narrator seems fascinated with the smokestacks and signs which clutter this man-made environment. As the narrator in "Zero Zero" rhapsodizes, "smoke curled black and feathery like a horse's tail from a thousand chimney pots" in this world "before popsicles and paperbacks." While the social order has been tamed, posing few dangers, Duncan has not rid these worlds of their more disreputable elements. The guy in the candy shop in "Chop Suey" has covered his body with tattoos. The Frenchmen in "Zero Zero" are suitably bored, ill-tempered, and insulting; even flowers hurl abuse at us. The man in the antlered hat sings rowdy songs about "bones" and "guts" when we visit the catacombs, and the women puff on cigarettes, wear too much make-up, flash their cleavage, and hint about illicit rendezvous. Duncan (this volume) suggests:

> There's a sense of bittersweet experience in "Chop Suey," where not everyone has had a perfect life but they're all happy people. Vera has three ex-husbands all named Bob. . . . Vera has problems, but she's also filled with love. And she's just a very vibrant, alive person, and that's why she fascinates the little girls.

Duncan rejects our tendency to "project this fantasy of purity and innocence onto children," suggesting that all this "niceness" deprives children of "the richness of their lives" and does not help them come to grips with their "complicated feelings" towards the people in their lives.

Duncan's protagonists, June Bug ("Chop Suey") and Pinkee LeBrun ("Zero Zero"), are smart, curious girls, who want to know more than they have been told. Daring Pinkee scampers along the roofs of Paris and pops down chimneys or steps boldly through the doors of shops, questioning adults about their visions for the new century. Yet she is also interested in smaller, more intimate questions, such as the identity of the secret admirer who writes love poems to Bon Bon, the singer at the Follies. Clues unearthed in one location may shed light on mysteries posed elsewhere, allowing Duncan to suggest something of

Figure 12.2: Bon-Bon's Boudoir in "Zero Zero." Copyright Theresa Duncan, 1997. Used with permission.

the "interconnectedness" of life within a close community. Often, as in *Harriet*, the goal is less to evaluate these people than to understand what makes them tick. In that sense, the game fosters the character-centered reading practices which Segel (1986) associates with the girls' book genres, reading practices that thrive on gossip and speculation.

Duncan's games have no great plot to propel them. Duncan (this volume) said, "'Chop Suey' works the way that real life does: all these things happen to you, but there's no magical event, like there is sometimes in books, that transforms you." Lazy curiosity invites us to explore the contents of each shop, to flip through the fashion magazines in Bon Bon's dressing room, to view the early trick films playing at Cinema Egypt, or to watch the cheeses in the window of Quel Fromage that are, for reasons of their own, staging the major turning points of the French Revolution. (She also cites inspiration from the more surreal adventures of *Alice in Wonderland*.) The interfaces are flexible, allowing us to visit any location when we want without having to fight our way through levels or work past puzzling obstacles. "Zero Zero" and Duncan's other games take particular pleasure in anarchistic imagery, in ways we can disrupt and destabilize the environment, showering the baker's angry faces with white clouds of flour, ripping off the table cloths, or shaking up soda bottles so they will spurt their corks. Often, there is something vaguely naughty about the game activities, as when a visit to Poire the fashion designer has us matching different pairs of underwear. In that sense, Duncan's stories preserve the mischievous and sometimes antisocial character of Harriet's antics and the transformative humor of Lewis Carroll, encouraging the young gamers to take more risks and to try things that might not ordinarily meet their parents' approval. Pinkee's first act as a baby is to rip the pink ribbons from her hair! Duncan likes her characters free and "unladylike."

In keeping with the pedagogic legacy of the girls' book tradition, "Zero Zero" promises us an introduction to French history, culture, and language, and "Smarty" a mixture of "spelling and spells, math and Martians, grammar and glamour," but Duncan's approach is sassy and irreverent. The waxwork of Louis XIV sticks out its tongue at us, while Joan D'Arc is rendered in marshmallow, altogether better suited for toasting. The breads and cakes in the bakery are shaped like the faces of French philosophers and spout incomprehensible arguments. Pinkee's quest for knowledge about the coming century cannot be reduced to an approved curriculum, but rather expresses an unrestrained fascination with the stories, good, bad, happy or sad, that people tell each other about their lives.

Harriet, the Spy is ambivalent about its protagonist's escapades: her misadventures clearly excite the book's female readers, but the character herself is socially ostracized and disciplined, forced to more appropriately channel her creativity and curiosity. Pinkee suffers no such punishment, ending up the game watching the fireworks that mark the change of the centuries and taking pleasure in the knowledge that she will be a central part of the changes that are coming: "tonight belongs to Bon Bon but the future belongs to Pinkee."

Conclusion: Toward a Gender-Neutral Play Space?

Brenda Laurel and Theresa Duncan offer two very different conceptions of a digital play space for girls—one pastoral, the other urban; one based on the ideal of living in harmony with nature, the other based on an anarchistic pleasure in disrupting the order of everyday life and making the familiar "strange." Yet, in many ways, the two games embrace remarkably similar ideals—play spaces for girls that adopt a slower pace, are less filled with dangers, invite gradual investigation and discovery, foster an awareness of social relations and a search for secrets, and center around emotional relations between characters. Both allow the exploration of physical environments but are really about the interior worlds of feelings and fears. Laurel and Duncan make an important contribution when they propose new and different models for how digital media may be used. The current capabilities of our video and computer game technologies reflect the priorities of an earlier generation of game makers and their conception of the boys' market. Their assumptions about what kinds of digital play spaces were desirable defined how the bytes would be allocated, valuing rapid response time over the memory necessary to construct more complex and compelling characters. Laurel and Duncan shift the focus—giving priority to character relations and "friendship adventures." In doing so, they are expanding what computers can do and what roles they can play in our lives.

On the other hand, in our desire to open digital technologies as an alternative play space for girls, we must guard against simply duplicating in the new medium the gender-specific genres of children's literature. The segregation of children's reading into boy- and girl-book genres, Segel (1986) argues, encouraged the development of gender-specific reading strategies—with boys reading for plot and girls reading for character relationship. Such differences, Segel suggests, taught children to replicate the separation between a male public sphere of risk-taking and a female domestic sphere of care-taking. As Segel (1986) notes, the classification of children's literature into boys books and girls' books "extracted a heavy cost in feminine self-esteem," restricting girl's imaginative experience to what adults perceived as its "proper place." Boys developed a sense of autonomy and mastery both from their reading and from their play. Girls learned to fetter their imaginations, just as they restricted their movements into real-world spaces. At the same time, this genre division also limited boys' psychological and emotional development, insuring a focus on goal-oriented, utilitarian, and violent plots. Too much interest in social and emotional life was a vulnerability in a world where competition left little room to be "led by your heart." We need to design digital play spaces that allow girls to do more than stitch doll clothes, mother nature, or heal their friends' hurts, and boys to do more than battle barbarian hordes.

Segel's analysis of "gender and childhood reading" suggests two ways of moving beyond the gender-segregation of our virtual landscape. First, as Segel (1986) suggests, the designation of books for boys and girls did not preclude (though certainly discouraged) reading across gender lines: "Though girls when they reached 'that certain age' could be prevented from joining boys' games and lively exploits, it was harder to keep them from accompanying their brothers on vicarious adventures through the reading of boys' books" (p. 175). Reading boys' books gave girls (admittedly limited) access to the boy culture and its values. Segel finds evidence of such gender-crossing in the nineteenth century, though girls were actively discouraged from reading boys' books because their contents were thought too lurid and unwholesome. At other times, educational authorities encouraged the assignment of boys' books in public schools, since girls could read and enjoy them, while there was much greater stigma attached to boys reading girls' books. The growing visibility of the "quake girls," female gamers who compete in traditional male fighting and action/adventure games (Jenkins and Cassell, this volume), suggests that there has always been a healthy degree of "crossover" interest in the games market and that many girls enjoy "playing with power." Girls may compete more directly and aggressively with boys in the video game arena than would ever have been possible in the real world of backyard play, since differences in physical size, strength, and agility are irrelevant. And they can return from combat without the ripped clothes or black eyes that told parents they had done something "unladylike." Unfortunately, much as girls who read boys' books were likely to encounter the misogynistic themes that mark boys' fantasies of separation from their mothers, girls who play boys' games find the games' constructions of female sexuality and power are designed to gratify preadolescent males, not to empower girls. Girl gamers are aggressively campaigning to have their tastes and interests factored into the development of action games.

We need to open up more space for girls to join—or play alongside—the traditional boy culture down by the river, in the old vacant lot, within the bamboo forest. Girls need to learn how to explore "unsafe" and "unfriendly" spaces, and to experience the "complete freedom of movement" promised by the boys' games, if not all the time, then at least some of the time, to help them develop the self-confidence and competitiveness demanded of professional women. They also need to learn how, in the words of a contemporary bestseller, to "run with the wolves" and not just follow the butterflies. Girls need to be able to play games where Barbie gets to kick some butt.

However, this focus on creating action games for girls still represents only part of the answer, for as Segel (1986) notes, the gender segregation of children's literature was almost as damaging for boys as it was for girls: "In a society where many men and women are alienated from members of the other sex, one wonders whether males might be more comfortable with and understanding of women's needs and perspectives if they had imaginatively shared female experiences through books, beginning in childhood" (p. 183). Boys may need to play in secret gardens or toy towns just as much as girls need to explore adventure islands. In the literary realm, Segel points to books such as *Little House on the Prairie* and *A Wrinkle in Time* that fuse the boy and girl genres, rewarding both a traditionally masculine interest in plot action and a traditionally feminine interest in character relations.

Sega Saturn's "Nights into Dreams" represents a similar fusion of the boys' and girls' game genres. Much as in "Secret Paths," our movement through the game space is framed as an attempt to resolve the characters' emotional problems. In the frame stories that open the game, we enter the mindscape of the two protagonists as they toss and turn in their sleep. Claris, the female protagonist, hopes to gain recognition on the stage as a singer, but has nightmares of being rejected and ridiculed. Elliot, the male character, has fantasies of scoring big on the basketball court, yet fears being bullied by bigger and more aggressive players. They run away from their problems, only to find themselves in Nightopia, where they must save the dream world from the evil schemes of Wileman the Wicked and his monstrous minions. In the dreamworld, both Claris and Elliot may assume the identity of Nights, an androgynous harlequin figure who can fly through the air, transcending all the problems below. The game requires players to gather glowing orbs that represent different forms of energy needed to confront Claris's and Elliot's problems—purity (white), wisdom (green), hope (yellow), intelligence (blue), and bravery (red)—a structure that recalls the magic stones in "Secret Paths in the Forest."

The tone of this game is aptly captured by one Internet game critic, Big Mitch: "The whole experience of "Nights" is in soaring, tumbling, and freewheeling through colorful landscapes, swooping here and there, and just losing yourself in the moment. This is not a game you set out to win; the fun is in the journey rather than the destination." Big Mitch's response suggests a recognition of the fundamentally different qualities of this game—its focus on psychological issues as much as on action and conflict, its fascination with aimless exploration rather than goal-driven narrative, its movement between a realistic world of everyday problems and a fantasy realm of great adventure, and its mixture of the speed and mobility associated with the boys' platform games with the lush natural landscapes and the sculpted soundtracks associated with the girls' games. Spring Valley is a sparkling world of rainbows and waterfalls and Emerald Green forests. Other levels allow us to splash through cascading fountains or sail past icy mountains and frozen wonderlands, or bounce on pillows and off the walls of the surreal Soft Museum, or swim through aquatic tunnels. The game's 3D design allows an exhilarating freedom of movement, enhanced by design features, such as wind resistance, that give players a stronger than average sense of embodiment. "Nights into Dreams" retains some dangerous and risky elements that are associated with the boys games. There are spooky places, including nightmare worlds full of day-glo serpents and winged beasties, and enemies we must battle, yet there is also a sense of unconstrained adventure and the experience of floating through the clouds. Our primary enemy is time, the alarm clock that will awaken us from our dreams. Even when we confront monsters, they don't fire on us; we must simply avoid flying directly into their sharp teeth. When we lose "Nights'" magical, gender-bending garb, we turn back into boys and girls and must hoof it as pedestrians across the rugged terrain below, a situation that makes it far less likely we will achieve our goals. To be gendered is to be constrained; to escape gender is to escape gravity and to fly above it all.

Sociologist Barrie Thorne (1993) has discussed the forms of "borderwork," which occurs when boys and girls occupy the same play spaces: "The spatial separation of boys and girls [on the same playground] constitutes a kind of boundary, perhaps felt most strongly by individuals who want to join an activity controlled by the other gender" (pp. 64–65). Boys and girls are brought together in the same space, but they repeatedly enact the separation and opposition between the two play cultures. In real-world play, this "borderwork" takes the form of chases and contests on the one hand and "cooties" or other pollution taboos on the other. When "borderwork" occurs, gender distinctions become extremely rigid and nothing passes between the two spheres. Something similar occurs in many of the books Segel identifies as gender neutral—male and female reading interests coexist, side by side, like children sharing a playground, and yet they remain resolutely separate, and the writers, if anything, exaggerate gender differences in order to proclaim their dual address. Wendy and the "lost boys" both travel to Never-Never-Land, but Wendy plays house and the "lost boys" play Indians or pirates. The "little house" and the "prairie" exist side by side in Laura Wilder's novels, but the mother remains trapped inside the house, while Pa ventures into the frontier. The moments when the line between the little house and the prairie are crossed, such as a scene in which a native American penetrates into Ma Wilder's parlor, become moments of intense anxiety. Only Laura can follow her pa across the threshold of the little house and onto the prairie, and her adventurous spirit is often presented as an unfeminine trait she is likely to outgrow as she gets older.

As we develop digital play spaces for boys and girls, we need to make sure this same pattern isn't repeated, that we do not create blue and pink ghettos. On the one hand, the opening sequences of "Nights into Dreams," which frame Elliot and Claris as possessing fundamentally different dreams (sports for boys and musical performance for girls, graffiti-laden inner-city basketball courts for boys and pastoral gardens for girls), perform this kind of borderwork, defining the proper place for each gender. On the other hand, the androgynous "Nights" embodies a fantasy of transcending gender and thus achieving the freedom and mobility to fly above it all. To win the game, the player must become *both* the male and the female protagonists, and they must join forces for the final level. The penalty for failure in this world is to be trapped on the ground and fixed into a single gender.

Thorne finds that aggressive "borderwork" is more likely to occur when children are forced together by adults than when they find themselves interacting more spontaneously, more likely to occur in prestructured institutional settings like the schoolyard than in the informal settings of the subdivisions and apartment complexes. All of this suggests that our fantasy of designing games that will provide common play spaces for girls and boys may be illusive and as full of its own complications and challenges as creating a "girls only" space or encouraging girls to venture into traditional male turf. We are not yet sure what such a gender-neutral space will look like. Creating such a space would mean redesigning not only the nature of computer games but also the nature of society. The danger may be that in such a space, gender differences are going to be more acutely felt, as boys and girls will be repelled from each other rather than drawn together. There are reasons why this is a place where neither the feminist entrepreneurs nor the makers of boys' games are ready to go, yet as the girls' market is secured, the challenge must be to find a way to move beyond our existing categories and to once again invent new kinds of virtual play spaces.

References

Booth, A. and Johnson, D. 1975. "The Effect of Crowding on Child Health and Development." *American Behaviourial Scientist* 18: 736–749.

Burnett, F. H. 1911. *The Secret Garden*. New York: Harper Collins.

Cavallo, D. 1981. *Muscles and Morals: Organized Playgrounds and Urban Reform, 1880–1920*. Philadelphia: University of Pennsylvania Press.

"Critical Depth." 1998. Advertisement, *Next Generation*, January.

"Die by the Sword." 1998. Advertisement, *Next Generation*, January.

Donaldson, F. 1970. "The Child in the City." University of Washington, mimeograph, cited in M. H. Matthews 1992, *Making Sense of Place: Children's Understanding of Large-Scale Environments*. Hertfordshire: Barnes and Noble.

Farley, W. 1941. *The Black Stallion*. New York: Random House.

Feinstein, K. and Kent, S. 1997. "Towards a Definition of 'Videogames.'" http:www.videotopia.com/errata1.htm.

Fitzhugh, L. 1964. *Harriet, the Spy*. New York: Harper & Row.

Formanek-Brunnel, M. 1996. "The Politics of Dollhood in Nineteenth-Century America." In H. Jenkins, ed., *The Children's Culture Reader*. New York: New York University Press.

Friedman, T. 1995. "Making Sense of Software: Computer Games and Interactive Textuality." In S. G. Jones, ed., *Cybersociety: Computer-Mediated Communication and Community*. Thousand Oaks, Calif.: Sage Publications.

Fuller, M. and Jenkins, H. 1995. "Nintendo and New World Travel Writing: A Dialogue." In S. G. Jones, ed., *Cybersociety: Computer-Mediated Communication and Community*. Thousand Oaks, Calif.: Sage Publications.

Hart, R. 1979. *Children's Experience of Place*. New York: John Wiley and Sons.

Holland, N. N. and Sherman, L. F. 1986. "Gothic Possibilities." In E. A. Flynn and P. P. Schweickart, eds., *Gender and Reading: Essays on Readers, Texts and Contexts*. Baltimore: Johns Hopkins University Press.

Jenkins, H. and Cassell, J. (this volume). "Chess for Girls?: The Gender Politics of the Girls Game Movement."

Katz, J. 1997. *Virtuous Reality*. New York: Random House.

Kinchloe, J. L. 1997. "*Home Alone* and 'Bad to the Bone': The Advent of a Postmodern Childhood." In S. R. Steinberg and J. L. Kincheloe, eds., *Kinder-Culture: The Corporate Construction of Childhood*. New York: Westview.

Kinder, M. 1996. "Contextualizing Video Game Violence: From 'Teenage Mutant Ninja Turtles 1' to 'Mortal Kombat 2.'" In P. M. Greenfield and R. R. Cocking, eds., *Interacting with Video*. Norwood: Ablex Publishing.

Matthews, M. H. 1992. *Making Sense of Place: Children's Understanding of Large-Scale Environments*. Hertfordshire: Barnes and Noble.

Moore, R. C. 1986. *Childhood's Domain: Play and Place in Child Development*. London: Croom Helm.

Newson, J. and Newson, E. 1976. *Seven Years Old in the Home Environment*. London: Allen and Unwin.

Rheingold, H. L. and Cook, K. V. 1975. "The Content of Boys' and Girls' Rooms as an Index of Parents' Behavior." *Child Development* 46: 459–463.

Rotundo, E. A. 1994. *American Manhood: Transformations in Masculinity from the Revolution to the Modern Era*. New York: Basic.

Searles, H. 1959. *The Non-Human Development in Normal Development and Schizophrenia*. New York: International Universities Press.

Segel, E. 1986. "'As the Twig Is Bent. . .': Gender and Childhood Reading." In E. A. Flynn and P. P. Schweickart, eds., *Gender and Reading: Essays on Readers, Texts and Contexts*. Baltimore: Johns Hopkins University Press.

Seitzer, E. 1996. Transcript of Expert Panel Meeting, Sega of America Gatekeeper Program. Los Angeles, June 21.

"Sonic R." 1998. Advertisement, *Next Generation*, January.

Henry Jenkins

Tapscott, D. 1997. *Growing Up Digital: The Rise of the Net Generation*. New York: McGraw Hill.

Thorne, B. 1993. *Gender Play: Girls and Boys in School*. New Brunswick: Rutgers University Press.

van Staden, J. F. 1984. "Urban Early Adolescents, Crowding and the Neighbourhood Experience: A Preliminary Investigation." *Journal of Environmental Psychology* 4: 97–118.

Van Vliet, W. 1983. "Exploring the Fourth Environment: An Examination of the Home Range of City and Suburban Teenagers." *Environment and Behavior* 15: 567–88.

"VR Sports." 1998. Advertisement, *Next Generation,* January.

Ward, C. 1977. *The Child in the City.* London: Architectural Press.

West, E. 1992. "Children on the Plains Frontier." In E. West and P. Petrik, eds., *Small Worlds: Children and Adolescents in America, 1850–1950.* Lawrence: The University Press of Kansas. p. 26–41.

Chapter 13

Storytelling as a Nexus of Change In the Relationship between Gender and Technology: A Feminist Approach to Software Design
Justine Cassell

Narrative might well be considered a solution to a problem of general human concern, namely, the problem of how to translate *knowing* into *telling*, the problem of fashioning human experience into a form assimilable to structures of meaning that are generally human rather than culture-specific.

—(White 1981)

Women repeatedly used the metaphor of voice to depict their intellectual and ethical development; and for them the development of a sense of voice, mind, and self were intrinsically intertwined.

—(Finke 1993)

What Girls Really Want and Who They Really Are

Recently, at a large technical computer conference where I was giving a talk on the nature of play and how to design computer games in such a way that children could appropriate technology to their own ends, a Very Famous Person stood up and made a Very Critical Remark. I had just finished describing one of the systems that my students and I have built within the framework of feminist software design—a storytelling system that encourages children first to program a computer persona to represent the wise old person of the children's own culture, and then to tell to that person the story of their lives, and the problems that they are currently facing. The VFP stood up and said, "Justine, why are you training children to entertain computers? And, besides, you are taking away the job of mothers, to listen to children." I was thrilled that this VFP knew my name, but dismayed that he understood the act of constructing one's ideal listener, and then telling the story of one's life to that listener, to be no more than entertaining a computer (let alone that he believed that the sole job of mothers—and only of mothers—was to listen to their children). The work that my students and I have done is largely about allowing children to entertain *themselves* and, in the process, to engage in the serious business of learning about themselves, constructing a social identity, and collaborating with others in the process of understanding that identity, all the while attaining technological fluency. Girls tend to like the computer games we build, but so do boys. This chapter is about the kind of software that asks children to do the entertaining, about its politics and its practice: about how we build girls' games in such a way that the game itself participates in the construction of a child's gender and other aspects of the self, without a preconceived notion of what a girl is.

The premise underlying much of the critical analysis and industry work presented in this volume is that it is a good thing for girls to begin to use computers at a young age. This premise is well supported by reports of how much more likely boys are than girls to use a computer at home, participate in computer clubs or activities at school, or attend a computer camp; by evidence of the links between early computer use and later career choices involving technology; by the current paucity of women designing technology; and by the increasing technologization of work (see Cassell and Jenkins, this volume, for a discussion of these trends). For these reasons (or because a large segment of the market is not purchasing their products), software designers have turned to software that girls will use. And these types of software have been lumped under the title "girl games."

Much of what we read concerning this new software for girls describes how important it is to know what girls really want ("each company's extensive focus-group testing shows, as Philips Media Home president Sarina Simon puts it, 'this is what girls want'" (Tanaka 1996)), and how girls play ("years of research into gender differences in play patterns show that boys, in general, like competitive win-lose situations, high scores and body counts. It's almost the opposite for girls"). When we read about these efforts, we may worry about *which* girls and *which* vision of girls. But all of this research assumes that there is a gender of "girl"—as if what "girls" is is static and ontological rather than dynamic and performative. And yet much research in the social sciences has come to see gender as *constituted* rather than preexistent. That is, "the notion of gender centers on the premise that the notions of men and women/male and female are sociocultural transformations of biological categories and processes" (Ochs 1992, p. 339). And, further, these sociocultural transformations are not constant across an individual's lifespan, or across the different contexts in which one acts, but rather "[O]ne's experience of gender emerges in participation as a gendered community member with others in a variety of communities of practice" (Eckert and McConnell-Ginet 1995, p. 469).

Gender, then, involves possibilities that are always in flux and that are determined by many things (race, class, age, peers, immediate context). Thus, the kinds of activities that have been described as "what girls really do" are not neutral or isolated acts but part of the construction of a complex identity. In this case, we might argue that designing "games for girls" misses the point. If we come up with one activity, or complex of activities that girls want, then we know that we must have only tapped into one context in which girls are girls. To avoid this paradox, and to create access to computers for children who engage in a variety of gendered activities, we must expand the range of the activities that are available. In fact, we might use the computer as the very site for children to make meanings, express themselves, and play out the range of identities that will constitute themselves. That is, children can use computers in order to try out identities and to explore the possibilities of expression, in such a way to make sense of their social sphere and develop an understanding of themselves.

How do we design in such a way that children can do gender and other social constructions of identity? One approach is Kinder's work (this volume), where the user chooses parameters of gender, and the parameters are explicitly split from one another (sex, gender identity, appearance). I wish to propose an alternative approach, one in which children or users of technology do not explicitly specify their gender. Rather, the technology participates in children's construction of their own gender identity just as it does in the construction of their identity as a whole, by asking them to tell the story of who they are. This approach has two theoretical antecedents: the first, briefly described above, is the postmodern view of gender as *performative*—socially constructed and yet capable of being explored on a personal level and *played* in different ways in different contexts (Butler 1990; Sedgewick 1993). The second theoretical antecedent is feminist pedagogy, which claims that there exist alternative but equal views of reality, that the importance of experiential as well as objective knowledge must be admitted, that in all organizations—indeed in all structures—

authority must be distributed among the participants, and that collaboration is essential to all work and play. Here "feminist" does not mean "for women" but "from the feminist movement," and is seen as benefiting both boys and girls.

If we rely on such an approach to design computer games for girls, what might be the best genre for our games? Many games for girls are educational (often for historical reasons having to do with how game designers see girls; see Cassell and Jenkins, this volume), many entail play situations that have traditionally been associated with girls such as those involving dolls, horoscopes, clothing, and make-up. I argue that the ideal playing field for the construction of self is storytelling and other kinds of narrative activity. That is, one very important way for children to learn about themselves, and to construct their selves, is through first-person storytelling and other kinds of participatory narratives. As Ochs and Taylor (1995) write, "[G]ender identities are constituted through actions and demeanors . . . among other routes, children come to understand family and gender roles through differential modes of acting and expressing feelings in narrative activity" (p. 98).

Many of the new computer games for girls involve narrative, including "American Girls," Purple Moon's titles, "Barbie Storyteller," HerInteractive's "Mc-Kenzie & Co.," and "Chop Suey." The narratives are stories familiar to girls in the target age groups, with characters that girls can relate to. Why do these narratives not suffice, then, to allow the child to construct a flexible and performative gender identity? Why are they so specifically games for *girls,* rather than for girls to be who they wish? First of all, many of the games for girls have been designed to exclude or turn off boys (and hence girls who do not fit stereotypical notions of girlhood?). Second, these narratives are not about the child's own self, nor are they flexibly designed to allow a range of gendered constructions. Some, such as "American Girls," are designed simply to tell a traditional story of "girlhood" to an all-too-familiar type of ideal "girl" audience. Other software, such as Purple Moon's "Rockett's New School" or HerInteractive's "McKenzie & Co.," instead allow girls vicariously to enact the roles in the stories—to imagine that they are the heroine, or the heroine's friend, and to exercise their social intelligence to make the story proceed in a particular direction. There is also software, such as "Chop Suey," that encourages girls to act as explorers to learn more about the subplots in the story, and the setting. Some of these stories are quite strong narratively, and quite engaging. Purple Moon's stories deal with issues of the self in sensitive and reflective ways, clearly mirroring Laurel's philosophy that "Stories are wonderful gifts. They're empowering for the teller and the hearer" (Laurel, this volume). No matter how engaging, however, the stories are about the lives of imaginary characters and not the user. And the user plays the listener, and not the teller of the tale. A story that a child tells herself will always be the most active construction of the child's self. This does not mean that the experience of being a listener is not without value. For reading (or watching) is also an active process, of appropriation and reflection, and self-making. Stories by others may be resources for storytelling and for constructing oneself through stories. But the teller of the tale holds the power of construction—of meaning-making—in her hands. Of course, CD-ROMs, and the concept of book on which they are based, are meant to be professional fiction, aesthetically crafted by artists and writers. However, telling a story to girls via a CD-ROM, whether or not the story is appealing to girls, or familiar, or important, still maintains the locus of control in the designer of the software, who decided what story to tell. An approach consonant with construction of social identity would give girls the role of narrator, and also allow them to choose whether to be the subject of the narration—that is, would give them voice. This would let them tell whatever story they like, while the computer constructed a willing listener. In this case we only risk having the child tell a narratively unprofessional story, which might not be aesthetically appealing to the everyday listener. But it is the child's own story, told in the child's own voice. It is a way for a child to represent his or her unique perspective on the world—the first-person perspective—to the world.

In fact, such an approach mirrors the "linguistic turn" (Fraser 1994) in social theory, including theory of gender. Here it is claimed that language is fundamental, indeed unique, in constructing social reality. That is, reality as described in language is given more weight than any objective reality. So giving the child the role of narrator and asking her to tell any story she chooses is asking her to create the world and her existence, in language.

This chapter is centered around two main points. First, I'm proposing a feminist vision of game software design as a space in which authority can be distributed to users, by allowing most of the design and construction to be carried out by the user rather than the designer—in fact, to have the game be *about* design and construction.[1] Second, I'm proposing that interactive storytelling games be the field on which we practice feminist game software design, because telling one's own stories and constructing one's own storytelling software can allow the finding of one's voice, a key way to distribute authority, and an important tool to give to girls (and to boys).

What Is a "Feminist Approach"?

The terms "feminism" and "feminist" have, for some, acquired a negative connotation recently, and the authors represented in this volume are as divided as the general population. (See, for example, Gesue.) At a recent talk that I gave on feminist software design, an audience member asked afterwards whether, if I was mainly interested in getting my ideas across, I could simply drop the label "feminist." I replied that I saw the label and the content as intrinsically linked. An hour later, he found me in the hall and gave me a carefully constructed sign: the suffix -ism inside a circle with a red bar across it. "You just don't realize how many people you have upset by using the term 'feminist,'" he said.

The modern feminist movement arose out of and alongside the civil rights and peace movements of the 1960s. The feminist movement fights for political, economic and social equality between men and women. As part of feminism's challenge to male hegemony, feminists have developed radical methodologies for studying social structures and instituting change. These methodologies, which may be called the "feminist approach," in recent years have been brought to bear on education, linguistics, philosophy, history, and many other disciplines. Feminist approaches share some of the following themes:

• A rejection of "the desirability or even the possibility of value-free research" (Weiler 1988). That is, it is impossible to factor out the point of view of the researcher in studying a particular problem.
• A focus on the subjective, experiential, everyday lived experiences of individuals. Thus, a feminist approach moves away from objective single-truth-oriented beliefs about the world.
• A strong emphasis on collaboration, which is seen as a key value in the construction of political movements and alliances between researchers in sometimes different fields. Collaboration in this context is often contrasted with competition, but *conflict* is not excluded (Jarratt 1991).
• An attempt to showcase a multiplicity of viewpoints and perspectives.
• An attempt to promote the distribution of authority among the members of a community. In particular, feminist research attempts to correct traditional imbalances of power between researcher and researched, teacher and students, and so on.

It is important to note that none of these themes pertains exclusively, or even particularly, to gender. Feminist approaches may be applied to any kind of hegemonic practice.

What Is Feminist Pedagogy?

Feminist pedagogy applies the tenets of feminist research to the practice of education. Feminist pedagogy is perhaps the domain in which the tenets of feminism have had the most success in changing institutions. Feminist teachers have wrought changes in the American classroom since the mid-1960s. Feminist pedagogy relies on the premise that authority should not be found primarily on the teacher's side of the desk (Lewis 1993). The feminist teacher says, "I am an expert, but I am not the only expert." Feminist pedagogy also strives to institute structures of collaboration in the classroom, despite the realities of grading individual performance. Feminist pedagogy teaches that theorizing can be based on the experience of real people with different experiences. In *Women's Ways of Knowing*, Belenky et al. argued that

> educators can help women develop their own authentic voices if they emphasize connection over separation, understanding and acceptance over assessment, and collaboration over debate; if they accord respect to and allow time for the knowledge that emerges from firsthand experience; if instead of imposing their own expectations and arbitrary requirements, they encourage students to evolve their own patterns of work based on the problems they are pursuing. These are the lessons we have learned in listening to women's voices. (1986, p. 229)

We might summarize these principles as follows:

- Transfer authority to the student
- Value subjective and experiential knowledge
- Allow a multiplicity of viewpoints
- Give the student voice to express the truth of her life as she experiences it
- Encourage collaboration

What Is Feminist Software Design?

If we extrapolate the principles of feminist pedagogy to the design of technology, we arrive at the following tenets:

- Transfer design authority to the user
- Value subjective and experiental knowledge in the context of computer use
- Allow use by many different kinds of users in different contexts

- Give the user a tool to express her voice and the truth of her existence
- Encourage collaboration among users

Thus, as in feminist pedagogy, where the authority is distributed throughout the classroom, in feminist software design, it is not the technologist who retains authority—or design-principles—but the user, who is given a free hand in deciding the use and structure of the game (but is not abandoned alone with the technology). Rather than positing an intrinsic link between computers and math and science, feminist software design looks for intrinsic links between computers and subjective and experiential topics such as storytelling. Likewise, rather than insisting on one right answer—one path through the software, for example—feminist software design conceives of users as diverse, and their paths through technology as equally diverse (this principle is well expressed by Turkle and Papert 1990). Feminist software design concentrates on the computer as a tool of expression, or a mirror of the self (Turkle 1984). And, finally, feminist software design looks for ways to allow many users to collaborate.

The vision of feminist software design that I am proposing here has several points of contact with other current perspectives on the design of new media. In terms of politics, and in terms of the types of collaborative tools envisaged, feminist software design is similar to user-centered, or participatory design. Participatory design, like feminist research, is not a single theory or technique for accomplishing software design. Rather, it is a set of perspectives that share concern for a "more humane, creative and effective relationship between those involved in technology's design and its use" (Suchman 1993). The goal of the participatory design movement is to encourage active participation in the design process by people using computer systems, and to make this participation empowering (Greenbaum and Kyng 1991). The movement grew out of the realization that, whereas in the early days of digital technology engineers were designing technology for other engineers, today's end users may not have the same goals or practices as the designers of their technology. In practical terms, this stance translates into conceiving of users as an essential part of the design team, and therefore bringing them in early during the design phase of new technology. In practice, the tools of participatory design are frequently used to design collaborative technologies. Examples are the successful Whiteboard technology that allows two architects, artists, or other designers to see each other's designs, and CommonSpace, software for collaborative writing. The points of contact between participatory design and feminist software design are not surprising given their political commonalities—both raise questions about

democracy, power, and control in the workplace (Balka 1996)—and the participation of many feminists in the founding of participatory design (Suchman
1991).[2] However, while advocates of participatory design do bring users into the
lab early in the product-development cycle, the product itself is still constructed
in the absence of the users, and no commitment is expressed to making a
product that allows different kinds of uses by different users at different
moments.

Another approach, that does advocate users' construction of their own
technology is *constructionism* (Papert 1980). Born of Piaget's theory of cognitive
development, constructionism claims that children are likely to have access to
more and different kinds of new ideas when they are building things that they
can reflect on and share with others in their learning community. The constructionist theory has been applied to math and science education, and more recently to learning about computation. Mitchel Resnick and his colleagues have
given children computational construction kits that support children's design
and construction of their own projects using on-screen software and also mini-
computers embedded in small Lego constructions (Resnick et al. 1996). Kafai
(this volume) has extended the paradigm to the design and construction of
educational video games. Constructionist technology design shares with the
feminist software design principles proposed here an emphasis on personal
appropriation of programming, and of technology in general (Papert 1980). Examples of software built within this framework include educational software
such as Logo, which supports direct manipulation and creation of computational artifacts as well as reflection about the programming process. Starlogo is
an extension of Logo that allows parallel processing and invites children to
create and reflect on decentralized systems. All of these tools leverage children's understanding of the world to help them learn how to program, and use
children's increasing understanding of programming to change their understanding of the world. However, the kinds of computational construction kits
proposed to children have focused heavily on science, math, and computer
science, and not on literature, culture, or self-knowledge. Math, science, and
computer science are fields where objective truth is very much privileged, and
for the most part where experiential knowledge is given little place.

What Is Storytelling and What Function Does it Serve?

I have argued that we must look to feminist pedagogy for a way to make software support experiential, first-person, collaborative activity that encourages

finding one's voice. Now I turn to the second part of the argument, that we must look to narrative for the specifics of that activity: allowing children to tell their own story. Computer environments can encourage people to share their personal stories, if we as designers of technology can set the appropriate context.

First, however, I lay out three functions of storytelling that make it a nexus of change in the relationship between gender and technology: informing others about our beliefs or experiences, exploring our role in the social world, and defining and negotiating norms that govern our behavior and our participation in communities of practice. I argue that storytelling is an important activity for the construction of self, for the construction of the world, and for the construction of the norms by which we lead our lives, and thus an activity that encourages storytelling is a potential space for the maintenance of an identity that is not voiceless. In other words, I claim that storytelling might be the *ur*-place to raise one's voice gladly.

During my first semester as faculty at MIT, an undergraduate asked about doing graduate work with me. During our conversation it came out that, after three and one-half years at MIT, she was taking her first course with a female professor. The student confided that until then, she had thought that she was unfit to be an academic herself. But seeing a woman on the other side of the desk had made her think that she could do it, too, and so she now wanted to apply to graduate school. The young woman told me this story in the context of her pleasure at finding out that I was taking graduate students, but I believe she felt the story was appropriate given the conversation we were having about research on gender and science. This kind of storytelling is powerful stuff. The act of confiding has powerful effects on the teller (Pennebaker 1990, Linde 1993); in this instance it created a bond between the teller and the listener (I admitted her as a graduate student) and, as witnessed by its inclusion in this chapter, affected the listener, too. We engage in this kind of storytelling all the time, yet as powerful as it is, and as ubiquitous, it has not had a technological home—there has existed no particular body of technology to support it, enhance it, or engage people in its practice.

I use the term "storytelling" rather than "stories" because we are interested here in a four-way relationship among the teller of a tale, the listener, the act of telling, and the tale itself. The literary fields have wished to denude the tale of its relationship with the teller and instead focus on its narrative aspects, and perhaps its effect on the listener. But if our interest is in voice, in giving children the chance to be heard, we must focus more on the production of tales than on their reception. But concentrating on production does not mean that we ignore the essential presence of a listener. All tales are produced for a listener—the storyteller herself or another (Polanyi 1989). Concentrating on production also doesn't mean that we ignore the important experience of consuming other people's stories: it can be incredibly validating to see in print a story similar to one's own, or to recognize aspects of oneself in a television character. In fact, as I will discuss below, it is a powerful experience for children to play both the teller and the listener of a same story. But children are quite often only given the role of listener, as a way of socializing them into the appropriate way to use their voice. Here we give them the role that is least expected. Finally, concentrating on production does not mean that we will ignore the narratives themselves—what the stories convey. Stories can be about events in the world around us, about events that we have experienced, or about the events that take place in our imaginations. In all cases, stories impose a structure on those events so that listeners (including the storyteller) can understand them and take away from them some particular perspective. Stories have these properties because of their essential duality. On the one hand, stories are made up of events that are narrated in a particular order and told from a particular point of view. On the other hand, stories are *about* events that took place in a particular order and were experienced by particular people. The order of events in the telling need not mirror the order of the events themselves, nor does the perspective on events need to mirror the original perspective of the teller. Having the order or perspective not be identical is what creates narrative effects. We build suspense ("what I have not mentioned until now is that . . ."), give our evaluation of what is happening ("all of this happened this way because. . ."), and make the story relevant to the interaction at hand ("this reminds me of what happened to us last summer"). These narrative effects, which in most everyday storytelling are included more or less unconsciously, are how tellers explore and convey knowledge and experience. We may use storytelling to inform others about our experiences or beliefs or to get enough distance from those experiences to be able to reflect on them (what Bruner and Lucariello (1989) refer to as the "cooling off function" of narrative).

Storytelling is also a way to explore the demands of different roles in the social world. As Turner (1981, p. 163) suggests, "narrative is . . . experiential knowledge." The young woman who came to see me was telling a story about exploring the role of scientist and academic. Through telling stories we can express how children and parents, girls and boys, each are expected to act. This function is apparent in the tales that parents tell about their children ("[My husband] said [to my daughter] 'tell your mother she's a creep' and that's when she said, 'nuh uh, Daddy.' She said, 'You're the creep.'"), and the tales that children come to tell about themselves ("[I] didn't want other kids to play on [the slide]. I want I myself, I myself to play on it") (both examples from Miller et al. 1990). In storytelling we can also experiment with developing notions of roles—how we are coming to believe that children act and adults act. This function is apparent in pretend play, an early version of storytelling. In fact, pretend play is a kind of coproduced storytelling, in which children share out the character roles and take turns being the narrator: "You be the teacher and and I'll be the student, and I'll say I didn't do my homework and then you'll yell at me, and then. . . ." Thus, in storytelling we experiment with, construct, and express our identities. Gender is a key aspect of that identity, and one that we can see young children exploring in their narrative play: "Planning and enacting co-constructed narrative play with same sex peers provides daily opportunities to observe, learn about, transmit and practice gender-stereotyped knowledge as well as others sorts of knowledge about the world" (Sheldon and Rohleder 1996, p. 629). In sum, storytelling is a means not only for projecting oneself to others, but also for constructing and interpreting aspects of the self.

Thus far I have talked about stories told by individuals, and stories told by pairs (a parent and a child, two children engaging in pretend play). Here I turn to stories that are told by groups of people, that are used to construct loci of power and structures of social organization. Eckert (1993) argues that gossip and "girl talk" serve to keep track of who is—or isn't—behaving in accordance with societal norms, and to create those norms. Thus, "girl talk can be seen as an agent of social change, as well as of social control." Eckert argues that girls in particular engage in this type of monitoring of norms because personal influence, defined as the ability to set behavioral norms and monitor other people's behavior, is women's symbolic capital (as opposed to men's capital, which is defined with respect to their accomplishments, possessions, and institutional status). Girl talk, in this instance, is a way of constructing power.

Compare this description of high school girls, however, with any one of a number of popular books on adolescent girls. Pipher (1994), for example, argues that at adolescence "girls become 'female impersonators' who fit their whole selves into small, crowded spaces." They lose interest in the subjects that they once loved, do less well in school, and in many different ways lose their authentic voices. Girl talk would appear to be a space in which girls can maintain their voices. In fact, as Gal (1991) convincingly argues, many women's genres, and women's everyday talk, manifest "subtlety, subversion and opposition to dominant definitions." Eckert and Gal both argue that language is not only an organ for silencing women, but also a weapon that has belonged particularly to women, as other kinds of power have been denied to them. And although common lore about girls being better at verbal tasks than boys from their first school days has been largely disproved (Sheldon 1993), it has been found that one enduring difference between boys and girls, and men and women, in different cultural and ethnic contexts, has been the attention that girls pay to the contextualization of language. For example, in looking at fantasy play among three-year-old children, Sheldon (1993) finds that girls focused more on negotiation around pretend play—who would play whom, what each child would say—and in some instances focused on it more than on the play itself. (See also Sachs 1987.) Johnstone (1993) reports similar findings for adult women and men producing conversational stories—women place greater emphasis on who said what. This research shows that the function of voice—who speaks and who says what—is particularly important to girls and women, in fantasy play and storytelling, and that it appears to be a site for the construction of power.

Raising One's Voice

The term "voice" in narrative theory has referred to whether an author speaks through a narrator or a character, or speaks as herself—it is intrinsically linked to the notion of *character* in narrative. But popular books on adolescence, and much feminist theory, use the terms "voice," "words," "language" in a metaphoric sense

> to denote the public expression of a particular perspective on self and social life, the effort to represent one's own experience, rather than accepting the representations of more powerful others. (Gal 1991, p. 176)

The two meanings come together when we consider storytelling as a place where one decides who to be—where one constructs a social self—and where a perspective is maintained on one's own life—where one resists the attempts by more powerful others to silence that perspective. Stories are not only a commonly available means to create, interpret, and publicly project culturally constituted images of self in face-to-face interaction, but also places to defy others' versions of who one is.

I am referring to stories that are told, as opposed to being painted or sung, for example. Stories are, in part, such a powerful vehicle for self-construction because they are told in language. And language is particularly capable of constructing reality because the same thing can be expressed in different ways, with each alternative allying the speaker with a particular community and particular discursive practices.

In sum, storytelling is an important activity for the development of knowledge about the self, particularly in relationship to others. It is where we learn to tell what we know about social interaction and ourselves to others who matter. If narrative is experiential knowledge, as Turner says, then in stories we can learn to know our own experience as primary, we can try out versions of ourselves, we can tell our stories, we can describe our version of the world, and we can learn to trust the value of our perceptions. When the storytelling voice is our own, we retain our perceptions of who we are, in the face of opposition to those perceptions. I am arguing that the way to get voice in computer games is to turn the storytelling over to the player, rather than leading the player through a narrative that others have built. That is, the child should be allowed to be the storyteller and not the story listener, to be the actor and not the acted upon.

What Has Computer Storytelling Been?

As mentioned earlier, many computer games for girls are narrative in nature. In fact, most video games for boys and girls are described as interactive fantasy play, or narrative-based. One might think, then, that these applications would allow children to engage in the kind of storytelling just described: experiential storytelling that constructs the self through the use of language and the mastery of voice. Why is this not the case? In classically "boy games" such as those produced for Nintendo, Fuller and Jenkins (1995) argue that "most of the criteria by which we might judge a classically constructed narrative fall by the wayside when we look at these games as storytelling systems. . . . The character is little more than a cursor that mediates the player's relationship to the story world. . .[they are] forms of narrative that privilege space over characterization or plot development." The user is invited to imagine himself the hero, conquering bad guys galore, but there is no narrator. In the case of the new girl games, as described above, many are "spatial stories" ("Chop Suey," for example; see Jenkins, this volume). The spatial story, as Fuller and Jenkins convincingly argue, is a valid narrative tradition with its own history (and roots in travelogue) and cultural functions. The cultural function of such stories, however, is not the construction of or reflection on the self but rather the experience of conquest, finding new frontiers, and so on.

Others, as discussed earlier, do indeed privilege characterization and problems concerning the construction of self in the social world (for example, Purple Moon's characters' dilemmas about what to wear to school to look cool, who to be friends with and so on). However, in these cases, the dilemmas are firmly in the third person. They are certainly relevant to the projected players, but not by any means in the player's own voice.

What about the new genre of interactive fiction? This refers to a short story or novel in a hypertext format, the branching nodes allowing users to read a different story each time by choosing different links. Once again, although there is room for vicarious experience and perhaps, in the better interactive fiction, for an experience approaching that of authorship, there is no place to deploy one's voice, or represent one's self (although some disagree. See the discussion of this point in Don 1990; Laurel 1993). Of course, as Fuller and Jenkins (1995) and Gailey (1993) have pointed out, children do not always work toward the goal intended by the toy designer. Children may "play crazy" with Nintendo and make characters bounce around the screen. In fact, Gailey suggests that girls may get around the strongly passive stereotypes of women in many video games by seeing themselves as stage managers of the video game narrative rather than adopting the role of key players in the story.

So storytelling with technology is tantalizingly close to what we might wish, and the current alternatives are exactly the places where boys are getting their exposure to computers. If technology can play a role in storytelling, then perhaps it can play a role in girls' storytelling of the self.

What Could Interactive Storytelling Be: Storytelling Systems Built on Feminist Principles

Mary Lyons, the founder of the women's college Mt. Holyoke, believed in the fundamental importance of lab courses in teaching science to women. The science courses at Mt. Holyoke are still based on this principle. However, Lyons' position has often been misunderstood to mean that girls are able to deal with the world only in practical terms. One often hears this same position cited in support of designing games for girls that are based on the real world, and not geared towards the fantastical. (This position is further discussed in the introduction to this volume.) In fact, what Mary Lyons said was that lab courses were important in teaching girls the independence of their intellect, that their perceptions of the world were valid, and their scientific intuitions valuable. Today, girls and women still can use playing grounds on which to learn to trust their perceptions of the world, their intellect, and their intuitions. And thus the utility of a tool to tell their own stories and hence to find their voices.

In the remainder of this chapter I discuss three of the storytelling tools that my students and I have built on the basis of feminist software design principles. Our storytelling games are built for research purposes and don't need to meet the exigencies of the market. They do, however, meet the exigencies of the children who come to my laboratory to test them. We provide storytelling tools that will allow children to test their theories of who they are, with respect to others and with respect to themselves. We intend to give them a lab for story design—and this is how we distribute authority.

The three storytelling tools that I am going to describe differ along the dimensions of first-person or third-person voice, the nature of collaborative activity that is encouraged, and the extent of design activities that are put in the hands of the children.

Renga

Turkle (1986) interviewed women who were struggling with their unwillingness to become hackers, proficient in programming and computer science. In "Computational Reticence: Why Women Fear the Intimate Machine," Turkle claims that their unwillingness arises from women's fear of entering into a relationship with an object: an entity without feelings that might consume their lives and not leave room for social interaction and love. One student, who to her surprise has been very successful in a computer science class, says: "I wanted to work in worlds where languages had moods and connected you with people" (p. 44).

The first storytelling system that I am going to describe has the simple goal of connecting children with one another through a collaborative storytelling activity. This Internet-based system is called "Renga" (http://mythos. media.mit.edu), and it allows children around the world to tell a story collaboratively in real time. Renga (from the Japanese word meaning "linked poem" or "linked image") resembles the game played in primary schools in which the class sits in a circle, one child begins a story, and each of the other children adds a sentence. Renga incorporates many of the linguistic, imaginative, and community aspects of the old-fashioned round-robin story, but allows for children all over the world to share in the circle. As children type in sentences, they are immediately added to the end of the story. If more than one child submits a sentence at once, a situation potentially threatening the cohesion of the story, one of the sentences is added where it is intended, and the others are held in a queue and added later according to discourse rules that ensure that the sentence fits in syntactically and semantically. We have begun the story with a seed sentence, "Once upon a time a little girl was sitting in front of her computer," and we end the story once it is so long that children seem to be no longer reading it all before they add their sentence. When one story has been finished, we add it to a page of previous stories that children can read, and begin the story again, with the same seed sentence. The beginning sentence we chose limits very little the directions that the story can go in, and also allows children to tell a first-person or third-person story. As shown in Plate 23, some children continued "and she decided to tell a story. She wanted to tell about unicorns and dragons and castles and princesses." Other children, on the other hand, took the "little girl" to refer to themselves, and continued "when suddenly the computer sucked her in the screen. The computer took her to a magical land with funny animals. I saw amazing things! It was very strange."

In our initial introduction of Renga, we invited the participation of every school in the world that had any web presence (214 schools in October 1995). Children from fourteen schools in eleven countries used Renga to collaborate on a story during one twenty-four-hour period in October 1995. While in general children found the system easy to use and enjoyable, our early experiences with Renga led us to realize how hungry for voice children really are. In our first trials with this system we found that, while children were happy to add sentences to the story, they also tended to punctuate the story with statements about themselves. Thus, in the middle of a segment about a little girl running away from a monster in the woods, one girl added, "Hi, I'm Tracy and I like ice cream. I live in Australia. Does anybody else like ice cream." The realization that collaboration on the story did not suffice, but that children also needed to collaborate on community—on expressing who they were to one another—led us to change the format and add a separate window where information about the author of each sentence is displayed. Clicking on a sentence now reveals information about the child who wrote that sentence, including whatever description of himself or herself the child chooses to add. We also added a list of the last five children who submitted sentences, in order to give children a sense of who is in the "room" at any one time.

Rosebud

This system takes a toy that is loved by both boys and girls—the stuffed animal—(Asakawa and Rucker 1992; Dyl and Wapner 1996) and makes it the child's ally and partner, facilitating the use of technology with which the child may not be familiar and making the computer no longer just a tool but one voice in a multiparty conversation. The stuffed animal is unique in a number of ways that are important for the different kinds of narratives that children (and adults) tell. First, since it represents a sentient being, the child can attribute to the stuffed animal social goals, thus giving the child an imaginary partner to share experiences. Second, the stuffed animal plays an early role in the child's narrative life: the listener of children's early stories, the subject of other stories, and the hero of plays put on by groups of children. Third, stuffed animals are solidly gender-neutral toys until preadolescence (at which point boys deny liking them anymore, but often refuse to throw them out). Finally, stuffed animals become keepsake objects that continue to play a role in people's memories.

In the Rosebud system (Glos 1997; Glos and Cassell 1997), the computer recognizes children's stuffed animals (via an infrared transmitter in the toy, and receiver in the computer) and asks the child to tell about the stuffed animal or, in a subsequent interaction, calls the stuffed animal by name and recalls what it has heard. The child is asked to tell a story about the stuffed animal, any story at all, with prompts along the way. The computer is an encouraging listener, as well as a teacher, pushing the child to write, write more, edit, and improve. (See Plate 24.) The child is in charge of the interaction, deciding which stuffed animal to play with and what story to tell. We have found this paradigm of the technologically enhanced stuffed animal as *ally* to be a powerful way to engage children in the active use of technology.

The collaboration among child, computer, and stuffed animal ends with the child recording the story in her own voice—the story is saved into the stuffed animal, which can then be asked to repeat the story back to her. Rosebud supports storytelling by one child and one stuffed animal, but also by multiple children each with his or her own stuffed animal, working together. In this literal sense of "voice," and in the metaphoric sense, Rosebud encourages the establishing of voice through an open-ended storytelling framework. It values subjective and experiential knowledge, as well as participatory creativity, supporting writing of personal stories. It promotes collaborative learning, among several users and through peer review, and presents the computer as a supportive learning partner rather than as an authoritative viewpoint, avoiding a hierarchical positioning. Contrary to traditional uses of computers as mathematical machines, Rosebud does not view the child's input as right or wrong, but rather gives only limited structure and guidance. Rosebud focuses on collaboration by allowing multiple-toy use and multiple-author storybooks, so that

Figure 13.1: Child using Rosebud to tell a story about Eeyore

several children can write a story together about all of their stuffed animals. Likewise, since the toy serves as a storage device, children can trade their stories by lending their stuffed animals to a friend.

Early testing of the Rosebud system focused, among other things, on whether stuffed animals that evoked highly commercialized narratives of their own, such as Pooh Bear and Eeyore, elicited less personal stories than stuffed animals with no commercial or narrative associations, such as a platypus. (See Figure 13.1.) We found that any stuffed animal was likely to elicit a highly personal, highly emotionally charged story, such as the following story told by a nine-year-old girl playing with a Pooh Bear and an Eeyore:

> Once upon a time a very long time ago there were two friends named pooh bear and eeyore. They liked each other very much and let nothing get in there way. One day eeyore felt sad because his mother passed away. So he went to his good friend pooh bear to ask for advice. Eeyore asked pooh bear and pooh bear said to take it easy and relax. Eeyore said ok I will.

Here the emotional bond that often exists between a child and a stuffed animal appears to be more important than any preexisting identity of the stuffed animal.

It should be noted that Rosebud is not the only existing computer application that relies on a stuffed animal or toy as interface device. Actimate's "Barney" and Mattel's "Talk with Me Barbie" both use toys as output devices for the computer, with differing amounts of personalization. Barney can talk to the child about a TV show that the child is watching; Barbie can use answers previously entered into a computer to work into her speech facts about the child such as her name, birthday, and favorite color. In both cases, however, the toy is the speaker and the child is once again firmly in the position of listener. Rosebud puts the child in the role of narrator of her own experience, allowing her an infinite range of narrative possibilities, stretching from telling a story that she has made up about her stuffed animal to telling a story about her experience with her stuffed animal to telling her own story as if it were the story of her stuffed animal (as seems to be the case in the story above).

SAGE

Like Rosebud, SAGE (Umaschi and Cassell, under review) invites children into a three-way interaction among the child, computer, and a stuffed animal. (See Plate 25.) Once again the stuffed animal serves as the child's ally, in this case with respect to a wise old person who lives in the computer, and who knows traditional stories. SAGE supports the creation of and interaction with the kind of wise old storytellers who always have the perfect story to tell in response to a child's problems. Children can engage with SAGE in two modes: by choosing from a library of sage storytellers and then telling a personal story to that persona, and by creating their own characters and types of storytelling interactions. In the first mode, children interact with a wise old sage, who asks them their problems, listens, and then offers a relevant traditional tale in response. In the second, children are invited to add to the library of wise old sages by designing their own personal storyteller for themselves and other children to interact with. This dual kind of interaction required implementing a visual programming language that allows children to design and program the actual words of scripts that the storyteller says; the conversational structure or flow of the interaction; the behaviors of the stuffed animal (its body language), which behaves as the storyteller's assistant and the child's ally; and the database of stories that the storyteller draws on to comfort his or her interlocutor. The stuffed animal can be programmed to exhibit some of the types of nonverbal behaviors that humans use to indicate engagement, and that are commonly found in conversational narratives between people. For example, the rabbit nods. Unlike humans, however, the rabbit can also show interest by raising its ears. In interaction mode, children can watch the stuffed animal move as they converse with it. In design mode, children can decide on the toy's communicative behaviors as well as the different personalities and conversational styles that it might demonstrate.

The SAGE system allows children to learn about themselves both through the appropriation of another's story, when they are listening to a traditional tale picked out for them by the wise old storyteller, and through first-person storytelling, when they are telling their own story to the sage. In addition, the power of children being able to design their own storytellers is that in doing so, they design their ideal listeners. They express those parts of themselves that know how to listen to the stories that they themselves tell. When interacting with one of the sages that we had designed, children were quick to reveal their problems. In building a sage, children designed that person to whom they wished they could turn with their problems. But it is essential to note that since the children were creating their own characters and databases of stories, they were also playing with different notions of self, and creating or imitating the narrative voices they wanted or needed to hear. Children used the SAGE system to build role models, soothing wise adults, family dogs, and other characters from their inner world. These projections allowed the children to practice presenting themselves to themselves as well as to others. One child built a storyteller called "Big Orange Fox" who, in response to the user's problems, tells stories about hard things that have happened to him. Big Orange Fox interviews the person interacting with him to find out if that person has "school problems, learning problems, teasing problems, subject problems, friendship problems, religion problems, and relative problems." Another child built a storyteller called "Mother Nature" (Plate 26). Mother Nature calls up a myth about nature (written by the child who designed the sage) in response to the user's description of her favorite thing in nature, as shown below:

SAGE: Hello, I'm Mother Nature. What is your name?
USER: Mira
SAGE: I am very old. I am already 3,183! How old are you? Please tell me in numbers.

USER: Twenty-four

SAGE: Well you're not too old, honey! So, do you like to be in nature? I live in it!

USER: Yes

SAGE: That is very nice! So have you ever done something good for nature?

USER: Yes

SAGE: Oh, OK, now I will tell you some stories. First I need you to tell me what your favorite thing in nature is because I might know a story about it!

USER: Animals

SAGE: In school Julie had to list all the animals she could list not including insects or sea animals. Julie was a very creative girl and she thought it would be boring just listing them. She wanted to make up a creative story about them. So she asked her teacher if she could. Her teacher, Ms. Corty, said that was fine. As soon as Julie was home she started right on her story about animals. For each animal she wrote an adventure. Her first animal was the dog. Julie loved dogs! The story was about a little dog who could not talk nor make a sound. He thought he had the worst life but he really had the best a puppy could have! Even though he could not talk he had a special talent. He could dance better than any dog or human being. Now he knew this but no one else did. The little puppy thought dogs should not dance so he did dance in an alley where almost no one goes. But one day a superstar searcher was doing his job and found the puppy. Soon the little dog was bigger than Michael Jackson! Julie finished the stories of the animals and brought it to school. She got an A+. Julie was so happy! The End!

USER: Thanks!

SAGE: I hope you liked my story! I have to go and make it rain in Hong Kong! Good-bye.

In using SAGE, children always tell stories in the first person. That person might be the child herself using SAGE in storytelling mode, or might be the child assuming the persona of a character to respond to other people's stories. It is revealing that once children had built a storyteller, they preferred to tell the stories of their problems to the storyteller they themselves had built.

Possible Objections

All this is well and good. But a number of counterarguments come to mind with respect to the arguments presented in this chapter.

First and foremost, one might ask if the computer is indeed the best partner with whom to discover who one is. As I was asked during the talk I gave, why are we training children to entertain computers? Why are we encouraging them to spend their time in front of a screen? Shouldn't children get out more? Shouldn't they spend more time with other children? Shouldn't parents be listening to children's stories? These questions have been asked regularly over the decades as new technologies have been introduced. It was asked of television, and the jury is still out. It was asked of radio and there probably isn't anybody today who thinks that radio is a danger to the family and the fabric of American society. In a couple of years, the jury will probably rule that television isn't intrinsically a danger to children either. And, in a couple of decades, the same ruling will come back with respect to computers. However, whereas television and radio were always output devices, I'm proposing that the computer serve as an input device, that it become a listener to children's stories, to their problems, to their deepest secrets. Shouldn't parents be playing that role? The truth is that children have never told their deepest secrets to their parents. In the past it was stuffed animals or pillows who listened to children's secrets. Computers have the advantage of remembering the secrets, giving children the option of later sharing those stories with adults or even later in their lives, remembering the children they were. In one workshop we ran using the SAGE storyteller, an eleven-year-old boy built a storyteller who told only horrific tales of mutilation, fear, and anger. The boy chose to share the storyteller with his parents, who promptly sat him down to talk about what was going on in his inner life.

What about the emphasis on equity for girls? A recent article in the *Boston Globe* asked if the push for gender equity for girls was hurting boys. Will boys be left behind now that we're spending so much research time on helping girls? Such a backlash response may be a sign that we are forgetting that bringing to girls traditionally male activities—such as science, math, design of technology—should not be our only goal in designing new kinds of computer activities. Boys have just as much of a need to be given access to traditionally female activities, such as using storytelling to talk about feelings. All children have a need to explore the nonstereotypical aspects of themselves.

Finally, do we need to call this a "feminist" enterprise? Isn't this just humanism? Or computer-supported collaborative work? Or any one of a number of other theoretical stances? To this, I have to reply that feminism's roots have stretched into neighboring fields, such as education and the design of human-computer interfaces. There is no one "feminism," just as there is no one "humanism." But the tenets of feminism have had a powerful effect on how we view relations of power, and they continue to be a useful lens through which to examine the distribution of authority and whose voices are privileged.

Conclusions

I've demonstrated that, based on feminist principles of design that I have laid out here, new kinds of storytelling applications can be built for children that extend the range of narrative voices, and narrative activities that the computer can support. I believe that these activities allow a range of girlhoods (and boyhoods) to coexist, ultimately extending the notion of what "girl" is to a more dynamic context-dependent, performative notion.

Women who show a positive attitude toward computers score higher on masculinity trait scales (Colley, Gale, and Harris 1994). When I interviewed undergraduates at MIT for a research position in gender and technology, several of the young women told me that they were video game enthusiasts, but then again they "hadn't been raised as girls," since they had been given computers to play with from a young age. Such an attitude maintains the gender stereotype ("real girls don't like computers"), and defines oneself as abnormal ("therefore I'm not a real girl"). Real change in girls' attitudes toward computers will be seen when this kind of thinking becomes unnecessary—the definition of "girl" will no longer have anything to do with liking computers. Real change in gender roles in general will be demonstrated by even broader movement— there will be no single narrow definition of "girl."

I'd like to design computer games that are as attractive to girls who love Nintendo as they are to girls who can't stand it. My approach is twofold: to aim for a new generation of toys and games with children as codesigners, in the sense that they can decide the story that they wish to tell and the games will listen; and to encourage a new generation of girls and boys who value equally what technology can do, and what the narrative self has to offer.

The girls' games movement has brought a change from stories with no representation of girls whatsoever to stories about girls. But these stories often serve to show girls what they are expected to be, and to encourage them to model expected behavior. The next stage in girls' games, as in children's storytelling, is stories that girls choose to tell for themselves.

Notes

1. While the feminist approach proposed here has many points of intersection with user-centered, or participatory design, it differs in that participatory design brings users in during the design of a system, and then sends the system off to be built by experts. Feminist software design, on the other hand, makes the system about design, so that the design and construction cycle continues into the use of the system itself.

2. Thanks to Anita Borg for bringing this point to my attention.

References

Asakawa, G. and Rucker, L. 1992. *The Toy Book*. New York: Alfred Knopf.

Balka, E. 1997. "Participatory Design in Women's Organizations: The Social World of Organizational Structure and the Gendered Nature of Expertise." *Gender, Work and Organizations* 4(2): 99–115.

Belenky, M., Clinchy, B., Goldberger, N. and Tarule, J. 1986. *Women's Ways of Knowing: The Development of Self, Voice, and Mind*. New York: Basic Books.

Bruner, J. and Lucariello, J. 1989. "Monologue as Narrative Recreation of the World." In K. Nelson, ed., *Narratives from the Crib*. Cambridge: Harvard University Press.

Butler, J. 1990. *Gender Trouble*. New York: Routledge.

Colley, A. M., Gale, M. T., and Harris, T. A. 1994. "Effects of Gender Role Identity and Experience on Computer Attitude Components." *Journal of Educational Computing Research* 10(2): 129–137.

Don, A. 1990. "Narrative and the Interface." In B. Laurel, ed., *The Art of Human-Computer Interface Design*. New York: Addison Wesley, 383–391.

Dyl, J. and Wapner, S. 1996. "Age and Gender Differences in the Nature, Meaning, and Function of Cherished Possessions for Childrens and Adolescents." *Journal of Experimental Psychology* 62: 340–377.

Eckert, P. 1993. "Cooperative Competition in Adolescent 'Girl Talk.'" In D. Tannen, ed., *Gender and Conversational Interaction*. New York: Oxford University Press.

Eckert, P. and McConnell-Ginet, S. 1995 "Constructing Meaning, Constructing Selves: Snapshots of Language, Gender, and Class from Belten High." In K. Hall and M. Bucholtz, eds., *Gender Articulated: Language and the Socially Constructed Self*. New York: Routledge.

Finke, L. 1993. "Knowledge as Bait: Feminism, Voice, and the Pedagogical Unconscious." *College English* 55: 9–27.

Fraser, N. 1994. "Pragmatism, Feminism, and the Linguistic Turn." In *Feminist Contentions: A Philosophical Exchange Between Seyla Benhabib, Judith Butler, Drucilla Cornell and Nancy Fraser*. New York: Routledge, 157–171.

Fuller, M. and Jenkins, H. 1995. "Nintendo and New World Travel Writing: A Dialogue." In S. G. Jones, ed., *CyberSociety: Computer-Mediated Communication and Community*. New York: Sage Publications, 57–72.

Gailey, C. 1993. "Mediated Messages: Gender, Class, and Cosmos in Home Video Games." *Journal of Popular Culture* 27(1): 81–97.

Gal, S. 1991. "Between Speech and Silence." In M. di Leonardo, ed., *Gender at the Crossroads of Knowledge: Feminist Anthropology in the Postmodern Era*. Berkeley: University of California Press, 175–203.

Glos, J. 1997. "Digital Augmentation of Keepsake Objects: A Place for Interaction of Memory, Story, and Self." Master's Thesis, Media Arts and Sciences, Media Laboratory, Massachusetts Institute of Technology. Cambridge, MA.

Glos, J. and Cassell, J. 1997. "Rosebud: A Place for Interaction between Memory, Story, and Self." Proceedings of Cognitive Technologies '97, IEEE Press, August, at Aizu, Japan.

Greenbaum, J. and Kyng, M., eds., 1991. *Design at Work: Cooperative Design of Computer Systems*. Hillsdale, N.J.: Lawrence Erlbaum Associates.

Jarratt, S. 1991. "Feminism and Composition: The Case for Conflict." In P. Harkin and J. Schilb, eds., *Contending with Words: Composition and Rhetoric in a Postmodern Age*. New York: MLA.

Johnstone, B. 1993. "Community and Contest: Midwestern Men and Women Creating their Worlds in Conversational Storytelling." In D. Tannen, ed., *Gender and Conversational Interaction*. New York: Oxford University Press.

Keller, E. F. 1985. *Reflections on Gender and Science*. New Haven: Yale University Press.

Laurel, B. 1993. *Computers as Theater*. New York: Addison Wesley.

Lewis, M. 1993. *Without a Word: Teaching Beyond Women's Silence*. New York: Routledge.

Linde, C. 1993. *Life Stories: The Creation of Coherence*. New York: Oxford University Press.

Miller, P., Potts, R., Fung, H., Hoogstra, L., and Mintz, J. 1990. "Narrative Practices and the Social Construction of Self in Childhood." *American Ethnologist*: 17(2): 292–311.

Ochs, E. 1992. "Indexing Gender." In A. Duranti and C. Goodwin, eds., *Rethinking Context.* Cambridge: Cambridge University Press, 335–358.

Ochs, E. and Taylor, C. 1995. "The 'Father Knows Best' Dynamic in Dinnertime Narratives." In K. Hall and M. Bucholtz, eds., *Gender Articulated: Language and the Socially Constructed Self.* New York: Routledge.

Papert, S. 1980. *Mindstorms: Children, Computers and Powerful Ideas.* New York: Basic Books.

Pennebaker, J. W. 1990. *Opening Up.* New York: Morrow.

Pipher, M. 1994. *Reviving Ophelia: Saving the Selves of Adolescent Girls.* New York: Putnam.

Polanyi, L. 1989. *Telling the American Story.* Cambridge: MIT Press.

Resnick, M., Bruckman A., and Martin, F. 1996. "Pianos Not Stereos: Creating Computational Construction Kits." *Interactions* 3(6) (September-October): 41–49.

Sachs, J. 1987. "Preschool Boys' and Girls' Language Use in Pretend Play." In S. Philips, S. Steele, and C. Tanz, eds., *Language, Gender and Sex in Comparative Perspective.* Cambridge: Cambridge University Press, 178–188.

Sedgewick, E. 1993. *Tendencies.* Durham: Duke University Press.

Sheldon, A. 1993. "Pickle Fights: Gendered Talk in Preschool Disputes." In D. Tannen, ed., *Gender and Conversational Interaction.* New York: Oxford University Press.

Sheldon A. and Rohleder, L. 1996. "Sharing the Same World, Telling Different Stories: Gender Differences in Co-Constructed Pretend Narratives." In D. I. Slobin, J. Gerhardt, A. Kyratzis, and J. Guo, eds., *Social Interaction, Social Context, and Language: Essays in Honor of Susan Ervin-Tripp.* Mahwah, N.J.: Lawrence Erlbaum Associates.

Suchman, L. 1991. "Closing Remarks on the 4th Conference on Women, Work and Computerization: Identities and Differences." In I. V. Ericksson, B. A. Kitchenham, and K. G. Tijdens, ed., *Women, Work and Computerization: Understanding and Overcoming Bias in Work and Education.* Amsterdam: Elsevier Science Publishers, 431–437.

Suchman, L. 1993. "Foreword." In D. Schuler and A. Namioka, eds., *Participatory Design: Principles and Practices.* Hillsdale, N.J.: Lawrence Erlbaum Associates, vii-x.

Tanaka, J. 1996. "No Boys Allowed." *Newsweek,* October 28.

Turkle, S. 1984. *The Second Self: Computers and the Human Spirit.* New York: Simon & Schuster.

Turkle, S. 1986. "Computational Reticence: Why Women Fear the Intimate Machine." In C. Kramerae, ed., *Technology and Women's Voices.* New York: Pergamon Press.

Turkle, S. and Papert, S. 1990. "Epistemological Pluralism: Styles and Voices within Computer Culture." *Signs* 16: 128–157.

Turner, V. 1981. "Social Dramas and Stories about Them." In W.J.T. Mitchell, ed., *On Narrative.* Chicago: University of Chicago Press.

Umaschi, M. 1997 "Soft Interfaces for Interactive Storytelling: Learning About Identity and Communication." Master's Thesis, Media Arts and Sciences, Media Laboratory, Massachusetts Institute of Technology. Cambridge, MA.

Umaschi, M. and Cassell, J. (under review). "Interactive Storytelling Systems for Children: Using Technology to Explore Language and Identity." *Journal of Interactive Learning Research.*

Wahlstrom, B. J. 1994. "Communication and Technology: Defining a Feminist Perspective in Research and Practice." In C. Selfe and S. Hilligoss, eds., *Literacy and Computers: The Complications of Teaching and Learning with Technology.* New York: ULA.

Weiler, K. 1988. *Women Teaching for Change: Gender, Class and Power.* South Hadley, MA.: Bergin & Garvey.

White, H. 1981. "Narrative and History." In W.J.T. Mitchell, ed., *On Narrative.* Chicago: University of Chicago Press.

Winnicott, D. W. 1971. *Playing and Reality.* London: Tavistock Publications.

Chapter 14

Voices from the Combat Zone: Game Grrlz Talk Back
Compiled by Henry Jenkins

Barbie doesn't live here anymore!

If 1997 became the "year for girls" in the game industry, much as Brenda Laurel and others had predicted, then, by year's end, another set of voices were being heard who also claimed to speak for girls and also sought to address what they wanted from digital media. Web pages are appearing that reflect the still nascent "game grrlz" movement. The game grrlz are older than those being targeted by Purple Moon, Girl Games, and the others, and certainly more self-confident than those described in their audience research. They have never felt left out of the digital realm and they take pleasure in beating boys at their own games, sometimes using their own gameboys. They don't want a "rom of their own"; they simply want a chance to fight it out with the others. Their voices are nineties kinds of voices—affirming women's power, refusing to accept the constraints of stereotypes, neither those generated by clueless men in the games industry nor those generated by the girls' game researchers. These female gamers are bluntly questioning the assumptions being made by the girls' game movement and asserting their own pleasures in playing fighting games like "Quake." These women are also demanding to be taken seriously by the game industry, questioning the gender stereotypes at the roots of existing games, and insisting that their younger sisters have access to the computer. In this next section, as a snapshot of an emerging subculture that commands the attention of anyone interested in gender and games, we reprint several editorials by female gamers that appeared on the web in late 1997 and early 1998. We let these gamers speak last to suggest that the debates this book has documented are far from over.

But . . . Girls Don't Do *THAT!*
Stephanie Bergman, Game Grrlz

A few days ago, I was sitting on the subway, heading uptown. It's a local—a really dreary ride, stopping every few minutes. A bunch of school kids got onto the train, probably about eight years old, shepherded by their teachers. Now, I love children. But on subways? I hate children, or more specifically, I hate the parents/baby-sitters/teachers who let the kids climb all over everything in sight, including the nearest person (me).

So I tried to ignore them, read my book in peace, when I hear someone start talking about "Super Mario" and Nintendo 64. I look up, and five boys are huddled around the pole in front of me, discussing the relative merits of the Nintendo joystick with the annoying thumb thingy (they loved it; I hate it). The girls are gathered in the corner for the most part, but, looking over, I see one girl watching the boys' conversation as closely as me. She slowly began making her way over to them, step by step, ignoring the strange looks the other girls were giving her.

Finally, with one big step, she walked over to the pole and asked the boys, "Do you have Sony Playstation?" Four of the boys flat out ignored her and continued their Nintendo talk. But the fifth boy turned to her and said, "No." She began rambling about how great Playstation is, and how "Tomb Raider" is the best game, getting into a pretty intense (for an eight-year-old) conversation with the boy.

The boy's friends notice him talking to (ew!) a girl, and ask him what he's doing. The boy tells his friends, "She has a Playstation."

One of the friends stares at the girl and asks, "Yeah, but do you have a Nintendo 64?" The girl (and here's where I began to laugh out loud, despite my attempts not to) looks at the boy, and with the greatest smirk, told him, "Nintendo 64s are for babies. Playstation. 'Tomb Raider.' Kill things, not jump on things." Another little boy asked, "What about that Barbie game?"

The girl rolled her eyes (I swear, it's only in New York that little kids can be THAT obnoxious. . .and no, that's not a good thing) and replied, "Barbie's not a game." And with that, she flipped her hair and walked back over to her girlfriends, who huddled around her, giggling, asking her what she had been doing talking to (ew!) boys.

After the kids got off the train, I was able to laugh in peace.

What I found the most surprising about what I'd witnessed, was the games referred to. The boys were talking about racing (Andretti, I think?), and "Mario

64." The girl was talking about "Tomb Raider," bucking all stereotypes right on their face.

What Purple Moon and other "girlie games" companies have to understand is that although there is a market for games like "Barbie Fashion Designer," there is just as big a market for girls who like to do the same things the boys do. There is nothing wrong with a little girl who enjoys a first-person shooter game. The little girl on the train was right. Barbie's not really a game. You point, click, do all sorts of things, but where's the competition? Where's the adrenaline rush of WINNING? It's not there. Because "girls don't like that."

Well, guess what? We sure do! Little girls like the one I saw on the train are the "great untapped market" that these companies should be shooting for. Let the future fashion designers of the world, male or female, have their Barbie. I have nothing against the game. In fact, I'm sure I would have loved it as a kid myself. The "girl games" companies have their place, they really do. But I think as long as they refuse to acknowledge that they're only making "games" to satisfy SOME little girls, they're enforcing a stereotype. Little girls like the one I saw are becoming more and more commonplace. Why did she pick "Tomb Raider" to play instead of, say, "Final Fantasy"? Maybe because of Lara. Or maybe because, as she put it, it just "is killer." We need to have companies making games for children, not for girls.

As a kid, I loved "PacMan." I loved "Ms. PacMan" even more. Not because she was female, but because the gameplay was better (I still think so, actually). "Pong," which I think everyone played at sometime or another as a child, had it's moments, but overall, it was boring (apologies to all those "Pong" lovers out there). "Space Invaders" had me sitting in front of the television for hours. In a way, I almost think gaming was better for girls back then. Games were games. No girl games, no boy games. The concept of "girl games," on its face, is detrimental to the little girls who game. It's because companies are creating games "for girls" that the boys had such a hard time understanding how this girl could be playing something other than Barbie.

I can only hope that someone from the girl game companies sees what I saw, a little girl, trying to make the boys understand that she liked something other than Barbie. One little boy accepted her. The others laughed. There is nothing wrong with her loving "Tomb Raider" (as much as I hate Lara), and fortunately, she knew that. But how many little girls are pushed away from playing it in favor of the games meant for girls? How many mothers buy their daughters the girlie games instead of a more "male" game? Yes, the mere fact that little girls are playing games is good. But pushing them into a certain type of game based on sex itself is a dangerous trend, one that other areas are getting out of. Women are doctors, women are lawyers. Fifty years ago, girls were taught not to even consider either profession. Now we're teaching girls that "these are their games" and "these are the boys' games." We're teaching these girls to see things based on their gender. Which is exactly what we're trying to avoid. People are people, right? Then why is it suddenly so acceptable to split little children up based on gender alone when it comes to games?

THINK before you tell your daughter, "That's a boys' game." THINK before you tell your son, "But that's for girls." It starts with games. Where does it end? I'm worried that it's back where we started fifty years ago.

Grrls & Gaming on ABC News
Nikki Douglas, Grrl Gamer

I have nothing against Brenda Laurel (from Purple Moon software, a maker of games specifically designed for young girls) and the other women who were quoted in the ABC News *Nightline* feature that recently aired about Girls and Gaming, but some of their quotes (not to mention some of the bon mots from John Romero, but I'll get to that later), had me reaching for the virtual airsickness bag.

Let me take them head on:

> "Girls' objection to computer games isn't what you'd expect. It's not that they're too violent, it's that they're too boring. They're extremely bored by them."
>
> —Brenda Laurel, Purple Moon Software

What exactly is boring about creative strategy and 3D virtual environments? What is boring about figuring out how to decimate nasty aliens that have taken our planet hostage? How is that boring? What about adventure games like "Tomb Raider" and "Blade Runner"? Is it boring to be part of a story that unfolds and asks questions about our humanity and empathy? Boring to jump across a ledge where there is a bear waiting to eat you? I'll tell you what boring is—it was waiting for those little cakes to come out of the Easy-Bake oven. It was trying to get Barbie to stand in those high heels. It was the fact that Ken was not anatomically correct. It was going to Child World at Christmas to pick out toys for Santa to bring us and my brother always got the coolest ones—like the *Star Trek* Enterprise that I coveted one year. That was the year I got the Barbie Townhouse. But I really loved *Star Trek*. I really wanted to have the Enterprise. All I got was Barbie and the townhouse with the elevator and my Mom saying to me, "But *Star Trek* is for boys, Barbie is for girls. Isn't this a cute little outfit?"

> "We find that a lot of male gamers are playing games like "Quake" and "Duke Nuke 'Em," where you basically get on and you shoot lots of monsters. It's a good way to relieve stress. Whereas women who are playing games I think are more interested in achieving goals. They like to figure out that they've solved a problem or they've done something."
> —Charlotte Panther, News Editor, Computer Gaming World

Lord knows we, as women, don't need to relieve stress. We just go shopping or eat or color code our underwear drawers, right? And I want all my gaming to be about achieving goals, just like my life is, not some escape. Oh, no, why would I want to temporarily escape all the stress and problem solving that I'm faced with every day? Why would I just once like to answer some insipid question like "I thought you were going to make dinner?" with a spray of automatic gunfire? There's your dinner, baby!

I think Charlotte just didn't want anyone to think she was, you know, one of those tough computer geek grrls or something. "OK, I'm on ABC News, my hair looks good, but I don't want to appear too butch, too Ellen." Personally, Char, I think kicking alien ass is doing something.

> "The Web and the Internet are about community, collaboration, who can form consensus. Those are the skills you need. And these are skills that women bring to the table."
> —Sherry Turkle, MIT

Yawwwwnnn. Community and collaboration are what women bring to the table? God, that is so 1950s, so retro, so family and hearth and Donna Reed. We're good little community makers and collaborators. We don't ever really do anything ground breaking, just create nice little places to live and work and raise our babies! That's what women are good at! If we work together we can all be friends. Well, screw that! I don't want to be friends! I want to be King! That's right, King, Hail to the King, baby! I want all the best stuff and I want it all for me and I will knock the hell out of anyone who tries to take a piece of my action. Not very community driven and collaborative, am I?

> "One interesting statistic at AOL is women tend to use e-mail 32 percent more than males. And when I look at the rest of my life, you know, and the patterns I see around me, that's not really surprising. In most households, you know, the woman mails the birthday card, the woman writes the thank-you notes and that behavior translates online."
>
> —Katherine Borsecnik, AOL

Shoot me if I ever write anyone a freakin' thank-you note. This statement really grates on me. Basically ol' Kath here believes that these are not surprising roles for women, to be caregivers, sending birthday cards, cheerful e-mails, and thank-you notes. Instead of challenging this and saying e-mail has been great, because we can keep in touch with people and get more work done (that's what I use it for), the thing it's best used for is the same mundane things I'm expected to do just because I'm a woman. Well, surprise, Kath, you aren't getting a birthday card from ME this year! I'm too busy using my e-mail for work to just gab in the coffee klatch with all the other Ladies who have nothing better to do.

> "Men tend to surf around. It's more like, you know, men with the channel changer, whereas women want everything in one place. So you have to make it very simple. And it's not because women are more simple creatures. It's just they want things very well organized. They want it laid out cleanly and clearly and they want a label to mean what it says."
>
> —Joy Every, AOL

AOL is apparently a great place to find women who are quite content in their little stereotypical roles. I'd just as soon as knock him out than relinquish the clicker, OK? I don't want everything in one place! How can you make a statement like that, that women want everything in one place? That's one of the most unbelievable generalizations I've ever heard. Then she slips and says it has to be simple and then backpedals by saying it's not because women are simple creatures, just more organized. Well maybe Joy is, but I sure as hell am not, and neither are most of the women I know. Some are, true. Like, my mom is very organized. She is the queen of organization. But she's also extremely anal-retentive. She doesn't like computers and asks me all the time, how can I remember where everything is in my e-mail in-box which has over ten-thousand e-mails? I just say, because I know who sent me what and when. She would end up filing all of them and I'd never remember which file they were in.

> "It's a problem that little boys like to play games that slaughter entire planets. It's not particularly a problem just of the computer culture."
> —Sherry Turkle, MIT

Maybe it's a problem, Sherry, that little girls DON'T like to play games that slaughter entire planets. Maybe that's why we are still underpaid, still struggling, still fighting for our rights. Maybe if we had the mettle to take on an entire planet, we could fight some of the smaller battles we face everyday. Women are not Men and Men are not Women, but all Women are not members of the doily of the month club either.

THE CASE FOR SHERRY'S ARGUMENT
> "Men design games for themselves because they understand what they know is fun. They don't understand what women find fun."
> —John Romero

So what do you think a date with John Romero is like? Bass fishing? A couple of hours at the shooting range? A case of beer and ESPN?

Here's a suggestion for all game makers out there: Women like action and adventure games. Get used to it. Sell them to us. Make more money. It's as simple as that.

This Girl Wants Games
Aliza Sherman, Cybergrrl

I got to sleep really late last night. But it wasn't work that kept me in the office. It wasn't insomnia that kept me awake. I was playing a computer game. And not your usual "Tetris," mind you. I was playing a multi-user, networked game called "Carmaggedon." I think the name says it all, but for those who don't know, I'll elaborate. Fast, wicked cars, elaborate maneuvering around impossible terrain, and gory, bloody hit-and-runs that leave roadkill in their wake. What's a nice grrl like me doing playing a violent, graphic game like this? It's fun!

Ever since I was in school, I loved arcade games. First it was pinball, then "Space Invaders," "Asteroids," "PacMan" and "Ms. PacMan," and then I discovered my niche with "Defender," the intergalactic shoot-'em-up game that ate up most of the rolls of quarters my mom sent me at college for laundry. I was hooked.

In video arcades, I found that I had an aptitude for the games that took a degree of hand-eye coordination and the ability to work small buttons quickly. Who knew how handy my typing lessons could be? I'd spend hours playing "Millipede" and "Galaga," promising myself that I'd stop playing if I got a higher score the next game. But of course, if I got a higher score, I'd just have to play "one more game" to see if that last high score was a fluke or if I could consistently make a better score.

Looking at the games on the market today for girls, I get a little concerned. Where are the games that teach them competitiveness? Assertiveness? And that take advantage of a female's natural hand-eye coordination? I think that as a society, we have a big taboo against strong women and a greater fear of women as warriors. Instead of making fashions with Barbie, why can't girls have a shoot 'em up game such as a Western based on Annie Oakley, or a fantasy rough and tumble game based on *Xena*, or a scary, evil "stab them in the heart with a stake" game based on *Buffy the Vampire Slayer*? Or how about a "Glass Ceiling" game for women, where they can take an array of automatic weapons to oppressive corporate offices?

I keep reading about articles and studies where experts say girls don't like shooting and blasting games but instead prefer quiet, contemplative games with well-rounded characters and storylines that stimulate their imagination. I'd venture to say, however, that these studies are a reflection of how we condition girls to be passive. The image of woman with gun is too shocking, too disruptive and threatening to the male dominant order of things.

Do I think violent video games for girls will change the way we view aggression in females? Will they cultivate a strength in girls or women? Will they positively influence women's role in society? Well, no. But I do think a good "blow them to bits" computer game is not a bad thing for girls. And I know I'm not the only grrl that thinks so.

Why GameGirlz?
Aurora, GameGirlz

My parents just don't quite understand. They do try, though. Two years ago for Christmas they stopped sending me peach bubble bath and sent the number-one-selling Mac game. They were so excited about finding a gift I would love that I still haven't had the heart to explain the Mac/PC thing and why to this day I still haven't played the game. My female friends think I'm a geek-freak. My male friends sit down on the LAN with me and try to kick my ass. *C'est la vie!*

It wasn't until the beginning of "Quake" and the online playing that I actually realized that there were other female gamers out there, and that I wasn't the only little girl who, once upon a time, had a hard time explaining to her friends why playing "Dolphin" on the Atari was so much more fun than dressing Barbie up in a very sleek new sparkly dress.

Online gaming has brought me hundreds of new friends, both male and female, who all share a love of fragging, slaying, and taking over worlds.

GameGirlz is something I have wanted to do for a very long time. Not to push females and say we're better (that certainly isn't the case), but to show people there are many female gamers in the world and to give those girlz a place on the net where they can get information, reviews, and resources. Plain and simple. What a girl wants out of a game is different than what a guy wants, and what each wants to see in a game is just as different. When I looked around at all the gaming-related sites online, I found one thing lacking. There was very little input from females in the industry and female gamers.

The other issue I wanted to address with this site is the *nature* of the content that is available. The majority of girls I talked to didn't find the games-related content on other sites that they were interested in. I have taken all the "Have you seen this anywhere?" and "Where can I find out how to do this?" e-mail that female gamers have sent me over the past year and included it in GameGirlz.

Over the next couple weeks I will be looking at setting up online tourneys, chat areas, and providing a place where genderless log-ins aren't needed. We also have female "Quake" and "Warcraft" "tutors" coming aboard and lots more fun and exciting things.

GameGirlz is not just me. It is a network of many male and female gamers who have an interest in online gaming and who think we girlz needed a few more resources. I'm just the one who tries to put it all together. My wonderful online (and offline) friends contributed a lot to this site. The staff of Planet

Quake also spent a lot of time helping me get GameGirlz up and running. So thank you to everyone who helped me get what I needed to do GameGirlz and to all the wonderful people who took time out of their busy schedules to do interviews. Also, thank you to the folks who stopped by to check out GameGirlz.

Cheers and Happy Fragging!

The Image of a Female Gamer
Aurora, GameGirlz

"...but...girls shouldn't be gamers...they are supposed to be Horse-Riders and Doll Fans!"

—quoted from e-mail sent to GameGirlz

Somebody needs to point him in the direction of the 1900s I think . . .

The sad thing is, with today's computer games' market overflowing with "games created for girls" full of things like dolls, make-up, boys, and fashion, this kind of theory is common. When you add that to the image of the beautiful, sexy, no-brains bimbo chick the computer gaming industry likes to promote . . . it's no wonder people look at me funny when I say I play games like "Quake" and "Dark Reign."

I ran across a *Wired* article by Janelle Brown, in which Bridget Massey, a spokeswoman for Attitude Networks, is quoted as saying, "Modeling is something all female teens are interested in." I love that quote. Just like all female teens are interested in modeling, all young girls are interested in games about make-up and all women are interested in fashion and beauty. I personally couldn't care less what the hottest color for summer wear is and I don't run out to buy the latest edition of *Seventeen* so I can find out if there is a 33.8 percent chance my boyfriend is cheating on me.

Like many other women gamers out there, I dislike the image of females that many software companies have set. This image is a topic I have discussed at length with many of the women (both game players and women working in the industry) who sent me e-mail about this site. In the eyes of the computer gaming industry, if you are a young girl, your only interests are boys and make-up. If you are an adult female, you wear leather and a bra big enough to double as a dust cover for your monitor.

Computer gaming companies need to market their games to the majority of the consumers. If that targeted audience consisted of a wide margin of adult males with a tiny percentage of females, I could understand the portrayal of the bimbo fantasy chick image. In saying that, I think many computer games companies need to take a second look at that targeted group and see how it has changed over the past year.

I'd like to quote the most recent and valid statistics I have found to date: 72 percent of game players are over eighteen, and of those half are over thirty-five; 40 percent of PC gamers and 27 percent of console gamers are women. Video games are no longer the domain of teenage boys.

Cheers & Happy Fragging!

Lara Croft, Female Enemy Number One?
Cal Jones, Reviews Editor for PC Gaming World

When it comes to weight and body image, most women are pretty insecure. Show me a woman who is happy with the size of her thighs and I'll show you a rarity. Much of the blame for this has been put on the media's portrayal of women—ultrathin models who live on a diet of Marlboro Lights and coffee, actresses who have their own personal trainer and enough time to work out for four hours a day, and heiresses who can afford cosmetic surgery, figure-enhancing designer togs, and celebrity hairdressers. These are not realistic role models for women who work eight or more hours a day or have children to bring up, yet we feel pressured into looking like them.

The bad news is that womankind has met an even more dangerous foe. She isn't a supermodel or a movie star—she isn't even real. No, this threat comes in the form of a silicon chick—none other than the Tomb Raider herself, Lara Croft.

The problem with Lara is that she was designed by men for men. How do I know this? Because Lara has thin thighs, long legs, a waist you could encircle with one hand, and knockers like medicine balls. Show that to a guy and although he may not admit it (since he suspects it may be sad to fancy a character in a game), deep down he finds Lara pretty sexy. Show that to a woman and she will complain that Lara is anatomically impossible. Which is true, because if you genetically engineered a Lara-shaped woman, she would die within around fifteen seconds, since there's no way her tiny abdomen could house all her vital organs.

More to the point, thin women do not have big jugs. Period. Breasts, as any woman knows, are composed mainly of fatty tissue, and one of the hazards of dieting is that your tits get smaller before your bum does. Any woman who is skinny and appears to have big hooters is either a) surgically enhanced, or b) wearing a Wonderbra with padding in it. End of story.

Of course, Eidos is marketing Lara Croft as a character who will appeal to both sexes. Obviously her figure will appeal to blokes (the straight ones anyway), but apparently women will like her because she's tough enough to climb up rock faces, shoot men in the face, and wander around in the freezing cold in only a pair of shorts and a vest without so much as a pointy nipple in evidence. Lara, you see, has gone from being a female character in an entertaining game to (post-Eidos marketing campaign) Girl Power incarnate.

Well, to hell with that. Women don't buy it. In fact, Lara could very easily make us feel inadequate. Not only does she have an impossible figure, but she is capable of feats of strength that most men couldn't muster. I mean, Lara can not only pull her bodyweight up from arms length, but she can do it whilst going into a handstand. I mean, I've been weight training seriously for ten years and I can't do that, and doubt very many women could.

Now, you may well ask why such a ridiculous creature like Ms. Croft is threatening to women. Obviously, we're sensible enough as a sex not to take her seriously, but the same cannot be said of impressionable teenage boys. It's a well-known fact that most youngsters get their first good look at the female anatomy via porn mags, and come away thinking women have jutting bosoms, airbrushed skin, and neatly trimmed body hair. Now, thanks to Lara, they'll also think women are superfit, agile gymnasts with enough stamina to run several marathons back to back. Cheers.

Seriously though, Lara is not the great feminist icon Eidos would have you believe. She's just a fantasy, and one that is pretty damned impossible for us women to live up to. Does she inspire me? Absolutely not, but I'm afraid she'll inspire a lot of other games companies who will see her success and try to emulate with their own over-inflated heroines. Fortunately, I've heard that the female "Quake II" character is a lot more realistic as far as anatomy's concerned, and she still kicks ass. Now that's one girl I'm looking forward to playing. Lara, get those melons out of your vest and I'll like you a whole lot better . . .

Where Do Girls Fit in the Gaming Scene?
Michelle Goulet, Game Girlz

A recent article in the gaming magazine *Next Generation* inspired me to form thoughts on a subject I have been pondering for quite some time: Where do girls fit in on the gaming scene? With this question out in the open you can safely assume that I am a girl, because from what I understand, most guys don't lose a lot of sleep thinking about this subject. The answer I have come to is not an easy one to accept: Girls don't really "fit" anywhere. They are not excluded from the boys' club of PC and Console Gaming, but they aren't included either, at least not the way they should be. You see girls everywhere in games. They are the bouncing blondes holding your trophies at the end of the race, the scantily clad heroines who wiggle and wear next to nothing, and the models in magazine ads wearing thigh-high black boots, holding a game box between their legs and a devilishly flirtatious look on their faces.

Don't get me wrong, I am not a "feminist" or a male-basher. I am, for all intents and purposes, a humanist, as I would and do stand up for the rights of people, not sexes. Having said that, I have to say that this issue of using women as sexual playthings in the gaming industry strikes a chord with me. Not only because I am a girl, but because I have experienced my share of sexual harassment in the gaming world. The majority of people with whom I talk about the subject seem to have a "does it really matter?" attitude. I say it does. I don't see anything productive coming out of this "trend" and I would even venture to say it is actually counterproductive for everyone involved. I think it needs to change, and so I vent my opinions in hopes of helping change along.

One of the counterarguments I have heard many times is that characters for guys are ideal, most times unnatural or near impossible-to-achieve body images, and that it should be no different for girls. I agree completely. I don't think I would want to play a homely looking three-hundred-pound female anymore than I would want to play a 105 pound blonde with enormous breasts. The point of contention here is deciding whose ideal body image it is. Most male characters that fit this ideal body image are based on the body image that is ideal to a lot of guys, not girls. Looking at the "Quake II" males, I would have to say that although they rock, they are nowhere near my ideal man. The same goes for most, though not all, female characters. They are the man's ideal image of a girl, not a girl's ideal image of a girl. I think this is the reason why the bimbo with big lips and a matching set of bazooms upsets a lot of gaming girls.

My thoughts on this matter are pretty straightforward. Include females in making female characters. Find out what the ideal female would be for both a man and a woman and work with that. Respect the females the same as you would the males. I'm not sure if I am alone on this, but I don't see many male characters running around wearing thongs and wiggling their butts for the player. Fabio's stereotype just doesn't make it into a lot of games, and if this were the case, I don't think I would have as big of a problem with the "big-busted bimbo."

Respecting the female characters is hard when they look like strippers with guns and seem to be nothing more than an erection waiting to happen. Believing that the industry respects females in general is hard when you see ads with women tied up on beds. In my opinion, respect is what most girls are after, and I feel that if the gaming community had more respect for their female characters they would attract the heretofore elusive female market. This doesn't mean that the girls in games have to be some kind of new butch race. Femininity is a big part of being female. This means that girls should be girls. Ideal body images and character aspects that are ideal for females, from a females point of view. I'd be willing to bet that guys would find these females more attractive than the souped-up bimbos they are used to seeing. If sexuality is a major selling point, and a major attraction for the male gamer, then, fine, throw in all the sexuality you want, but doing so should not preclude respect for females.

After taking a casual survey of sorts, I found out that most guys I talked to, while not unhappy for the most part with the female stereotypes now found in a multitude of games, wouldn't be any less happy with a character they could respect. A sexy, intelligent, classy woman. Some guys were even a little passionate about wanting to see women that had more than big boobs going for them. I heard things like, "I wouldn't not play a game because the chick had small tits," and, "There is more to being sexy than big boobs." I would have to say that apart from the odd wisecrack about beanpoles and naked bodies, I agreed with these guys. Makes me wonder if the gaming industry is even catering to what guys want in the first place. Maybe it's just what they think the guys want.

To sum up, I have to say that I think the gaming industry should give guys a little more credit, and girls a lot more respect, and I hope this will help move the tide in that direction.

Index

Family relationships, 20, 54, 157

Fantasies, 57

technological, 73–80, 92

Femininity, 22, 27, 73, 87, 144, 235, 280, 303–304, 341

decision making and, 82–84

gender diversity, 72, 146, 161

in play, 232, 233(fig.), 234

Feminism, feminist, 17, 138, 221–222, 320–321

activist, 168–169

entrepreneurial, 4, 7, 8, 14, 16, 167, 183, 211

equity, 129, 235

pedagogy, 300–301, 305–306, 307

software design and, 303–304, 313

Fienstein, Keith, 263

"Fighters Megamix" (game), 202

"Final Fantasy" (game), 330

Fitzhugh, Louise, 175, 177, 285–286, 287

"Flight Simulator" (game), 134, 143

Free to Be . . . You and Me (book, record), 19

Friday the Thirteenth (film), 31

Gailey, C., 312

"Galaga" (game), 335

Galatea, 160

Game companies, 16. *See also* by name

Game design, 7, 13, 58, 64, 72, 81, 96(table), 127, 187–188, 190, 194, 199, 202, 289, 300, 305. *See also* designers by name

alternative scenarios, 82–85, 159, 182, 274, 276

audio in, 224, 283

children and, 48, 52, 55–56, 90–110, 154, 225

developers, 17, 20, 23, 183, 195

feminine perspective, 85–86, 87, 200–221, 313

gender appropriate design, 238, 245

genre, 52, 53–54, 65, 148, 189

of girl games, 60–61, 299, 330

girl's preferences in, 29, 124, 130–131, 133, 141, 143, 246–248

interactivity and, 162, 185, 227

intrinsic motivation and, 92–93, 177